THE AMERICAN CIVIL WAR: 365 DAYS

Margaret E. Wagner

Introduction by Gary W. Gallagher
Vincent Virga, Picture Editor

Abrams, New York, in association with the Library of Congress

PREFACE

In 1861, the staff of the Library of Congress conducted an inventory and found that 856 of the 70,000 volumes in the Library's collections were absent from the shelves. Nearly 300 of those books, the inventory noted, had been charged to "persons belonging to the so-called seceded states." That January, several senators from Southern states—including future Confederate president Jefferson Davis—had withdrawn from the U.S. Senate. A month later, the Confederate States of America was established. Two months after that, Confederate cannon in Charleston, South Carolina, fired the opening salvos in what would become the costliest war, in American lives, that this nation has ever fought. Sundering families and friendships, devastating large sections of the South, creating great waves of refugees seeking escape from the war's destruction or the brutality of human servitude, this terrible, rending conflict eventually decided the future course and character of the nation. At its end, the scourge of slavery was erased from this land, and the United States of America was firmly established as one nation, *indivisible*.

Fulfilling the primary role for which it was founded in 1800, the Library of Congress served throughout the war as a vital resource for the national legislature, President Abraham Lincoln, and other government figures as they grappled with the complex problems involved in waging a war for the survival of the American nation and the great democratic experiment it embodies. In the years since the war, the Library has grown to become the largest library in the world. Mainly housed in three large buildings on Capitol Hill and holding nearly 130 million items, it continues to serve the legislature as it also serves—in person and via the Internet—the American people and visitors from overseas. At the heart of our vast and wide-ranging collections, which are drawn from around the world, is a huge store of written, visual, recorded, and electronic materials that chronicle the origins and development of the United States. The section of our Web site that delivers some ten million of these primary materials free to local users everywhere is properly called "American Memory."

For *The American Civil War: 365 Days*, we have delved into our store of American memories—including the millions of items not yet available online—and selected more than 500 images that provide telling glimpses into the world of mid-nineteenth-century America. This volume includes photographs and lithographs; battlefield drawings, political cartoons, and music covers; recruitment, political, and theatrical posters; the contents of President Lincoln's pockets on the night he was mortally wounded at Ford's Theatre; manuscript maps, illustrated letters, and Lincoln's handwritten Gettysburg Address. Excerpts from among the many published Civil War–era letters, diaries, and memoirs that are included in the vast store of books known as the General Collections—and from manuscript letters of Northern and Southern soldiers and civilians—lace through the text and reveal the passionate eloquence and utter conviction that characterized Americans on both sides of this brutal conflict.

In these three buildings on Capitol Hill, the scenes and voices of the Civil War years are not remote. Here, the past, with its riveting stories, is always present, engaging, and instructive—as you will discover in the pages of *The American Civil War: 365 Days*.

James H. Billington
The Librarian of Congress

INTRODUCTION

The Civil War bequeathed to subsequent generations of Americans a fabulous store of images that evoke the compelling personalities and events of the nation's great watershed. These images produced during and after the conflict include, among other things, scores of thousands of photographs, paintings, sculpture, broadsides, political and patriotic cartoons, decorated sheet music, and engravings in illustrated periodicals. The collections of the Library of Congress, unmatched in the number and variety of images they contain, have supplied illustrative material for innumerable books on the Civil War era. Whether used to supplement the prose of scholars or to add a visual dimension to the vast written record of the generation that experienced the war, the images have influenced the ways in which people think about the conflict. This selection of items from the Library's holdings conveys the richness of the material, as well as affording modern readers an opportunity to understand how Americans saw the war in 1861–65 and remembered it in the postwar decades.

Photographs have heavily influenced public perceptions of the struggle. During and shortly after the conflict, they offered a stark departure for Americans whose visual understanding of warfare had come from highly stylized, and often overtly romantic, renderings of valiant soldiers following mounted officers into action amid fluttering banners. Photographers accompanied Union armies into the field, sometimes reaching battle sites in time to take pictures that stripped away civilians' illusions about war as a glorious test of manhood and valor without ghastly consequences. The Union soldier disemboweled by an artillery shell at Gettysburg and the bloated corpses of Confederate attackers in front of Battery Robinett at Corinth, Mississippi, typify the photographs that shocked and fascinated Civil War–era viewers in equal measure. Beyond studies of soldiers killed in action (some of them, such as the Confederate sharpshooter in the "Devil's Den" at Gettysburg, carefully arranged to achieve the best possible composition), photographers recorded many other graphic scenes—few more disturbing than the row of skulls atop a collection of bones, limbs, and uniform fragments gathered by workers disinterring bodies at Cold Harbor for reburial shortly after the end of the war. The camera also preserved more mundane dimensions of military life, including men at drill, at ease in their camps, and aboard naval vessels. These pictures document a great deal about the men's clothing, their tents and cabins, and other aspects of mid-nineteenth-century material culture.

Photographic portraits afford an especially rich body of imagery. Few resonate more powerfully than the two taken of Abraham Lincoln in February 1860 and April 1865. In the first, by Mathew Brady, Lincoln gazes toward the camera with an expression that combines purpose and strength. His angular face carries no extra flesh but appears almost youthful for a man of fifty-one years. The second portrait, from a sitting just days before Lincoln's assassination, leaves no doubt about the physical toll exacted by the war. Deep lines mark the president's forehead and cheeks, and his sunken eyes, even at the moment of final triumph over the Confederacy, seem to be haunted by tragedy and loss. Far better than even the most gifted artist or writer, these portraits reveal how profoundly the war affected untold Americans.

Because technology did not permit photographers to capture subjects in motion, that task fell to sketch artists who witnessed many memorable incidents. London-born Alfred R. Waud stood out among a talented group that included, among many others, Winslow Homer, Waud's brother William, Edwin Forbes, and another Englishman named Frank Vizetelly. Their interests ranged from camp scenes, where Homer and Forbes excelled, to life on the march and in combat. Alfred Waud's sketch of Union soldiers carrying comrades away from menacing fires during the second day of the battle of the Wilderness matches the best photographs in terms of its ability to convey the horror of war. One soldier crawls toward safety, another raises his arm in hopes of securing help, and two of the four principals, with a wounded man slung in a blanket held by muskets, look over their shoulders toward the encroaching flames. Away from the battlefield, Waud's sketch of Major General George B. McClellan's farewell to the Army of the Potomac in the autumn of 1862 crackles with the emotion of a heartfelt parting. More subdued than these two examples of his brother's work is William Waud's study of Pennsylvania soldiers voting in the field in 1864, which underscores the vitality of a democratic republic that sought to maintain electoral rhythms amid the dislocation of a massive internal conflict.

The war disrupted the lives of civilians as well as soldiers, a fact well represented in the Library of Congress material. It hit hardest in the Confederacy, where the armies carried out most of their major military operations. Much of the Confederacy's economic infrastructure and transportation network suffered significant damage, as indicated by George Barnard's photograph of William Tecumseh Sherman's soldiers destroying railroad tracks, Alfred Waud's sketch of Union soldiers dismantling a luckless farmer's fence for firewood, and Adalbert J. Volck's propagandistic treatment of a woman, reduced to living in a cave, kneeling in prayer during the siege of Vicksburg. Artists also examined disaffection with the war that plagued both the United States and Confederate governments. Eighteen months after Appomattox, *Harper's Weekly* drew on an overly dramatic sketch by Alfred Waud to show a clandestine meeting of southern Unionists in wartime eastern Tennessee. Unhappiness with the Northern war effort erupted most infamously in New York City in July 1863, when mobs, as shown in a pair of wartime illustrations, rampaged through much of the city protesting the draft and attacking African Americans.

Black people figured prominently in the war as refugees, laborers, and Union soldiers. A conflict that began as a struggle to restore the Union took on a more radical character when the United States made a commitment to emancipation. Long before Lincoln issued his Emancipation Proclamation or the U.S. Congress passed the Thirteenth Amendment ending slavery, hundreds of thousands of slaves made their way to Union lines in search of freedom. Called contrabands during the war, these refugees denied their labor to the Confederacy and frequently worked to support Northern military forces. A memorable photograph caught a group of contrabands crossing Virginia's Rappahannock River in the summer of 1862. Union troopers water their horses in the background as black men, women, and children, their goods filling a wagon beyond the top of the side rails, stop and pose for the camera. Once behind Union lines, African American refugees often lived in camps such as the one sketched near Washington, D.C. Crowded and subject to outbreaks of killing diseases, the camps proved a difficult stopping point on the road from slavery to freedom.

Most slaves in the Confederacy did not win their freedom before the end of the war. Some lived too far from the liberating presence of Union armies to risk an escape; others chose to make the best of difficult circumstances in familiar surroundings. Like white Confederates, they coped with changes in old patterns of living occasioned by the conflict while continuing to carry out their prewar tasks. Many were put to work in direct support of Confederate armies, as shown by William Waud's drawing of black men mounting artillery pieces on Morris Island, near Charleston, South Carolina, in 1861. An undetermined number of slaves and free black men worked as teamsters and cooks and in other noncombatant roles with armies in the field—though not, as is sometimes mistakenly claimed, as soldiers serving alongside white Confederates.

An array of images chronicles the experience of black soldiers in United States service. Portraits of Sergeants Powhatan Beaty and James H. Harris, both of whom won Medals of Honor, and of Robert Smalls, who made the pages of *Harper's Weekly* by piloting the rebel vessel *Planter* into Union waters in 1862, put individual faces on the phenomenon of 180,000 African American men donning blue uniforms. Photographs of units of U.S. Colored Troops stand in striking contrast to Kurz & Allison's highly unrealistic postwar lithograph of the storming of Battery Wagner on July 18, 1863. Few images caught the transformative nature of the conflict more surely than an illustration in the February 21, 1865, issue of *Harper's Weekly*. It featured the Fifty-fifth Massachusetts Infantry, a black regiment, marching into Charleston, South Carolina, where secession had first exploded into national headlines in December 1860. Alfred Waud's drawing of black soldiers embracing their wives and children after being mustered out at Little Rock, Arkansas, in 1866 similarly highlights the importance of a war that placed muskets in the hands of former slaves whose loyal service gave them a solid claim to citizenship. Images of the Freedmen's Bureau and the Ku Klux Klan from *Harper's Weekly* bring coverage of African Americans to an equivocal close, suggesting the tensions in a postwar United States where various forces worked for and against the just treatment of freed people.

Although less revolutionary than its effect on enslaved African Americans, the war also wrought significant changes in the circumstances of innumerable women. On small farms North and South, women shouldered additional burdens in coping with the absence of husbands and sons. Others entered the workplace as clerks, as members of the U.S. Sanitary Commission and other soldier's aid organizations, and as workers in war-related industries (a number lost their lives in accidents at ordnance facilities). Most famously, thousands of women became nurses, a profession thoroughly dominated by men before the war. The photographic record is especially rich in likenesses of women engaged in medical service—including prominent figures such as Clara Barton, Dorothea Dix, and Dr. Mary E. Walker, as well as Margaret Elizabeth Breckinridge and other ordinary women who attended to sick and wounded soldiers. In her portrait, Barton's benign expression masks a fierce determination that allowed her to triumph over a military medical establishment that sought to frustrate her at every turn. A few women, among them Pauline Cushman and Rose Greenhow, served as spies whose activities often were cloaked in an aura of exaggerated danger and romance.

Americans looking back to the war in the decades after Appomattox created a demand for both realistic and romantic images. Wartime photographs of battlefield carnage and other military subjects sold well as stereo views that produced the illusion of three dimensions. In 1911, Francis Trevelyan Miller's *The Photographic History of the Civil War* gathered several thousand images in ten volumes. Although the quality of reproduction was uneven, Miller's massive set reached a wide audience. So did prints and lithographs of famous battles and leaders published by Currier & Ives and Kurz & Allison. Harking back to prewar depictions of military action, these firms sacrificed authenticity for color and drama. In *Battle of Bull Run . . . Gallant*

Charge of the Zouaves and Defeat of the Rebel Black Horse Cavalry, for example, Currier & Ives featured Union soldiers in striking Zouave uniforms patterned after French units in North Africa, a huge artillery explosion, and a carnival of combat that any veteran would have dismissed as wildly inaccurate. Kurz & Allison's lithographs of Wilson's Creek, Fredericksburg, the attack on Battery Wagner, and Cedar Creek similarly engage the eye with brightly colored uniforms, flapping flags, shell bursts, rolling clouds of powder smoke, and officers and soldiers striking gallant poses.

Americans seeking a middle ground between photographs and gaudy prints could select from several options. Various books reprinted engravings based on the work of sketch artists from *Harper's Weekly, Frank Leslie's Illustrated Newspaper,* and other periodicals. Louis Prang also issued a series of chromolithographs devoted to campaigns and generals that hewed closer to historical accuracy and boasted far more artistic merit than anything from Currier & Ives or Kurz & Allison. Perhaps luckiest of all were people who had access to the work of artists such as Winslow Homer, Julian Scott, and Edwin Forbes, whose paintings amply rewarded anyone with the opportunity to study them closely.

By the time of the fiftieth anniversary of the battle of Gettysburg in 1913, reconciliation had carried the day in terms of remembering the war. White Americans North and South, typified by the aged veterans shaking hands at the Gettysburg reunion, preferred to extol the glory and bravery of soldiers on both sides rather than dwell on the depth of old antagonisms. The highly contentious political issues of the 1850s and 1860s and the two sides' motives in going to war gave way to a shared insistence that white soldiers in blue and gray had manifested the best *American* virtues. Black people played only the smallest part in this narrative, though they remained a presence in photographs and artworks produced during and after the war (Kurz & Allison's lithograph of the charge of the Fifty-fourth Massachusetts Infantry at Battery Wagner, published in 1890, focused on the death of the regiment's white colonel, Robert Gould Shaw, rather than on his black soldiers). The irony of a gathering at Gettysburg that neglected emancipation could not have been lost on any perceptive person who recalled Lincoln's stirring call for "a new birth of freedom" in his address at the battlefield in November 1863.

Just eight years shy of a century after the veterans marked the fiftieth anniversary of Gettysburg, the tumultuous era of the Civil War continues to fascinate many Americans. Some have come to their interest in the subject, at least in part, because of gripping images from the nineteenth century. In my own case, the dead Confederate sharpshooter in the Devil's Den, a photograph of Ulysses S. Grant leaning against a tree at City Point, Virginia, in 1864, and several of Alfred Waud's sketches deeply impressed me as a boy. This collection from the Library of Congress almost certainly will have the same effect on readers, who should profit from it in at least two ways: they will encounter a splendid array of beautifully reproduced images that helped define the war for those who experienced it, and they will find that the images retain enormous descriptive and interpretive power.

Gary W. Gallagher

Gary W. Gallagher is the John L. Nau III Professor of History at the University of Virginia and the author or editor of more than two dozen books on Civil War history, including *The Confederate War* and *Lee and His Army in Confederate History*.

ABOUT THIS BOOK

The American Civil War: 365 Days considers the conflict not as a strictly chronological narrative, but from the perspective of twelve broad themes (in order of presentation): Irrepressible Conflict (the buildup to, and beginning of, the war), Gathering Momentum, War in the East, Wartime Politics, War on the Water, Fighting for Freedom (focusing on the complex struggles of African Americans), Turning Points, Army Life, War in the West, Behind the Lines, Valor and Sacrifice, and An Uneasy Peace (the end of the war and its aftermath). The main text and images within each month pertain to the theme introduced on the first day of the month.

The daily events found at the bottom of each left-hand page are generally *not* connected to the text and images on the same two-page spread; instead, these entries constitute a separate running diary of noteworthy Civil War–related events that happened on a particular day, from the birth dates of future Civil War political and military leaders to battlefield clashes, important activities on the home front, and intriguing lesser-known incidents during the war.

JANUARY: IRREPRESSIBLE CONFLICT

Eight decades after thirteen American colonies eloquently declared their independence from Great Britain in 1776, the booming and boisterous United States of America was enmeshed in an accelerating crisis that threatened to tear it apart. The country's two major regions, the industrial North and the agrarian South, had been growing estranged for years. The single most divisive issue was the South's devotion to, and increasing reliance upon, its "peculiar institution" of slavery. Compromise measures promulgated by Congress after furious debate in 1820 and 1850 maintained a balance between slave and free states and helped preserve peace between the regions. But with many in the South advocating the spread of slavery into new territories, and with the North's abolition movement—organizations of white and free black people who were passionately committed to ending slavery—gathering strength and engaging in bolder action, the peace was tenuous at best. Southern fears of Northern interference with the South's way of life increased support for the drastic measure of disunion, which had been threatened by some Southern politicians for years.

In 1858, a leader of the four-year-old Republican Party, Senator William H. Seward of New York, declared that the United States was in the throes of "an irrepressible conflict between opposing and enduring forces, and . . . must and will, sooner or later, become either entirely a slaveholding nation, or entirely a free-labor nation." A rising Republican star, Abraham Lincoln

{ **JANUARY 1** 1863: The Emancipation Proclamation is issued. }

The United States Senate, A.D. 1850. Henry Clay addresses the U.S. Senate; Daniel Webster is seated to the left of Clay, and John C. Calhoun is to the left of the Speaker's chair. The fiercely debated Compromise of 1850 postponed the North-South conflict. Engraving (in sepia tints) by R. Whitechurch of a drawing by P. F. Rothermel, c. 1855

of Illinois, agreed. "A house divided against itself cannot stand," Lincoln stated during his unsuccessful campaign against Democrat Stephen A. Douglas for a seat in the U.S. Senate that same year. "I believe this government cannot endure permanently half slave and half free." But this need not mean war. Like many others, Lincoln believed that restricting slavery "to the old states where it now exists" would put it "in course of ultimate extinction"—a fate that was anathema to Southerners.

By 1860, Lincoln was the Republican nominee for president, and Southerners were uttering threats of secession with such frequency and virulence that, to many in the North, the right of states to secede had become the crucial question. "I could agree to no compromise [on slavery]," Republican senator James W. Grimes of Iowa wrote, "until the right to secede was fully renounced, because it would be a recognition of the right of one or more States to break up the government at their will."

On December 20, 1860, less than two months after Lincoln's election (see January 15–17), South Carolina became the first of eleven Southern states that eventually seceded to form the Confederate States of America (see April 6 map). Less than four months later, on April 12, Confederate cannon fire aimed at the U.S. garrison under siege inside Fort Sumter, in Charleston Harbor, South Carolina, ignited the conflict that would rend families, rupture friendships, ravage much of the South, and appall the world as it consumed hundreds of thousands of lives over four long and terrible years.

Born five years before the United States Constitution was signed at Philadelphia in 1787, the renowned orator and constitutional lawyer Daniel Webster was a staunch defender of the Union of the American states through a long political career that included service as secretary of state, several terms in the U.S. House of Representatives, and nearly twenty years in the U.S. Senate. In a January 1830 debate with a leading states' rights proponent, Senator Robert Y. Hayne of South Carolina, Webster had declared for "Liberty *and* Union, now and forever, one and inseparable!" Twenty years later, the looming evil of disunion was foremost in his mind when he supported the Compromise of 1850, "not as a Massachusetts man, nor as a Northern man, but as an American." The year of that compromise, states' rights advocate Robert Barnwell Rhett Sr. of South Carolina began two years' service in the Senate after twelve years in the House. Throughout the 1850s, the provocatively opinionated publisher of the *Charleston Mercury* fanned the flames of sectionalism and secession, as he had been doing for twenty years. "There exists a great mistake . . . in supposing that the people of the United States are, or ever have been, one people," he declared four days after Abraham Lincoln's election as president in 1860. "On the contrary, never did the sun shine on two people as thoroughly distinct as the people of the North and . . . South."

Daniel Webster (1782–1852). Photograph by Mathew Brady, 1851–52

Robert Barnwell Rhett Sr. (1800–1876). Woodcut illustration in *Frank Leslie's Illustrated Newspaper*, February 9, 1861

{ **JANUARY 2** 1861: South Carolina state troops seize the inactive Fort Johnson in Charleston Harbor. }

The territories of Kansas and Nebraska became prime battlegrounds in the struggle between slave and free states after passage of the Kansas-Nebraska Act of 1854. Engineered by Senator Stephen A. Douglas, the act for the first time allowed slavery north of the dividing line between future slave and free states that had been established as part of the 1820 Missouri Compromise—if the territorial settlers themselves voted to permit it. This policy of "popular sovereignty" inspired abolitionists in the North to send adherents to settle in the territories, while Southerners crossed into Kansas from Missouri to vote illegally in territorial elections and engage in armed attacks on free-state settlers. As violence escalated, an "Anti-Nebraska" political party, opposed to the spread of slavery into the territories, formed in the North. Soon renamed the Republican Party, it was represented in the 1856 presidential election by soldier-explorer John C. Frémont, who won eleven Northern states but lost to Democrat James Buchanan. This 1856 political cartoon, by John L. Magee of Philadelphia, blames Democrats for violence against the antislavery settlers in the disputed territories. Buchanan is one of the figures holding the Free-Soiler; Douglas is one of the figures shoving slavery down the Free-Soiler's throat.

Forcing slavery down the throat of a freesoiler. Lithograph on wove paper of a political cartoon by John L. Magee, 1856

{ **JANUARY 3** 1861: Georgia troops seize Fort Pulaski before Federal troops can garrison it. }

FORCING SLAVERY DOWN THE THROAT OF A FREESOILER

A fanatic abolitionist and supporter of the Kansas Free-Soil movement, John Brown stunned the nation—and horrified the South—when he led twenty-one men in an unsuccessful October 1859 raid on the Federal arsenal at Harpers Ferry, Virginia, in a plot to issue stolen weapons to slaves and foment a slave rebellion. Thwarted by Federal troops under Lieutenant Colonel Robert E. Lee and Lieutenant J. E. B. Stuart, Brown's raid was denounced by most Northern politicians—including virtually every Republican leader. This did not prevent Southerners from labeling Lincoln and his party "John Brown Republicans" in 1860—the same year Southern-backed "filibuster" William Walker was executed in Honduras. Filibustering (mounting military expeditions to secure American proslavery interests on foreign soil) flourished during the 1850s, and doctor-lawyer-journalist Walker was the most notable of these adventurers. In 1856, he established a dictatorship in Nicaragua, but his plan to create a broader empire supported by slave labor was defeated when a coalition of four Central American states drove him out of the region. Celebrated throughout the South, Walker launched three more Central American expeditions. On the third, the British, who had their own interests in the region, captured Walker and turned him over to Honduran authorities.

John Brown (1800–1859). Photograph by Levin C. Handy from an earlier daguerreotype, date unknown

William Walker (1824–1860). Photograph by Mathew Brady, 1855–60

{ **JANUARY 4** 1861: Alabama forces take over the Federal arsenal at Mount Vernon, Alabama. }

The common belief that emancipated slaves would never be accorded equal status with whites in the United States—and a desire on the part of some white citizens to keep the free black population from growing—inspired a movement to encourage black emigration and colonization outside the country. In 1821, the American Colonization Society, established four years earlier to raise funds to send free blacks to Africa, purchased land and founded Liberia on Africa's west coast, at Cape Mesurado. In 1847, the colony became the independent Republic of Liberia; by 1860, more than ten thousand free African Americans had emigrated. Many slave owners favored colonization, believing that the emigration of free blacks would reduce the likelihood of slave rebellions. Most free blacks, however, opposed emigration to Africa—as well as later schemes to establish African American colonies in Haiti and Central America. "Does any one pretend to deny that this is our country?" the African American lawyer and orator John Rock said in 1862. "Or that much of the wealth and prosperity found here is the result of the labor of our hands? Or that our blood and bones have not crimsoned and whitened every battlefield from Maine to Louisiana? It is true, a great many simple-minded people have been induced to go to Liberia and to Hayti, but, be assured, the more intelligent portion of the colored people will remain here . . . where we have withstood almost everything."

Rev. Philip Coker, chaplain of the Senate of Liberia. Daguerreotype, 1856–60

Fish Town at Bassau, Liberia. Watercolor by Robert K. Griffin, c. 1856

{ **JANUARY 5** **1861:** A merchant vessel, the *Star of the West,* leaves New York for Fort Sumter carrying 250 troops and supplies. }

We are an agricultural people: we are a primitive but a civilized people. We have no cities—we don't want them. We have no literature—we don't need any yet. We have no press—we are glad of it. We do not require a press because we go out and discuss all public questions from the stump with our people. We have no commercial marine—no navy—we don't want them. We are better without them. Your ships carry our produce, and you can protect your own vessels. We want no manufactures: we desire no trading, no mechanical or manufacturing classes. As long as we have our rice, our sugar, our tobacco, and our cotton, we can command wealth to purchase all we want from those nations with which we are in amity, and to lay up money besides.

Sunny South. Color lithograph, Calvert Litho. & Engr. Co., 1883

—Louis T. Wigfall (1816–1874), U.S. senator from Texas (1859–61) and Confederate senator from Texas (1862–65), as quoted by British correspondent William Russell

{ **JANUARY 6** **1865:** Irate over General Benjamin Butler's failure to follow orders regarding the Union assault on Fort Fisher, North Carolina, which guards the last port through which General Robert E. Lee's Confederate army can receive supplies, General Ulysses S. Grant asks President Lincoln to remove Butler from command of the Army of the James. }

SUNNY SOUTH

"What, to the American slave, is your Fourth of July?" former slave
Frederick Douglass asked in a speech on July 4, 1852. "I answer: A day that reveals to him,
more than all other days in the year, the gross injustice and cruelty to which he is the constant
victim. To him your celebration is a sham." As he spoke, nearly four million people were
enslaved in the United States, and the South's reliance on slave labor was growing. Congress
had ended the African slave trade in 1808 (the domestic slave trade flourished), but a brisk
illegal African operation continued; it is estimated that more than fifty thousand slaves were
smuggled into the country between 1808 and the start of the Civil War. Southerners defended
their "peculiar institution," with elaborate arguments based on religion, science, history, and
economics—averring that slavery supported the entire American economy, not just the South's.
Senator John C. Calhoun of South Carolina claimed that slavery was "a positive good" and "the
most safe and stable basis for free institutions in the world." A rising Northern politician could
not have disagreed more. "This is a world of compensations," Abraham Lincoln wrote on April 6,
1859, "and he who would be no slave must consent to have no slave. Those who deny freedom to
others deserve it not for themselves, and, under a just God, cannot long retain it."

The Lash and *The Parting* "Buy
us too." Color lithograph cards
by H. L. Stephens, in William
A. Stephens, *Stephens' Album
Varieties no. 3: The Slave in
1863* (1863)

{ **JANUARY 7** **1861:** Senator John J. Crittenden of Kentucky, a Unionist, gives a speech urging passage
of his compromise to end secession and avoid war. }

No. 5.

THE LASH.

Enterd accord'g to act of Cong's in the year 1863, by Wm. A. Stephens, in the Clerks Office of the Dist. Court of the U.S. for the E. Dist. of Pa.

No. 4

THE PARTING "Buy us too."

Enterd accord'g to act of Cong's in the year 1863, by Wm. A. Stephens, in the Clerks Office of the Dist. Court of the U.S. for the E. Dist. of Pa.

In May 1856, as violence between proslavery and free-state factions escalated in the territory of Kansas, Congress debated whether to admit the territory to the Union under its recently promulgated free-state constitution, ignoring a proslavery territorial legislature elected largely by Southerners who had crossed into Kansas and voted illegally. Senator Charles Sumner, Republican from Massachusetts, delivering a tempestuous speech titled "The Crime against Kansas," called the architect of the Kansas-Nebraska Act, Senator Stephen A. Douglas, "the squire of Slavery, its very Sancho Panza, ready to do its humiliating offices," and referred to Senator Andrew P. Butler of South Carolina as a man "who has chosen a mistress . . . who, though ugly to others, is always lovely to him. . . . I mean the harlot, Slavery." Two days later, Preston S. Brooks, a South Carolina representative and Butler's nephew, stormed onto the floor of the Senate after it had adjourned for the day, told Sumner the speech was "a libel on South Carolina, and Mr. Butler," and beat Sumner insensible with a gold-headed cane, inflicting injuries that plagued the senator for years. Indignation surged across the North. In the South, however, resolutions approving Brooks's action were passed. An attempt to expel Brooks from Congress failed to achieve the necessary two-thirds vote. Still, the congressman resigned—and was promptly returned to Congress by his constituents.

Democratic Platform Illustrated.
Lithograph on wove paper,
James G. Varney, 1856

Preston S. Brooks (1819–1857).
Mezzotint engraving by A. B.
Walter, c. 1857

Charles Sumner (1811–1874).
Reproduction of a photograph
possibly by Mathew Brady,
1861–74

{ **JANUARY 8** 1861: U.S. Secretary of the Interior Jacob Thompson of Mississippi, the last Southerner in the cabinet, resigns. }

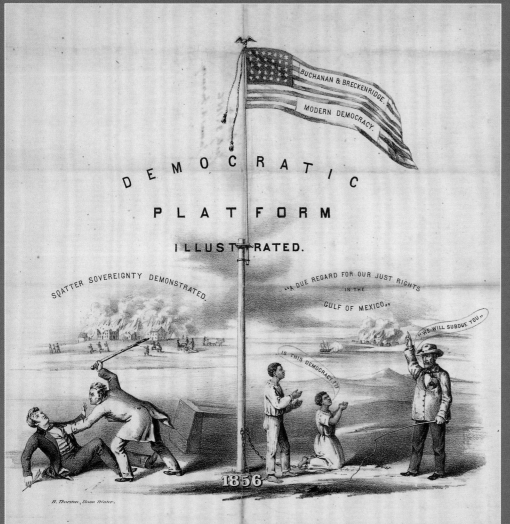

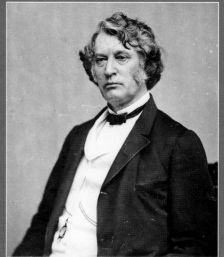

As debate over the extension of slavery into the territories increased, so did abolitionist activities that resulted in courtroom battles. Perhaps the most famous of these cases was the May 1854 trial of Anthony Burns. A slave of Charles Suttle of Alexandria, Virginia, he had fled to the freedom of Boston, where Suttle soon found him. Burns's arrest on a trumped-up charge of robbery, as well as his treatment as a fugitive slave, led to a mass protest meeting by sympathetic Bostonians, who then marched on the jail and made an unsuccessful attempt to release him—during which a deputy was killed. With police and military reinforcements called in, Boston had the aura of a city under martial law. This changed to an aura of mourning as buildings were draped with black crepe after Burns was legally declared a fugitive slave and ordered back to Virginia. A year later, Passmore Williamson, the secretary of the acting committee of the Pennsylvania Anti-Slavery Society, assisted by several free black men, boarded a ship getting ready to depart from the Philadelphia docks and escorted Jane, a slave of the U.S. minister to Nicaragua, John H. Wheeler, and her two sons off the ship after she let it be known that she wished to be free. During the resulting confusion of legal cases, Williamson was kept in jail from mid-July to early November for providing inaccurate testimony—though, in fact, he had testified truthfully. Williamson became an abolitionist hero, his incarceration purportedly demonstrating the proslavery bias of Federal courts.

Cover of *The Boston Slave Riot, and Trial of Anthony Burns* (1854)

Passmore Williamson, in Moyamensing Prison [Philadelphia] for Alledged Contempt of Court. Lithograph with watercolor on wove paper by Augustus Kollner of artwork by Emil Luders, c. 1855

{ **JANUARY 9** **1861:** Mississippi secedes from the Union, following the lead of South Carolina three weeks earlier. }

THE
BOSTON SLAVE RIOT,
AND
TRIAL
OF
Anthony Burns,

CONTAINING THE

REPORT OF THE FANEUIL HALL MEETING; THE MURDER OF
BACHELDER; THEODORE PARKER'S LESSON FOR THE DAY;
SPEECHES OF COUNSEL ON BOTH SIDES, CORRECTED
BY THEMSELVES; VERBATIM REPORT OF JUDGE
LORING'S DECISION; AND, A DETAILED AC-
COUNT OF THE EMBARKATION.

BOSTON:
FETRIDGE AND COMPANY.
1854.

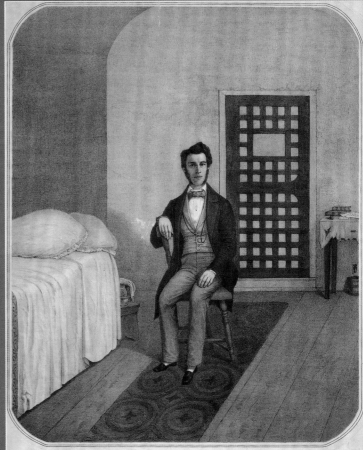

My return is the truth & the whole truth. It will neither be retained nor amended. Keep Eyous to. P. Williamson

PASSMORE WILLIAMSON,
IN MOYAMENSING PRISON FOR ALLEDGED CONTEMPT OF COURT.

One of America's foremost nineteenth-century families, whose American roots extended back to 1637, the Beecher family included some of the strongest and most influential antislavery voices heard in the antebellum era and during the Civil War. Patriarch Lyman Beecher, a Presbyterian minister who believed in education for women as well as men, shared his moral opposition to slavery with his thirteen children. His son Henry Ward Beecher, pastor of the Congregational Plymouth Church of Brooklyn, was a leading clerical voice in the abolitionist movement; the guns he helped provide to Free-Soilers in the disputed territory of Kansas were quickly dubbed "Beecher's Bibles." His sister Harriet Beecher Stowe, a teacher and writer, became the preeminent Beecher of her generation after the publication of her best-selling anti-slavery novel *Uncle Tom's Cabin, or Life among the Lowly* in 1852. "I wrote what I did because as a woman, as a mother I was oppressed and broken-hearted with the sorrows and injustices I saw," she said, "because as a Christian I felt the dishonor to Christianity—because as a lover of my country I trembled at the coming day of wrath."

Beecher family group: Harriet Beecher Stowe (1811–1896), Rev. Lyman Beecher (1775–1863), Rev. Henry Ward Beecher (1813–1887). c. 1855–63

{ **JANUARY 10** 1861: Florida becomes the third state to secede from the Union. }

First published as a serial, then as a two-volume novel, *Uncle Tom's Cabin* was also produced as a stage drama several times before and during the Civil War. Northern audiences became deeply engaged by the struggles of Tom, an earnest and appealing old slave who is devoted to his kind, debt-ridden Kentucky master but is sold, eventually becoming the property of a cruel plantation owner, Simon Legree. In making a slave the title character and a hero, and in creating vivid characters who did not fit standard stereotypes (Legree is a Northerner who moved South, and some Southerners figure among the story's more sympathetic characters), Stowe presented a deeply human and particularly scathing indictment of the institution and the plight of slaves, both in bondage and as fugitives. Many Northerners were outraged by the cruelties of slavery depicted in the story. Most Southerners were outraged by the story itself, decried as a glaring example of Northern attacks against Southern honor and "domestic institutions." This outrage lasted for years. In November 1862, Confederate soldier Rufus Cater wrote of Mrs. Stowe and her novel, "I wonder if her pharisaical heart feels no compunctious throb when she beholds such carnage and bloodshed, the work of those fierce flames of fanaticism which her ingenious brain labored so assiduously to enkindle."

Uncle Tom's Cabin. Poster for a theatrical production. Color lithograph, W. J. Morgan & Co., 1881

{ **JANUARY 11** 1861: Alabama is the fourth state—and the third in three days—to secede from the Union. }

THE FAMOUS JARRETT & PALMER LONDON COMP'Y
SLAVINS ORIGINAL AMERICAN TROUPE
CONSOLIDATED WITH
UNCLE TOM'S CABIN.
W.J. MORGAN & CO. LITH. CLEVELAND.O.
LC-USZ62-2655

Beginning his quest for emancipation in 1846 after residing for a time with his master in the free state of Illinois and the free territory of Wisconsin, Dred Scott was declared a free man by a St. Louis jury in 1850—but the Supreme Court in Missouri, a slave state, reversed the decision two years later. Scott appealed the reversal to the U.S. Supreme Court, where the case was argued in February 1856 and reargued that December. It was finally decided on March 6, 1857, two days after the inauguration of President James Buchanan—who had been apprised of the decision before it was announced and urged the public to support it. Instead of deciding the issue on narrow grounds, the Court, which included a number of slaveholders, ruled against Scott, seven to two, in a breathtakingly broad decision now generally regarded, as noted by legal scholar Geoffrey Stone, "as the greatest legal and moral blunder in the Court's history." The majority decision, written by Chief Justice Roger B. Taney (who had freed his own slaves), was an attempt to settle, at one stroke, the troubling issue of slavery and the Federal territories. Instead, the long and complex ruling—which included the stipulation that black people could not be citizens and thus could not claim any of the rights and privileges of citizenship—sparked widespread outrage and political action. Many Republicans began to publicly support black citizenship and other fundamental rights; some called for full equality for blacks, including the right to vote. The ruling also pushed some Northern Democrats into the Republican Party.

Dred Scott (c. 1799–1858).
Wood engraving in *Century* magazine, 1887

Roger B. Taney (1777–1864). 1855–64

James Buchanan (1791–1868). 1850–68

{ **JANUARY 12** 1863: The First Confederate Congress gathers at Richmond for its third session, hearing President Jefferson Davis speak optimistically on the state of the Confederacy. }

The Dred Scott decision was among the issues addressed in the rambunctious contest between Republican challenger Abraham Lincoln and Democratic incumbent Stephen A. Douglas in the 1858 campaign for one of the Illinois seats in the U.S. Senate. Lincoln lost by a vote of fifty-four to forty-six (at the time, state legislatures elected U.S. senators). But during more than two months of verbal jousting with the five-foot-four-inch Douglas, an able and pugnacious politician known as the "Little Giant," the six-foot-four-inch, self-educated Lincoln, a former one-term congressman, won national attention.

"Mr. Lincoln advocates boldly and clearly a war of sections," Douglas charged in Chicago on July 9, "a war of the North and the South, of free states against the slave states—a war of extermination—to be continued relentlessly until the one or the other shall be subdued."

"Judge Douglas . . . says that I am in favor . . . of inviting (as he expresses it) the South to a war upon the North for the purpose of nationalizing slavery," Lincoln replied the next day. "I did not say that I was in favor of anything. . . . I only said what I expected would take place. . . . I did not even say that I desired that slavery should be put in course of ultimate extinction. I do say so now, however. . . . I have always hated slavery."

Abraham Lincoln (1809–1865) in Pittsfield, Illinois, two weeks before the final Lincoln-Douglas debate. Photograph from an ambrotype by Calvin Jackson, October 1, 1858

Stephen A. Douglas (1813–1861). Daguerreotype by the Mathew Brady Studio, 1844–60

{ **JANUARY 13** 1863: Federal officials formally authorize the raising of Negro troops for the Union army's South Carolina Volunteer Infantry. }

Born into slavery, Harriet Tubman escaped to Philadelphia in 1849, navigating her course to freedom, she said, by following the North Star. Returning south at least nineteen times, she rescued more than two hundred slaves—including her own mother and father—via the Underground Railroad. White abolitionists and free blacks operated this secret, loosely organized system to help slaves flee from captivity in the South to the relative safety of the free states or the more secure freedom of Canada. Danger was a constant; any form of assistance to runaways was illegal. Escaped slaves who were recaptured risked being tortured, maimed, and sold far away from family and friends, while those helping them might be sued, fined, or imprisoned. Tubman's exploits were so successful—"I never ran my train off the track," she said, "and I never lost a passenger"—that the State of Maryland offered a $40,000 reward for her capture. "In point of courage, shrewdness, and disinterested exertions to rescue her fellowman," declared William Still, a fellow leader of the Underground Railroad, "she was without equal." Tireless, Tubman gave antislavery speeches and, in 1858, helped John Brown plan his raid on Harpers Ferry. During the Civil War, as a spy and scout, she provided valuable intelligence to Union forces, and she was also a nurse for soldiers and black refugees.

Harriet Tubman (1821?–1913). Photograph by H. B. Lindsley, 1860–75

Harriet Tubman, disguised as a man, aiding an escape. Ink-and-watercolor drawing by Bernarda Bryson, 1934–35. Art © Estate of Bernarda Bryson Shahn / Licensed by VAGA, New York, N.Y.

{ **JANUARY 14** 1861: Louisiana state troops seize Fort Pike, near New Orleans. }

Shaken by crisis after crisis as rancor grew between the regions, the country lurched toward the 1860 presidential campaign. The Democratic Party divided, with Northern and Southern factions unable to agree on a candidate. After two stormy conventions, Stephen A. Douglas emerged as the candidate of the Northern Democrats, while Vice President John C. Breckinridge of Kentucky represented Democrats in the South. A new and destined-to-be-short-lived organization, the Constitutional Union Party—which recognized "no political principle other than the Constitution of the country, the union of the states, and the enforcement of the laws"—also entered a candidate: John Bell, a former U.S. senator from Tennessee. Republicans chose "dark horse" Abraham Lincoln as their candidate, believing he would be the Republican most likely to win states such as Illinois and Indiana, which Democrat James Buchanan had carried in 1856. Lincoln also clearly reflected the strong Republican position against the expansion of slavery, and his articulate attacks on the Dred Scott decision had made him a party hero. Outside the party, however, many were less happy about the prospect of Lincoln as president. In November, the candidate received a letter signed by "Johny Coyle," written in a child's hand and decorated by a small hand-drawn bird. "Mr. Lincoln," Coyle wrote, "please to withdraw. We do not want you for president of the United States. The Spirit says so."

[Dividing the] National Map. Depicted are, left to right, presidential candidates Lincoln, Douglas, Breckinridge, and Bell. Lithograph on wove paper. 1860

{ **JANUARY 15** 1862: The U.S. Senate confirms the appointment of Edwin M. Stanton as secretary of war, succeeding the much-criticized Simon Cameron. }

In the hard-fought 1860 presidential contest, only three candidates ran in each section of the country: Lincoln, Douglas, and Bell in the North; Breckinridge, Douglas, and Bell in the South. At the time, it was traditional for presidential candidates to remain above the fray, letting others do the campaigning for them. Stephen A. Douglas broke with this tradition. Deeply concerned that the country was about to come apart, he embarked on a speech-making campaign that exhausted his health, did little to further his own presidential bid, and failed to deter those who were determined that their states would secede from the Union if the Republican candidate were successful. The equally worried Abraham Lincoln, meanwhile—in the midst of much correspondence on weightier matters—received a letter, dated October 15, from eleven-year-old Grace Bedell of New York that contained an intriguing suggestion for the clean-shaven Republican candidate: "I have got 4 brothers and part of them will vote for you anyway and if you will let your whiskers grow I will try and get the rest of them to vote for you you would look a great deal better for your face is so thin. All the ladies like whiskers and they would tease their husbands to vote for you and then you would be President."

For President, Abram Lincoln. Woodcut or lithograph on cotton by H. C. Howard as poster/campaign banner, 1860

{ **JANUARY 16** 1861: The Arkansas legislature finishes a bill seeking a referendum on secession. }

For President

ABRAM LINCOLN.

For Vice President

HANNIBAL HAMLIN.

"Your eighteen Northern non-slave-holding States nominate two of the most fanatical of your sect as candidates for President and Vice-President," U.S. Senator—and "fire-eating" Southerner—Louis T. Wigfall of Texas thundered during a Senate debate. "And now you tell us they shall be inaugurated. Previously to the election and to the anticipated inauguration you organized a Praetorian guard. . . . That . . . its members do undergo military drill; that it is a military organization, no man who has looked upon them . . . and heard their regular military tramp, does or can doubt." Hardly an official creation of the six-year-old Republican Party, hundreds of Wide-Awake Clubs sprang into being in 1860. Dressed in capes and carrying lighted oil lamps mounted atop four-foot poles (which could easily be converted to cudgels), the Wide-Awakes marched in support of Lincoln and other Republican candidates, monitored polling places on Election Day, and added zest, excitement, and—among some non-Republicans—bitterness to what was already a crucial, and harrowing, political campaign.

Free speech, free soil, free men. Membership certificate for the Republican Wide-Awake Club. Lithograph on wove paper, Gavit & Co., 1860

{ **JANUARY 17** 1865: General William Tecumseh Sherman prepares to march his army north from Savannah, Georgia, through South Carolina, though bad weather delays his campaign for two more days. }

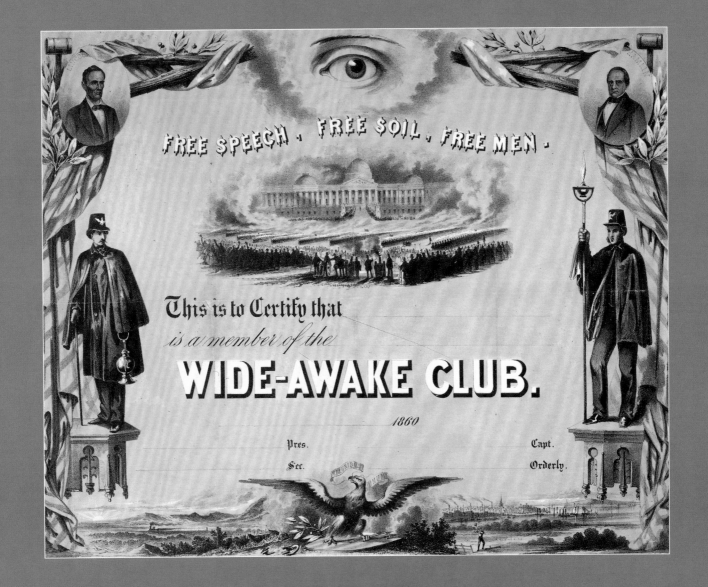

It is seventy-two years since the first inauguration of a President under our national Constitution. During that period fifteen different and greatly distinguished citizens have, in succession, administered the executive branch of the government. They have conducted it through many perils, and generally with great success. Yet, with all this scope of precedent, I now enter upon the same task for the brief Constitutional term of four years under great and peculiar difficulty. A disruption of the Federal Union, heretofore only menaced, is now formidably attempted. . . . In *your* hands, my dissatisfied fellow countrymen, and not in *mine*, is the momentous issue of civil war. The government will not assail *you*. You can have no conflict, without being yourselves the aggressors. *You* have no oath registered in Heaven to destroy the government, while *I* shall have the most solemn one to "preserve, protect, and defend" it.

 I am loth to close. We are not enemies, but friends. We must not be enemies. Though passion may have strained, it must not break our bonds of affection. The mystic chords of memory, stretching from every battle-field, and patriot grave, to every living heart and hearth-stone, all over this broad land, will yet swell the chorus of the Union, when again touched, as surely they will be, by the better angels of our nature."

     —President Abraham Lincoln, First Inaugural Address, March 4, 1861

Abraham Lincoln delivers his first inaugural address at the U.S. Capitol. March 4, 1861

{ **JANUARY 18** 1862: The Confederate Territory of Arizona is formed out of the southern half of the Union's New Mexico Territory. }

"The tea has been thrown overboard," Robert Barnwell Rhett's *Charleston Mercury* proclaimed after Lincoln's election. "The revolution of 1860 has been initiated." South Carolina soon became the first of eleven states to declare it had left the Union, beginning a process that would lead to a confederation of the seceded states. (Two additional border states, Missouri and Kentucky, were represented by stars on the Confederate flag, but they did not actually secede.) In early 1861, at about the time the Confederate States of America (CSA) was being officially organized at a convention in Montgomery, Alabama, this Northern political cartoon appeared, portraying leaders of the states that had thus far left the Union—South Carolina, Mississippi, Florida, Alabama, Georgia, and Louisiana—as a band of competing opportunists and affording them little sympathy. The *Baltimore American*, meanwhile, reflected the growing fears of actual conflict between the alienated regions when it passionately editorialized on January 7 for restraint and conciliation: "What new and unspeakable horrors are involved in the idea of civil war! Does it not become all good men, all men who have humanity, to besiege the throne of Heaven with their supplications, that this hitherto the happiest of all nations may be saved from such an unnatural collision and fearful catastrophe?"

The Dis-United States. Or the Southern Confederacy. Lithograph on wove paper of a political cartoon, Currier & Ives, 1861

{ **JANUARY 19** 1807: Robert Edward Lee (CSA) is born in Stratford, Virginia.
1861: Georgia is the fifth state to secede from the Union. }

THE DIS-UNITED STATES.

OR THE SOUTHERN CONFEDERACY

Published by Currier & Ives, 152 Nassau St. N.Y.

As President Franklin Pierce's secretary of war (1853–57), former soldier Jefferson Davis strove with little success to reorganize the small yet hidebound antebellum military establishment. As a U.S. representative and senator, Davis became a champion of the entire South by stoutly defending states' rights. A wealthy Mississippi planter, and the owner of many slaves, Davis had built a life that was deeply intertwined with the South's "peculiar institution." But after being chosen provisional president of the Confederate States of America on February 9, 1861, by delegates to the Montgomery, Alabama, convention that formed the Confederacy, he did not mention slavery in his inaugural address on February 18. Instead, he emphasized the right of each sovereign state to determine its own course. Davis stated: "Through many years of controversy with our late associates, the Northern States, we have vainly endeavored to secure tranquillity, and to obtain respect for the rights to which we were entitled. As a necessity, not a choice, we have resorted to the remedy of separation; and henceforth our energies must be directed to the conduct of our own affairs."

Jefferson Davis (1808–1889). Hand-colored lithograph, Blelock & Co., 1850–70

The Hon. Jefferson Davis, president-elect of the new Southern Confederacy, addressing the citizens of Montgomery, Alabama, from the balcony of the Exchange Hotel, on the night of Feb. 16, 1861, and previous to his inauguration. From a sketch by our special artist. Wood engraving in *Frank Leslie's Illustrated Newspaper*, March 16, 1861

{ **JANUARY 20** 1861: Mississippi secessionists take over the Federal installations on Ship Island, in the Gulf of Mexico. }

FRANK LESLIE'S
ILLUSTRATED
NEWSPAPER

Entered according to the Act of Congress, in the year 1861, by Frank Leslie, in the Clerk's Office of the District Court for the Southern District of New York.

No. 277.—Vol. XI.]   NEW YORK, MARCH 16, 1861.   [Price 6 Cents.

LITH & PUBLISHED BY B.E. LOCK & CO. 110 CANAL ST. NEW ORLEANS.

"How strange how romantic life is now in Charleston!" Southerner Caroline Howard Gilman wrote to her "Aunt Lala" early in 1861. "Almost every man is dressed in some uniform—all are so anxious and solemn." As tensions rose and the possibility of war increased, excitement was high, and much heed was paid to uniforms and other martial accoutrements. This was particularly true in the South, with its cherished military traditions. (Ninety-six military schools were founded in the South between 1827 and 1860, compared to fifteen in the North.) A rare and colorful reflection of these traditions, and a vision of the Confederate army in its infancy, is found in *Uniform and Dress of the Army of the Confederate States*, published the year the war began. As the war wound on, uniforms became more patchwork affairs, especially in the South's armies, due to shortages imposed by the North's naval blockade. (It was reportedly on a quest for shoes manufactured at a Gettysburg factory that Lee's Army of Northern Virginia entered that town in 1863.) Material problems did not dim the spirit of the Confederate fighting man, however. After the battle of Gettysburg, one retreating Confederate soldier is said to have told his officer, "We'll fight them, sir, till hell freezes over. And then, sir, we will fight them on the ice."

Infantry. Color lithograph by B. Duncan of a drawing by E. Crehen, in *Uniform and Dress of the Army of the Confederate States* (1861)

{ **JANUARY 21** 1824: Thomas Jonathan "Stonewall" Jackson (CSA) is born in Clarksburg, Virginia. }

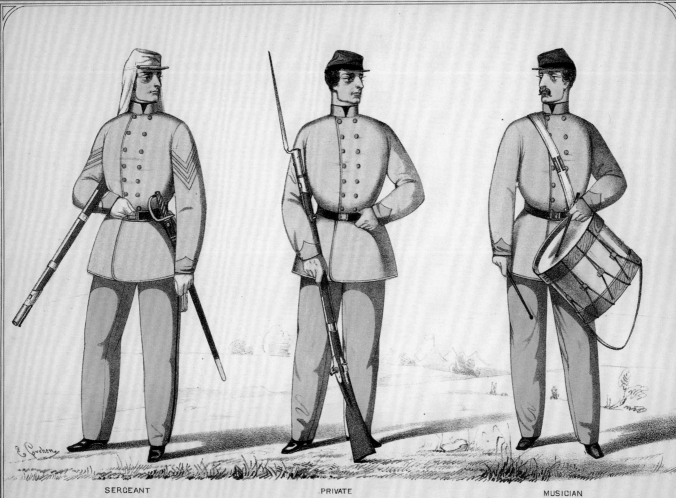

SERGEANT .PRIVATE MUSICIAN

INFANTRY

Unable to fulfill his dream of attending West Point, New Yorker Elmer Ellsworth went west, eventually settling in Illinois. Enthusiastic for military pursuits, he secured command of a lackluster band of voluntary military students and turned them into the U.S. Zouave Cadets, a group that became famous for its precision drills. (Zouaves were particularly ferocious Algerian soldiers whose exotic uniforms were widely imitated.) In 1860, Ellsworth entered the law office of Abraham Lincoln as a law student. After working on Lincoln's presidential campaign, he followed the new president to Washington, D.C., where he proposed the formation of a militia bureau. He also raised, trained, and brought back to Washington a regiment of New York volunteers recruited from the city's volunteer firemen. The reciprocal devotion between Ellsworth and his New York Fire Zouaves drew the attention of Lincoln's secretary, John Hay, who wrote of the volunteers' "respectable demeanor to their Chief and his anxious solicitude for their comfort & safety." Rowdy when off duty in the capital city but well disciplined on duty, the Fire Zouaves soon won particular favor because of their special expertise. On the night of May 9, 1861, Willard's Hotel, a prime Washington gathering place for politicians and favor seekers, caught fire. The Fire Zouaves rushed to the rescue, fought the fire with dash and determination for more than two hours, and saved the hotel. (See also January 29, February 2.)

Ellsworth's Campaign & Barrack or Dress Uniforms. Color print, date unknown

{ **JANUARY 22** 1864: Major General William Rosecrans is named commander of the Union's Department of the Missouri. }

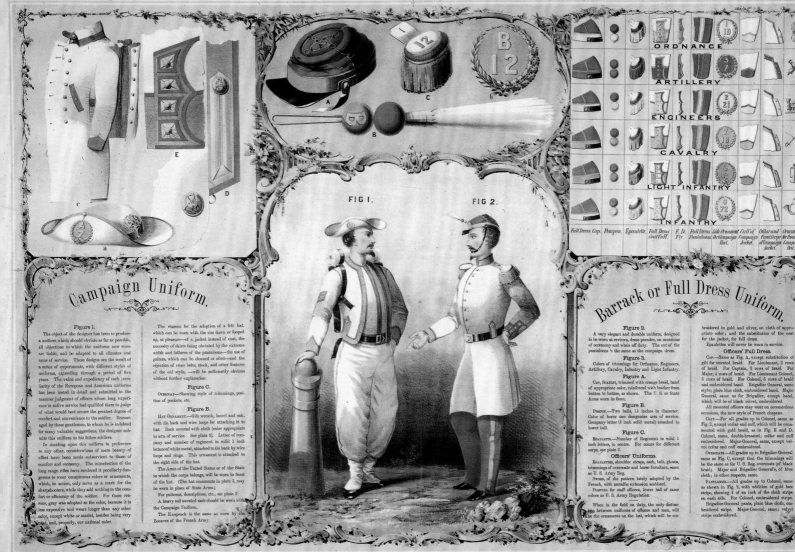

ELLSWORTH'S CAMPAIGN & BARRACK OR DRESS UNIFORMS.

On December 20, 1860, delegates to the South Carolina secession convention solemnly signed a parchment declaring "that the union now subsisting . . . under the name of 'The United States of America' is hereby dissolved." Then the convention dispatched three commissioners, James L. Orr, Robert W. Barnwell, and James H. Adams, to Washington to negotiate the removal of "foreign" troops from its soil. The commissioners insisted that President James Buchanan remove the Federal garrison at Charleston, which had recently shifted from Fort Moultrie to Fort Sumter. After Lincoln's inauguration on March 4, 1861, they continued negotiations, usually via an intermediary, with the new Republican secretary of state, William H. Seward—who, in 1858, had described an "irrepressible conflict" between the nation's slave-labor and free-labor factions. A man of acute political instincts and a firm believer in his own abilities, Seward had embarked on his cabinet service acting more independently than he would after Lincoln proved a far stronger and abler chief executive than Seward initially believed him to be. This caused confusion, and then indignation, among Confederate authorities after Seward declared, in early April, "I am satisfied the government will not undertake to supply Fort Sumter without giving notice to [South Carolina] Govr. Pickens." A few days earlier, however, Lincoln had ordered that preparations be made for a relief expedition that would resupply—though not reinforce—the besieged Federal garrison there.

"The Union is Dissolved!" *Charleston Mercury*, broadside extra, December 20, 1860

William H. Seward (1801–1872). Engraving by John Chester Buttre, 1843–93

{ **JANUARY 23** 1863: Major General Ambrose Burnside's Union army pulls back to Fredericksburg, Virginia, ending its abortive "mud march," an attempt to advance across the Rappahannock River. }

CHARLESTON
MERCURY
EXTRA:

Passed unanimously at 1.15 o'clock, P. M., December
20th, 1860.

AN ORDINANCE

To dissolve the Union between the State of South Carolina and
other States united with her under the compact entitled "The
Constitution of the United States of America."

We, the People of the State of South Carolina, in Convention assembled, do declare and ordain, and
it is hereby declared and ordained,

That the Ordinance adopted by us in Convention, on the twenty-third day of May, in the
year of our Lord one thousand seven hundred and eighty-eight, whereby the Constitution of the
United States of America was ratified, and also, all Acts and parts of Acts of the General
Assembly of this State, ratifying amendments of the said Constitution, are hereby repealed;
and that the union now subsisting between South Carolina and other States, under the name of
"The United States of America," is hereby dissolved.

THE
UNION
IS
DISSOLVED!

As negotiations between Confederate and Federal authorities continued in Washington, the attention of the citizens of Charleston—and, increasingly, much of America—was focused on one of the fortifications protecting Charleston Harbor: Fort Moultrie, where a small garrison of U.S. soldiers commanded by Major Robert Anderson (1805–1871) was stationed. As representatives of a government the people of South Carolina now considered alien, the men of the garrison were more than unwelcome; their presence was considered an affront. Caught in this dangerous situation and determined that his command would stay in place as long as that was the will of the Federal government, Major Anderson surveyed Fort Moultrie's defenses—including low walls that could easily be breached by fire from sharpshooters hidden in the nearby houses and sand hills—and found them inadequate. Acutely aware of the intense Confederate interest in his garrison's activities, he stealthily transferred his men to the much stronger Fort Sumter in Charleston Harbor on the night of December 26, 1860, informing the adjutant general of this move in a report that did not reach Washington until December 29: "I have the honor to report that I have just completed, by the blessing of God, the removal to this fort of all of my garrison. . . . The step which I have taken was, in my opinion, necessary to prevent the effusion of blood."

Sketch of Charleston's defense. Ink-and-watercolor drawing by [Frank] Vizetelly, 1863

{ **JANUARY 24** 1861: Georgia state troops take over the Federal arsenal at Augusta. }

Among those present in Charleston as attention focused on Major Robert Anderson's Fort Sumter garrison was the avid secessionist Edmund Ruffin, a Virginia native who had long defended "the institution of negro slavery" as the foundation "on which the social & political existence of the south rests" and, in 1860, had decried the South's "present submission to northern domination." Severely disappointed when Virginia did not immediately secede after South Carolina did, Ruffin had moved in 1861 to Charleston, where he joined the Palmetto Guard. "Taken altogether, this is a most singular state of war," he reported on March 17, before actual war had begun. "Fort Sumter is surrounded by batteries prepared to batter or shell it. . . . The officers of the fort & the besieging C.S. army even exchange friendly visits, & dine at each other's quarters." Meanwhile, Southerner John J. Crittenden was witnessing the final defeat of his eleventh-hour attempt to preserve the Union: the House of Representatives voted down the "Crittenden Compromise" in January, and his fellow senators followed suit in March. Returning to Kentucky, Crittenden labored successfully to keep his state in the Union. But he would be among the Americans whose families were torn apart by the Civil War: his son George became a Confederate general; his son Thomas, a general for the Union.

Edmund Ruffin (1794–1865).
c. 1860–65

John J. Crittenden (1787–1863).
Daguerreotype by the Mathew
Brady Studio, 1844–46

{ **JANUARY 25** 1825: George Edward Pickett (CSA) is born in Richmond, Virginia. }

[April 12, 1861] I do not pretend to go to sleep. How can I? If Anderson does not accept terms—at four—the orders are—he shall be fired upon.

I count four—St. Michael chimes. I begin to hope. At half-past four, the heavy booming of a cannon. . . .

[April 13] Fort Sumter has been on fire. He has not yet silenced any of our guns. . . . But the sound of those guns makes regular meals impossible. None of us go to table. . . .

[April 15] I did not know that one could live such days of excitement. . . .

The crowd was shouting and showing these two [Colonels Chesnut and Manning] as messengers of good news. They were escorted to Beauregard's headquarters. Fort Sumter had surrendered.

—Mary Boykin Chesnut, diary entries

Bombardment of Fort Sumter, Charleston Harbor, 12th & 13th of April, 1861. Hand-colored lithograph, Currier & Ives, 1861?

{ **JANUARY 26** 1861: Louisiana becomes the sixth state to secede from the Union. }

As would often be the case in the war that began with the cannonades at Charleston Harbor, the two men commanding the opposing Union and Confederate forces were not strangers to each other. Both Major Robert Anderson, commander of the garrison in Fort Sumter, and P. G. T. Beauregard, commander of Confederate forces in Charleston, were West Point graduates—Anderson, class of 1825; Beauregard, class of 1838—and, at one time, Anderson had been Beauregard's much-respected artillery instructor. Both had served on General Winfield Scott's staff during the Mexican War (1846–48), and both the Louisianian Beauregard and the Kentuckian Anderson (who was married to a woman from Georgia) had deep ties to the South. The staunch Confederate Beauregard, temperamental and confrontational, had been appointed commandant of West Point in January—with the assistance of his politically influential brother-in-law, Senator John Slidell (see May 7). He was relieved of that command after five days, in large part because of his obvious Southern sympathies, and he resigned from the U.S. Army a month later. The staunch Unionist Anderson, steady and forthright, exhibited the sorrowful grace and absolute determination to prevail in the end that would characterize many on both sides during the war. "Our Southern brethren . . . have attacked their father's house and their loyal brothers," he wrote. "They must be punished and brought back, but this necessity breaks my heart."

Major Robert Anderson, USA, in command of Fort Sumpter [sic], *Charleston Harbor, SC.* Woodcut of a photograph by Webster & Bros., in *Frank Leslie's Illustrated Newspaper,* February 2, 1861

Pierre Gustave Toutant Beauregard (1818–1893). 1860–65

{ **JANUARY 27** 1862: President Lincoln issues General War Order No. 1, directing Union armies to advance against Confederate forces after a long period of inaction. }

FRANK LESLIE'S
ILLUSTRATED
NEWSPAPER

Entered according to the Act of Congress in the year 1860, by FRANK LESLIE, in the Clerk's Office of the District Court for the Southern District of New York.

No. 271—Vol. X.]   NEW YORK, SATURDAY, FEBRUARY 2, 1861.   [PRICE 6 CENTS.

MAJOR ROBERT ANDERSON, COMMANDING AT FORT SUMPTER, CHARLESTON.

MAJOR ANDERSON, at present one of the first among the foremost of American names, was born in Kentucky, September, 1805. Graduating at West Point in 1825, he joined the army as a second lieutenant. It is somewhat remarkable that, in 1832, he was Inspector-General of the Illinois Volunteers, in the Black Hawk war, Abraham Lincoln being a captain in the same body. He was promoted to a first lieutenant, and became instructor and inspector at West Point in 1835. He became Aide-de-Camp to General Scott in 1838, and a few months afterwards published his book, "Instruction for Field Artillery, Horse and Foot," arranged for the service of the United States. This work very greatly extended his reputation; it was pronounced admirable and thorough, and passed at once into general use. In the year 1838 Lieutenant Anderson received his commission as Captain, which was honorably earned by his gallant and successful services in the Florida War. The brevet bears the date of April 2d, 1838. He afterwards served as Assistant Adjutant-General, having the rank of Captain; but on being promoted to the Captaincy of his own regiment he relinquished the office in 1841.

He was actively engaged through the whole Mexican War, serving, as will be seen, with marked ability, and with conspicuous success. He took part in the siege of Vera Cruz, where he served under Major-General Scott with the Third Regiment of Artillery. In this siege he had command of one of the batteries, which was distinguished for the precision of its fire and its unceasing activity.

He went on with the conquering army during its whole triumphal march and final occupation of the city of Mexico and the halls of the Montezumas. On several occasions during that eventful march the conduct of Captain Anderson called forth the hearty commendations of his superior officers. He was severely wounded during the attack of El Molino del Rey, and his conduct is thus commented upon in the despatches of Captain Blake, his next superior officer: "Captain Robert Anderson (acting field officer) behaved with great heroism on this occasion. Even after receiving a severe and painful wound, he continued at the head of his column, regardless of pain and self-preservation, and setting a handsome example to his men of coolness, energy and courage." He was also highly spoken of by General Garland in his report, not only as being among the first to force an entrance into the strong position of El Molino del Rey, but also for his gallant defence of the captured works.

Captain Robert Anderson won his brevet rank as Major by his intrepid and gallant conduct in the action at El Molino del Rey. The brevet bears the date of September 8th, 1847. He was afterwards promoted to the Majority of the First Regiment of Artillery, on October 5th, 1857, a position which he still holds, to his own credit and the honour of his country.

It will be seen by our brief sketch that Major Robert Anderson has been no "carpet knight;" he has seen service in the heated field, and has known and braved the discomforts of every a campaign. He is, in fact, not only an accomplished theorist, but a tried and able practical soldier. During the past year he was appointed to the command of the

facts in the harbor of Charleston, and occupied Fort Moultrie while superintending the completion of the formidable battery, Fort Sumpter, which is the key to the avenue of defence in the harbor. His subsequent action in evacuating Fort Moultrie and taking possession of Fort Sumpter on Christmas night, 1860, is familiar to all our readers. It was a strategical movement which, however offensive it may have been to the authorities of South Carolina, was considered by military authorities to be fully justified by the position in which he was placed. He took the only course which could assure to him the command of the position entrusted to his charge. Since his possession of Fort Sumpter his course has been eminently conservative, displaying that caution, calmness and decision as necessary in a military commander. A less able or more impracticable officer would, beyond the possibility of a doubt, have involved our country in a bloody fratricidal war, which has been, so far, happily prevented by the clear head and true heart of Major Robert Anderson.

The personal appearance of Major Anderson is very striking. In height he is between five feet nine and five feet ten inches, and his figure is firmly knit and very military. His complexion is dark; his eyes, very dark; his manners are very courteous, and his voice rich and full. We have, however, said so much about him in our last few papers that it is unnecessary to lengthen our notice. He is a soldier of whom the republic may well be proud, and enjoys the respect of both North and South. That he may never be called upon to test his courage and endurance against his own countrymen is the sincere prayer of every true American.

All parties have perfect confidence in his

MAJOR ROBERT ANDERSON, U. S. A., IN COMMAND OF FORT SUMPTER, CHARLESTON HARBOR, S. C.—PHOTOGRAPHED BY WENZLER & ZIEN.

Although songs published before the Civil War remained in the popular repertoire, the conflict also inspired a surge of musical creation, almost from the opening salvos. More than 9,000 new songs were printed in the North, 750 in the South (where publishing materials were much scarcer). "Dixie," which appeared just before the war, became wildly popular in the South; Julia Ward Howe's poem "The Battle Hymn of the Republic" was equally so in the North after it was set to the familiar tune "John Brown's Body" in 1862. Some songs became miniature battlefields, with Northerners and Southerners singing different lyrics. Some battlefields were briefly united by familiar songs: before the battle of Stones River (Murfreesboro), Tennessee, at the end of 1862, the opposing armies, encamped close to each other, joined in singing "Home Sweet Home"—an interlude that did not prevent them from waging a close and hard-fought battle in the following days. "Taps"—not a song but a poignant and dignified bugle call marking the end of a soldier's day—was among the lasting musical creations of the Civil War; it was adapted from an earlier call ("Tattoo") by Union major general Daniel Butterfield, with the assistance of bugler Oliver Willcox Norton of the Eighty-third Pennsylvania Regiment.

"Beauregard's March" (sheet-music cover). Color engraving, Miller & Beacham, 1861

"All Hail to the Flag of Freedom" (sheet-music cover). Color lithograph, Skaats & Knaebel, 1861

{ **JANUARY 28** 1863: A mass meeting in St. Louis declares support for the Emancipation Proclamation. }

To Genl. P. G. T. BEAUREGARD,
C. S. A.

BEAUREGARD'S MARCH.

BY

COMPOSED FOR THE PIANO

BY

CHAS. LENSCHOW.

PUBLISHED BY MILLER & BEACHAM, BALTIMORE.

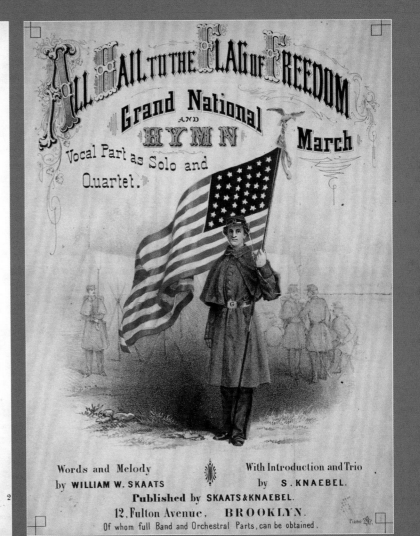

ALL HAIL TO THE FLAG OF FREEDOM

Grand National
AND
HYMN March

Vocal Part as Solo and
Quartet.

Words and Melody
by **WILLIAM W. SKAATS**

With Introduction and Trio
by **S. KNAEBEL.**

Published by SKAATS & KNAEBEL.

12, Fulton Avenue. BROOKLYN.

Of whom full Band and Orchestral Parts, can be obtained.

When Abraham Lincoln arrived in Washington for his inauguration (having traveled incognito near the end of his journey because of a rumored assassination attempt), he went straight to Willard's Hotel, owned by brothers Henry and Joseph C. Willard. As a young congressman in the mid-1840s, Lincoln had attended meetings at Willard's but could not afford to live there. In 1861, the president-elect was shown to the hotel's best suite, overlooking Pennsylvania Avenue. Already an important capital-city landmark, the hotel blossomed during the war into such a hub of commercial and political intrigue that Nathaniel Hawthorne wrote, in "Chiefly about War Matters," that it was "much more justly called the center of Washington and the Union than either the Capitol, the White House or the State Department." Among its appointments, Willard's included both ladies' and gentlemen's dining rooms and parlors. Strict segregation of the sexes was not observed, however—at least with regard to the rooms dedicated to the ladies. According to *Springfield Republican* correspondent Mary Clemmer Ames, gentlemen could behave as they would when they were in their own facilities, but when they joined the ladies, they were expected to allow time "to masticate their food in a Christian manner; time to read the newspaper and to discuss the news with their lady friend over their coffee." (See also January 22, November 13.)

Ladies parlor at Willard's Hotel, Washington, DC. Ink and opaque white drawing by Thomas Nast, March 6, 1861

{ **JANUARY 29** 1861: Kansas is admitted to the Union as the thirty-fourth state, with a constitution prohibiting slavery. }

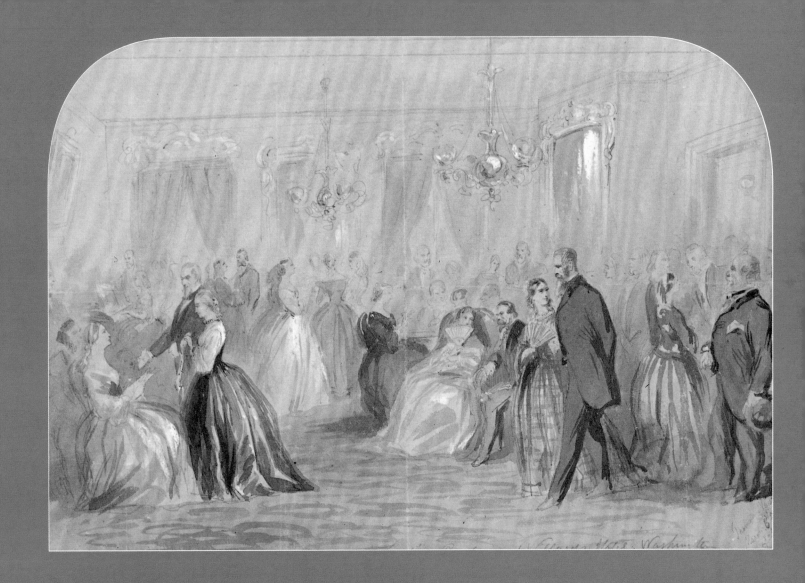

A hero of the War of 1812, Winfield Scott was general-in-chief of the U.S. Army from July 1841 to November 1861. Architect of the American victory in the Mexican War (1846–48), Scott commanded many officers in that conflict who would face one another on home soil less than twenty years later, including P. G. T. Beauregard, George B. McClellan, Jefferson Davis, Winfield Scott Hancock, Braxton Bragg, and Ulysses S. Grant. Scott considered one of his staff officers during that earlier war, Captain Robert E. Lee, "the very best soldier that I ever saw in the field" and saw to it that Lee was offered command of the U.S. Army in April 1861. Instead, Lee resigned from the army and returned to his beloved "country" of Virginia. Scott, meanwhile, was advising the government to be prudent in the event of actual war with the breakaway states. He knew that a full-scale invasion of the South would be terribly costly; such an invasion, he estimated, "might be done in two or three years . . . with 300,000 disciplined men, estimating a third for garrisons, and the loss of yet a greater number by skirmishes, sieges, battles and Southern fevers." Scott's estimate was considered unrealistically inflated by many of those who were aware of it at the time. In fact, it proved to be conservative: more than two million men served in the Union army during the brutal four-year conflict.

General Winfield Scott (1786–1866) and staff. c. 1860?

{ **JANUARY 30** 1816: Nathaniel Prentiss Banks (USA) is born in Waltham, Massachusetts. }

In May 1861, when war was a fact, General-in-Chief Winfield Scott proposed a Union strategy that would avoid an invasion of the South, which he knew would be extremely costly for both sides. Combining a naval blockade of seaports on the Atlantic and Gulf coasts with moves to establish U.S. military control of the Mississippi River, this strategy, Scott said, would "envelop the insurgent states and bring them to terms with less bloodshed than by any other plan." Ridiculed and quickly dubbed the "Anaconda Plan" in the press, after the snake that kills by constriction, Scott's scheme was rejected as too slow. Most in the North (and many in the South) were convinced that the war would be short—and their own side would emerge victorious. Later that year, after Union defeats at First Bull Run and Ball's Bluff, Winfield Scott retired. As the war progressed, the plan he had outlined in 1861 essentially became the Union's winning strategy.

Scott's Great Snake. Color lithograph map by J. B. Elliott, 1861

{ **JANUARY 31** 1865: General Robert E. Lee, commander of the Army of Northern Virginia, is appointed general-in-chief of all the Confederate armies. }

FEBRUARY: GATHERING MOMENTUM

The conflict began with great bursts of patriotic fervor in both warring regions; so many men enlisted in the North and the South that initial government manpower quotas were quickly exceeded. People on each side assumed a short conflict would end with their primary goal secured: for the North, preservation of the Union; for the South, establishment of a separate confederation of slave-labor states. Those in the North believed the Union would be saved with the assistance of Southern Unionists, whose influence would help bring the seceded states back into the Union. Thus, at this early stage of the war, Union troops often protected the property of secessionists and Southern sympathizers—including slaves. Even General William Tecumseh Sherman, famous in the later years of the conflict as a practitioner of "total" or "hard" war, adhered meticulously to this conciliatory policy, insisting that all property taken for Federal use must be paid for and seeing to it that Union soldiers who stole or vandalized anything were punished.

Southern Unionist influence did not prove strong enough, however, and the determined majority in the South clung to the belief that if they just held on a bit longer, the North would tire of expending human and financial resources on a futile effort and let the Confederate states go. Yet at the end of 1861, with hundreds of thousands of Americans under arms, the Lincoln administration showed no inclination to agree that the South had a right to secede. As the

{ **FEBRUARY 1** 1865: Illinois is the first state to ratify the Thirteenth Amendment, abolishing slavery. }

Off to the War. Poster advertising the play *Gettysburg.* Calhoun Show print, c. 1890

divided nation moved toward a second year of war, a year of battles so brutal and costly that they would horrify European observers, conciliation remained at the foundation of Northern military strategy. "Be careful so to treat the unarmed inhabitants as to contract, not widen the breach existing between us & the rebels," General-in-Chief George B. McClellan instructed the new Department of the Ohio commander, Brigadier General Don Carlos Buell, on November 12, 1861. "It should be our constant aim to make it apparent to all that their property, their comfort and their personal safety will be best preserved by adhering to the cause of the Union."

In 1862, the Union endured some costly battlefield victories along with bitter and bloody losses that bolstered Southern resolve to prevail. "We are told by various and sundry Editors that the war will ere long be brought to a close by the intervention of European powers and the bankruptcy of the Yankee government," Confederate soldier Rufus Cater wrote on June 22. "An honorable Peace which brings to us a glorious independence is truly desirable for we are tired of war, but we want it on no other terms. Peace must bring with it all the blessings of a free people." The lengthening war, as well as an increase in vicious guerrilla warfare, inspired a slow transformation in Northern strategy. Conciliation gave way to pragmatism, taking whatever strict measures were deemed militarily necessary. This, in turn, eventually yielded to the "hard war" policy that was to prevail in the last two years of the war—in which all the militarily useful resources of the South, such as crops, railroads, and livestock, were regarded as acceptable targets.

As war began, Washington, D.C., was a vulnerable city. Embraced on three sides by Maryland, a slaveholding state sympathetic to the South, the city also faced hostile Virginia just across the Potomac River. On the night of May 23, 1861, as Virginians celebrated popular ratification of their state convention's earlier vote to secede, thousands of Union troops moved through Washington streets toward the Potomac. Crossing the river in four coordinated thrusts, the Federal troops quickly gained footholds on Virginia soil and began digging fortifications that would make the nation's capital far more secure. There was so little opposition to the unexpected operation that the Federal forces suffered only one casualty—but it was a loss that plunged the Union into mourning. Colonel Elmer Ellsworth, Abraham Lincoln's friend and protégé and the renowned leader of the New York Fire Zouaves (see January 22), was shot and killed by James Jackson after Ellsworth removed a Confederate flag from the roof of the Marshall House, Jackson's Alexandria inn. (Fire Zouave private Francis E. Brownell immediately killed the innkeeper.) Ellsworth, whose funeral was held at the White House, had written his parents before the operation: "I am perfectly confident to accept whatever my fortune may be, and confident that He who noteth even the fall of a sparrow, will have some purpose even in the fate of one like me."

Elmer Ellsworth (1837–1861). c. 1860

Death of Col. Ellsworth after hauling down the Rebel flag, May 24, 1861. Hand-colored lithograph, Currier & Ives, 1861

{ **FEBRUARY 2** 1864: Confederate navy men capture the Union gunboat *Underwriter* and set it afire near New Berne, North Carolina. }

As soon as war broke out, President Lincoln called for seventy-five thousand U.S. militia to serve for ninety days. The defense of Washington was a prime worry: more troops were urgently needed to bolster the city's defenses. These reinforcements had no choice but to travel through Maryland, where sympathy for the Southern cause and ill feeling toward Lincoln and the Union ran high. On April 19 (coincidentally, the anniversary of the first shots fired in the American Revolution, at Lexington, Massachusetts, in 1775), the Sixth Massachusetts Regiment was attacked as it marched through Baltimore on its way to the capital city. Some soldiers opened fire; four soldiers and twelve Baltimore civilians were killed, and many others were wounded. Just over a month later, when the Ninth New York State Militia marched through Baltimore, the city had calmed down somewhat, but apprehension remained high: "Arrived in Baltimore, Md., about mid-day," Private John W. Jaques of the Ninth New York wrote in his diary on May 28, 1861, "expecting to meet there the 'Eighth New York, volunteers,' who having their arms with them, were to escort us through the city, but we were disappointed in not meeting them, so we pursued our march . . . passing through Pratt street, where the 'Sixth Massachusetts, volunteers,' were attacked by a mob, in April, while on their way to Washington; but our regiment was not molested, although many a black look was cast upon us, they freely offered us ice-water and other refreshments, but Colonel Stiles had ordered the men not to accept anything from them, as he was afraid they would try to poison us."

The Lexington of 1861. Hand-colored lithograph, Currier & Ives, 1861?

{ **FEBRUARY 3** 1807: Joseph Eggleston Johnston (CSA) is born at "Cherry Grove," Prince Edward County, Virginia. }

The men who volunteered to fight for either the North or the South joined the armies for a variety of reasons: a quest for adventure, a desire to experience combat, a wish to see more of the world—or, for many, a sense of obligation to support the state and region in which they lived and the ideals in which they believed. Basically, these were ideals shared by the men of both sides. But Northerners and Southerners had come to view them in radically different lights. "We all declare for liberty," Abraham Lincoln said in 1864, "but in using the same word we do not mean the same thing. With some, the word liberty may mean for each man to do as he pleases with himself and the product of his labor; while with others the same word may mean for some men to do as they please with other men and the product of other men's labor. Here are two, not only different, but incompatible things, called by the same name, liberty. And it follows that each of the things is by the respective parties called by two different and incompatible names, liberty and tyranny."

Illustrated Union artillery recruitment poster. Date unknown

Confederate recruitment poster from Tennessee. May 1861

{ **FEBRUARY 4** 1861: The first session of the Provisional Congress of the Confederate States of America convenes in Montgomery, Alabama. }

HEAVY ARTILLERY

Raised by authority of the State, at the request of the Secretary of War and Major-General McCLELLAN.

ONLY FIRST-CLASS RECRUITS

WANTED FOR THE

FIRST REGIMENT NEW-YORK HEAVY ARTILLERY

FOR GARRISON DUTY.

Col. T. D. DOUBLEDAY,
Lieut. Col. S. GRAHAM,
First Major H. H. HALL,
Second Major THOS. ALLCOCK.

Companies to be ordered to proceed at once to Washington.

GOOD POSITIONS GIVEN TO SOLDIERS WHO HAVE SEEN SERVICE.

JAS. B. GRANT,
Recruiting Officer.

GEORGE F. NESBITT & CO., Printers and Stationers, corner of Pearl and Pine Streets, N. Y.

FREEMEN!

OF

TENNESSEE!

The Yankee War is now being waged for "beauty and booty." They have driven us from them, and now say OUR TRADE they must and will have. To excite their hired and ruffian soldiers, they promise them our lands, and tell them our women are beautiful---that beauty is the reward of the brave.

Tennesseans! your country calls! Shall we wait until our homes are laid desolate; until sword and rape shall have visited them? NEVER! Then

TO ARMS!

and let us meet the enemy on the borders. Who so vile, so craven, as not to strike for his native land?

The undersigned propose to immediately raise an infantry company to be offered to the Governor as part of the defense of the State and of the Confederate States All those who desire to join with us in serving our common country, will report themselves immediately.

J. B. Murray.
H. C. Witt.

May 17th, 1861.

Neal & Roberts, Printers, Morristown, Tenn.

When the nation's new First Family moved into the White House, they were immediately surrounded by a hum of disapproving Washington gossip: the president was too tall, too awkward, too unsophisticated; his wife was unfashionable and suspect—her brother-in-law was a Confederate general, and three half brothers were also fighting for the South. When Mary Lincoln overspent the $20,000 congressional allotment for redecorating the White House, even her husband objected that so much money had been expended to redo their grand residence "when the poor freezing soldiers could not have blankets." That furor soon passed, as the president's attention was ever more deeply absorbed in the war, which in 1861–62 was not going nearly as well as expected for the North. Lincoln's worry and frustration evaporated, however, when his two young sons, Willie and Tad, barreled through White House offices and played tricks on grave-looking cabinet members and visiting army officers. In February 1862, both boys contracted typhoid fever, dampening even the good news of General Ulysses S. Grant's first notable Civil War victories, at Forts Henry and Donelson in Tennessee. When eleven-year-old Willie died, on February 20, the family was nearly overwhelmed by grief. Mary Lincoln suffered convulsions of anguish and took to her bed for three weeks; the president twice ordered that Willie's body be exhumed so that he could look on the boy's face again. Eight-year-old Tad, still feverish but beginning to recover, would wake up and cry that he could never talk to Willie again.

Abraham Lincoln and his son Tad. Color lithograph of a photograph, Louis Prang & Co., 1860–1909

Mary Todd Lincoln (1818–1882). 1860–65

{ **FEBRUARY 5** 1864: Major General William T. Sherman's Union army marches into Jackson, Mississippi, en route to Meridian. }

Home to the U.S. Congress and an architectural expression of American democracy, the U.S. Capitol was also a temporary military barracks in the first months of the war, as Washington braced for an expected Confederate attack. At the peak, some four thousand volunteers were billeted in and around the Capitol, their marches and drills giving great comfort to Washingtonians. But the mass of temporary residents provided little but aggravation to the architect who was in charge of the ongoing project to replace the Capitol dome. Besides the irritation caused by "about 100 drummers all the time drumming," Thomas U. Walter grumbled to his wife in letters, sanitation was far from ideal. "The smell is awful. The building is like one grand water closet. Every hold and corner is defiled." Vast stores of supplies cluttered rooms and corridors, but at least better odors soon emanated from the basement, where twenty newly built brick ovens began turning out fifty-eight thousand loaves of bread a day for the men; the ovens remained in service even after the soldiers had moved into regular camps. The bakery was finally moved in October, due to growing complaints about bread-delivery wagons cluttering Capitol driveways—and after smoke damage had been detected in some books in the Library of Congress, located in rooms directly above the ovens.

"The Capitol a barrack." Captain Tate and militia troops. May 1861

{ **FEBRUARY 6** 1833: James Ewell Brown "Jeb" Stuart (CSA) is born in Patrick County, Virginia. }

May 13 1861

The half-replaced dome of the U.S. Capitol building loomed behind the procession on May 21, 1861, that escorted the body of Colonel Abram S. Vosburgh, commander of the Seventy-first Regiment, New York State Militia, to the train that would return his body to New York. President Lincoln was among the dignitaries and family members who attended the colonel's funeral at the Washington Navy Yard and remained with the procession, and the ceremonies drew heavy coverage by the press. Colonel Vosburgh's death from natural causes came just days before Colonel Elmer Ellsworth became the Union's first well-known battle casualty of the war (see February 2). The elaborate ceremonies that attended these early deaths contrasted sharply with the often hasty and rough burials that would be accorded tens of thousands of other soldiers as the armies of the North and South met in increasingly brutal clashes more costly than any battles fought before or since on the American continent. In these early days, very few anticipated the terrible casualties this fratricidal conflict would inflict; both sides generally expected the war to be over by Christmas.

Funeral of Col Vosburgh. The Hearse approaching the R.R. Depot. Pencil, Chinese white, and black ink wash drawing on brown paper by Alfred R. Waud, May 1861

{ **FEBRUARY 7** 1861: The Choctaw Indian nation declares allegiance to the Confederacy. }

Even though Southerners initially believed the North would offer little, if any, effective objection to secession, men began to arm and drill almost immediately after their states passed secession ordinances. The Confederacy's Palmetto Battery was organized, and initially funded, by Captain Hugh Richardson Garden of Sumter, South Carolina, after he had fought at First Bull Run (First Manassas). In the thick of campaigns in the eastern theater throughout the war, the battery contributed to the Confederate victory at Second Bull Run (Second Manassas); fought at Antietam, after which the Army of Northern Virginia retreated to its home ground, ending General Robert E. Lee's first incursion into Maryland; returned with Lee to Northern territory and fought at the pivotal three-day battle of Gettysburg (after which Lee again retreated); and later saw action during the bitter contest in Virginia's entangled woodland called the Wilderness (May 1864). Defending Petersburg, Virginia, during the months-long Union siege of that city, the battery also took part in the battle of the Crater, where an audacious Federal attempt to breach the city's defenses by tunneling and rigging explosives underground turned into a Union disaster when Northern troops became trapped in the crater that the explosion created (see June 26).

The Palmetto Battery, near Charleston, South Carolina. Photograph by George S. Cook, 1863

{ **FEBRUARY 8** 1820: William Tecumseh Sherman (USA) is born in Lancaster, Ohio. }

In the North, where many believed that the South could not possibly stand up to the United States for very long, men trooped to the colors, eager for a chance to "see the elephant"—experience combat—before the war ended in a glorious victory. Like their counterparts in the South, most of these citizen soldiers entered service in regiments raised by the states and led, especially in the beginning, by political appointees or elected officers whose knowledge of military science was far from reliable. As it became clear that the war would continue beyond Christmas, President Lincoln signed bills authorizing a vast expansion of the army, with new volunteers generally to be enlisted for a term of three years. After First Bull Run in late July, the lack of proper training, especially among the largely amateur officers, was acknowledged as a formidable problem. By 1862, the Union required examinations and other measures to ensure that officers had an acceptable amount of military knowledge. Earlier, while organizing the Army of the Potomac, the veteran soldier George B. McClellan had instituted training programs to instill basic military skills in volunteers, and these programs became common practice in all U.S. armies after McClellan became general-in-chief in November 1861.

Group of men from Company A, Eighth New York State Militia, in Arlington, Virginia. June 1861

{ **FEBRUARY 9** 1864: Led by Colonel Thomas E. Rose, 109 Union officers tunnel out of Libby Prison in Richmond, Virginia; 59 of the men will eventually reach Union lines. }

"The proscribed Americans (and there are many), attached to this regiment have, since their encampment here, formed themselves into a defensive association. They propose to cultivate a correct knowledge of the manual of arms and military evolutions, . . . actuated by the conviction that the time is not far distant when the black man of this country will be summoned to show his hand in the struggle for liberty." African American William H. Johnson sent this report to the Boston-based newspaper *Pine and Palm* at the end of November 1861, while serving with the Eighth Connecticut Volunteers as an "independent man" (a status that was not clearly defined). Black men had served in American forces from the Revolution through the War of 1812, but they were initially forbidden to serve in the Union army during the Civil War. Some joined white regiments anyway—occasionally as regular soldiers, but more often as servants of white officers or as teamsters who drove supply wagons. As the war progressed, many escaped or liberated slaves also attached themselves to Northern units. Meanwhile, spokesmen, both white and black, urged the U.S. Congress and the president to alter the policy that made the North's military campaign to reconstruct the Union a "white man's war." But complex political currents, and prevailing assumptions about the suitability of African Americans for military service, made Union authorities reluctant to consider the proposition—especially when they believed that the war would be short.

John Henry, servant, at headquarters, Third Army Corps, Army of the Potomac (possibly at Bealton, Virginia). October 1863

{ **FEBRUARY 10** **1862:** The remainder of the Confederate "Mosquito" fleet, which had unsuccessfully resisted the Federal amphibious landing on Roanoke Island, is destroyed at Elizabeth City, North Carolina. }

On June 10, 1861, "political general" Benjamin F. Butler, commander of the Federal garrison at Fort Monroe, opposite Norfolk, Virginia, dispatched several Union regiments comprising some forty-four hundred men to drive away twelve hundred Confederates who had constructed a battery emplacement only eight miles from the fort, near Bethel Church (Big Bethel). Butler's elaborate battle plan added to the confusion of the inexperienced Union troops, who, at this early stage of the war, were not all clothed in what later became the standard blue uniform. One New York regiment, wearing gray uniforms, was fired on by another New York regiment, whose commander did not know the recognition sign (the watchword "Boston") and so did not cease fire when he heard it. This skirmish between two Federal units warned the Confederates of the pending attack. Though of little lasting significance, the ensuing engagement (which Union colonel Joseph B. Carr described as "the disastrous *fight* at Big Bethel—battle we may scarcely term it") was an embarrassing debacle for the North that provided a boost in morale for the South. The Confederate battery's commander, Major George W. Randolph, came to the notice of his superiors and later became a brigadier general and Confederate secretary of war. Among the eighteen Union men killed in the abortive assault was Major Theodore Winthrop, a thirty-three-year-old poet and novelist whose books, all published posthumously, included *John Brent*, one of the earliest novels of the American West.

Plan of the Battle of Bethel (battle of Big Bethel, 1861). Hand-colored map, c. 1861

{ **FEBRUARY 11** 1812: Alexander Hamilton Stephens, vice president of the Confederacy, is born in Wilkes (Taliaferro) County, Georgia. }

Presented to Mrs. M. C. Taylor with filial respect by her son
Wm. B. Taylor

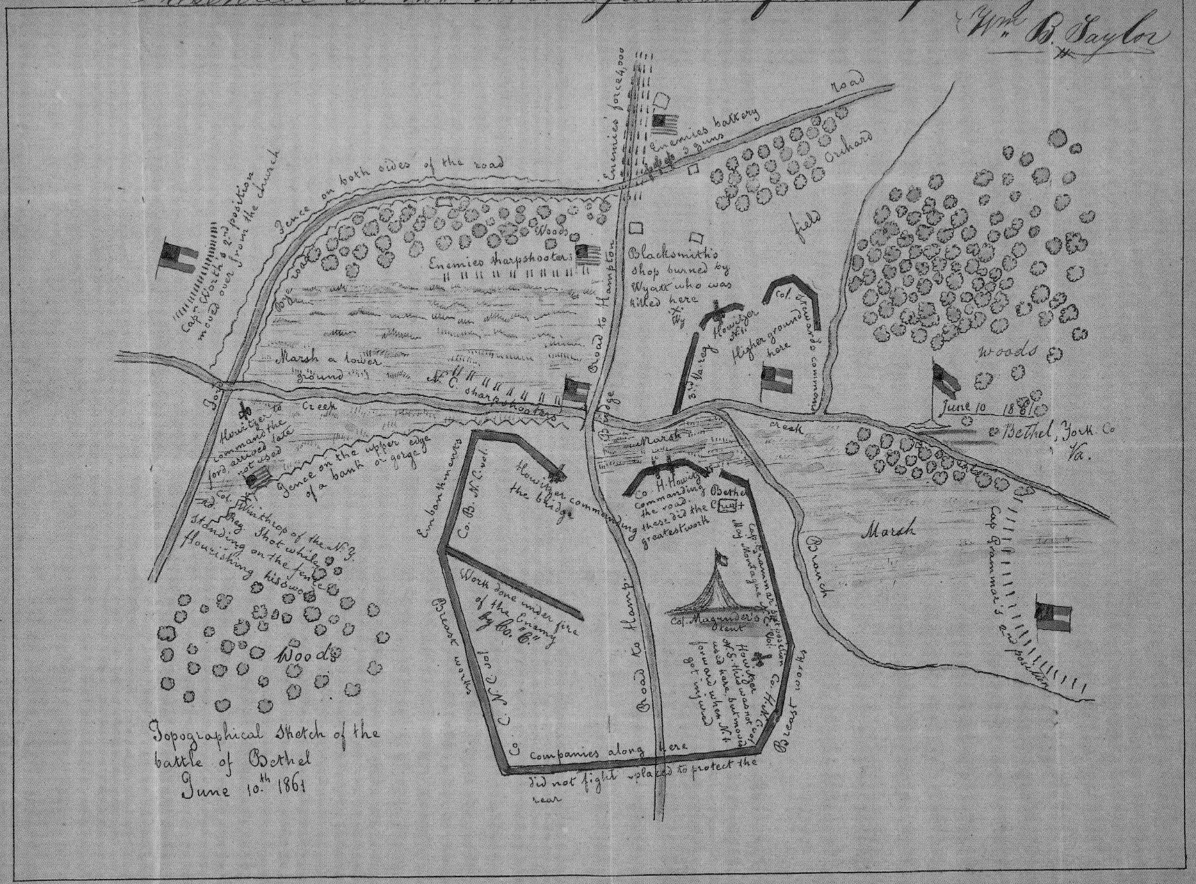

Enemies force 4,500
Enemies battery 3 guns

Fence on both sides of the road

Capt Werth's 4th position
moved over from the church

Enemies sharpshooters

Woods

Blacksmith's shop burned by Wyatt who was killed here

field
Orchard

Marsh a lower ground

N.C. sharpshooters

Higher ground here

Col. forward to command

woods

June 10 1861

Bethel. York. Co. Va.

Howitzer command the ford used

Creek

Fence on the upper edge of a bank or gorge

Winthrop of the N.Y. shot while standing on the fence flourishing his sword

Woods

Howitzer commanding the bridge

Embankments

Co. B. N.C. vol.

Breast walls

Work done under fire of the enemy by Co. C.

Marsh

Bethel

Col. Magruder's tent

Breast works

Marsh

Branch

Capt Brown's 2 position

Co. B. N.C. vol.

3 companies along here did not fight placed to protect the rear

Topographical Sketch of the battle of Bethel June 10th 1861

Plan of the Battle of Bethel

Bowing to home-front pressures (including banner headlines in Horace Greeley's *New York Tribune* demanding that Union forces move "Forward to Richmond! Forward to Richmond!"), General-in-Chief Winfield Scott sent Brigadier General Irvin McDowell and a Union army of some thirty-five thousand poorly trained men into the war's first major battle. Bull Run (named for a stream near Manassas Junction, Virginia, and the site of a second battle about a year later; Manassas was the Confederates' name for both) was an attempt to push thirty thousand Confederates under Generals Joseph E. Johnston and P. G. T. Beauregard, then within twenty-five miles of Washington, away from the nation's capital. Leaving Washington on July 16, the Union soldiers made very slow progress. By July 21, they were in position—accompanied by Northern civilians who were so confident that they had followed the troops to witness the Confederate defeat. Union troops first heard the unnerving "rebel yell" at First Bull Run, and Confederate brigadier general Barnard Bee, who was subsequently killed in the battle, bestowed the nom de guerre "Stonewall" on Brigadier General Thomas J. Jackson, whose troops were holding fast under a furious Union assault. In the face of such stiff resistance, the inexperienced Federal troops eventually broke and ran, their retreat turning into a rout as soldiers became entangled with fleeing civilians. The humiliating loss at Bull Run sent shock waves through the Union, which over the next few months concentrated on organizing and training its armies.

Battle of Bull Run, Va, July 21ˢᵗ 1861. Gallant Charge of the Zouaves and Defeat of the Rebel Black Horse Cavalry. Hand-colored lithograph, Currier & Ives, 1861?

{ **FEBRUARY 12** 1809: Abraham Lincoln, sixteenth president of the United States, is born in Hardin (Larue) County, Kentucky. }

"I have made arrangements for the [newspaper] correspondents to take the field," Irvin McDowell, the Union commander at First Bull Run, reportedly said. "And I have suggested to them that they wear a white uniform to indicate the purity of their profession." Included in Civil War correspondent William Russell's book *My Diary North and South* (1863), McDowell's perhaps apocryphal suggestion that reporters be clothed in a manner likely to attract the unfortunate attentions of the enemy might have stemmed from Northern newspaper reports before the Union defeat on July 21, 1861. Articles that included details about U.S. regiments and their prebattle positions in and around Washington quickly found their way into Confederate hands, providing information at least as valuable as that reported by such Washington-based Confederate agents as Rose O'Neal Greenhow. In addition to the hard-won knowledge that Union armies required better training, First Bull Run provided irrefutable evidence that military intelligence garnered from newspapers, cavalry reconnaissance, signalmen, balloonists, and spies in the developing "secret service" organizations of each side would be a major factor in the burgeoning conflict.

Map of the Bull Run battlefield. Drawing by Leon J. Fremaux, August 24, 1861

{ **FEBRUARY 13** **1862:** Union forces under Ulysses S. Grant, including naval support commanded by Andrew Foote, attack the Confederate-built Fort Donelson, Tennessee, on the Cumberland River. }

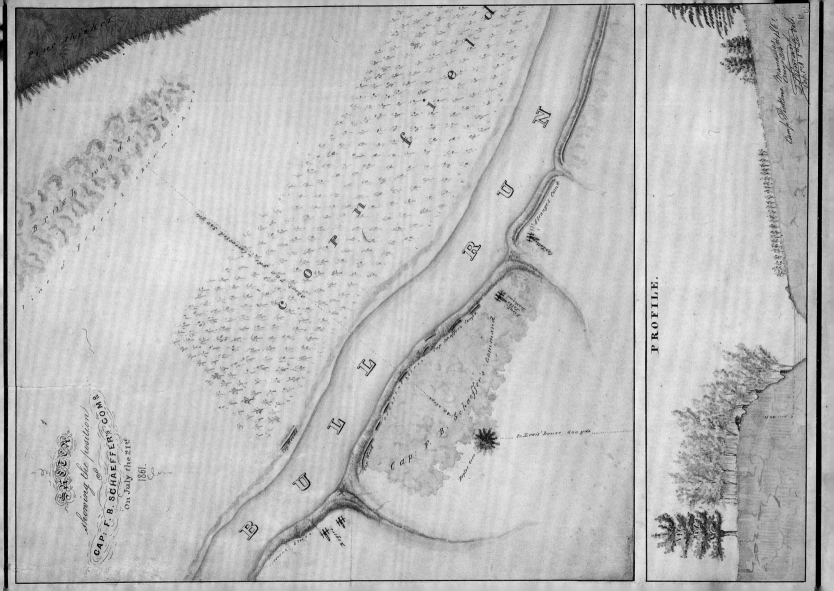

Pine thicket.

B u l l R u n

S t o n e f i e l d

woods

line of fence 3 or 4 feet high

line of fence past, stone wall on one side, low ground some 500 yds wide

Strange's Cove

Cap: F. B. Schaeffer's command

to Lewis' house 600 yds

SKETCH
Showing the Position
OF
CAP. F. B. SCHAEFFER'S COM.
On July the 21st
1861.

PROFILE.

Camp Perkins, Va.

General Irvin McDowell had served in the Mexican War (1846–48) with the two main Confederate commanders he faced at First Bull Run, Joseph E. Johnston and P. G. T. Beauregard—and Beauregard had been a classmate of McDowell's at West Point. After his unprepared soldiers were routed at Bull Run, McDowell was replaced by George B. McClellan—but he was also promoted to major general, perhaps an acknowledgment that public and high-command pressures had forced the battle before his army was ready. After commanding a corps that protected Washington while McClellan's Army of the Potomac was engaged in the Peninsula campaign aimed at Richmond (March–July 1862), McDowell faced Confederates again at Second Bull Run. Also a Union defeat, this encounter marked the end of his Civil War battlefield service. Johnston, meanwhile, had been replaced in the field three months earlier by Robert E. Lee because of wounds sustained as he faced McClellan's forces on the Virginia Peninsula. Transferred to the western theater of operations after he recovered, Johnston presided over the loss of Vicksburg, Mississippi, then proceeded to fight a defensive war, trying to keep his forces intact and battle-worthy as he was pressed back toward Atlanta by William T. Sherman's Union army.

Irvin McDowell (1818–1885). Photograph by the Brady National Photographic Art Gallery, 1860–65

Joseph E. Johnston (1807–1891). c. 1865

{ **FEBRUARY 14** 1864: William T. Sherman's Union troops capture Meridian, Mississippi. }

With two proclaimed governments—one Unionist and one secession-ist—Missouri was the site of particularly bitter Civil War struggles between armies and among Missourians to gain military control of the state. The major clash was the battle of Wilson's Creek on August 10, 1861, a fierce encounter pitting fifty-four hundred Union troops under Brigadier General Nathaniel Lyon against eleven thousand Confederates under Brigadier General Ben McCulloch and Major General Sterling Price. Centering on a fight for a piece of strategic high ground called Bloody Hill, the battle turned in the Confederates' favor after General Lyon was killed leading a counterattack against Confederates who had tried to push Federal troops off the crest of the hill—from which Federal troops had earlier evicted Confederate cavalry. Low on supplies and having suffered heavy casualties, the Union forces retreated, leaving a huge section of Missouri under Confederate and pro-secessionist sway. Coming less than a month after the Union defeat at First Bull Run (July 21), this was another bitter setback for the North.

Battle of Wilson's Creek, Aug. 10, 1861. Color lithograph, Kurz & Allison, 1893

{ **FEBRUARY 15** **1865:** Heavy skirmishing occurs as General William T. Sherman's Union troops continue their rapid march toward Columbia, South Carolina. }

"President, Cabinet, Genl. Scott & all deferring to me," Major General

George B. McClellan wrote to his wife, Ellen, in 1861. "By some strange operation of magic I seem to have become the power in the land." An able soldier who had served on Winfield Scott's staff during the Mexican War, McClellan had received few lessons in humility while in the antebellum U.S. Army or during his brief civilian career as a railroad official (1857–61). Appointed in May 1861 to lead the Union's Department of the Ohio, where some modest battlefield successes by men under him added luster to his reputation, McClellan was summoned to Washington after the Union defeat at First Bull Run and given command of the Military Division of the Potomac. In November, he succeeded the seventy-five-year-old Scott as general-in-chief of all U.S. land forces. McClellan proved an able organizer and administrator, providing Union troops with much-needed training that gave a firm boost to army morale. But his reluctance to aggressively employ these stronger and better-trained forces provoked increasing impatience in President Lincoln, who, on January 27, 1862, took the unprecedented step of issuing General War Order No. 1. This "Ordered that the 22d of February 1862, be the day for a general movement of the Land and Naval forces of the United States against the insurgent forces." The president's Special War Order No. 1, issued four days later, was specifically aimed at forcing McClellan to begin offensive operations in Virginia.

General George B. McClellan (1826–1885), fourth from right, and staff. c. 1862

{ **FEBRUARY 16** 1862: In an important Federal victory in the western theater, Confederates surrender Fort Donelson, Tennessee, to General Ulysses S. Grant, who becomes famous throughout the Union. }

On October 21, 1861, Union forces under Colonel Edward D. Baker—an influential former Republican congressman and senator and a close friend of President Lincoln—engaged in what was to have been a diversionary maneuver while a larger Union force moved against Confederates encamped near Leesburg, Virginia. After climbing onto a high bluff overlooking the Potomac River, the Union soldiers met unexpectedly fierce opposition from Confederates under Brigadier General Nathan G. "Shanks" Evans and were forced back over the edge of the bluff. More than half the brigade—including Baker—became casualties. Baker's death turned the battle of Ball's Bluff (Leesburg), which had limited military significance, into an event with tremendous political repercussions. Coming just three months after the rout of Union troops at First Bull Run, it prompted the establishment of the congressional Joint Committee on the Conduct of the War, which became a powerful force throughout the conflict.

Edward D. Baker (1811–1861). Engraving by J. A. O'Neill, c. 1861

Death of Col Edward D. Baker at the Battle of Balls Bluff near Leesburg, Va, Oct 21ˢᵗ 1861. Hand-colored lithograph, Currier & Ives, 1861?

{ **FEBRUARY 17** **1865:** Union troops capture Columbia, South Carolina, and fires spread through sections of the city. Meanwhile, Confederate forces withdraw from Charleston, South Carolina. }

The most unremittingly contested ground of the Civil War was in the northernmost Confederate state, Virginia. The state capital, Richmond, located less than one hundred miles from Washington, D.C., became the capital city of the Confederacy in mid-1861, and from the beginning it was a prime target of Union military campaigns. It was protected primarily by the Southern force that Robert E. Lee renamed the Army of Northern Virginia when he assumed command, after Joseph E. Johnston was wounded during the Union's first concentrated effort to take the Confederate capital, in March–July 1862. Like the Federal capital at Washington, Richmond was fairly bursting at the seams during the war. The city was filled with government offices, war-related industries, refugees, wounded soldiers, spies, and Union prisoners confined in various facilities, including the notorious Libby Prison. Among Richmond's wartime residents was Mrs. Judith W. McGuire, who wrote in her diary on April 21, 1862, with McClellan's Union army on the Peninsula, "The ladies are now engaged making sand-bags for the fortifications at Yorktown; every lecture-room in town crowded with them, sewing busily, hopefully, prayerfully." A month later, as Union soldiers moved closer, she reported: "The anxiety of all classes for the safety of Richmond is now intense, though a strong faith in the goodness of God and the valour of our troops keeps us calm and hopeful."

Sketch of the city of Richmond, Va. Drawing by R. K. Sneden, Topographical Headquarters, Third Corps, December 1861

{ **FEBRUARY 18** 1865: Charleston, South Carolina, surrenders to Union troops under Brigadier General Alexander Schimmelfennig. }

On November 7, 1861, a huge combined land-and-sea expedition under Union brigadier general Thomas W. Sherman and U.S. Navy captain Samuel F. Du Pont attacked, captured, and began to secure the Hilton Head–Port Royal area, between Savannah, Georgia, and Charleston, South Carolina. Remaining in Union hands for the rest of the war, this area became an important base for coaling and supplying U.S. ships blockading the Southern coast. Port Royal also became a testing ground for educational and agricultural programs to assist freed slaves, some ten thousand of whom had been left behind when their masters fled inland. Having been long isolated from other communities, these former slaves had developed a unique way of life, and few whites expected them to succeed on their own. Northern missionaries and teachers soon began arriving in the Union enclave, determined to establish schools. In May 1862, well before President Lincoln issued the Preliminary Emancipation Proclamation (September 22, 1862), Major General David Hunter made a first—unauthorized and unsuccessful—attempt to form a Union regiment of freed slaves, the First South Carolina Volunteer Infantry (Colored), at Hilton Head (see June 11). An authorized First Carolina was formed later in the year and placed under the command of a noted abolitionist, Colonel Thomas Wentworth Higginson.

Victorious bombardment of Port Royal, SC Nov 7th 1861 by the United States fleet under command of Commodore Dupont. Hand-colored lithograph. Currier & Ives, c. 1861–62?

{ **FEBRUARY 19** 1862: The new Confederate Congress, replacing the Provisional Congress of 1861 after elections in the fall, orders the release of two thousand Federal prisoners of war. }

Proscribed and declared "infamous" by the legislature of his native
South Carolina when he chose to fight for the Union, Percival Drayton had entered the U.S. Navy
as a midshipman in 1827 and seen service with the Brazil, Mediterranean, and Pacific squad-
rons before the outbreak of the Civil War. Given command of USS *Pocahontas*, Drayton participated in the successful 1861 expedition against Port Royal, South Carolina, during which the
defending Confederate troops—under the command of his brother, Brigadier General Thomas
Drayton—were forced to withdraw inland, with the general himself leaving behind a house
and slaves.

General Drayton, a West Point classmate and longtime friend of Jefferson Davis, had
resigned from the military in 1836. But he returned to service on September 25, 1861, receiving
a commission as brigadier general in the Provisional Army of the Confederate States. Less than
two months later, he was facing Union naval forces led by his brother. His withdrawal inland was
the precursor to a wartime military career served primarily behind the lines. "He is a gentleman
and a soldier in his own person," Robert E. Lee wrote to Davis, "but seems to lack the capacity
to command."

Percival Drayton (1812–1865),
above left. 1855–65

Thomas F. Drayton (1808–
1891). 1861–65

"Slaves of the rebel Genl.
Thomas F. Drayton, Hilton
Head, SC." Photograph by
Henry P. Moore, May 1862

{ **FEBRUARY 20** 1865: The Confederate House of Representatives authorizes the use of slaves as soldiers. }

In February 1862, President Lincoln received good news from the western theater: Union forces had captured two forts, Henry and Donelson (along with several thousand Confederate troops), that were crucial to the Confederate defensive line on the Tennessee and the Cumberland rivers, respectively, thus opening those waterways for transport of troops and supplies deeper into the South. The major battle took place at Fort Donelson, on February 13–15. The day after the battle ended, Brigadier General Ulysses S. Grant, the Union commander, responded to an attempt by Brigadier General Simon Bolivar Buckner (left in command when his Confederate superiors fled) to negotiate terms of surrender by writing, "Sir: yours of this date proposing armistice and appointment of commissioners to settle terms of capitulation, is just received. No terms except an unconditional and immediate surrender can be accepted. I propose to move immediately upon your works." Buckner—who had served with Grant in the Mexican War (the two had climbed Mount Popocatépetl together) and helped him through some financial difficulties in 1854—unhappily accepted those terms. "Unconditional Surrender" Grant became a Northern hero. Buckner was briefly a prisoner of war but went on to other Southern commands. The two men did not meet again until Buckner visited Grant on July 10, 1885, thirteen days before Grant died of throat cancer.

Battle of Fort Donelson—Capture of General S. B. Buckner and his army, February 16th 1862. Color lithograph, Kurz & Allison, 1887

{ **FEBRUARY 21** 1862: Confederates successfully engage Union forces at Valverde, New Mexico Territory. }

Coming soon after some painful Union military setbacks, General Ulysses S. Grant's victories at Forts Henry and Donelson in Tennessee were widely celebrated, and Grant was lionized by the Northern press—in stories sometimes illustrated by woodcuts based on early wartime photographs such as this one, in which Grant wore a much longer beard than he did later on. A West Point graduate, Grant was also a veteran of the Mexican War, where he had served with a number of men whom he would later face across Civil War battlefields (including Simon Bolivar Buckner, the general who surrendered Fort Donelson; see February 21). "The acquaintance thus formed was of immense service to me in the war of the rebellion," Grant later wrote in his memoirs, "I mean what I learned of the characters of those to whom I was afterwards opposed. . . . The natural disposition of most people is to clothe a commander of a large army whom they do not know, with almost superhuman abilities. A large part of the National army, for instance, and most of the press of the country, clothed General Lee with just such qualities, but I had known him personally, and knew that he was mortal; and it was just as well that I felt this."

General Ulysses S. Grant (1822–1885), center, and staff. October 1861

{ **FEBRUARY 22** 1862: Jefferson Davis, the provisional Confederate president for the past year, is sworn in as president of the Confederacy in Richmond, Virginia, after being elected by Southern voters in November 1861. }

Civil War-era women were not allowed to be soldiers, but a small number, estimated at between four hundred and six hundred, did campaign with the armies. Some disguised themselves as men and enlisted as regular soldiers. Others went into battle—but only to save lives. Several had accompanied their husbands or relatives to army camps and were moved by circumstances to bear arms. "Michigan Bridget" Devens (or Divers), for example, traveled throughout the war with the First Michigan Cavalry Regiment, in which her husband was a private. Although she usually served behind the lines, Devens occasionally participated in combat. "She became well known throughout the brigade for her fearlessness and daring, and her skill in bringing off the wounded," reported L. P. Brockett and Mary C. Vaughan in their book *Woman's Work in the Civil War* (1867). "Occasionally when a soldier whom she knew fell in action, after rescuing him if he was only wounded, she would take his place and fight as bravely as the best. In two instances and perhaps more, she rallied and encouraged retreating troops and brought them to return to their position, thus aiding in preventing a defeat."

A Woman in Battle—"Michigan Bridget" Carrying the Flag. Illustration in Mary A. Livermore, *My Story of the War: A Woman's Narrative* (1888)

{ **FEBRUARY 23** **1861:** Texas voters approve secession by a three-to-one margin, ratifying a state convention's action on February 1. }

Ambrose Burnside—whose long side whiskers inspired the term "side-burns"—graduated from West Point in 1847 but left the U.S. Army after six years and went into business. Active in local military organizations, Burnside organized the First Rhode Island Regiment and became its colonel at the outbreak of the Civil War. After First Bull Run, he was commissioned brigadier general of volunteers. In early 1862, he won a promotion and much prestige for leading a successful expedition to the North Carolina coast. After the battle of Antietam and the dismissal of George B. McClellan, Burnside accepted command of the Army of the Potomac (see July 8). He led it to a costly defeat at Fredericksburg in December 1862 (see March 17 and 18) and was himself relieved of command after a dispute with his subordinates. Transferred to the Department of the Ohio (where his arrest of the antiwar politician Clement L. Vallandigham prompted one of the great Northern political furors of the war; see April 19), Burnside proved an effective commander at Knoxville, Tennessee. But in 1864, he was blamed for the bloody fiasco after the great mine explosion at Petersburg, Virginia (see June 26), an event that marked the close of his military career.

Ambrose Burnside (1824–1881) and other officers of the First Rhode Island Volunteers, Camp Sprague, near Washington, D.C. 1861

{ **FEBRUARY 24** 1862: Union troops under General Nathaniel P. Banks occupy Harpers Ferry, Virginia. }

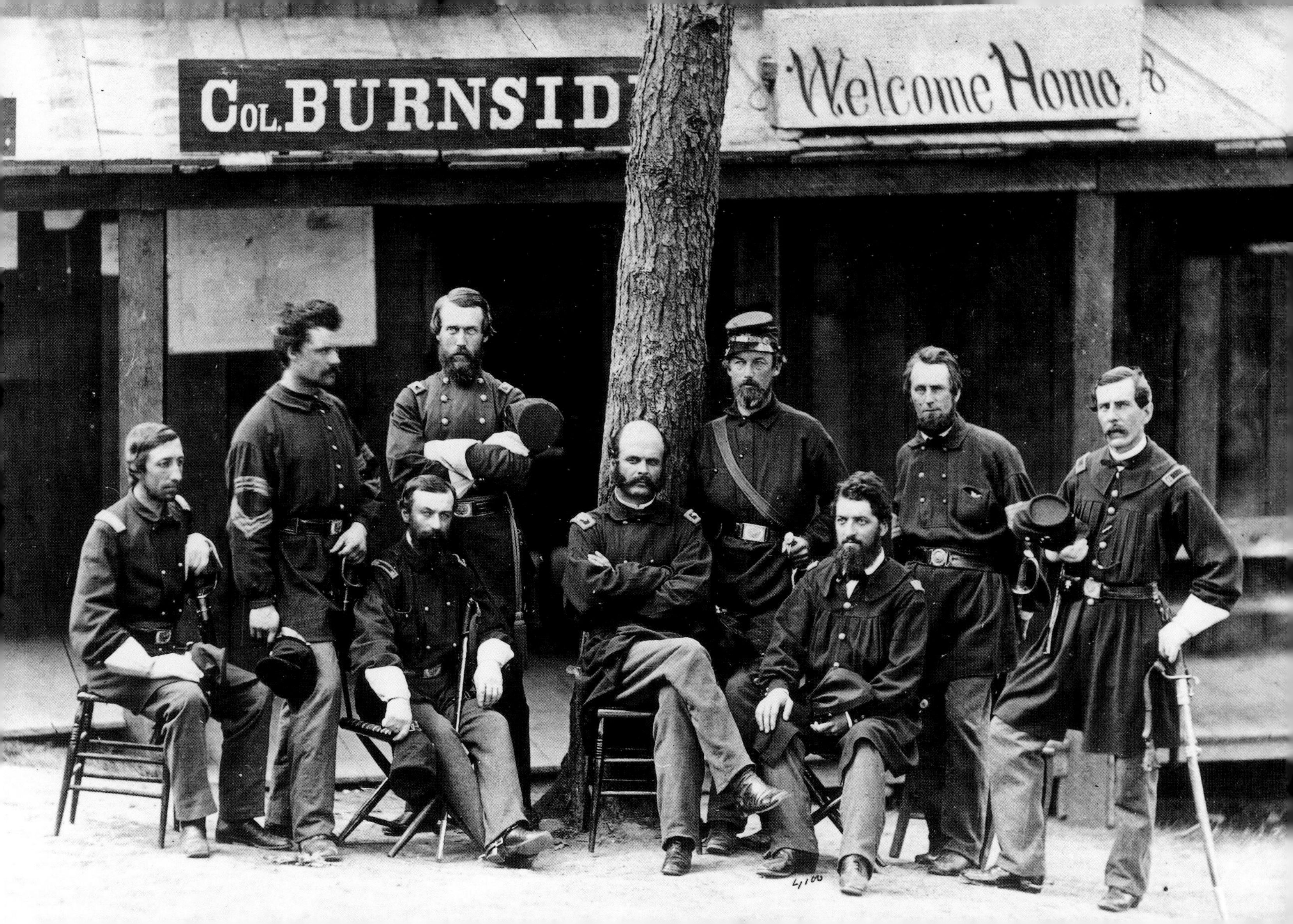
Col. BURNSID
Welcome Home.

After the Northern victories at Forts Henry and Donelson pierced the Confederacy's western defensive line, Confederate troops regrouped, bringing reinforcements by railroad to their base at the transport center of Corinth, Mississippi. Moving toward the Tennessee-Mississippi border, Grant's army camped—but did not fortify its position at Pittsburg Landing, near Shiloh Church, Tennessee. Waiting for his own reinforcements, Grant concentrated on drilling the many inexperienced soldiers included in his force. Neither he nor his army foresaw the Confederate attack on April 6, 1862. Led by Albert Sidney Johnston (who would be killed during the first day's fighting), the Confederates pushed Grant's troops to the river's edge—though stubborn action by Union troops at what became known as the "Hornets' Nest" bought valuable time for Grant to regroup. Reinforced by the second day and outnumbering the Confederates, Grant forced the Southern troops, now under P. G. T. Beauregard, to withdraw to Corinth on April 7. Inflicting almost twenty-four thousand casualties, more than all previous U.S. wars combined, the costly and desperate battle of Shiloh—a precursor of the huge Civil War battles to come—was regarded as a Northern victory.

Battle of Shiloh (April 6–7, 1862). Color lithograph, Louis Prang & Co., 1888

{ **FEBRUARY 25** 1862: Union troops under General Don Carlos Buell occupy Nashville, Tennessee, without bloodshed. Meanwhile, the U.S. War Department takes control of all telegraph lines to facilitate military movements. }

I have a little flag; it belonged to one of our cavalry regt's; presented to me by one of the wounded. It was taken by the Secesh in a cavalry fight, and rescued by our men in a bloody little skirmish. It cost three men's lives, just to get one little flag, four by three. Our men rescued it, and tore it from the breast of a dead Rebel—all that just for the name of getting their little banner back again. The man that got it was very badly wounded, and they let him keep it. I was with him a good deal; he wanted to give me something, he said, he didn't expect to live, so he gave me the little banner as a keepsake. I mention this, mother, to show you a specimen of the feeling. There isn't a reg't, cavalry or infantry, that wouldn't do the same on occasion.

—Poet Walt Whitman, letter to his mother, April 10, 1864

Confederate Battle-Flags and *Famous Union Battle-Flags.* Illustrations in Mary A. Livermore, *My Story of the War: A Woman's Narrative* (1888)

{ **FEBRUARY 26** 1863: The Cherokee Indian National Council repeals its ordinance of secession and declares its support for the Union. }

In the early years of the war, Abraham Lincoln—a "hands-on" and often frustrated commander in chief—elevated several generals to high responsibility. In the eastern theater, where Robert E. Lee's Army of Northern Virginia outfought Union forces at Second Bull Run (August 1862) and Chancellorsville (May 1863), the Army of the Potomac changed commanders numerous times. The fourth, George Gordon Meade, assumed command just before the battle of Gettysburg (July 1863). Meanwhile, in the western theater, Ulysses S. Grant rose in Lincoln's estimation as he proved his mettle at Forts Henry and Donelson, Tennessee (February 1862); with the capture of Vicksburg, Mississippi (July 1863); and with the dramatic victories of Lookout Mountain and Missionary Ridge in Tennessee (November 1863). In March 1864, Grant was made lieutenant general, a permanent rank held only by George Washington before him (Winfield Scott had been a brevet lieutenant general), and became general-in-chief of all Union armies. In the bloody months that followed, Grant—with Philip Sheridan, William T. Sherman, George H. Thomas, and other talented subordinates—pressed Confederate forces ceaselessly on all fronts.

Famous Union Commanders of the Civil War, 1861–65. Left to right, top row: Thomas, Kearny, Burnside, Hooker, Logan, Meade, McClellan; middle row: McDowell, Banks, Sheridan, Grant, Sherman, Rosecrans, Sickles; bottom row: Farragut, Pope, Butler, Hancock, Sedgwick, Porter. Color lithograph, Sherman Publishing Co., 1884

{ **FEBRUARY 27** **1864:** Federal prisoners of war begin arriving at the unfinished Camp Sumter, near Americus, Georgia—the infamous prison camp that came to be known as Andersonville. }

At the center of these assembled portraits, as he was at the heart of the Confederacy's military efforts, Robert E. Lee is surrounded by other prominent and capable Confederate commanders—including Stonewall Jackson, Jeb Stuart, Richard Ewell, Braxton Bragg, Wade Hampton, and Jubal Early. The efforts of these Southern military leaders were eventually eclipsed by the superior strategy of the North under Ulysses S. Grant, and by the South's own supply and manpower problems. The character of the Confederate commander in chief, Jefferson Davis, was also a factor in the South's defeat. A graduate of West Point (1828), a veteran of the Black Hawk War (1832) and the Mexican War (1846–48), and U.S. secretary of war (1853–57) under President Franklin Pierce, Davis had much more practical military experience than the Union's commander in chief. But he did not have the diplomatic skills, the ability to select talented subordinates and then delegate to them, the pragmatic flexibility—or the sense of humor—that marked Abraham Lincoln. Davis went through six secretaries of war in four years, engaged in what today would be called micromanaging, and feuded with his generals, particularly Joseph E. Johnston and P. G. T. Beauregard—and particularly *excepting* Robert E. Lee, whom he named general-in-chief of all Confederate armies on January 31, 1865.

Famous Confederate Commanders of the Civil War, 1861–65. Left to right, top row: Hood, A. P. Hill, A. S. Johnston, Ewell, Longstreet, Hardee, Price; middle row: Stuart, Beauregard, Jackson, Lee, J. E. Johnston, Fitzhugh Lee, Bragg; bottom row: Early, Breckinridge, Polk, Hampton, E. K. Smith, Semmes. Color lithograph, Sherman Publishing Co., 1884

{ **FEBRUARY 28** | 1862: The Confederacy observes a day of fasting and prayer. }

MARCH: WAR IN THE EAST

Roughly comprising the area east of the Appalachian Mountains, in the vicinity of the rival capitals of Washington and Richmond, the eastern theater was the area in which General Robert E. Lee's Army of Northern Virginia confronted the Union's powerful Army of the Potomac, commanded, in turn, by Generals George B. McClellan, Ambrose E. Burnside, Joseph Hooker, and George Gordon Meade. When Ulysses S. Grant became general-in-chief of all Union armies (March 1864), he made his headquarters with the Army of the Potomac and determined its movements (as well as supervising the movements of all other Federal forces), but General Meade was in command of the Army of the Potomac itself until the Confederate surrender at Appomattox. Warfare in the eastern theater included the crucial battles of Antietam and Gettysburg, the long siege of Petersburg, Virginia, and the very mobile Shenandoah Valley campaigns of 1862 and 1864. Although guerrilla warfare is often most closely associated with the conflict in the West, partisan rangers and guerrilla bands were active in the eastern theater throughout the Civil War, and the U.S. Navy conducted raids and enforced the Union blockade along the Atlantic coast. Stonewall Jackson, James Longstreet, Jubal A. Early, Joseph E. Johnston, and P. G. T. Beauregard were among the Confederate generals who held commands in this theater. (Johnston and Beauregard also saw duty in the western theater; see also September, "War in the West," and, for crucial operations in all theaters, July, "Turning Points.")

George B. McClellan (1826–1885). A hero to many, McClellan provoked impatience in his commander in chief with his failure to move aggressively. Color lithograph, c. 1862

{ **MARCH 1** 1864: President Lincoln nominates Major General Ulysses S. Grant for the recently revived regular army rank of lieutenant general. }

Abraham Lincoln before delivering his Cooper Union address in New York City. Photograph by Mathew Brady, February 27, 1860

The war's first major battle, First Bull Run (First Manassas), occurred in the eastern theater—and demonstrated painfully to the Union, as other circumstances were demonstrating to commanders in the South, that the volunteers pouring into their armies required much better training. On both sides, it also proved necessary, particularly in the first year of the war, to weed out incompetent officers, many of whom had been elected by their regiments—usually because of skillful electioneering or personal popularity rather than martial ability. "It would be safe to trust men of the intelligence & character of our volunteers to elect their officers," Lee wrote to Andrew G. Magrath on December 24, 1861, "could they at the time of election realize their dependent condition in the day of battle. But this they cannot do, & I have known them in the hour of danger repudiate & disown officers of their choice & beg for others."

"As a general rule the officers (and, of course, the non-commissioned officers) of volunteer regiments were entirely ignorant of their duties," McClellan wrote in his postwar memoir (*McClellan's Own Story*, 1887) of the Union army's situation after First Bull Run. "Many were unfitted, from their education, moral character, or mental deficiencies, for ever acquiring the requisite efficiency. These latter were weeded out by courts-martial and boards of examination, while the other were instructed *pair passu* as they instructed their men." As incompetent officers were discharged or made more competent, McClellan instituted much tougher training regimens for the men in the ranks. "The first thing in the morning is drill," new Union soldier Oliver Willcox Norton wrote in a letter home in October 1861, "then drill, then drill again. Then drill, drill, a little more drill. Then drill, and lastly drill. Between drills, we drill and sometimes stop to eat a little and have a roll-call."

On March 11, 1862, President Lincoln issued War Order No. 3, relieving George B. McClellan as general-in-chief of all Union armies but leaving the major general in command of the Department and Army of the Potomac. This measure was ostensibly taken to ease McClellan's burden as he prepared for the first major Union attempt to take Richmond, Virginia, the Confederate capital. Six days later, McClellan started transporting the 105,000-man Army of the Potomac by ship to the Virginia Peninsula, between the York and the James rivers, to initiate what became known as the Peninsula campaign. Lasting through July 1862, the campaign began with a siege of Yorktown, where McClellan was reluctant to attack what he was certain were superior forces (the Confederates were actually badly outnumbered); continued through a brutal encounter at Williamsburg; and ended when McClellan withdrew from the Peninsula after a series of battles known as the Seven Days, believing it was necessary to "save this army" from Southern forces he continued to assume were vastly more numerous. Throughout the campaign, the general peppered the president—whom he once described as "nothing more than a well-meaning baboon"—with complaints of insufficient manpower and inadequate support. "Your dispatches complaining that you are not properly sustained, while they do not offend me, do pain me very much," Lincoln replied as McClellan dithered at Yorktown. "Let me tell you that it is indispensable to you that you strike a blow. . . . You must act."

A view in Williamsburg, Virginia (wagons on Duke of Gloucester Street). Watercolor drawing by William McIlvaine, 1862

{ **MARCH 2** 1867: Overriding President Andrew Johnson's veto on the same day, Congress passes the Reconstruction Act, setting conditions for reintegration of Southern states into the Union. }

Ever reluctant to delegate responsibility for the military conduct of the war, President Jefferson Davis nonetheless recognized the overwhelming character of his duties as Confederate commander in chief. On March 3, 1862, he summoned to Richmond a general officer in whom he had utmost confidence—Robert E. Lee. Although he was named the president's military adviser, Lee was given more than advisory duties: he was charged with "the conduct of military operations in the armies of the Confederacy" and given "control of military operations, the movement and discipline of the troops, and the distribution of supplies among the armies of the Confederate states"—the same responsibilities specified in early proposed legislation that would have established the office of Confederate commanding general, had Davis not vetoed it. Thus, acting as an ad hoc chief of staff, Lee was able to bring some centralized military planning and expertise to the Confederacy's high command—but only for three months. On May 31, when General Joseph E. Johnston was severely wounded at the battle of Seven Pines (Fair Oaks), during the Union's Peninsula campaign, Lee left Richmond to assume command of Johnston's force, which he renamed the Army of Northern Virginia. Lee's aggressive tactics and his success in keeping a numerically superior army away from Richmond formed the foundation of the faith that the Southern people would have in him, and in his army, for the rest of the war.

Jefferson Davis (1808–1889). c. 1855

Robert E. Lee (1807–1870). Photograph by Julian Vannerson, 1863

{ **MARCH 3** 1863: President Lincoln signs the first Federal draft act, imposing liability on all able male citizens between twenty and forty-five years old. }

On a relatively quiet day during the Peninsula campaign, photographer James F. Gibson was able to set up his cumbersome equipment and convince members of General Fitz-John Porter's staff to hold still long enough for him to create this picture of military relaxation. Included in the group is recent West Point graduate George Armstrong Custer (reclining at right, next to his dog), a veteran of First Bull Run who was in the process of proving himself a talented and courageous warrior. Not long before this picture was taken, Custer had become one of the first Union officers to observe the field of battle from a balloon. And this same month, he waded across the uncertain waters of the Chickahominy River to determine a safe ford for Union forces, then reconnoitered the enemy's position on the other side—so impressing General George B. McClellan that, in early June, Custer was appointed one of the general's aides, with the rank of captain of volunteers. Headstrong and daring, Custer would continue to impress his superior officers, and the Northern public, throughout the war as he stayed in the thick of fighting in the eastern theater (see also November 10 and 12).

The staff of General Fitz-John Porter on the Peninsula, Virginia: the two reclining figures are Lieutenant William G. Jones, left, and Lieutenant George A. Custer. Photograph by James F. Gibson, May 20, 1862

{ **MARCH 4** 1861: Abraham Lincoln is inaugurated.
1865: President Lincoln is inaugurated for a second term. }

The Civil War occurred in an era of change in battle strategy and tactics.
The increased range and accuracy of rifled weapons (those with spiral grooves inside the barrel)
meant that the advantage in battle now typically rested with the defender armed with these
longer-range weapons; as a result, the cavalry charges and massed frontal assaults common
at the beginning of the century were employed much less frequently, for they were far too
costly. The widespread, routine use of breastworks and trenches became a natural response to
the improvements in weaponry. On the Peninsula, Civil War artist Alfred R. Waud sketched
these Union soldiers on their way to dig trenches that they would then inhabit while besieging
Yorktown—facing Confederate troops equally well dug in. Two years later, and not far away,
elaborate trench systems were constructed during the ten-month Union siege of Petersburg,
Virginia. Trenches were also used in the western theater. "All day yesterday & today we were at
work on the trenches, most of the time in the middle of the mud and the rain," James B. Mitchell,
a Confederate lieutenant, wrote to his father from Tullahoma, Tennessee, on June 20, 1863.
"The ditches . . . are now about completed and we are taking a little rest. . . . It seems to be the
general opinion that if the enemy advance upon us in this position, they will be beaten back with
terrible slaughter. I hope & pray that it may be so & I may come out safely & I wish you to join
your applications to mine."

*Going to the trenches—a sketch
in Camp Winfield Scott. Before
Yorktown* (on the Peninsula).
Pencil drawing on brown paper
by Alfred R. Waud, May 1862

{ **MARCH 5** 1862: General Pierre Gustave Toutant (P. G. T.) Beauregard assumes command of the Confederate Army of the Mississippi. }

From late March through mid–June 1862, Thomas Jonathan "Stonewall" Jackson realized, to brilliant effect, a plan that Robert E. Lee suggested while still President Davis's military adviser in Richmond. With the aid of maps prepared by his skilled topographical engineer, Jedediah Hotchkiss (pictured at left, near the top), Jackson led his Confederates in a dazzling series of maneuvers and battles that diverted Union troops from reinforcing McClellan's army on the Virginia Peninsula—and earned Jackson a reputation among his Northern opponents as a nearly invincible foe. Although it began with a tactical defeat for the Confederates at the battle of Kernstown (March 23), the Shenandoah Valley campaign quickly developed into a Southern triumph, one of military history's greatest strategic campaigns. Jackson's men marched so often and so far—defeating Union forces at McDowell (May 8), Front Royal (May 23), the first battle of Winchester (May 25), Cross Keys (June 8), and Port Republic (June 9)—that they became known as "Jackson's Foot Cavalry." Jackson himself emerged from the campaign as the Confederacy's foremost hero.

General Thomas Jonathan "Stonewall" Jackson (1824–1863) and staff, Richmond, Virginia. Photograph by Vannerson & Jones from original negatives, c. 1861–63

{ **MARCH 6** 1831: Philip Henry Sheridan (USA) is born in Albany, New York. }

Lieut. T. J. Jackson & Staff

With huge armies maneuvering over vast areas, accurate topographical information was of crucial importance in the Civil War. Yet of the few maps readily available in 1861, most were out-of-date or lacked information vital to the war's prosecution. In seeking to improve the situation, Federal authorities at least had the benefit of existing mapmaking organizations (such as the army's Corps of Topographical Engineers and the navy's Hydrographic Office), as well as adequate supplies of materials necessary to produce maps once accurate information was secured. The South lacked those advantages. But the Confederates' difficult situation was ameliorated by the efforts of dedicated topographical engineers. Prominent among them was Jedediah Hotchkiss (1828–1899), a native of New York who had moved in 1847 to Virginia, where he and his brother established a school. A man of utmost integrity and tireless dedication, Hotchkiss provided indispensable geographic intelligence for Stonewall Jackson and other Confederate commanders, including Robert E. Lee. He began his maps by sketching topographical notes—a process that at least once caused him some trouble. "I went on to Luray [Virginia], sketching the road," he wrote in his diary on November 20, 1862. "Came near being arrested. . . . A boy saw me sketching, by the rode [*sic*] side, and reported me to the Provost Marshal . . . as having on blue pants, etc., so he got Capt. Macon Jordan and some others to come and take me prisoner. When the Captain road [*sic*] up he broke into a big laugh, recognizing me, having been one of my Mossy Creek pupils."

Pages from the sketchbook of the Second Corps, Army of Northern Virginia. Pen and ink, pencil, and watercolor by Jedediah Hotchkiss, 1864–65

{ **MARCH 7** 1862: The battle of Pea Ridge (Elkhorn Tavern), Arkansas, the biggest battle west of the Mississippi River, begins, ending in a strategically important Union victory the next day. }

21

Williamsport
Aug. 25th

65
Col. 92

dism—

3rd 2nd Res. Munford

Johnson's

4th

Aug. 27th
Fitz Lee came to Leetown—
28th had engagement at Smithfield

Col. 92

Aug. 29th Fitz Lee remained on N. bank of Opequon

Lomax

JoC

Smithfield

Wickham Munford

Sept. 18th Wickhams Br. drawn up all day on right of Millwood Road— 4th on picket & Both Brs in Support

(Winchester or Opequon Sept 19-1864)

Sept 19th Fitz Lees Div. ordered at daylight to some position as yesterday—on right of Pegram— about 8 am Pegram went to left of Munford & Munford went to left Payne & Supported Breathed.
About 11 am. Moved to Millwood Rel. at gallop to Support Lomax

Payne

Breathed's Battn fired at flank of enemy

Pond

Rodes

Col 92
71

22

(Winchester- Sept. 19-1864)   Under shelling for 3 hours

Pegram

Munford then ordered at gallop Wm Lomax to Martinsburg Rd—

at 5 P.M. stampede having taken place—found Yanks in Fort Jackson Charged & took it & put

2nd Shoemaker

Munford 3rd   Charged fort—

Col. 92
73

1st Regt. in first 2d Div of enemy In cav. in front— infantry held Fort until all had left then came to Milltown on the ridges— when Yankees Charged his flank & he turned & drove across the pike just at dark—

Ft. Collyer

75
Col 92

Milltown

night of 19th 1st 2nd & part of 4th went to Kernstown & then to Front Royal— under Munford— the evening of the 20th the Yanks drove picket from Guard Hill & put Batt. there— Torbert & Pow attacked Munford before day at River

(Guard Hill Sept 19 & 20, 1864)

Despite George B. McClellan's constant conviction that he was facing overwhelming forces, and the general's attendant caution, his army made slow progress up the Peninsula toward Richmond, coming near enough that the reverberations from cannon fire caused great shudders of apprehension in the Confederate capital. The Army of the Potomac's advance also resulted in at least brief surges of optimism among some who read newspaper reports in Washington. "McClellan seems to be doing his whole duty now," wrote Commissioner of Public Buildings Benjamin Brown French in the midst of the Peninsula campaign. "He is making the Rebels skip down on the Peninsula. . . . I think now, the rebellion is on its last legs." Replacing the badly wounded General Joseph E. Johnston on June 1, 1862, Robert E. Lee proceeded to wage a creative and stubborn defense with the revivified and renamed Army of Northern Virginia—aided by Stonewall Jackson, recalled from the Shenandoah Valley, and Jeb Stuart, whose cavalry made a spectacular reconnaissance foray completely around the more numerous Union forces on June 12–15. After the often heavy fighting in a series of battles that became known as the Seven Days (June 25–July 1), McClellan proceeded to pull his army away from Richmond and the destruction that he feared from far greater Southern strength. He continued to blame Washington for his supposedly precarious position: "I have seen too many dead and wounded comrades to feel otherwise than that the government has not sustained this army," he wrote to Secretary of War Edwin M. Stanton and President Lincoln. "If you do not do so now the game is lost."

Yorktown, Virginia (with Union encampments). Watercolor drawing by William McIlvaine, 1862

{ **MARCH 8** **1862:** The U.S. Navy suffers the worst day in its eighty-six-year history when the Confederate ironclad frigate *Virginia* (formerly USS *Merrimack*) destroys two wooden Union vessels and runs others aground in Hampton Roads, the narrow channel between Norfolk and Fort Monroe, Virginia. }

Camp near Richmond, Va., June 26, 1862.

. . . The enemy threw shells all about our camp yesterday and killed two horses, but only one man. It was a great day between our batteries and those of the enemy. They fired all day long, but as it was all at long taw little damage was done. I went out this morning to view the enemy, and could see them and their breastworks very distinctly.

Since I began writing this letter I hear a terrific cannonading on the left wing of our army, and I believe the battle has opened. I am informed that General Jackson is about there and that a fight will certainly take place this week.

You must be cheerful and take things easy, because I believe the war will soon be ended. [June 29] . . . I was correct in my last letter to you when I predicted that the great battle had commenced (Chickahominy or Gaines Mills). The conflict raged with great fury after I finished writing, and it lasted from three o'clock until ten that night. The cannonading was so continuous at one time that I could scarcely hear the musketry at all. . . . A Yankee officer (a prisoner) told me that they had no idea General Jackson was anywhere about here, and he acknowledged that General McClellan was completely outwitted. I tell you the Yankee "Napoleon" has been badly defeated.

—Dr. Spencer Glasgow Welch, surgeon (CSA), letters to his wife

"Yorktown, Va., vicinity. 13-inch seacoast mortars of Federal Battery No. 4 with officers of 1st Connecticut Heavy Artillery." Photograph by James F. Gibson, May 1862

{ MARCH 9 } 1862: A new age in naval warfare is foreshadowed when two ironclad ships, the squat USS *Monitor* and CSS *Virginia* (also known as the *Merrimack*), fight each other. The battle is inconclusive, but it eases Union fears of the armored Confederate vessel (see also May 8–10).

Preparing to pull back from the Peninsula after the Seven Days battles, George B. McClellan shifted his supply base to Harrison's Landing on the James River. He called the movement a "strategic withdrawal"; others termed it the "great skedaddle." Richmond remained safe and would not be as seriously threatened for another two years. Yet Robert E. Lee's Confederate army had not destroyed or even crippled the Army of the Potomac, which remained a potent force. Both sides paid a heavy price in casualties for the months-long Peninsula campaign, and both had to scramble to cope with their thousands of wounded. "The most saddening sight was the wounded at the hospitals, which were in various places on the battlefield," wrote Confederate surgeon Spencer Glasgow Welch toward the end of the campaign. "Not only are the houses full, but even the yards are covered with them. There are so many that most of them are much neglected. The people of Richmond are hauling them away as fast as possible." So many Union wounded were taken to Washington that some twenty-two emergency hospitals were established during the summer—with Peninsula campaign casualties soon joined by those from Second Bull Run. Churches, schools, even at one point the Capitol building were used to house battered soldiers, for whom medical care was slowly improving as organizations such as the newly formed U.S. Sanitary Commission and compassionate individuals such as Clara Barton began providing much-needed supplies and nursing services.

The Army of the Potomac. The wagon trains of the Army of the Potomac en route from Chickahominy to James River, Va. during the Seven Days Fight (fording Bear Creek one mile below Savage Station) June 29th 1862. Color lithograph, date unknown

{ MARCH 10 1863: President Lincoln issues a proclamation of amnesty to soldiers absent without leave, if they report before April 1. **}**

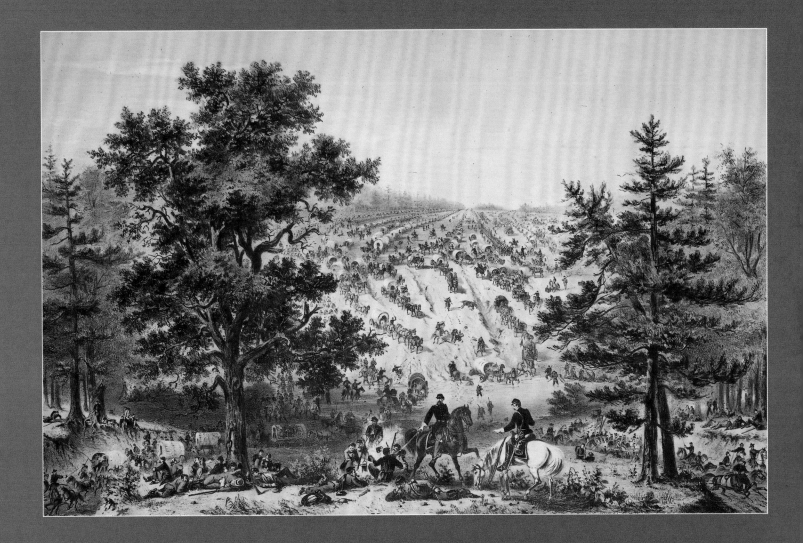

Following the Peninsula campaign, Robert E. Lee moved his army to north-central Virginia, where the Confederates faced a newly organized Union force: the Army of Virginia, commanded by Major General John Pope. Smaller than the Army of the Potomac, Pope's force might more easily be pushed back, thus allowing the Confederates to recover lost territory and supplies and more effectively secure the area north of Richmond, with its vital railroads to the Shenandoah Valley. The Second Bull Run campaign (Second Manassas, August 26–September 1, 1862) opened after Stonewall Jackson's "foot cavalry" defeated a smaller Union force under Nathaniel P. Banks at Cedar Mountain (Slaughter Mountain) on August 9, then followed that achievement with a spectacular fifty-mile march that took the Confederates around Pope's right flank, to the well-stocked Union supply depot at Manassas Junction. Suffering from a dearth of supplies themselves, Jackson's men ate and drank, stuffed everything they could carry into their knapsacks, and burned the rest. A confused pursuit by Federal forces ended when a Union division neared Jackson's concealed lines just north of the First Bull Run battlefield, and Jackson decided to engage. The battle of Groveton (Brawner's Farm) on August 28 turned into an hours-long musket-fire duel that ravaged the lines of both sides. As night fell and the firing stopped, Pope determined to attack Jackson. Meanwhile, another Confederate force under James Longstreet was approaching Pope's army from the west.

Battle of Groveton. Drawing by Edwin Forbes, August 30, 1862

 MARCH 11 1862: President Lincoln relieves Major General George B. McClellan from his post as general-in-chief of all U.S. armies. McClellan still commands the Union's powerful force in the eastern theater, the Army of the Potomac.

Infantry open the left wing at Battle of Bull Run — Regt 30th P.V. 1863, 4th P.V.

Recently transferred from the enclave that Union forces had established on South Carolina's Sea Islands, Major General Isaac Ingalls Stevens arrived in Virginia in time for the Second Bull Run campaign. First in his class at West Point (1839) and a veteran of the Mexican War, Stevens had served as governor of the Washington Territory (1853–57) and as a territorial delegate to Congress (1857–60) before reentering military service at the outbreak of war. At Second Bull Run, he served with distinction, his men covering the Union retreat as the Confederates won the field. Among his opponents was William E. Starke, a veteran of campaigns in western Virginia. Recently promoted to brigadier general, Starke assumed command of a division at Second Bull Run after its commander, Brigadier General William B. Taliaferro, was wounded. Stevens was killed by a gunshot wound immediately after Second Bull Run, during the battle of Chantilly (September 1, 1862)—in which his son, Hazard Stevens (1842–1918), was wounded. (Hazard Stevens later received the Medal of Honor for leading the assault that captured Fort Huger, Virginia, in 1863.) Starke was killed just over two weeks later, in the furious fighting that made the battle of Antietam (Sharpsburg), Maryland, the bloodiest single day of the war.

Isaac Ingalls Stevens (1818–1862). Photograph by Timothy H. O'Sullivan, March 1862

William E. Starke (1814–1862). Steel engraving, 1861–65

{ **MARCH 12** 1864: The Union's Red River campaign into Louisiana begins under the command of General Nathaniel P. Banks. }

Just over one year after the war's first major battle, the Federal defeat at First Bull Run, the Union suffered another humiliating loss at Second Bull Run, as Robert E. Lee continued his successful campaign against John Pope's Army of Virginia. On August 29–30, 1862, Pope made a series of misjudgments that effectively ended his Civil War battlefield service. Beginning with the erroneous conviction that he had trapped Stonewall Jackson, and continuing with his failure to believe General Fitz-John Porter's report that thirty thousand Confederates under James Longstreet had arrived on the battlefield, Pope ended the first day of the battle by mistaking Confederate moves to consolidate their lines as evidence the Southerners were retreating. He quickly reported to Washington that his army had won the battle. The next day, Lee's army disabused him of that notion when Pope sent his men to pursue the fleeing Confederates—and found them still in their line of battle. After a full day of ferocious fighting that reverberated with the demoralizing rebel yell, Pope's army was in full retreat, saved from complete disaster only by stubborn rearguard action.

The Second Battle of Bull Run, Fought Aug. 29th 1862. Hand-colored lithograph, Currier & Ives, 1862?

{ **MARCH 13** 1863: An accidental explosion at the Confederate Ordnance Laboratory in Richmond kills or injures sixty-nine people, nearly all of them women. }

After the 1860 presidential election, as it became clear that the United States would quite probably be split by war, the North and the South began to develop secret service organizations—an activity that bloomed, at times haphazardly, during the conflict. Among the women who engaged in what had previously been viewed as an unsavory and "ungentlemanly" pursuit was Rose O'Neal Greenhow, a superb Washington hostess and influence peddler, whose charmed circle included presidents, congressmen, and military leaders. A fervent proponent of the Southern cause, Mrs. Greenhow provided information helpful to Confederate generals Beauregard and Johnston before First Bull Run—and was subsequently imprisoned for her Confederate fervor. (This picture was taken in Washington's Old Capitol Prison, where she spent several months before being released in a prisoner exchange.) Farther west, in the troubled border state of Kentucky, actress Pauline Cushman was performing services for the Union that would earn her the sobriquet "Spy of the Cumberland." After boldly toasting Jefferson Davis and the Confederate cause while on stage in Louisville, she began an undercover effort among Southern troops that secured information valuable to Federal forces. The timely arrival of Union troops rescued Cushman from being hanged after her true loyalties were discovered. She later received an honorary major's commission from President Lincoln.

Rose O'Neal Greenhow (1815–1864) with her daughter. 1862

Pauline Cushman (1833–1893). 1860–80?

{ MARCH 14 1863: Admiral David G. Farragut leads his Union flotilla up the Mississippi River at night, past the batteries of Port Hudson, Louisiana, but the flotilla is too heavily damaged in the passage to successfully blockade the city. **}**

Continuing to push north after his victory at Second Bull Run, Robert E. Lee led his army across the Potomac River into the Union state of Maryland in early September 1862, hoping to secure supplies, acquire thousands of recruits from among residents who were sympathetic to the South, encourage European recognition of the Confederacy, and demoralize the Union into suing for peace. "Our army has come among you," Lee stated in a proclamation issued in Frederick, Maryland, on September 8, "and is prepared to assist you with the power of its arms in regaining the rights of which you have been despoiled." However, Lee issued the proclamation in an area of the state where there were not many slaves and there was little feeling of being despoiled, and few Marylanders swelled his army's ranks. The Federal government, meanwhile, mustered forces to interfere with Lee's progress. Some Union troops took shelter in this church at Chambersburg, Pennsylvania, a Northern town, not far from Gettysburg, that would have the distinction of being invaded by Confederates twice during the war. This September, however, it remained under Union control as Lee's first major invasion of the North culminated in the pivotal battle of Antietam (Sharpsburg) on September 17 (see July 1–5). After that costly battle, Lee led his army back to Virginia.

Union troops preparing to bivouac in church pews, Chambersburg, Pennsylvania. Watercolor by James Fuller Queen, 1862

{ **MARCH 15** 1863: Authorities in San Francisco take control of the schooner *J. M. Chapman*, about to leave with twenty alleged secessionists and six Dahlgren guns. }

Near Brooks's Station, Va., . . . our brigade left Rappahannock Station on the afternoon of November 19th, and after marching about five miles through mud and rain, we at eleven o'clock encamped for the night. On the next day we marched about ten miles through mud two inches deep—on guard that night in a rain storm; started next morning and marched ten miles in mud three inches deep. It rained nearly all day with great violence. After a halt of two days we came down here to draw rations; we had a march through mud about five inches deep. During our halt we were posted on a hill where the winds blew bitter cold, but we fixed our tent up in such a way that we slept warm. We were constantly drilling leaving us hardly time to cook our food. To-day we broke camp and moved into a warmer position, and the boys commenced putting up their tents with a view of remaining here for some days, but orders came to-night to be ready for a march in the morning. . . . I am well, with the exception of a headache to-night. Our next move will be toward Fredericksburg, to participate in the grand battle expected to take place there in a few days. Please give my remembrance to all who inquire after.

—Sergeant Warren H. Freeman (USA), letter to his father, December 4, 1862

A Union officer looks across the river toward Fredericksburg, Va. Pencil and Chinese white drawing on brown paper by Alfred R. Waud, December 1862

{ **MARCH 16** 1862: The Federal government institutes martial law in San Francisco in response to rumors of a possible attack. }

In early November 1862, President Lincoln finally relieved George B. McClellan of battlefield command (see April 14, July 8) and named Major General Ambrose Burnside commander of the Army of the Potomac. As he reorganized the army, Burnside secured the president's approval for a new campaign against Richmond. The effort disintegrated into failure along the Rappahannock River, at Fredericksburg, Virginia, when, on December 13, the Union suffered one of its worst defeats of the entire war. In this encounter, Burnside sent the one-hundred-thousand-man Army of the Potomac—in formation and over open ground—against Lee's smaller force (seventy-two thousand), which was well positioned on the high ground beyond the town. "When within some three hundred yards of the rebel works, the men burst into a cheer and charged for the heights," wrote Union soldier Josiah Marshall Favill in his diary, after participating in the battle. "Immediately the hill in front was hid from view by a continuous sheet of flame from base to summit. The rebel infantry poured in a murderous fire while their guns from every available point fired shot and shell and cannister. The losses were so tremendous, that before we knew it our momentum was gone, and the charge a failure. . . . I wondered while I lay there how it all came about that these thousands of men in broad daylight were trying their best to kill each other. Just then there was no romance, no glorious pomp, nothing but disgust for the genius who planned so frightful a slaughter."

Battle of Fredericksburg—the Army of the Potomac Crossing the Rappahannock in the morning of Dec. 13, 1862, under the command of Genls. Burnside, Sumner, Hooker, and Franklin. Color lithograph, Kurz & Allison, 1888

 { MARCH 17 1864: Lieutenant General Ulysses S. Grant formally assumes command of the armies of the United States. **}**

"It is well that war is so terrible," Robert E. Lee said, watching his troops wreak havoc on the Army of the Potomac at Fredericksburg, "or we would grow too fond of it." The cost of Fredericksburg was indeed terrible: casualties on both sides—eighteen thousand killed, wounded, or missing—amounted to three times the number of American men killed or wounded on D-Day in World War II; two-thirds of the casualties were on the Union side. "Not for 50 years to come will that scene ever fade from the memory of those who saw it," wrote *London Times* correspondent Francis Charles Lawley, who viewed the battle from the Confederate lines. "There, in every attitude of death, lying so close to each other that you might step from body to body, lay acres of the Federal dead. . . . [In the town itself,] layers of corpses stretched in the balconies of houses as though taking a *siesta*. In one yard a surgeon's block for operating was still standing, and, more appalling to look at than even the bodies of the dead, piles of arms and legs, amputated as soon as their owners had been carried off the field, were heaped in the corner." Throughout the Union, people were stunned by this terrible defeat. The people of the North, *Harper's Weekly* editorialized, "cannot be expected to suffer that such massacres as this at Fredericksburg shall be repeated."

"Burying the dead at a hospital in Fredericksburg, Va." December 1862?

{ **MARCH 18** 1865: Amid arguments and mutual finger-pointing with President Davis, the Confederate Congress adjourns its last session. }

Thursday, Jan. 29th [1863, in Virginia] . . . It has been a pleasant sunshiny day,—but cool,—the snow being about a foot deep. It broke down many trees last night and some horses were killed. It is freezing up tonight. . . . The papers say the enemy 'stuck in the mud' when they attempted to come over the 20th inst. The mud is deep. . . .

Saturday, Jan. 31st . . . The day has been very pleasant, thawed some but the snow is still deep. It appears that Burnside, the Fed. Commander here, was relieved from command the 26th and Jo. Hooker put in his place. Sumner and Franklin have also been recalled. Success to the derangement such changes must produce.

—Major Jedediah Hotchkiss (CSA), diary entries

Headquarters Twelfth Army Corps [Virginia], April 5, 1863. . . .

Last night a furious storm of wind, snow and hail set in, and continued till near noon to-day. It will melt very fast, of course, but the roads, which before were nearly dry, will go back to their former state of mud. I got caught in the storm last night; I had been over to the cavalry with Tom Robeson; when we came back, . . . the wind blew such a gale that the horses could hardly breast up against it.

I wouldn't have believed, two months ago, that popular feeling would be so unanimously for war. They have at last waked up to the fact that we've got to fight these rebels till we crush them, let it take one year or ten, and that there is no peace now but in dishonor and eternal disgrace.

—Major Charles Fessenden Morse (USA), letter to his family

Winter campaigning. The Army of the Potomac on the move. Sketched near Falmouth [Virginia,] Jan. 21. Pencil, Chinese white, and black ink wash drawing on tan paper by Alfred R. Waud, January 21, 1863

{ **MARCH 19** 1861: In Texas, Federal troops surrender Forts Clark, Inge, and Lancaster. }

Originally in the regular Confederate cavalry, where he was a favorite of General Jeb Stuart, John Singleton Mosby became widely known as the leader of a partisan band so effective that the area of Virginia in which it operated was called "Mosby's Confederacy." Mosby's Forty-third Virginia Battalion ("Mosby's Rangers"), organized under the Confederacy's unique Partisan Ranger Act (April 1862), conducted daring raids that earned Mosby and his men fame and affection in the South; their irregular tactics earned them the uncomplimentary label of "bushwhackers" in the North, where many considered them no better than outlaws. "The complaint has often been made against me that I would not fight fair," Mosby wrote after the war, adding that "in one sense this charge . . . is true. I fought for success and not for display." Union cavalry general Phil Sheridan also fought for success, with the feisty aggressiveness that characterized him from his West Point days, when he was suspended for chasing a fellow cadet with a fixed bayonet. Dubbed "little Phil" by his men, Sheridan became a celebrated figure throughout the North after what came to be known as "Sheridan's Ride," during the Union's 1864 Shenandoah Valley campaign. Color lithographs depicting his dash, on his warhorse Rienzi, to rally his troops during the battle of Cedar Creek, Virginia (October 19, 1864), abounded even well after the war. The ride was also the subject of a popular poem by Thomas Buchanan Read. Written immediately after the event, the poem was recited by actor James Edward Murdoch, almost before the ink was dry, to wartime Northern audiences that reportedly sprang to their feet applauding furiously (see also March 28).

John Singleton Mosby (1833–1916). c. 1861–65

Philip H. Sheridan (1831–1888). c. 1861–65

{ MARCH 20 1862: Stonewall Jackson pursues withdrawing Union troops toward Winchester, Virginia. **}**

"A devoted champion of the South was one who possessed a heart intrepid, a spirit invincible, a patriotism too lofty to admit a selfish thought and a conscience that scorned to do a mean act," Major General Jeb Stuart wrote in a letter to R. H. Chilton on December 3, 1862. "His legacy would be to leave a shining example of heroism and patriotism to those who survive." The commander of the cavalry that were the "eyes" of Robert E. Lee's army and, with Stonewall Jackson, one of Lee's most trusted and accomplished subordinates, Stuart was describing the "chivalry" professed by many in the South's wealthy, slaveholding aristocracy. All three of these Confederate generals had graduated from the U.S. Military Academy at West Point; all three distinguished themselves fighting against the U.S. Army—in the process becoming the foremost Confederate heroes of the Civil War. These three generals also reflected the South's deeply rooted military traditions, represented most concretely in the region's many military schools. Among the best known of these schools was the Citadel, established as the South Carolina Military Academy in 1842. Citadel cadets no doubt admired Lee, Jackson, and Stuart and perhaps thought of them as their studies were interrupted for war service. The Citadel's Corps of Cadets participated in eight Civil War engagements—beginning before the formal onset of the war when, in January 1861, they fired on USS *Star of the West*, which was attempting to resupply Fort Sumter but was forced to withdraw from Charleston Harbor and return to New York.

Three Heroes. Robert E. Lee, flanked by Stonewall Jackson, left, and Jeb Stuart. Black pastel drawing by F. C. Buroughs, 1893?

The Citadel Cadets, of Charleston, South Carolina. Wood engraving in *Frank Leslie's Illustrated News,* February 9, 1861

{ **MARCH 21** 1861: Louisiana ratifies the Confederate Constitution. }

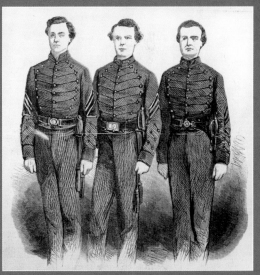

Nicknamed "Fighting Joe" for his display of bravery during the 1862 Peninsula campaign, Major General Joseph Hooker was not renowned for humility or circumspection. Two of his least attractive qualities—unqualified ambition and a tendency to backbite—were noted by President Lincoln in a letter he sent to Hooker after naming the general to replace Ambrose Burnside as commander of the Army of the Potomac: "You have taken counsel of your ambition, and thwarted him [Burnside] as much as you could, in which you did a great wrong to the country, and to a most meritorious and honorable brother officer." Lincoln also knew of Hooker's comments regarding the country's need for a dictator: "Of course it was not for this, but in spite of it, that I have given you the command. Only those generals who gain successes can set up dictators. What I now ask of you is military success, and I will risk the dictatorship." After reorganizing the Army of the Potomac—and instituting measures that markedly raised its morale—Hooker was supremely confident that he could comply with the commander in chief's request. "My plans are perfect," he told his staff as he prepared to take his 130,000 men across the Potomac River. "May God have mercy on General Lee, for I will have none." Shortly thereafter, Hooker's army confronted Robert E. Lee's 60,000-man Army of Northern Virginia in the "Wilderness" area of Virginia, near a large dwelling known as Chancellorsville Inn—and after four days of fighting was roundly whipped.

Joseph Hooker (1814–1879). Photograph by the Brady National Photographic Art Gallery, 1860–65

8th Penn Cavalry crossing at Elys [?] Ford before battle of Chancellorsville. Pencil and Chinese white drawing on olive paper by Alfred R. Waud, April–May 1863

{ **MARCH 22** 1817: Braxton Bragg (CSA) is born in Warrenton, North Carolina. }

Aware that Joseph Hooker had led the Army of the Potomac across the Rappahannock River into Virginia in another attempt to outflank the strong Confederate position in Fredericksburg, Robert E. Lee moved to counter the Federal action—leaving a covering force under Major General Jubal Early in the town itself. In consultation with Stonewall Jackson, Lee made the daring decision to split his main force, sending Jackson around to flank Hooker. This Jackson accomplished on May 2, striking the unprepared Union force at about 6 P.M. However, riding forward in a small party through the gloom of that evening, Jackson was mistaken for a Union officer and wounded by his own soldiers. The battle continued, ending two days later in a stunning victory for the Confederates—with the help of Hooker's own cautious movements and poor reconnaissance. But the resounding Southern victory became bittersweet when Jackson's wound proved mortal: his arm was amputated on the night of May 2, and he died of pneumonia on May 10. A distraught General Lee said, "I know not how to replace him." In Washington, news of the terrible Union defeat nearly overwhelmed President Lincoln. "One newly risen from the dead could not have looked more ghostlike," a friend of Lincoln's, newspaper correspondent Noah Brooks, later wrote. "Clasping his hands behind his back, he walked up and down the room, saying, 'My God! My God! What will the country say? What will the country say?'"

Battle of Chancellorsville (Stonewall Jackson is wounded). Color lithograph, Kurz & Allison, 1889

{ **MARCH 23** 1862: The first battle of Kernstown, Virginia, marks the opening of Stonewall Jackson's Shenandoah Valley campaign. }

The Civil War was the first conflict in which the electric telegraph played a major role. Operational in the United States since the 1840s, the telegraph changed the manner in which commanders exercised their authority: they could now be made almost instantly aware of developments along a wide front and quickly issue orders accordingly. In Washington, President Lincoln could often be found in the War Department's telegraph office, where he eagerly awaited news from all theaters of operation—many times, in the first half of the war, trooping back to the White House utterly discouraged. Telegraph lines to Richmond likewise kept President Davis informed. Each side tapped the other's telegraph lines. (By one account, Robert E. Lee's personal telegraph operator, C. A. Gaston, tapped General Grant's line for six weeks during the siege of Petersburg.) And each side combated the other's telegraphic intelligence gathering by developing ciphers. The Union's more extensive telegraph net included commercial telegraph companies, the Signal Corps Field Telegraph, and the Military Telegraph Service. The small Confederate military telegraph system depended on civilian companies, and most operators were civilians.

"Field telegraph station, Wilcox's Landing, Va., vicinity of Charles City Court House." 1864 (probably May or June)

{ **MARCH 24** 1864: President Lincoln meets with Ulysses S. Grant, general-in-chief of the U.S. armies, at the White House. }

In early May 1864, General-in-Chief Ulysses S. Grant, headquartered with George Gordon Meade's Army of the Potomac, embarked on the Overland campaign, a relentless pursuit of Lee's Army of Northern Virginia that pushed the Confederates back to Petersburg, Virginia. The first clash of this bloody five-week campaign was the battle of the Wilderness, on May 5–6, which participant Josiah Marshall Favill of the Union army described in his diary:

> The enemy came rushing up to our breastworks, some climbing over them. I saw a rebel officer mount the rampart with a flag in his hand, waving it over the heads of his men. The woods had taken fire in front and now spread to the log breastworks, which added renewed terrors and excitement to the situation. As the rebel flag was flaunting over the burning ramparts, Carrol's brigade came sweeping up at the double quick, and with a wild hurrah drove the rebels back into the mass of flames and smoke and recovered everything that had been temporarily lost. . . . As soon as the enemy was driven back we devoted ourselves to saving the wounded from roasting to death in the woods and in front. This is one of the horrors of fighting in dense woods, where the bursting shells invariably in dry weather set fire to the dead leaves and branches.

Wounded soldiers escaping from the burning woods of the Wilderness, May 6, 1864. Pencil and Chinese white drawing on brown paper by Alfred R. Waud, May 6–7, 1864

{ **MARCH 25** **1865:** Confederates attack and briefly capture Fort Stedman, part of the Union siege fortifications at Petersburg, Virginia. Meanwhile, Union troops begin their siege of Mobile, Alabama. }

"The position I am now placed in I feel will prove a trying one," Ulysses S. Grant wrote on March 15, 1864, as he assumed command of all Union armies. "But by having an eye to duty alone I shall hope to succeed." The aggressiveness, tenacity, and skill with which Grant pursued the preservation of the Union are reflected in his famous definition of the art of war: "Find out where your enemy is. Get at him as soon as you can. Strike at him as hard as you can and as often as you can, and keep moving on." This philosophy was evidenced in his conduct of the Overland campaign. It began with the bloody battle of the Wilderness, which left about eighteen thousand Union soldiers killed, wounded, or missing. Previous Federal commanders in the eastern theater had typically pulled back to regroup and reoutfit their armies after a major encounter. But Lieutenant General Grant had promised President Lincoln that "whatever happens there will be no turning back." As he pushed forward after the Wilderness, Grant ordered General William T. Sherman to press on into Georgia. In August, after a Confederate incursion led by Jubal Early that had reached the outskirts of Washington, Grant initiated Philip Sheridan's successful Shenandoah Valley campaign in pursuit of Early's force. "I shall not give my attention so much to Richmond as to Lee's army," Grant said to his staff as the Overland campaign began, "and I want all commanders to feel that hostile armies, and not cities, are to be their objectives."

General Ulysses S. Grant with members of his staff. 1864

{ **MARCH 26** 1863: West Virginia voters approve the gradual emancipation of slaves. }

Immediately after the bitterly fought battle of the Wilderness, Grant and Meade's Army of the Potomac smashed into Lee's Army of Northern Virginia again in a series of brutal encounters constituting the battle of Spotsylvania, which took place around the village of Spotsylvania Court House, Virginia, on May 8–21, 1864. Ferocious fighting was the hallmark of these encounters, as Union soldiers attacked positions that the Confederates had worked frantically to fortify with nearly impenetrable fieldworks. Twelve regiments, formed in columns and led by Colonel Emory Upton, forced their way through the Confederate defenses on May 10 but were compelled to withdraw that night; on May 12, Grant sent Winfield Scott Hancock's corps against a nearby position, which would become known as the "Bloody Angle." Although Lee was forced back to a new position, fierce fighting continued until Grant disengaged on May 19. Two days later, Union forces advanced again, trying to move around the Confederate right flank.

Battle at Spottsylvania [*sic*]. Reproduction of a painting by E. Packbauer, in *Deeds of Valor* (1901)

{ **MARCH 27** **1865:** President Lincoln meets with Generals Ulysses S. Grant and William T. Sherman and Admiral David Dixon Porter aboard the *River Queen* at City Point, Virginia. }

After Jubal Early's Confederate troops menaced Washington in July 1864, Ulysses S. Grant formed a new fighting force, the Army of the Shenandoah, and ordered its commander, Major General Philip Sheridan, to "pursue Early to the death." The other major objective of Sheridan's Shenandoah Valley campaign was to destroy the fertile valley's capacity to continue serving as the "Breadbasket of the Confederacy." The "hard war" was to be brought home to its inhabitants under Grant's orders that nothing "should be left to invite the enemy to return." Beginning in August, the campaign included the third battle of Winchester (September 19) and the battle of Fisher's Hill (September 22), and it culminated in the battle of Cedar Creek (October 19). In this encounter—which began as Sheridan was riding to Washington for a strategy conference—Early took the initiative, launching a daring surprise attack that had been proposed by Major General John Brown Gordon and Stonewall Jackson's former mapmaker, Major Jedediah Hotchkiss. This initial attack broke Union lines and forced a retreat. But the Confederates did not press the Federal troops hard enough to prevent their regrouping. Hearing of the battle, General Sheridan rode back on his warhorse, Rienzi, and inspired his men as they counterattacked—an action that thrilled the North, where it was widely celebrated. The Union counterattack smashed the Confederates. (See also March 20, November 23–26.)

Jubal Early (1816–1894). 1861–65

Battle of Cedar Creek, Oct 19, 1864. Color lithograph, Kurz & Allison, 1890

{ **MARCH 28** 1818: Wade Hampton (CSA) is born in Charleston, South Carolina. }

"We must destroy this army of Grant's before it gets to the James River," Robert E. Lee said to Jubal Early in June 1864, as Ulysses S. Grant's Overland campaign pushed the Army of Northern Virginia back to the Confederate cities of Richmond and Petersburg. "If he gets there it will become a siege, and then it will be a mere question of time." Grant's army began crossing the James on June 12, and by June 15, Lee's predicted siege had begun. The Petersburg campaign (June 15, 1864–April 3, 1865) foreshadowed the trench warfare of the western front during World War I, as each side dug in for what would become the longest sustained operation of the Civil War. Gradually extending the lines of their own numerically superior Union force, Generals Grant and Meade forced Lee to stretch his own lesser resources; by February 1865, Confederate lines extended thirty-seven miles. "The boys are all very diligently engaged throwing up fortifications in the front," Richard Lewis, a Confederate lieutenant, wrote to his mother from Petersburg on September 18, 1864, "being gone every day from 6 o'clock until about two or three, and will soon have the noble and brave old city almost impregnable, though the stout hearts around it are almost strong enough bulwark."

Confederate fortifications, with chevaux-de-frise beyond, at Petersburg, Virginia. 1865

{ **MARCH 29** 1865: The Appomattox campaign—the final Union push against Robert E. Lee's army—begins. }

By the end of March 1865, Robert E. Lee's position at Petersburg had become untenable, and the leader of the Army of Northern Virginia (and, as of January, the Confederate general-in-chief) sought ways to breach Union lines and lead his men out, with the hope of linking with the Confederate force, led by Joseph E. Johnston, that was then in North Carolina—being hotly pursued by William T. Sherman's Federal troops. On March 25, Lee's men unsuccessfully attacked Fort Stedman, on the right of the Union's lines, and sustained more than four thousand casualties. On April 1, one day after Union forces had suffered a tactical defeat at Dinwiddie Court House, Federal troops led by Philip Sheridan and Gouverneur Warren attacked Five Forks, a key position on what was to be Lee's route of retreat from Petersburg. Although Lee had ordered Major General George Pickett to "hold Five Forks at all hazards," this proved impossible. The left flank of the outnumbered Confederates crumbled, and a division of Union cavalry charged the Confederate rear and captured more than one thousand prisoners. The victory at Five Forks allowed Grant to launch an all-out assault the next day, which finally forced Lee's withdrawal from the Petersburg-Richmond area. Both cities were in Union hands by April 3.

Battle of Five Forks, Va.—Charge of General Sheridan April 1st 1865. Color lithograph, Kurz & Allison, 1886

{ **MARCH 30** 1864: Confederates attack Snyder's Bluff, Mississippi. }

When the Civil War started, neither side possessed the facilities to house and care for vast numbers of prisoners over extended periods of time. This lack of preparedness led to one of the war's great horrors: tens of thousands of the more than four hundred thousand Americans who became prisoners during the war were corralled into unsanitary pens, often exposed to the elements, without the food, exercise, shelter, or clean water needed to sustain them—the most infamous example of poor prison facilities being Andersonville (see August 22). One large Federal facility that housed Confederate prisoners was Point Lookout, Maryland (officially, Camp Hoffman, for Colonel William Hoffman, U.S. commissary general of prisoners). Also used as a hospital complex, this former resort was not very healthful for its prisoner population: unsanitary water and exposure to harsh weather off Chesapeake Bay took a severe toll, primarily because prisoners were housed in often inadequate tents instead of wooden barracks, as was the case in most other Union military prison facilities. More than thirty-five hundred Confederate prisoners died there between July 1863 and May 1865. Some twenty-two thousand Confederates were still imprisoned at Point Lookout when the war ended. (See also August 20 and 21.)

Rebs taking the oath [of loyalty to the United States] at Richmond. Pencil and Chinese white drawing on olive paper by Alfred R. Waud, April–May 1865

Point Lookout, Md. Color map (bird's-eye view) by George Everett, 1864

{ MARCH 31 1862: With Stonewall Jackson active in the Shenandoah Valley, President Lincoln recalls some of General George B. McClellan's troops from Virginia's Peninsula to help protect Washington. **}**

464

POINT LOOKOUT, MD

VIEW OF HAMMOND GENL. HOSPITAL & U.S. GENL. DEPOT FOR PRISONERS OF WAR.

1. Light house,
2. Dining cars & kitchen,
3. Hospl. Headquarters,
4. Baggage house,
5. Heating room,
6. Half Diet kitchen,

7. Chapel,
8. Reservoir,
9. Circle of wards,
10. Ward G.
11. " D.
12. " P.

13. West R.
14. K. L. Donnelly Stores,
15. Dead house,
16. Barber house,
17. Wharf & Post-Com. buildings,
18. Ice house.

34. Line of railng. Hosp. & Mlitry.
35. Qrs. of Capt. Lucas, C. S.
36. " of Mr Tompkins a. m. Clerk,
37. Qrs. of Capt. Craft C. S.
38. " of Lt. Sargent Ord. officer,
39. " of Capt. Guthrey, Q. M.

40. Office of Com. of Musters
41. Office of Capt. Patterson Provost Marshal
42. Brig. Gen. Marston Headquarters,
43. 2nd Wisconsin battery,
44. Cluster of stables,

45. Convalescent quarters,
46. Star Spangled Masonic Lodge,
47. Murphy's farm house,
48. Office of 12th. N. H. V.
49. Qrs. of Dr. Marrow, Sur. 2nd. N. H. V.

50. Qrs. of Col. Bailey 2nd. N. H. V.
51. Camp of 2nd. N. H. V.
52. " of 12th. N. H. V.
53. Hospital 2nd N. H. V.
54. Camp of New Langley. Cmry.

55. Qrs. of Union recruits from invd. prisoners,
56. Guard house,
57. Relief Camp,
58. Camp 5th. N. H. V.
59. Qrs. of Col. Crum. 5th. N. H. V.

60. Burying ground,
61. Small pox hospital,
62. Worlds diverse Peninsula & Block houses,
63. Cook house,
64. Misssdrliment as Office,
65. Camp for hired officers.

15. Laundry,
16. Guard quarters,
17. Hosp. Com. a. Clerks Store room,
18. Old hotel — ward A & B,
19. " — ward A & B,
20. Commissary building,

26. Ward I,
27. " G,
28. " S,
29. Row of P-avenue boarding house
30. Africas boarding house,
31. Russell up's photograph gallery,

31. Qrs. of W. H. Gurine, &c.
32. " S,
33. Teleg. U. S. A. & Ex officers,
34. Qrs. of A. Heger, Surg. U. S. A. in charge of hospital,
35. Qrs. of Surg. Thompson, in charge of Prisoners Camp.

APRIL: WARTIME POLITICS

More immediately and painfully than during any other American conflict—save, perhaps, the revolution that gave birth to the United States—political and battlefield campaigns affected each other during the Civil War. Political considerations, of course, governed the choice of sides—which was not always a simple matter of proclaiming loyalty to a state or a region or joining an army. Loyal Unionists in the South and Southern sympathizers in the North often found themselves in difficult, sometimes dangerous, circumstances. Some Indian nations joined the Confederate cause, hoping for recognition and better treatment than they were receiving from the Union; a few of those nations became as divided as the country at large.

As the war dragged on, political pressure to affect movement on the battlefield was applied officially, through such vehicles as the Union's congressional Joint Committee on the Conduct of the War and the actions of certain Confederate state governors. Pressure was also applied unofficially, via citizens' organizations and newspapers such as Horace Greeley's *New York Tribune*, which helped propel ill-prepared Federal troops into battle at First Bull Run.

Some political moves could be made only in the light of favorable news from the battlefield. In 1862, the Preliminary Emancipation Proclamation stayed in President Lincoln's desk drawer from July to September—a period of Union setbacks and disappointments—until a dearly purchased victory at Antietam made it possible for Lincoln to release this controversial

{ **APRIL 1** **1865:** At the battle of Five Forks, outside Petersburg, Virginia, General Robert E. Lee's forces are defeated by the Union army, which now threatens the withdrawal of Lee's Confederate troops from around the long-besieged city. }

Prominent Union and Confederate generals and statesmen as they appeared during the great Civil War, 1861–5. Color lithograph, Kurz & Allison, 1885

and crucially important document. The proclamation, which added the abolition of slavery to preservation of the Union as a Northern war objective, made it much less likely that the antislavery European nations would recognize the Confederate States of America. It also provided an added basis for the Union's recruitment of African American soldiers—a measure by no means universally welcomed in the North, and violently condemned in the South. Yet as the war continued and its material and human resources dwindled, Southern politicians, too, began debating whether to add slaves to the fighting ranks of its armies.

Congressional and gubernatorial races in both the North and the South reflected this close entanglement of politics and the battlefield, as did the 1864 U.S. presidential contest. When the Union battlefield successes at Gettysburg and Vicksburg were followed, in 1864, by General-in-Chief Ulysses S. Grant's costly Overland campaign and the seemingly inconclusive siege of Petersburg, Virginia, Lincoln appeared to be facing almost certain political defeat. Just six weeks later, however, General William T. Sherman's Union troops were in Atlanta, and General Phil Sheridan's Union army was besting Jubal Early's Confederate force in the Shenandoah Valley. On November 8, the National Union Party, with Republican Abraham Lincoln as its candidate, won 55 percent of the popular vote and all but three Union states. Lincoln also received the three-to-one support of Union soldiers. Six months later, on May 7, 1865, one of those soldiers, Lieutenant Oliver Willcox Norton, noted, in a letter to his sister, the mixed feelings with which many Northerners greeted the end of the conflict: "Well, we may say the war is over—'this cruel war is over.' The joy of the nation is tempered by its grief at the base assassination of the President, but we can console ourselves by the thought that he had accomplished his work."

After he assumed office, Abraham Lincoln appointed a cabinet that included some exceptionally talented and able administrators. Among them were a few strong personalities with political ambitions, most notably Secretary of the Treasury Salmon P. Chase and Secretary of State William H. Seward, whose actions sometimes tested Lincoln's patience and diplomatic skills. Another of his initial cabinet appointments, Secretary of War Simon Cameron, presented a different sort of problem. Promised a cabinet post at the 1860 Republican national convention in exchange for ending his presidential candidacy and supporting Lincoln, Cameron revealed a marked bent toward corruption. As the U.S. Army expanded, requiring huge amounts of food, clothing, and equipment, he favored his friends with jobs and contracts that they were ill equipped or little inclined to fulfill. Cameron's political ineptitude also led him to publicly advocate freeing the slaves of rebellious citizens at a time when Lincoln felt it necessary to tread very carefully on the issue of emancipation. By January 1862, Cameron had been appointed U.S. minister to Russia and the prickly but politically astute Edwin M. Stanton had replaced him as secretary of war.

President Lincoln and His Cabinet, with [brevet] Lieut. Genl. [Winfield] Scott (in 1861). Left to right: Attorney General Edward Bates, Secretary of the Navy Gideon Welles, Postmaster General Montgomery Blair, Secretary of State William Seward, Secretary of the Treasury Salmon Chase, Lincoln, Scott, Secretary of the Interior Caleb Smith, and Secretary of War Simon Cameron. (The unfinished Washington Monument is visible at far left.) Lithograph, 1866

{ **APRIL 2** 1865: The Confederate government evacuates Richmond, Virginia. Confederate general A. P. Hill is killed outside Petersburg, Virginia. }

President Lincoln's first vice president was attorney Hannibal Hamlin, who had abandoned the Democratic Party in 1856 to join the new Republican Party because its platform was more in line with his fervent opposition to slavery. At times impatient with the president's slow progress toward emancipation, Hamlin nevertheless respected Lincoln and served effectively as vice president—while edging ever closer to the Radical Republicans, who favored harsher treatment for secessionists than did the president. A much more tempestuous relationship existed between President Jefferson Davis and the Confederate vice president, former congressman Alexander H. Stephens of Georgia—who had long foreseen the trials that disunion would bring. "You may think that the suppression of an outbreak in the southern States would be a holiday job for a few of your northern regiments," he stated during a congressional debate in the 1850s, "but you may find to your cost, in the end, that seven millions of people fighting for their rights, their homes, and their hearth-stones cannot be 'easily conquered.'" Physically frail but strong-minded, Stephens opposed Davis on a variety of issues, including conscription and the suspension of habeas corpus.

Hannibal Hamlin (1809–1891).
Daguerreotype by the Mathew
Brady Studio, 1844–60

Alexander H. Stephens
(1812–1883). 1865–80

{ **APRIL 3** 1865: Union troops occupy Richmond and Petersburg, Virginia. }

From February 4 to May 21, 1861, delegates from the first six states to secede from the Union met in Montgomery, Alabama, to create a new Confederate government. After adopting a provisional constitution, the convention established critical national departments. These mirrored the governmental organization of the United States, with some divergences. The U.S. and Confederate governments each had a State Department, Treasury Department, War Department, and Post Office. Unlike the Union, however, the Confederacy added a Justice Department (the United States, which had an attorney general, would not create a Justice Department until 1870). Of the Confederacy's original cabinet appointments, only two remained in office throughout the war: Secretary of the Navy Stephen R. Mallory and Postmaster General John H. Reagan. A procession of six secretaries of war in four years reflected President Davis's hands-on approach to military affairs, something that led to clashes with a number of Confederate generals—but not with Robert E. Lee, who ultimately became Confederate general-in-chief in January 1865.

Jefferson Davis and His Cabinet—with General Lee in the Council Chamber at Richmond (in early 1861). Left to right: Secretary of the Navy Stephen Mallory, Attorney General Judah Benjamin (later, secretary of war and then secretary of state), Secretary of War Leroy Walker, Davis, Lee, Postmaster General John Reagan, Secretary of the Treasury Christopher Memminger, Vice President Alexander H. Stephens, and Secretary of State Robert Toombs. Lithograph, Thomas Kelly, 1866

{ **APRIL 4** 1865: Making his way through streets crowded with celebrating African Americans, President Lincoln visits the former White House of the Confederacy in Richmond, then meets with former Confederate official John A. Campbell. }

Through the pages of his *New York Tribune,* Horace Greeley had become one of the North's most influential editors in the years leading up to the war. Passionate in his belief that all Americans should be politically and economically free, Greeley spoke out against monopolies, for labor unions, in support of experiments in "constructive democracy"—and against slavery. Greeley's most famous wartime editorial, published on August 20, 1862, under the heading "The Prayer of Twenty Millions," strove to push President Lincoln toward emancipation. Lincoln quickly penned a reply that has since become famous, emphasizing his paramount objective of saving the Union (see April 15). As this exchange became the subject of public discussion, difficulties—some rooted in differing opinions regarding the conduct of the war—were building between Greeley and Charles A. Dana, the *Tribune*'s managing editor. Dana resigned and subsequently accepted a position with the War Department; in 1864, he was appointed assistant secretary of war. Often in the field, he became an effective liaison between frontline Union armies and their civilian commanders in Washington, D.C.

Editorial staff of the *New York Tribune.* Seated, left to right: George M. Snow, financial editor; Bayard Taylor, correspondent; Horace Greeley; George Ripley, literary editor. Standing, left to right: William Henry Fry, music editor; Charles A. Dana; Henry J. Raymond, special assistant. Daguerreotype by the Mathew Brady Studio, c. 1847–48

{ **APRIL 5** 1839: Robert Smalls (USA), the only African American naval captain during the Civil War, is born in Beaufort, South Carolina. }

Our colonial ancestors were forced to vindicate that birthright [to constitutional representative government] by an appeal to arms. Success crowned their efforts, and they provided for their posterity a peaceful remedy against future aggression.

The tyranny of an unbridled majority, the most odious and least responsible form of despotism, has denied us both the right and the remedy. Therefore we are in arms to renew such sacrifices as our fathers made to the holy cause of constitutional liberty.

—President Jefferson Davis, address at his second inauguration, February 22, 1862 (after a general election confirmed his selection as president of the Confederacy by delegates to the February 1861 convention of seceding states)

Bacon's Military Map of the United States Shewing the Forts & Fortifications. Free (nonslave-holding) areas are tinted green, border slave areas are yellow, and seceded (Confederate) areas are pink. Color map, Bacon & Co., London, 1862

Our popular Government has often been called an experiment. Two points in it our people have already settled—the successful establishing and the successful administering of it. One still remains—its successful maintenance against a formidable internal attempt to overthrow it. It is now for them to demonstrate to the world that those who can fairly carry an election can also suppress a rebellion; that ballots are the rightful and peaceful successors of bullets. . . . Such will be a great lesson of peace; teaching men that what they cannot take by an election, neither can they take it by war.

—President Abraham Lincoln, message to the U.S. Congress, July 4, 1861

{ **APRIL 6** 1865: Thousands of Confederates surrender at Sayler's Creek, Virginia, the last major engagement between the Army of Northern Virginia (Lee) and the Army of the Potomac (Grant). }

1ˢ BACON'S MILITARY MAP OF AMERICA. 1ˢ

BACON'S MILITARY MAP OF THE UNITED STATES Shewing the **FORTS & FORTIFICATIONS.**

Published by BACON & Cᵒ 48 Paternoster Row.

LONDON 1862

EXPLANATION.

Many Europeans closely followed the events of the American Civil War; some of them hoped the conflict would bring an end to the American experiment: "The great body of the aristocracy and the commercial classes are anxious to see the United States go to pieces," U.S. Minister to Great Britain Charles Francis Adams wrote to his son on December 25, 1862. "The middle and lower class sympathise [*sic*] with us [because they] see in the convulsion in America an era in the history of the world, out of which must come in the end a general recognition of the right of mankind to the produce of their labor and the pursuit of happiness." Europe's most powerful nation, Britain was central to both Union and Confederate diplomatic efforts. In May 1861, Queen Victoria proclaimed Britain's intention to remain neutral—but also declared that it would accord both sides belligerent status. For a time, it seemed possible that Britain would go further and formally recognize the Confederate States of America as a separate nation. But Federal successes on the battlefield, Lincoln's Emancipation Proclamation, and the South's continuing reliance on slavery finally led Britain and the other antislavery European powers to deny such recognition to the Confederacy.

England and America . . . (Queen Victoria visits an American naval vessel). Color lithograph of a painting by W. Simpson, Colnaghi, London, 1859

{ **APRIL 7** 1865: President Lincoln sends a wire to General Ulysses S. Grant: "General Sheridan says 'If the thing is pressed I think that Lee will surrender.' Let the thing be pressed." }

The Russian autocracy and the American democracy had enjoyed
excellent relations since the Crimean War (1853–56), when Washington had been benevolently
neutral toward Russia during its conflict with Britain and France, and Russia had signed a
treaty favorable to American shipping. The Russian government's own neutrality was markedly
benevolent toward the Union during the Civil War. In November 1862, after learning from Russia's ambassador to the United States, Baron Edouard de Stoeckl, that the United States flatly
rejected the idea of European mediation to end the war, the Russian government refused to
participate in a three-power (France, Russia, Britain) mediation conference, unless both warring
sides requested mediation. At that time, de Stoeckl's American counterpart was Simon Cameron,
recently appointed minister to Russia after his dismissal as secretary of war (see April 2). During most of the conflict, however, the U.S. minister to Russia was Cassius Marcellus Clay, the
son of a wealthy Kentucky slaveholder who had become, by the mid-1850s, an emancipationist
and a founder of the Republican Party. During Cameron's brief tenure in Russia, Clay was serving in the Union army. (See also October 21.)

Baron Edouard de Stoeckl
(1814–1869). 1855–65

Cassius Marcellus Clay (1810–
1903). Photograph by Mathew
Brady, 1844–60

{ **APRIL 8** 1864: Nathaniel Banks's Union troops "skedaddle" from Richard Taylor's Confederates at the battle of Sabine Crossroads, Louisiana. }

The huge Trans-Mississippi Department (the area of military activity west of the Mississippi River), scene of some of the most brutal guerrilla actions of the wartime era, also witnessed what devolved into separate civil wars within the larger one. Several Indian nations, including the Creek and the Cherokee, were divided by commitments to either the Confederacy or the Union, and they sometimes fought among themselves, as well as in North-South clashes. One battle in which Cherokee units fought alongside white Confederate troops was at Pea Ridge (or Elkhorn Tavern), Arkansas, on March 7–8, 1862, the culmination of a Union campaign by General Samuel R. Curtis to drive Major General Sterling Price's Confederates out of Missouri. The battle took place in northwestern Arkansas, near the town of Bentonville, where Price's men, joined by a force under Brigadier General Ben McCulloch and Major General Earl Van Dorn, found that Curtis had anticipated their planned attack against pursuing Federal troops. This Confederate defeat left Missouri securely in Union hands for more than two years.

Battle of Pea Ridge, Ark. March 5 to 8, 1862. Color lithograph, Kurz & Allison, c. 1885

{ APRIL 9 1865: Confederate general Robert E. Lee surrenders the Army of Northern Virginia to Union general Ulysses S. Grant at Appomattox Court House, Virginia. **}**

A nephew of the Cherokee chief Stand Watie (who was the only Indian to become a brigadier general in the Confederate army), Elias Cornelius Boudinot was born in the Cherokee Nation and reared in Vermont; in 1856, he settled in Arkansas, where he became a successful lawyer and politician. After serving as secretary to the Arkansas secession convention in 1861, he helped Stand Watie raise a Cherokee regiment and served briefly as its lieutenant colonel before the Cherokees elected him their representative to the Confederate Congress—which also included representatives of the Choctaw, Creek, Seminole, and Chickasaw nations. In the North, civil engineer and Seneca Indian sachem Ely Samuel Parker spent months overcoming anti-Indian prejudice before finally winning a captain's commission. First assigned as divisional engineer under General J. E. Smith, he was soon transferred to the staff of Ulysses S. Grant, whom he had befriended before the war. As the general-in-chief's military secretary, Parker was the officer who recorded the negotiated changes in the terms of Robert E. Lee's surrender at Appomattox Court House when the adjutant general assigned to the task proved to be too nervous to write.

Elias C. Boudinot (1835–1890). 1860–75

Ely Samuel Parker (c. 1828–1895). Date unknown

{ **APRIL 10** 1865: Robert E. Lee issues his last general orders, bidding "an affectionate farewell" to his troops. }

Told in the summer of 1862 that the Sioux people were hungry, Minnesota trader Andrew Myrick reportedly said that "they should eat grass or their own dung." Surrounded by white people with similar attitudes, restricted to a narrow strip of land, and deprived of their hunting privileges and thus dependent on government supplies that were not being delivered, the Sioux of south-central Minnesota staged a bloody monthlong uprising, from mid-August to mid-September—while the battles of Second Bull Run and Antietam were being fought in the East. Myrick was among the first of several hundred people to die in the uprising, as the Indians attacked both civilians and soldiers. By the end of September, the fighting had stopped and more than 1,000 Sioux were prisoners of the U.S. Army. A military tribunal sentenced 303 of them to die by hanging and expected quick authorization for the executions from the commander in chief. But President Lincoln asked two lawyers to determine, by reviewing records of the trials, which of the condemned men had actually led the uprising. The day after Christmas, 38 of the Sioux were executed.

The Siege of New Ulm, Minn.
Reproduction of a painting by
Henry August Schwabe, 1902

{ **APRIL 11** 1861: Confederate authorities visit Fort Sumter, in Charleston Harbor, South Carolina, and demand its surrender. }

Prominent among the Northern women active in the rough-and-tumble of wartime politics, women's rights activist Susan B. Anthony was a founder of the National Woman's Loyal League. "[This] is a war to found an empire on the negro in slavery," she declared to the members of that patriotic society, "and shame on us if we do not make it a war to establish the negro in freedom." The organization linked the quest for African American rights with women's causes. "There never can be a true peace in this Republic," its membership resolved, "until the civil and political rights of all citizens of African descent and all women are practically established." Wartime orator and antislavery activist Anna Dickinson had already assumed the right to speak out on "unfeminine" issues, including the military conduct of the war. Fiery and sometimes abrasive, Dickinson criticized Abraham Lincoln for his moderation and called General George B. McClellan her "pet peeve." In 1864, she earned a standing ovation for a speech, delivered on the floor of the House of Representatives, that helped raise $1,000 for the Freedmen's Relief Society.

Susan B. Anthony (1820–1906). Engraving, G. E. Perine and Co., date unknown

Anna E. Dickinson (1842–1932). 1855–65

{ **APRIL 12** 1861: Confederates in Charleston, South Carolina, fire upon Fort Sumter, and the U.S. Civil War begins. }

Eng⁰ by G E Perine & C⁰ N.Y.

A native of Virginia, historian, storyteller, and writer on Indian legends, Mary Henderson Eastman (1818–1887) expressed her support for the South's "peculiar institution" in a novel that appeared hard on the heels of Harriet Beecher Stowe's *Uncle Tom's Cabin* in 1852. But Eastman's defense of slavery in *Aunt Phillis's Cabin* was sometimes tepid. One of her characters, Mr. Weston, a plantation owner, acknowledges "the evils of slavery," for example, but he can see no way around it. "In our [Virginia] climate, white labor would answer," he says, "but farther South, only the negro can labor, and this is an unanswerable objection to our Southern States becoming free." During the war, politics also infiltrated schoolbooks. This page from the *Confederate Spelling Book* is headed by a simple patriotic message, but other textbooks were much more forthright. A Southern geography primer written by Marinda Branson Moore includes the following: "Q. What is the present drawback to our trade? A. An unlawful Blockade by the miserable and hellish Yankee Nation."

Title page of *Aunt Phillis's Cabin; or, Southern Life as It Is,* by Mary H. Eastman (1852)

Page from the *Confederate Spelling Book,* 5th ed. (Richmond, 1865)

{ **APRIL 13** 1861: The Federal garrison at Fort Sumter is compelled to surrender to the Confederates after sustaining thirty-four hours of bombardment. }

AUNT PHILLIS'S CABIN;

OR,

SOUTHERN LIFE AS IT IS.

BY MRS. MARY H. EASTMAN.

Philadelphia:
Lippincott, Grambo & Co.
1852.

A soldier is a man who fights for his country.

It is the duty of every man to love his country, and to defend it bravely against its enemies.

Accent on the first syllable.

A mi a ble	Ab so lute ly	Fash ion a ble
fa vor a ble	ac cu ra cy	lam en ta ble
va ri a ble	ac ri mo ny	man age a ble
Me di a tor	ad mi ra ble	mat ri mo ny
rea son a ble	ad ver sa ry	pat ri mo ny
sea son a ble	al a bas ter	man da to ry
trea son a ble	al le go ry	nat u ral ly
Cu mu la tive	al li ga tor	nav i.ga ble
cu li na ry	glad i a tor	pal at a ble
lu mi na ry	am i ca ble	prac ti ca ble
cu ri ous ly	ap pli ca ble	plan e ta ry
fu ri ous ly	an ti qua ry	sal u ta ry
du bi ous ly	cap il la ry	sanc tu a ry
du ti ful ly	an nu al ly	stat u a ry
ju di ca ture	car i ca ture	sal a man der
nu ga to ry	cat er pil lar	tab er na cle
nu mer a ble	char i ta ble	tran si to ry
su per a ble	hab it a ble	val u a ble

General George B. McClellan "has lain still twenty days since the battle of Antietam," General-in-Chief Henry W. Halleck complained in a letter to his wife on October 7, 1862. "I cannot persuade him to advance an inch." McClellan's continual and characteristic dallying had just taken President Lincoln to McClellan's camp—a visit that did not markedly improve the general's momentum in pursuit of General Robert E. Lee's Army of Northern Virginia. Lincoln's subsequent letters and telegrams encouraging McClellan to action were often countered by complaints and excuses. "I have just read your dispatch about sore-tongued and fatigued horses," Lincoln telegraphed McClellan testily on October 24. "Will you pardon me for asking what the horses of your army have done since the battle of Antietam that fatigues anything?" Two weeks later, the president finally relieved McClellan of duty—a move heartily approved by many Republicans, including those serving on the congressional Joint Committee on the Conduct of the War. Hearty disapproval came from many Peace Democrats (also called "Copperheads"), who were already distressed by President Lincoln's issuance of the Preliminary Emancipation Proclamation on September 22, five days after the Union victory at Antietam.

President Abraham Lincoln with General George B. McClellan and other officers, Antietam, Maryland. Photograph by Alexander Gardner, October 3, 1862

{ **APRIL 14** 1865: President Lincoln is mortally wounded by John Wilkes Booth, a zealous Southern sympathizer and member of a famous acting family, during a performance at Ford's Theatre in Washington, D.C. }

"My paramount object in this struggle is to save the Union . . . ," President Lincoln wrote to *New York Tribune* editor Horace Greeley on August 22, 1862 (see April 5). "If I could save the Union without freeing any slave, I would do it; and if I could save it by freeing all the slaves, I would do it; and if I could do it by freeing some and leaving others alone, I would also do that." Lincoln had run for president pledging not to interfere with slavery in the states where it existed—abhorring the South's "peculiar institution" but believing that it would eventually disappear. By July 1862, however, despite his subsequent letter to Greeley, the president had announced to his cabinet his determination to issue a proclamation of emancipation for all slaves in areas then held to be in rebellion. Waiting until his position was strengthened by the Union victory at Antietam, Lincoln issued the Preliminary Emancipation Proclamation on September 22. Six days later, he wrote the vice president that "while commendation in newspapers and by distinguished individuals is all that a vain man could wish, the stocks have declined, and troops come forward more slowly than ever. . . . The North responds to the proclamation sufficiently in breath; but breath alone kills no rebels." The stronger Emancipation Proclamation, issued on January 1, 1863, also sanctioned the employment of black soldiers. (See also June 15–17.)

The Emancipation Proclamation. Pen-and-ink manuscript by Abraham Lincoln, written in Washington, D.C., July 1862

{ **APRIL 15** **1865:** President Lincoln dies at 7:22 A.M.; Andrew Johnson, his second-term vice president, becomes the seventeenth president of the United States. }

In pursuance of the sixth section of the act of congress entitled "An act to suppress insurrection and to punish treason and rebellion, to seize and confiscate property of rebels, and for other purposes" Approved July 17. 1862, and which act, and the Joint Resolution explanatory thereof, are herewith published, I, Abraham Lincoln, President of the United States, do hereby proclaim to, and warn all persons within the contemplation of said sixth section to cease participating in, aiding, countenancing, or abetting the existing rebellion, or any rebellion against the government of the United States, and to return to their proper allegiance to the United States, on pain of the forfeitures and seizures, as within and by said sixth section provided—

And I hereby make known that it is my purpose, upon the next meeting of Congress, to again recommend the adoption of a practical measure for tendering pecuniary aid to the free choice or rejection, of any and all States which may then be recognizing and practically sustaining the authority of the United States, and which may then have voluntarily adopted, or thereafter may voluntarily adopt, gradual abolishment of slavery within such State or States— that the object is to practically restore, thenceforward to be maintain, the constitutional relation between the general government, and each, and all the states, wherein that relation

is now suspended, or disturbed; and that, for this object, the war, as it has been, will be, prosecuted. And, as a fit and necessary military measure for effecting this object, I, as Commander-in-Chief of the Army and Navy of the United States, do order and declare that on the first day of January, in the Year of Our Lord one thousand, eight hundred and sixty three, all persons held as slaves within any state or states, wherein the constitutional authority of the United States, shall not then be practically recognized, submitted to, and maintained, shall then, thenceforward and forever, be free.

On August 25, 1862, the U.S. government officially authorized Brigadier General Rufus Saxton, military governor of South Carolina's Sea Islands, to raise five regiments of African American soldiers. That order and the September 27, 1862, swearing into U.S. service of the First Regiment of the Louisiana Native Guards—the first black regiment officially mustered into service (in Union-occupied New Orleans)—were watersheds in the evolution of the Civil War from a conflict waged exclusively by white troops to preserve the Union to a broader war to preserve the Union without slavery. Fighting prejudice among Northerners as well as combating Confederate troops, the Union's black soldiers repeatedly proved their mettle. Sergeant James H. Harris, a Marylander and a member of Company B, Thirty-eighth U.S. Colored Troops, and First Sergeant Powhatan Beaty of Company G, Fifth U.S. Colored Troops, were among the twenty-three black Union soldiers and sailors who served in the Civil War with such distinction that they received the nation's highest military decoration, the Medal of Honor. They were both cited for gallantry in action at Chaffin's Farm, Virginia, on September 29, 1864.

James H. Harris (1828–1898). 1864–98

Powhatan Beaty (1837–1916). 1864–1900

{ APRIL 16 1862: President Lincoln signs a bill ending slavery in the District of Columbia. **}**

In February 1861, the *Times* of London sent William Howard Russell to the United States to report on the growing rift between the two American regions. Famous for his reports of the Crimean War, Russell had ready access to politicians and military commanders on both sides. His dispatches to the newspaper were followed by a book, *My Diary North and South* (1863), that was filled with acute, if sometimes jaded, observations. "A public man in the United States is very much like a great firework," he wrote in October 1861; "he commences with some small scintillations which attract the eye of the public, and then he blazes up and flares out in blue, purple, and orange fires, to the intense admiration of the multitude, and dying out suddenly is thought of no more, his place being taken by a fresh Roman candle or catherine wheel which is thought to be far finer." While Russell observed, other Europeans participated. The exiled pretender to the French throne, Louis Philippe d'Orléans, and his brother, Robert, joined the Union army in 1861 as unpaid captains and aides-de-camp. Serving with the Army of the Potomac through the 1862 Peninsula campaign, the brothers were the first Civil War officers whose principal duty was to summarize intelligence reports.

Sir William Howard Russell (1820–1907). 1855–65

Louis Philippe d'Orléans, comte de Paris (1838–1894), and Robert d'Orléans, duc de Chartes (1840–1910). Photograph by the Brady National Photographic Art Gallery, 1861–65

{ **APRIL 17** 1861: The state convention in Virginia adopts an ordinance of secession. }

A direct descendant of Presidents John Adams and John Quincy Adams, Charles Francis Adams Jr. joined the First Massachusetts Cavalry Regiment in 1861. At the end of the war, he was commanding officer of the Fifth Massachusetts Cavalry—the first African American cavalry regiment raised by his state. Harvard-educated, observant, and opinionated, Adams wrote vivid wartime letters, many addressed to his father, who was the U.S. minister to Great Britain (see April 7). "I pulled out your old letters and . . . re-read them with [the Union victories of] Gettysburg, Vicksburg, Port Hudson and [the action at] Morris Island . . . absorbing my thoughts," he wrote to his father on July 22, 1863. "Does Europe want more? If it does I think it will get more, but I am lost in astonishment at the strength the North is developing. . . . I may look at these things from too much of an army point of view, just as you take everything from your London watch-tower; but it does now seem to me that if any European nation, and especially England, and next to her France, wants hard knocks with little gain, they need only to meddle with us."

Charles Francis Adams Jr. (1835–1915), in rocking chair at left, with three unidentified fellow Union officers. c. 1864

{ **APRIL 18** **1865:** Generals William T. Sherman and Joseph E. Johnston, meeting near Durham Station, North Carolina, sign a "memorandum or basis of agreement" calling for an armistice by all armies in the field—along with several wide-ranging arrangements, such as a general amnesty for Confederates, that are subject to the approval of higher authorities. }

In April 1863, Major General Ambrose Burnside, then commanding the Union Department of Ohio, issued General Order No. 38, which stated, in part, that "the habit of declaring sympathies for the enemy will not be allowed in this Department." Ohio was the home of former congressman Clement L. Vallandigham, among the most outspoken "Copperheads" (Peace Democrats)—opponents of the war and the Lincoln administration. In May, Vallandigham challenged Burnside's order by giving a speech before a huge crowd in which he called the war "wicked, cruel, and unnecessary," and General Order No. 38 a "base usurpation of arbitrary authority." That night, Union soldiers smashed in Vallandigham's door and carted him away to be tried, not by a civil court but by a military tribunal—which quickly found him guilty and sentenced him to prison for the rest of the war. A furor ensued, in which even some of Lincoln's staunch supporters criticized the president and his general for suppression of the right of free speech. The debate raged well after the president ordered Vallandigham to be banished rather than imprisoned. Traveling via the Confederate states and Bermuda, Vallandigham went to Canada, from which he conducted an unsuccessful campaign to become governor of Ohio. He returned to his home state after a year in exile and remained an outspoken Peace Democrat.

Clement L. Vallandigham
(1820–1871). 1855–65

Ambrose Burnside (1824–1881).
Photograph by the Brady
National Photographic Art
Gallery, 1860–65

{ **APRIL 19** **1865:** Funeral services for Abraham Lincoln take place in the East Room of the White House, before his body is taken to the Capitol rotunda for public viewing until the next evening. }

As one of the North's special artist-correspondents, the staunch Unionist Thomas Nast covered Abraham Lincoln's 1861 trip to Washington and the bitter violence of the 1863 New York conscription riots (see October 22). After joining the staff of *Harper's Weekly* in 1862, Nast created sentimental images supporting the newspaper's patriotic campaigns. He also fired off salvo after salvo of sharp-edged editorial cartoons—including a ferocious barrage in favor of Lincoln and against Democratic candidate George B. McClellan during the 1864 presidential campaign. One of Nast's most powerful and much-reprinted illustrations appeared as the commanding feature of a broadside published by the Congressional Union Committee. Text below the illustration reiterated Confederate peace conditions cited in the *Richmond Enquirer* on October 16, 1863. The broadside admonished Northerners not to betray those fighting and dying for the Union cause by succumbing to the calls for a negotiated settlement that were being made by "Copperheads"—Peace Democrats, such as Clement L. Vallandigham, and others who favored settlement of the conflict short of the South's total surrender.

Thomas Nast (1840–1902). 1860–75

A Traitor's Peace that the Northern Copperhead leaders would force upon the Country. Broadside illustrated by Thomas Nast, 1864

{ **APRIL 20** 1865: General Robert E. Lee writes to President Davis, recommending a complete suspension of hostilities, rather than partisan warfare as some Confederates are advocating. }

On April 28, 1864, Lieutenant George G. Smith of the U.S. Army, stationed in Union-occupied Louisiana, noted in his diary that "we [have] found many men, and women too, throughout the South faithful to their country and flag: ready to sacrifice property, and life too, if need be to protect them from that wicked rebellion." At the beginning of the war, many in the North had believed that such faithfulness to the United States would be strong enough to win seceded states back to the Union without an extended conflict. This proved to be overly optimistic. Although Union loyalists were present in many Southern communities, they voiced their opinions at their own peril. William "Parson" Brownlow of Tennessee, editor of the *Knoxville Whig*, saw his presses destroyed and was briefly jailed by Confederate authorities for treason after he declared in an 1861 editorial that he would rather be imprisoned than "recognize the hand of God in the work of breaking up the American Government." Eventually sent to the North, Brownlow returned to Tennessee with General Ambrose Burnside's Union army in 1863 and reopened his paper—which he renamed the *Knoxville Whig and Rebel Ventilator*. In 1865, Brownlow became governor of the state.

William G. "Parson" Brownlow (1805–1877). 1860–75

Secret meeting of southern Unionists—sketched by our special artist, A. R. Waud. Illustration in *Harper's Weekly*, August 4, 1866

{ **APRIL 21** 1865: A train bearing Abraham Lincoln's body leaves Washington, D.C., taking a long route to Springfield, Illinois, with frequent stops to accommodate the huge numbers of mourners along the way (see December 12). }

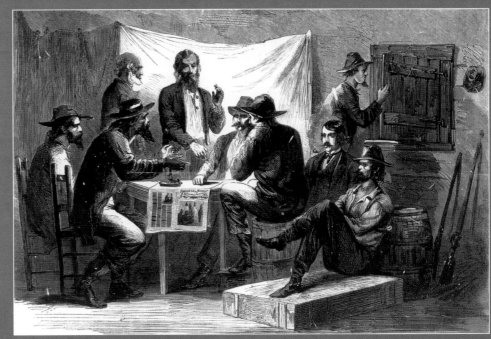

A prominent and capable lawyer, Edwin M. Stanton served briefly as attorney general under President Buchanan before his appointment as U.S. secretary of war in January 1862. He proceeded to reform this crucial department, which under Simon Cameron had grown rife with graft and corruption, and ran it with a grim efficiency dedicated to aggressive prosecution of the war. Not at first a Lincoln admirer, Stanton quickly forged an effective working relationship with the president. Two months after Stanton assumed his cabinet position, his Southern counterpart, former U.S. senator Judah P. Benjamin, was removed as the Confederate secretary of war amid a storm of criticism over a defeat at Roanoke Island (February 8, 1862). Enjoying the absolute confidence of Jefferson Davis, Benjamin immediately assumed the office of secretary of state, where he stayed for the rest of the war, focusing on the unsuccessful battle to win European recognition of the Confederacy.

Edwin M. Stanton (1814–1869). Photograph by the Brady National Photographic Art Gallery. 1860–65

Judah P. Benjamin (1811–1884). c. 1856

{ **APRIL 22** 1861: Robert E. Lee is named commander of the forces of his native state of Virginia. }

An influential Republican senator from Ohio, John Sherman usually
focused his wartime attention on backing financial measures such as the National Banking Act
of 1863 and working to ensure that the burgeoning Federal bureaucracy was efficiently supporting the war effort. When he was unhappy with the Union's progress on the battlefield, however,
he said so. At one point, casting a jaundiced eye toward the professional military, he announced
that he "did not believe that a military education at West Point has infused into the Army the
right spirit to carry on this war." This did not adversely affect the close relationship he enjoyed
with his West Point–graduate brother, Major General William T. Sherman—who regarded
most politicians with a jaundiced eye of his own. Steadily emerging as one of the Union's most
effective battlefield commanders, by 1864 General Sherman was leading his rough-and-ready
western army through the heart of the South. When he took Atlanta, Southern hearts grieved and
Northern morale surged. When another Confederate bastion fell to his forces that December, the
general sent a widely quoted telegram to President Lincoln that began, "I beg to present you, as
a Christmas gift, the city of Savannah."

John Sherman (1823–1900).
Daguerreotype, 1844–63

*Santa Claus Sherman Putting
Savannah into Uncle Sam's
Stocking.* Engraving in *Frank
Leslie's Illustrated Newspaper,*
December 1864

{ **APRIL 23** 1865: In Charlotte, North Carolina, President Jefferson Davis describes the state of the
Confederacy in a letter to his wife, Varina: "Panic has seized the country." }

"It seems exceedingly probable that this Administration will not be reelected," Abraham Lincoln wrote in a memorandum on August 23, 1864. "Then it will be my duty to so cooperate with the President elect, as to save the Union between the election and the inauguration; as he will have secured his election on such ground that he can not possibly save it afterwards." Beset by political factionalism—from radicals in his own Republican Party to "Copperheads," or Peace Democrats—Lincoln was also the focus of widespread civilian distress over sixty-five thousand Union casualties from General Ulysses S. Grant's five-week Overland campaign toward Richmond and General William T. Sherman's slow progress toward Atlanta. The Democratic nominee for president, chosen at the party's convention on August 29–31, was former Union general-in-chief George B. McClellan, whom the president had relieved of battlefield command in November 1862 for his failure to aggressively prosecute the war. The Democratic platform included a "peace plank" that demanded the immediate negotiation of a peace settlement with the Confederacy.

Grand National Democratic Banner. Peace! Union! And Victory! Lithograph with watercolor on wove paper, Currier & Ives, 1864

Grand National Union Banner for 1864. Liberty, Union and Victory. Lithograph with watercolor on wove paper, Currier & Ives, 1864

{ **APRIL 24** 1865: President Andrew Johnson rejects the terms of agreement in the "memorandum or basis of agreement" that Union general William T. Sherman and Confederate general Joseph E. Johnston signed on April 18, and he orders Sherman to resume hostilities if the Confederates do not surrender within forty-eight hours. }

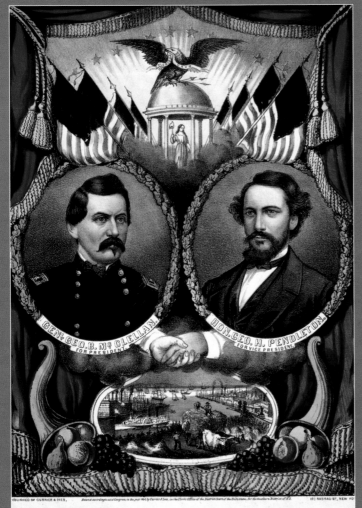

GRAND NATIONAL DEMOCRATIC BANNER.

PEACE! UNION! AND VICTORY!

GRAND, NATIONAL UNION BANNER FOR 1864.

LIBERTY, UNION AND VICTORY.

Ordinarily, army camps are not bastions of the democratic process. But in the presidential election of November 1864, Union soldiers were encouraged to vote. Nineteen states made provisions for absentee balloting; in those that did not, soldiers who received furloughs could vote at home. On September 8 (after General William T. Sherman's morale-boosting capture of Atlanta), Lincoln's opponent, former Union general-in-chief George B. McClellan, had repudiated the Democratic platform's "peace plank" and stated that "[the preservation of] the Union is the one condition of peace." Nevertheless, soldiers voted for "Old Abe" by a three-to-one margin, choosing to press through to victory in a war they believed the South had started and which, by 1864, had cost hundreds of thousands of lives. "Thank God, it is accomplished," Union soldier and fervent Lincoln supporter David Lane wrote in his diary after the polls had closed in his camp in Virginia. "Of 194 votes polled today, only 46 were cast for McClellan and Secession. One week ago they claimed a majority. . . . The day, with its overwhelming weight of responsibility, is passed beyond recall and I calmly await the announcement of the result."

Pennsylvania soldiers voting, Army of the James. Pencil, Chinese white, and black ink wash drawing on light green paper by William Waud, October 1864

{ **APRIL 25** 1865: Federal cavalry closes in on presidential assassin John Wilkes Booth in Virginia. }

Cap. WATTSON
Co Co I
3RD PENN ARTY

MESS

C S

Abraham Lincoln, who in 1860 had been dubbed the Illinois "rail-splitter" (a person who splits logs for rail fences), chose Andrew Johnson, a former tailor with a flair for debating, as the candidate for vice president who would best help him sew up the country in the 1864 election. (Vice President Hannibal Hamlin, unhappy in the office, was edging too close to the Radical Republicans, who advocated punitive policies toward the South that the president did not favor.) Johnson was a veteran politician by then: elected to the U.S. Senate (1857–62), he had remained in that post after Tennessee voters endorsed secession in June 1861. A supporter of the Lincoln administration, Johnson was appointed military governor of Tennessee in March 1862. His success in that difficult post did not go unnoticed in Washington. The inauspicious beginning to his brief tenure as vice president did not go unnoticed either. Tired after his journey from Nashville and not feeling well, Johnson fortified himself with three glasses of whiskey before the inauguration ceremonies at the Capitol. His subsequent behavior moved the recently appointed attorney general, James Speed, to whisper to Secretary of the Navy Gideon Welles, "The man is certainly deranged."

The "Rail Splitter" at Work Repairing the Union. Lithograph, Joseph E. Baker, 1864

{ **APRIL 26** 1865: John Wilkes Booth is shot and killed in a Virginia barn surrounded by Federal troopers. In North Carolina, General Joseph E. Johnston formally surrenders his Confederate troops to General William T. Sherman. }

A supremely effective Confederate battlefield commander whose admirers dubbed him "the Stonewall of the West," Major General Patrick Cleburne was respected by his men and renowned for his courage—which extended beyond the battlefield. In January 1864, as the South fought dwindling material and human resources in addition to Northern armies, Cleburne proposed freeing slaves so that the freed men could be employed as soldiers. The proposal touched off a bitter, and initially fruitless, debate among Southern military and political leaders. The camp adamantly opposed to the measure included Howell Cobb of Georgia, a former Speaker of the U.S. House of Representatives and secretary of the treasury. An early advocate of secession, Cobb served the Confederacy as both politician and soldier during the war. When the idea of accepting slaves into the fighting ranks of the Southern armies was again debated—this time by the Confederate Congress—in January 1865, Cobb protested to President Davis: "If slaves will make good soldiers, our whole theory of slavery is wrong." Nevertheless, in March, Davis signed the "Negro Soldier Law," authorizing the enlistment of slaves. But the measure came too late to have any real impact.

Patrick Cleburne (1828–1864). 1861–64

Howell Cobb (1815–1868). Daguerreotype, 1844–60

{ **APRIL 27** 1822: Ulysses S. Grant (originally Hiram Ulysses Grant) (USA), general-in-chief of U.S. armies during the Civil War and the eighteenth president of the United States, is born in Point Pleasant, Ohio. }

"Fondly do we hope—fervently do we pray," Abraham Lincoln said in his Second Inaugural Address, "that this mighty scourge of war may speedily pass away." The inauguration ceremonies on March 4, 1865, included parades and celebrations—and more followed. Hundreds of cannons fired salutes in early April as Petersburg and Richmond fell and General Robert E. Lee surrendered the Army of Northern Virginia; throngs crushed through the doors of the White House to be included in formal receptions. On April 11, contemplating Reconstruction, Lincoln addressed a crowd gathered on the White House lawn, asking everyone to "join in doing the acts necessary to restoring the proper practical relations between these [seceded] States and the Union." Discussing the Reconstruction of Louisiana, a state that had been partially occupied by the Union army since 1862 and had long had a literate and cosmopolitan free black population, Lincoln stated: "It is also unsatisfactory to some that the elective franchise is not given to the colored man. I would myself prefer that it were now conferred on the very intelligent, and on those who serve our cause as soldiers." Those words so enraged one man in the crowd that he vowed this would be Lincoln's final speech. The man's name was John Wilkes Booth.

Abraham Lincoln's last reception. Hand-colored lithograph of a painting by Anton Hohenstein, published by John Smith, 1865

{ **APRIL 28** 1862: The British ship *Oreto* reaches Nassau in the Bahamas, where the vessel will be outfitted as CSS *Florida*, a Confederate raider of Union merchant ships. }

Washington, DC. Dear Father: . . . Last Friday night at 10 o'clock, I witnessed the saddest tragedy ever enacted in this country. Notwithstanding my promise to you not to visit the theater, I could not resist the temptation to see . . . the President, and when the curtain at Ford's rose on the play of *Our American Cousin,* my roommate and I were seated . . . just beneath the President's box. The President entered the theater at 8:30 amid deafening cheers and the rising of all. Everything was cheerful, and never was our magistrate more enthusiastically welcomed, or more happy—Many pleasant allusions were made to him in the play, to which the audience gave deafening responses, while Mr. Lincoln laughed heartily and bowed frequently to the gratified people. Just after the third act, and before the scenes were shifted, a muffled pistol shot was heard, and a man sprang wildly from the national box, partially tearing down the flag, then shouting 'sic semper tyrannis, the south is avenged' with brandished dagger rushed across the stage and disappeared. . . . The shrill cry of murder from Mrs. Lincoln first roused the horrified audience, and in an instant the uproar was terrible. . . . Strong men wept, and cursed, and tore the seats in the impotence of their anger.

—James S. Knox, letter to his father, April 15, 1865

Contents of Abraham Lincoln's pockets on the night the president was assassinated, shown with the *New York Times* issue reporting the assassination

{ **APRIL 29** 1861: Despite strong pro-Southern sentiments in the state, the Maryland House of Delegates votes overwhelmingly against secession. }

The news of Lee's surrender is true. Better than all my hopes was the prospect of the end of the war. It was ended on the 9th and every one admitted it. New York, Philadelphia and Baltimore were jubilant. Joy on every face and tongue. I could not see or hear of a secession sympathizer. At the theater last night a band from Lee's army was present and played "Hail Columbia" and the "Red, White and Blue," and here in Baltimore those tunes were vociferously cheered. I went to bed happy, thinking of the glorious change, and came down this morning to be astounded by the news that President Lincoln was assassinated last night at Ford's Theater in Washington and Secretary Seward and his son were stabbed at almost the same hour. . . . The President died at 7:22 this morning.

It is too terrible to think of, and I cannot imagine the consequences. . . . What are we to do with such a president as Andy Johnson? What effect will it have on the question of peace?

Well, we can do nothing but wait. The nation's joy is changed to mourning and to mutterings of vengeance on the cowardly assassins and the infamous plotters who arranged the murders.

—Lieutenant Oliver Willcox Norton (USA), letter
to his brother and sister, April 15, 1865

Wanted poster for the Lincoln assassins, one of the first such posters to use suspects' photographs (see also December 10–14 and 16). April 1865

{ **APRIL 30** 1861: Like many other groups eager to demonstrate their patriotic fervor at the outset of the war, members of the New York Yacht Club offer the use of their vessels to the Federal government. }

SURRAT.   BOOTH.   HAROLD.

War Department, Washington, April 20, 1865,

$100,000 REWARD!

THE MURDERER

Of our late beloved President, Abraham Lincoln,

IS STILL AT LARGE.

$50,000 REWARD

Will be paid by this Department for his apprehension, in addition to any reward offered by Municipal Authorities or State Executives.

$25,000 REWARD

Will be paid for the apprehension of JOHN H. SURRATT, one of Booth's Accomplices.

$25,000 REWARD

Will be paid for the apprehension of David C. Harold, another of Booth's accomplices.

LIBERAL REWARDS will be paid for any information that shall conduce to the arrest of either of the above-named criminals, or their accomplices.

All persons harboring or secreting the said persons, or either of them, or aiding or assisting their concealment or escape, will be treated as accomplices in the murder of the President and the attempted assassination of the Secretary of State, and shall be subject to trial before a Military Commission and the punishment of DEATH.

Let the stain of innocent blood be removed from the land by the arrest and punishment of the murderers.

All good citizens are exhorted to aid public justice on this occasion. Every man should consider his own conscience charged with this solemn duty, and rest neither night nor day until it be accomplished.

EDWIN M. STANTON, Secretary of War.

DESCRIPTIONS.—BOOTH is Five Feet 7 or 8 inches high, slender build, high forehead, black hair, black eyes, and wears a heavy black moustache.

JOHN H. SURRATT is about 5 feet, 9 inches. Hair rather thin and dark; eyes rather light; no beard. Would weigh 145 or 160 pounds. Complexion rather pale and clear, with color in his cheeks. Wore light clothes of fine quality. Shoulders square; cheek bones rather prominent; chin narrow; ears projecting at the top; forehead rather low and square, but broad. Parts his hair on the right side; neck rather long. His lips are firmly set. A slim man.

DAVID C. HAROLD is five feet six inches high, hair dark, eyes dark, eyebrows rather heavy, full face, nose short, hand short and fleshy, feet small, instep high, round bodied, naturally quick and active, slightly closes his eyes when looking at a person.

NOTICE.—In addition to the above, State and other authorities have offered rewards amounting to almost one hundred thousand dollars, making an aggregate of about TWO HUNDRED THOUSAND DOLLARS.

MAY: WAR ON THE WATER

The naval history of the Civil War is a compendium of tedious but dangerous patrols and daring operations on rivers, along the Atlantic and Gulf coasts, and on the high seas. "Tin-clads," submersibles, "double-enders," "ninety-day gunboats," torpedo boats, "Davids" (small Confederate torpedo boats that attacked Goliath-like larger ships), and converted tugboats were among the many types of vessels that played an integral role in the strategies that the North and the South employed.

Union naval strategy, at the start, was primarily focused on the blockade of Southern ports on the Atlantic and Gulf coasts and the need to hunt down Confederate commerce raiders and privateers. These efforts—combined with larger joint army-navy operations to control the Mississippi River from Cairo, Illinois, to the Gulf, aimed at isolating the South—demanded enormous numbers of men and ships. Fortunately for the Union, U.S. shipbuilding facilities and the flourishing merchant marine—an invaluable pool of vessels and experienced seamen—were predominantly associated with Northern ports.

The Confederacy, which faced the necessity of building its navy from next to nothing, endeavored to overcome its significant disadvantages in personnel, money, and manufacturing capabilities by using the element of surprise to break the blockade. Under the stewardship of Secretary of the Navy Stephen R. Mallory, the Southern navy procured sleek cruisers from

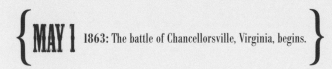

{ **MAY 1** 1863: The battle of Chancellorsville, Virginia, begins. }

Bombardment and Capture of the Forts at Hatteras Inlet, N.C., Aug. 27ᵗʰ, 1861. Following Union defeats at Big Bethel, First Bull Run, and Wilson's Creek, Missouri, this joint army-navy expedition garnered a sorely needed victory for the North. Hand-colored lithograph, Currier & Ives, c. 1861

British shipyards and used them with significant effect to prey on Union shipping; initiated a program to produce ironclad warships; and developed other innovative devices such as underwater explosives (called torpedoes) and submersible vessels—one of which, CSS *Hunley*, became the first submersible ever to sink an enemy warship. The Confederate navy reached its peak in early 1864, with 753 officers, 4,460 enlisted men, and 539 Marine Corps personnel, as opposed to the U.S. Navy's 6,759 officers, 51,357 sailors, and 3,850 U.S. Marines at about the same time.

As often happens in wartime, the Civil War prompted technological developments and hastened other advancements already under way. In the naval realm, steam engines were replacing sail power, efficient screw propellers were replacing paddle wheels, and iron was replacing wood: Civil War naval duels between ironclad vessels, beginning with the historic encounter between USS *Monitor* and CSS *Virginia* (previously USS *Merrimack*), presaged a new era in naval warfare. Another revolutionary innovation born of battle was the revolving gun turret, which gave warships greater flexibility to engage the enemy and defend themselves.

Ultimately, the U.S. Navy's overwhelming superiority stifled the fledgling, and exceptionally resourceful, Confederate navy. Although Southern commerce raiding did have an impact on Northern shipping, it never threatened to change the war's outcome. Rather, the U.S. Navy's blockade and successful river operations that shut down Confederate ports proved to be key elements in the Union victory.

In 1860, Abraham Lincoln chose moderate Republican Gideon Welles, former head of the Naval Bureau of Provisions and Clothing, to be the U.S. secretary of the navy. Welles proceeded—with the help of his assistant secretary, Gustavus Vasa Fox—to reorganize the Navy Department. He supported the development of ironclad vessels, heavy ordnance, and improved steam machinery. A longtime opponent of slavery, Welles ordered naval commanders to protect runaway slaves as early as July 1861; in September, he issued orders that allowed freedmen to enlist in the navy—an unsegregated force in which an estimated eighteen thousand African Americans served during the war. Welles's Confederate counterpart, Stephen R. Mallory, former chairman of the U.S. Senate's Committee on Naval Affairs, faced the necessity of building the South's navy essentially from scratch. Mallory worked, with mixed results, to purchase cruisers that could be employed as commerce raiders and to acquire ironclad vessels and rams (ships with iron ramming devices protruding beyond their prows). He also initiated ship construction in the South and established the Confederate Torpedo Bureau, which built torpedoes (naval mines) and torpedo boats.

Gideon Welles (1802–1878). 1855–65

Stephen R. Mallory (1813–1873). Photograph by the Brady National Photographic Art Gallery, 1860–65

{ **MAY 2** **1863:** Stonewall Jackson is mortally wounded during the battle of Chancellorsville, dying on May 10; command of his men passes to Jeb Stuart. }

CSS *Sumter*'s run to open waters past the Union blockade below New Orleans in June 1861 marked the start of Captain (later, rear admiral) Raphael Semmes's celebrated wartime exploits as the Confederacy's most accomplished commerce raider. Under his command, the *Sumter* took eighteen prizes (Union merchant vessels) in a six-month career that ended when Union ships effectively blocked the vessel from sailing out of Gibraltar. "Anniversary of the day of my resignation from the navy of the United States," Semmes wrote in his diary while aboard the *Sumter* on February 15, 1862. "And what an eventful year it has been! The Northern States have been making a frantic and barbarous war upon thirteen states, and nine millions of people; in face, too, of Madison's words, 'If there be a principle that ought not to be questioned in the United States, it is that every nation has the right to abolish an old Government, and establish a new one.' And then what floodgates of private misery have been raised by this war." With his next command, CSS *Alabama*, Semmes and his crew created their own special misery for the Union, seizing or destroying millions of dollars worth of cargo and ships (see also May 26 and 27).

Capt. Semmes of the pirate "Alabama." Lithograph (one tint stone), Louis Prang & Co., 1864

The Sumter running the blockade of Pass à l'Outre by the enemy's ship Brooklyn on the 30ᵗʰ June 1861. Color lithograph, Hoen & Co., published by Kelly, Piet & Co., 1869

 MAY 3 1865: After traveling a circuitous route since its departure from Washington, D.C., on April 21, the Lincoln funeral train reaches Springfield, Illinois.

Converted from a New York ferryboat, the 517-ton side-wheel steamer USS *Hunchback* entered service as a Union gunboat on January 3, 1862, at Hampton Roads, Virginia. One of many civilian vessels drafted into the navies of both sides during the war, it was assigned to duty with the North Atlantic Blockading Squadron. USS *New Hampshire* had been named the *Alabama* as it was being built in the 1820s but was renamed, for obvious reasons, when finally launched in April 1863. It became a supply ship for the South Atlantic Blockading Squadron. The naval war in which these two Union ships took part ranged from duels between Confederate commerce raiders and Union warships on the high seas, to cat-and-mouse games between blockaders and blockade-runners, to combined army-navy operations on American rivers. As was true on land, this American-versus-American naval war often brought sailors into conflict with men who had once been their comrades. "We are lying now . . . just beyond the range of the forts," U.S. Navy lieutenant George H. Perkins wrote his mother in 1862. "The rebel steamers come out and have a look at us, and positively it seems strange that they are our enemies."

On the deck of the U.S. gunboat *Hunchback*. 1862–65

"Powder Monkey" (USA), aboard USS *New Hampshire* off Charleston, South Carolina. c. 1864

{ **MAY 4** 1863: The battle of Chancellorsville ends with a Union defeat.
1865: Abraham Lincoln is buried in Springfield, Illinois. }

The vitally important Mississippi River was a bone of Union-Confederate contention until the Union secured control of the entire waterway in mid-1863. On October 1, 1862, command of the newly designated Mississippi Squadron was given to Commander (later, admiral) David Dixon Porter, who had played a prominent part in the successful campaign against New Orleans earlier that year. Another U.S. Navy participant in the New Orleans campaign, Lieutenant George H. Perkins, described river warfare in letters to his mother. "The rebels are continually sending down firerafts," he wrote on April 20, 1862, while aboard USS *Cayuga*, "and the bombardment from the mortars goes on night and day, so that we have hardly any sleep. I will write as soon as we reach New Orleans, and I hope you are not worrying, for by the time you get this everything will be over. . . . Unless we meet some unforeseen obstacle, New Orleans must fall, though perhaps it will take a week's hard fighting. We have just heard that Captain Bailey has taken the Cayuga for his flagship, so we shall lead the gunboats."

USS Alexandria, *of the Mississippi River Squadron.* Watercolor by Ensign D. M. N. Stouffer, c. 1864–65

{ **MAY 5** 1864: The battle of the Wilderness (Virginia) begins. }

U.S. Navy veteran Andrew Foote was a man of principle: after patrolling off the coast of Africa in the 1850s, he wrote two books based on his experiences that roused sentiment against the African slave trade. In 1862, his in-service temperance campaign resulted in the suspension of the navy ration of grog. Placed in command of Federal naval forces on the upper Mississippi River in 1861, Foote quickly built up and equipped this flotilla. The following February, in cooperation with a Union army commanded by General Ulysses S. Grant, Foote's unit was a crucial element in the victorious assaults on Forts Henry and Donelson, which broke the Confederate line of defense in northwestern Tennessee—and brought Grant to national attention. Several weeks later, Confederate navy officer James Waddell, recently resigned from the U.S. Navy after returning from duty in Asia, witnessed the capture of New Orleans by Admiral David G. Farragut's fleet. After serving on the Virginia Peninsula and at Charleston Harbor, South Carolina, Waddell took command of a fast high-seas vessel, the *Shenandoah*, which disrupted the New England whaling fleet in the Pacific before becoming the only Confederate vessel to circumnavigate the globe.

Andrew Hull Foote (1806–1863). 1855–63

James Iredell Waddell (1824–1886). 1861–65

{ **MAY 6** 1861: The state legislatures of Arkansas and Tennessee pass secession ordinances, making them the ninth and tenth states to leave the Union. Meanwhile, the Confederacy formally recognizes that a state of war exists with the United States. }

On November 8, 1861, the unarmed British vessel *Trent* was en route from Cuba to Europe with James Mason and John Slidell aboard—the men were Confederate envoys to Great Britain and France, respectively—when it was intercepted by the armed USS *San Jacinto*, under the command of Captain Charles Wilkes. Acting without first consulting higher authorities, and in violation of traditional U.S. regard for the rights of neutral vessels, Wilkes forced the *Trent*'s reluctant captain to relinquish his Confederate passengers—an action that was celebrated throughout the North. The outraged British, preparing for war if the envoys were not released, dispatched additional troops and naval vessels to their Canadian garrisons. The French, meanwhile, declared their support for the British position. Recognizing that the Union could ill afford to fight both the Confederates and the British, the Lincoln administration extricated itself from this dangerous situation via a note that Secretary of State William H. Seward dispatched to the British on December 27. While stating that the United States had done nothing illegal, Seward nevertheless agreed to release the Confederates—and congratulated the British on at last recognizing that the rights of neutral vessels should be respected.

Charles D. Wilkes (1798–1877).
Engraving, date unknown

John Slidell (1793–1871).
Photograph by Mathew Brady,
1860–70

James M. Mason (1798–1871).
Photograph by Mathew Brady,
1844–60

{ **MAY 7** 1864: General William T. Sherman begins his four-month-long march through Georgia to Atlanta. }

Stephen R. Mallory began his tenure as Confederate secretary of the navy expressing great faith in a type of vessel first used by the Koreans in the sixteenth century and most recently employed by the British and French during the Crimean War (to bombard Russian forts). "I regard the possession of an iron-armored ship as a matter of the first necessity," he wrote in May 1861. "Such a vessel at this time could traverse the entire of the United States, prevent blockades, and encounter with fair prospect of success, their entire Navy." Though perhaps an overstatement of the effect of one armored vessel, it is true that on March 8, 1862, the U.S. Navy suffered the worst day in its eighty-six-year history when the ironclad CSS *Virginia* (formerly USS *Merrimack*) destroyed two wooden Union vessels and ran others aground in the narrow channel of Hampton Roads, Virginia. But the Union was developing ironclads, too, and on March 9, USS *Monitor* engaged the *Virginia* in the first clash between ironclad naval vessels in history. Although the two-hour duel was inconclusive—with neither ship proving able to do the other great damage—it was the harbinger of a new era in naval warfare.

The Monitor and Merrimac: The first fight between ironclads. Color lithograph, Louis Prang & Co., 1886

{ **MAY 8** 1864: Fighting begins at Spotsylvania Court House, Virginia, where it will continue for nearly two weeks. }

Stimulated by the knowledge that the Confederates were creating the ironclad *Virginia* (formerly the *Merrimack*), the U.S. government commissioned an ironclad vessel of its own, designed by the Swedish-born inventor John Ericsson. The unique USS *Monitor* was essentially an armored raft equipped with a revolving turret holding twin eleven-inch Dahlgren guns (distinctive bottle-shaped smoothbore cannons named for their inventor, John Dahlgren; see May 25). Built in New York in record time (a little over three months), the *Monitor* arrived at Hampton Roads, Virginia, on the night of the *Virginia*'s victory over the Union's wooden-hulled blockaders. With the standoff battle between the two ironclads on March 9, 1862, technological balance had been restored between the two navies. This initial clash of ironclads led to "monitor fever" in the North. The Union developed dozens of variations of the original *Monitor*; in all, sixty Union ironclads (some called "monitors") were built during the war. Production of ironclads also remained a Confederate priority. Because of a lack of adequate shipyards and materials, however, fewer than two dozen of the approximately fifty ironclads intended for the Confederacy became available for service.

Fifteen officers on the deck of the Union ironclad *Monitor*. 1862

{ **MAY 9** 1865: A military commission established by the War Department opens the trial of the eight accused conspirators in the assassination of President Lincoln (and the attempted assassination of Secretary of State William H. Seward on the same night). }

On an April 1861 mission to Pensacola, Florida, Lieutenant John L. Worden became the first Federal officer taken prisoner by the Confederates. Exchanged after seven months, he took command of the *Monitor* in January 1862. With the aid of his executive officer, Lieutenant Samuel Dana Greene, Worden brought the ship through an angry storm on the way to its historic encounter with the *Virginia* on March 9. During that battle, an explosion partially blinded Worden, and Greene again stepped in to assist. In the *Virginia*'s devastatingly successful engagement with wooden-hulled Union vessels the day before, the ship's commander, Franklin Buchanan, had been wounded, so the *Virginia* was under the command of Lieutenant Commander Catesby ap Roger Jones during its historic engagement with the *Monitor*. Buchanan, the first superintendent of the U.S. Naval Academy (1845–47) and the commandant of the Washington Navy Yard at the outbreak of the war, had become the only full admiral in the Confederate navy after he resigned his U.S. commission. Once he recovered from his wounds, Buchanan was placed in command at Mobile Bay, Alabama—where he was again wounded, and also taken prisoner, during his stout but unsuccessful defense of the bay against Admiral David G. Farragut's naval assault in August 1864 (see May 28 and 29).

John L. Worden (1818–1897). Date unknown

Franklin Buchanan (1800–1874). 1855–62

{ **MAY 10** **1865:** Jefferson Davis is captured by Union troops near Irwinville, Georgia, effectively putting an end to the Confederate government. }

The Confederacy's first major defeat was the seizure of its largest city, the vital and cosmopolitan port city of New Orleans, in April 1862. The city's downfall was assured after Admiral David G. Farragut, aboard his flagship, USS *Hartford*, led his Union naval squadron past Forts Jackson and St. Philip, near the mouth of the Mississippi River, in a hair-raising, cannon-fire-punctuated predawn advance. The squadron arrived at New Orleans on April 25 and received something less than a warm welcome from the residents. They could do little beyond a vocal protest, however, because all major Confederate armies were occupied elsewhere. "The crowds on the levee howled and screamed with rage," young citizen George Washington Cable wrote later. "The swarming decks answered never a word; but one old tar on the *Hartford*, standing with lanyard in hand beside a great pivot-gun, so plain to view that you could see him smile, silently patted its big black breach and blandly grinned." After the mayor declined the honor of surrendering the city, Farragut sent marines in to raise the American flag on April 29. Two days later, Major General Benjamin F. Butler's army arrived to begin an eventful occupation.

The City of New Orleans, and the Mississippi River . . . (bird's-eye view). Color lithograph, Currier & Ives, 1885

{ **MAY 11** 1864: Confederate cavalry general Jeb Stuart is mortally wounded at the battle of Yellow Tavern, Virginia. }

Serving under Admiral David G. Farragut during the expedition to take New Orleans, the exceptionally talented naval officer David Dixon Porter made this imaginative sketch of the Union squadron's passage of Forts Jackson and St. Philip, which defended the city. Porter had done much of the preliminary planning for the expedition and was in direct command of a mortar flotilla. His drawing gives two points of view: Farragut's second-in-command, Captain Theodorus Bailey, sees a giant beast—a hybrid of the indigenous alligator and crayfish—protecting the Confederate ironclads while he leads the fleet into its lair; and an "eye witness" sees Bailey demolish the Confederate fleet with little effort. Bailey's subsequent description of the battle in a report to the secretary of the navy, as "a contest between iron hearts in wooden vessels and ironclads with iron beaks—and the iron hearts won," was widely quoted. And eyewitness George Washington Cable described Bailey's walk with Lieutenant George H. Perkins, through a hostile crowd to the city hall to demand the surrender of New Orleans, as "one of the bravest deeds I ever saw done." (See also May 22.)

Bailey leading the fleet as it appeared to an eye witness. Pen-and-ink drawing by David Dixon Porter, New Orleans, 1862

{ **MAY 12** 1865: The last land fight of the Civil War between sizable forces—ending the next day in a Confederate victory—takes place at Palmito Ranch, Texas. }

passage of the Forts as it appeared to Bailey and reported by him, leading! the fleet.

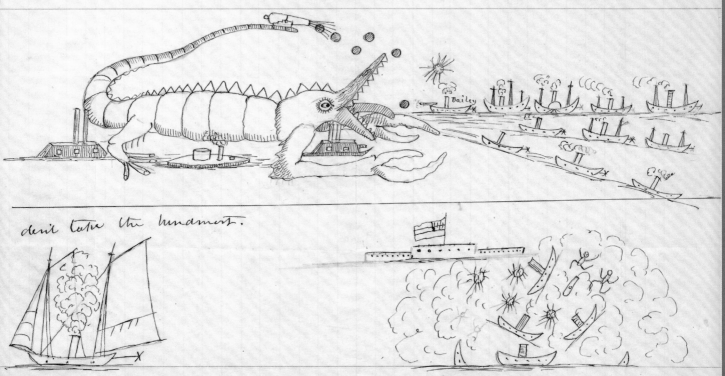

don't take the hindmost.

Bailey leading the fleet as it appeared to an eye witness

Moving swiftly across the water, civil engineer and author Herman
Haupt is piloting a special one-man pontoon boat that he invented for scouting and for extremely
close inspection of bridges. An 1835 graduate of West Point, Haupt had resigned from the U.S.
Army after only three months' service to become assistant engineer in the survey of a Pennsylvania railroad. Soon a celebrated expert on railroads and bridge construction, he was the man the
Union turned to when the Civil War broke out. Railroads became such crucial lifelines for the
military that in 1862, President Lincoln assumed unprecedented authority to control the Northern railway systems. As chief of construction and transportation of U.S. military railroads—with
military rank, though he accepted no pay so that he could work independently and continue
civilian pursuits—Haupt was the primary force in wresting organization from chaos. Sometimes
abrasive, always inventive, Haupt established repair crews that became so adept at rebuilding
lines the Confederates had damaged that it was said that "the Yankees can build bridges quicker
than the Rebs can burn them down."

General Herman Haupt in a
portable pontoon boat on the
Potomac River. Photograph by
A. J. Russell, 1860–65

 { MAY 13 1864: Confederate cavalry begin a new campaign north of the Arkansas River. **}**

As General George B. McClellan retreated from the Virginia Peninsula, shifting his base to Harrison's Landing on the James River, his Army of the Potomac was hotly pursued by General Robert E. Lee's Army of Northern Virginia. In a series of encounters that became known as the Seven Days, which marked the end of the Union's failed Peninsula campaign against Richmond, Lee sought to deal the Federal force a lethal blow. His final attempt occurred at the battle of Malvern Hill on July 1, 1862—but the Confederate attacks, launched against well-placed Union lines, were neither well planned nor well coordinated. Southern troops marched over open fields under lacerating and unrelenting fire from Union army artillery and river-based gunboats. "The vast aerial auditorium," one newspaper correspondent wrote, "seemed convulsed with the commotion of frightful sounds." General D. H. Hill, who watched as shells tore into his Confederate troops, later said of the battle, "It was not war—it was murder." But McClellan, rejecting suggestions from some of his officers that he take advantage of this bloody victory and push toward Richmond again, continued his retreat to Harrison's Landing, where navy gunboats protected the Union camps and communications.

Gunboats shelling the enemy at the battle of Malvern Hill—sketched from McClellan's headquarters. Pencil and Chinese white drawing on tan paper by Alfred R. Waud, July 1, 1862

{ **MAY 14** 1863: Union forces occupy Jackson, the capital of Mississippi. }

General McClellan went aboard while I was sketching
to change the position of the gunboats that
were shelling our infantry.

Gunboats shelling the enemy at the battle of Malvern hill   sketched from McClellan's head quarters   A. R. Waud

August 5th [1862, at Westover plantation, seven miles from Baton Rouge]. . . . About half-past nine, . . . a guerrilla told us the [Confederate] ram Arkansas was lying a few miles below, on her way to cooperate with [Confederate general John C.] Breckinridge, whose advance guard had already driven the pickets into [Union-occupied] Baton Rouge. . . . Mother threatened us with shot and shell and bloody murder, but the loud report of half a dozen cannon in slow succession only made us more determined to see the fun. . . . The [carriage] driver, being as crazy as we, fairly made his horses run along the road to catch a glimpse of our Ram. . . . We crossed to the outer levee, and there she lay at our feet . . . a heavy, clumsy, rusty, ugly flatboat with a great square box in the center, while great cannon put their noses out at the sides, and in front. The decks were crowded with men, rough and dirty, jabbering and hastily eating their breakfast. That was the great Arkansas! God bless and protect her, and the brave men she carries.

—Sarah Morgan, diary entry

Destruction of the rebel ram "Arkansas" by the United States gunboat "Essex," on the Mississippi River, near Baton Rouge, August 4th [sic] 1862. Hand-colored lithograph. Currier & Ives, 1862?

Its engines damaged and irreparable less than a month after its initial strikes against Federal ships, near Vicksburg, Mississippi, the ironclad *Arkansas* was set afire and abandoned by its crew on August 6, as the ironclad *Essex* and other Union vessels approached. (This print exaggerates their role in the demise of the *Arkansas*.)

{ **MAY 15** 1862: Heavy fire from the Confederate guns of Fort Darling, about eight miles from Richmond, defeats a Union naval effort to reach the Confederate capital via the James River. }

The U.S. Navy created the first floating hospital in June 1862, after the Union gunboat *Mound City* captured a Confederate steamer. The steamer, renamed USS *Red Rover* and depicted in these drawings, was refurbished and used to care for sailors of the Mississippi squadron—and to carry supplies for other Union vessels. The *Red Rover* featured bathrooms, windows covered with gauze blinds, an elevator between decks, and an icebox with a three-hundred-ton capacity. Among the staff were nurses from the order of Sisters of the Holy Cross, the first women to serve on a navy ship. (Nuns from several orders cared for the wounded of both sides during the war.) Nearly twenty-five hundred Union sailors received medical care on this vessel throughout the conflict. Onshore Union naval hospitals, most of them built in the 1830s, were located in Philadelphia; Chelsea, Massachusetts; and Brooklyn, New York. The Confederate navy operated hospitals at Richmond, Charleston, Wilmington, Savannah, and Mobile.

The Floating Hospital on the Mississippi (multiple views). Wood engraving of drawings by special artist Theodore R. Davis, in *Harper's Weekly*, May 9, 1863

{ **MAY 16** 1861: Tennessee is officially admitted to the Confederacy. }

The Naval Hospital "Red Rover."

Convalescent Ward.

"The Sister."

The Ward.

THE FLOATING HOSPITAL ON THE MISSISSIPPI.—Drawn by Mr. Theodore R. Davis.—[See Page 301.]

Union strategists considered control of the Mississippi River a major goal, for this would cut the Confederacy in two. Vicksburg, called "the key to the Mississippi," was the object of repeated Union attacks. General Ulysses S. Grant's first Vicksburg campaign (November 2–December 20, 1862) was thwarted, primarily by Confederate cavalry raids. But Grant kept pressing the well-fortified city's defenses—with the able assistance of the Mississippi Squadron, under the command of Captain David Dixon Porter. After failing in his attempt to blaze an indirect approach by water to the city via Steele's Bayou (March 14–25, 1863), Porter repaired and reorganized his squadron before Grant's second Vicksburg campaign, a three-month push that finally took the Confederate bastion. That campaign commenced on April 16 with a daring nighttime run past Vicksburg's guns by Porter's fleet, carrying troops and supplies to be landed south of the city. "New York conflagrations and Fourth of July pyrotechnics—they were nothing to it!" Ensign Elias Smith of USS *Lafayette* later reported. By 1:30 A.M., the squadron was safely past the city.

Siege of Vicksburg—13, 15, & 17 Corps, commanded by Gen. U. S. Grant, assisted by the Navy under Admiral Porter—[as Confederates prepare to] surrender, July 4, 1863. Color lithograph, Kurz & Allison, 1888

{ **MAY 17** 1863: Engaged by Union troops, Confederate forces burn bridges over the Big Black River, Mississippi, and continue to fall back toward Vicksburg. }

A product of the "monitor fever" that seized the North after the duel between the ironclads *Monitor* and *Virginia (Merrimack)* in March 1862, USS *Onondaga* was commissioned in March 1864, the same month Ulysses S. Grant assumed command of all Union armies. As Grant began planning his spring 1864 Overland campaign, which pushed Robert E. Lee's army back toward the Petersburg-Richmond line, the *Onondaga* joined the James River Flotilla, covering the waterway approaches to the Confederate capital. Lee had considered it imperative to destroy Grant's force before it crossed the James and laid siege to these two vital Southern cities. But the Union army crossed the James in mid-June—with the aid of 450 engineers. Under the command of Captain George H. Mendell, the engineers constructed, in record time, a temporary bridge spanning the twenty-one-hundred-foot-wide river—the longest continuous pontoon bridge ever built up to that time. (Their achievement was later eclipsed by the military engineering feats of World War II.)

A scene on the James River, Virginia, with the monitor USS *Onondaga* at anchor. 1864

{ **MAY 18** 1861: Arkansas is officially admitted to the Confederacy. }

Neither participant in the Civil War's most famous naval engagement survived long after their duel at Hampton Roads, Virginia. CSS *Virginia* (*Merrimack*) went back to base at the Norfolk Navy Yards, where it was repaired and strengthened before venturing into Hampton Roads on two other occasions, in April and May, without engaging in combat. By then, George B. McClellan's army was on the Virginia Peninsula. Left without a port when Federal troops took Norfolk, the *Virginia* was scuttled by its crew on May 11, after a last-ditch attempt to lighten the ship enough to move it up the James River failed. USS *Monitor*, meanwhile, was on the James River, supporting McClellan's campaign. After helping to cover the Army of the Potomac's final retreat, the *Monitor* was first assigned to blockade duty, then ordered to North Carolina for operations against the Confederate port city of Wilmington. En route, the *Monitor* was caught in a nighttime storm off Cape Hatteras on December 30, 1862, and it foundered shortly after midnight. Four officers and twelve crewmen went down with the ship; forty-seven others were rescued.

Destruction of the rebel monster "Merrimac" off Craney Island May 11, 1862. Hand-colored lithograph, Currier & Ives, 1862?

The Monitor *in a Storm.* Reproduction of a painting by Robert Hopkin, in *Deeds of Valor* (1901)

 MAY 19 1863: General Ulysses S. Grant launches the first attack against Vicksburg, a day after his army finally moves into position and begins a nearly seven-week siege. The assault is unsuccessful.

A 1,173-ton "double-ender" steam gunboat, the Brooklyn-built USS *Mendota* was commissioned in May 1864 and soon began service on the James River, Virginia, covering the Union army's campaign against the Confederate defenses of Richmond. A year earlier, on July 4, 1863, Lieutenant George H. Perkins, on duty along the Mississippi, had described in a letter what naval river action could entail:

Federal gunboat men on the deck of the *Mendota*. 1864

> I have been up all night, and have had a hard and lively time. Within two miles of Donaldsonville a rebel battery opened on us with artillery and sharp-shooters. We were struck several times and had quite a spirited engagement. I got the *North America* by all right, with only four shots through her, and then leaving her at Donaldsonville I returned to the scene of action, and kept it up till they stopped firing. On my way down I trained my guns on everything I could see, as I was determined to make them pay dear for their whistle this time; but the levee is so high that one is not able to see anything behind it, and the rebels mass their sharpshooters at different points, and fire into our gunboats when they pass; and although we blaze away back, we do not get a fair revenge.

{ **MAY 20** 1861: North Carolina becomes the eleventh state to join the Confederacy, the governor of Kentucky issues a proclamation of neutrality, and the Confederacy's Provisional Congress decides to move its capital from Montgomery, Alabama, to Richmond, Virginia. }

Robert Smalls (1839–1915) became one of the Union's most celebrated sailors—after stealing a Confederate ship. A former South Carolina slave, Smalls was impressed into the Confederate navy, where he was made part of the crew of the dispatch and transport boat *Planter*. In May 1862, Smalls expertly piloted the cargo-laden *Planter*, with sixteen other slaves aboard, past the watches of the Confederate fortifications and made his way out to the Union blockade fleet. When he turned his "contraband" crew and supplies over to the Union flag officer, he became an instant hero to the abolitionist forces in the North and an inspiration to both slaves and free blacks in the South. After his break for freedom, Smalls joined the U.S. Navy, staying on the vessel he had just liberated. His intimate knowledge of the shallow inland waters of the South Carolina and Georgia coasts proved indispensable to the Union campaign in and around Charleston. In December 1863, when the commander of the *Planter* deserted his post under fire, Smalls piloted the ship out of danger. As a result, he was promoted to captain and given command of the *Planter*, a post he held until the ship was decommissioned in 1866.

Robert Smalls and *The gun-boat "Planter."* Wood engravings in *Harper's Weekly,* June 14, 1862

{ **MAY 21** 1863: Union forces begin the siege of Port Hudson, Louisiana, north of Baton Rouge. }

Born at sea as his parents were emigrating from Ireland to the United States, John Newland Maffitt spent nearly thirty years in the U.S. Navy before resigning to serve the Confederacy. His swashbuckling Civil War service included command of a gunboat and several blockade-runners, as well as three months as engineering officer on the staff of General Robert E. Lee. Maffitt was particularly successful as captain of the commerce raider CSS *Florida*, which took twenty-two Union vessels as prizes. The *Florida*—at the time, lacking guns and carrying a crew ravaged by yellow fever—also made a spectacular run past Union blockaders into the port of Mobile, Alabama, in September 1862, an adventure that won Maffitt promotion to commander. An equally skilled seafarer with a zest for action, U.S. naval officer David Dixon Porter was promoted over some eighty officers to become commander of the Mississippi Squadron in 1862. After playing a crucial supporting role in General Ulysses S. Grant's successful second campaign against Vicksburg, Porter went on to command the North Atlantic Blockading Squadron, which forced the surrender of Fort Fisher, North Carolina. He was the only naval commander to receive the official thanks of the U.S. Congress three times for his wartime services (see also May 12, 17, and 31).

John Newland Maffitt (1819–1886). Date unknown

David Dixon Porter (1813–1891). 1860–65

{ **MAY 22** 1865: Jefferson Davis is imprisoned in a cell at Fort Monroe, Virginia, where he will remain for two years—later indicted, but never prosecuted, and eventually released. }

One of the North's leading Civil War naval officers, Admiral David G. Farragut enjoyed stellar and much-celebrated successes at New Orleans in 1862 and Mobile Bay in 1864. But his attempt to achieve an effective naval blockade of the Confederate Mississippi River bastion of Port Hudson, Louisiana, in March 1863 was a failure. Located 25 miles north of Union-occupied Baton Rouge, the small town of Port Hudson was at one end of a 110-mile stretch of the Mississippi River still controlled by the Confederacy (Vicksburg was at the other end). Fortified with earthworks and gun batteries well placed on the bluffs overlooking a severe bend in the river, Port Hudson was a prime—and formidably difficult—objective for Union forces. Farragut's attempt to run his entire squadron past the deadly accurate fire of Confederate guns on March 14 resulted in the loss of USS *Mississippi* and severe damage to two other vessels. Port Hudson remained in Confederate hands until a siege and costly land assaults finally resulted in its formal surrender on July 9, five days after the fall of Vicksburg (see also September 13).

Bombardment of Port Hudson.
Reproduction of a painting by
E. Packbauer, 1902

{ **MAY 23** 1824: Ambrose Everett Burnside (USA) is born in Liberty, Indiana. }

When the guns roared at Fort Sumter in April 1861, the U.S. Marine Corps, with fewer than nineteen hundred officers and enlisted men, was the smallest branch in the military. It became even smaller after nearly one-third of its officers resigned to join the Confederate service. By the end of the war, however, the U.S. Marine Corps numbered nearly four thousand. Not the specialists in amphibious assaults that they became between the two world wars (the few Civil War amphibious assaults—those against the Hatteras forts in 1861 and Fort Fisher in 1864–65, for example—were undertaken by army units), U.S. Marines served primarily on board navy vessels, manning the big guns in countless Civil War actions. Small groups of marines also assisted the army on shore. Established by an act of the Confederates' Provisional Congress in March 1861, the Confederate Corps of Marines never numbered more than six hundred. Southern marines manned the Potomac River batteries that attempted to close the river to Union naval traffic and operated, with superior efficiency, the batteries at Drewry's Bluff, Virginia, that guarded the southern approaches to Richmond. Confederate marine guard detachments were also stationed at several important Southern port cities.

Six U.S. Marines, Washington, D.C. 1865?

{ **MAY 24** 1863: U.S. Marines burn Austin, Mississippi. }

A scientist, mathematical scholar, and inventor, John Dahlgren became a U.S. Navy midshipman in 1826; served with distinction on the U.S. Coast Survey; published, anonymously, a controversial series of articles attacking new naval regulations; served in the Mediterranean; and was professor of gunnery at the U.S. Naval Academy at Annapolis, Maryland, while also performing the duties of ordnance officer that would bring him world recognition— and would help prepare the U.S. Navy for the Civil War. Dahlgren expanded and organized the ordnance establishment, designed heavy guns ("Dahlgren guns") that were widely adopted, published a number of ordnance-related books and articles, and completely revolutionized the armament of the navy. He assumed overall command of the Washington Navy Yard several days after the Civil War began; at his own request, he also saw active combat duty. As commander of the South Atlantic Blockading Squadron from July 1863, Dahlgren led sea attacks on Charleston and its fortifications and cooperated with General William T. Sherman in the capture of Savannah, Georgia.

Rear Admiral John A. Dahlgren (1809–1870), center, and staff aboard USS *Pawnee*, Charleston Harbor, South Carolina. c. 1864

{ **MAY 25** 1862: Stonewall Jackson overcomes his religious scruples and attacks Union troops on a Sunday at Winchester, Virginia—a Confederate victory. }

On July 19, 1862, at 9:15 A.M., CSS *Alabama* hoisted anchor in Liverpool, England, embarking on a career as a commerce raider that was to do great damage to U.S. shipping for nearly two years. Recently completed in a Liverpool shipyard with only the numerical designation "290," the ship was built for the Confederacy, like the *Florida* (see May 22), by a British manufacturer operating under an extremely narrow construction of British neutrality. Supposedly embarking on a trial run, the ship sailed to the Azores to be outfitted for combat. Anticipating the campaign against Federal ships, the *Alabama*'s captain, Raphael Semmes, had written earlier to the secretary of the Confederate navy: "I shall feel much more independent in [the *Alabama*] upon the high seas than I did in the little *Sumter*. I think well of your suggestion of the East Indies as a cruising ground, and hope to be in the track of the enemy's commerce in those seas as early as October or November next, when I shall doubtless be able to make other rich 'burnt-offerings' upon the altar of our country's liberties." (See also May 3 and 27.)

The Alabama (290) and the Brilliante. Pencil and black ink wash drawing by G. [probably Granville] Perkins, October 1862

{ **MAY 26** 1865: At New Orleans, General Simon Bolivar Buckner agrees to surrender terms for the Army of Trans-Mississippi, the last significant army of the Confederacy; his superior, General E. Kirby Smith, will officially accept the terms of surrender one week later. }

G. Perkins

The most famous and successful Confederate raider, CSS *Alabama*, Raphael Semmes's second command (see May 3 and 26), captured nearly seventy merchant vessels and destroyed or damaged more than $6 million worth of U.S. shipping. A primary target of the Union navy, the *Alabama* was finally cornered in the harbor of Cherbourg, France, on June 19, 1864, by USS *Kearsarge*, commanded by Captain John A. Winslow—with whom Semmes had shared shipboard quarters during the Mexican War (1846–48). In midmorning, in fine weather, Semmes sailed out of the harbor, and the war's greatest ship-to-ship combat in open seas took place before a host of civilians observing from the shoreline cliffs (possibly including the artist Édouard Manet, who painted the *Alabama and Kearsarge* in oil the same year). Circling and firing, the ships drew closer together, with the *Kearsarge* taking the offensive. By noon, the *Alabama* was too badly damaged to continue, and Semmes had to strike his colors, before his ship sank. "My crew seems to be in the right spirit," he had written in his diary before the engagement began. "God defend the right, and have mercy upon the souls of those who fall, as many of us must!" Nine *Alabama* crewmen were killed and thirty were wounded, but Semmes and some of his officers managed to escape to England.

Kearsarge and Alabama. Color lithograph, Louis Prang & Co., 1887

{ **MAY 27** 1865: President Andrew Johnson orders the release of most persons imprisoned by Federal military authorities for their activities on behalf of the Confederacy. }

A major entry way for supplies to the Confederacy from abroad, Mobile, Alabama, was served by Mobile Bay. The bay was guarded by the formidable Fort Morgan and a small naval contingent of three gunboats and the ironclad *Tennessee*, under the command of Admiral Franklin Buchanan (see May 10). As Admiral David G. Farragut led his Union fleet of fourteen wooden ships and four monitors in an attack on August 5, 1864, one of the ironclads, USS *Tecumseh*, struck a mine and foundered. Farragut maneuvered his flagship, USS *Hartford*, to lead his fleet through the minefield (see May 29). Despite determined resistance from Fort Morgan—and particularly from Buchanan's ironclad, which took on the entire Union fleet all by itself—the *Tennessee*, the fort, and the bay all soon fell to the Union forces, closing the port of Mobile to all shipping. "In the success which has attended your operations," Secretary of the Navy Gideon Welles wrote to Admiral Farragut, congratulating him for this important victory, "you have illustrated the efficiency and irresistible power of a naval force led by a bold and vigorous mind."

Battle of Mobile Bay. Color lithograph, Louis Prang & Co., 1886

{ **MAY 28** 1818: Pierre Gustave Toutant Beauregard (CSA) is born in St. Bernard, Louisiana. }

Among the dangers confronting Admiral David G. Farragut's fleet at Mobile Bay (see May 28) were fields of underwater explosive devices that are known as mines today but were called torpedoes during the Civil War. Confederate disadvantages in men and materials prompted the widespread use of these "infernal machines," which had been initially regarded as dishonorable or ungentlemanly weapons. First employed in the Potomac River in July 1861, they came to be the Confederacy's most effective weapons against ships: they were responsible for destroying or seriously damaging forty-three Union vessels—including USS *Tecumseh* at Mobile Bay. Clambering up a mast of his flagship, USS *Hartford*, to improve his perspective after the *Tecumseh*'s unhappy encounter, Admiral Farragut reportedly shouted the soon-to-be-legendary, "Damn the torpedoes, full speed ahead," and guided his ships to victory.

Infernal machines discovered in the Potomac [near Aquia] Creek by the flotilla. Pencil and Chinese white drawing on brown paper by Alfred R. Waud, July 7, 1861

Lashed to the shrouds—Admiral David Farragut passing the forts at Mobile in his flagship "Hartford." Color lithograph, Louis Prang & Co., 1870

MAY 29 **1865:** President Johnson issues a formal proclamation granting amnesty and pardon to everyone who participated in "the existing rebellion"—with certain exceptions, such as high-ranking Confederate military officers and civilian officials (and Johnson will eventually grant clemency to most of them).

On April 27, 1865, two weeks after Northern joy over Robert E. Lee's surrender had been lacerated by grief over Abraham Lincoln's assassination, the steamboat *Sultana* moved slowly northward on the Mississippi River. Designed to carry 376 passengers, it was packed that day with 2,000 recently released prisoners of war—as well as other passengers and equipment. Seven miles above Memphis, three of the steamboat's four boilers exploded, destroying the ship and setting its larger remnants afire. Passengers who had not been killed outright were plunged into the river. Many of the men could not swim, and nearly all of them were weak from long months of debilitating captivity; large numbers drowned in the muddy current. More than 700 people were ultimately pulled from the water and taken to Memphis hospitals, but over 200 of those rescued from the river did not survive. The loss of an estimated 1,500 to 1,700 lives made the destruction of the *Sultana* the deadliest maritime disaster in the nation's history.

Explosion of the Steamer "Sultana," April 28, 1865. Wood engraving in *Harper's Weekly*, May 20, 1865

MAY 30 1861: At Norfolk, Virginia, Confederates raise USS *Merrimack* (later armored and given new life as CSS *Virginia*), which Federal forces burned while evacuating the navy yard there.

Wilmington, North Carolina, with its vital railroads and shipyards, and surrounded by fortifications, was the South's most important blockade-running port—and, after Admiral David G. Farragut's August 1864 triumph at Mobile Bay (see May 28 and 29), the only major Confederate seaport open to trade with the outside world. Its most formidable defense was Fort Fisher, so well protected by a minefield and artillery emplacements that it was known as "the Gibraltar of the South." After an unsuccessful expedition against the fort in late December 1864, Union forces regrouped, and in January 1865, some ninety-six hundred men and more than sixty ships returned to try again. Under the joint command of Rear Admiral David Dixon Porter and General Alfred H. Terry, this expedition—the largest army-navy operation of the war—was successful. Beginning with a damaging bombardment (January 13–15), the expedition culminated in a land assault (January 15) that included some of the fiercest close-quarters fighting in the entire four-year conflict. With the fort in Union hands, Wilmington fell on February 22, depriving Robert E. Lee of his most vital supply line.

The bombardment and capture of Fort Fisher, NC, Jany. 15th 1865. Hand-colored lithograph. Currier & Ives, date unknown

{ **MAY 31** 1862: The battle of Seven Pines (Fair Oaks), Virginia, begins. }

JUNE: FIGHTING FOR FREEDOM

The greatest wedge between the industrial North and the agrarian South, slavery had
been the focus of American political and social struggles long before it was eradicated by means
of the actual clash of arms. At the time of the American Revolution, slavery was legal in all
thirteen colonies—a fact that inspired opposition to slavery as early as 1688, especially within
some religious groups, most notably Quakers. As free black people joined with white abolitionists in antislavery societies, and an eloquent black press joined white abolitionist newspapers
in editorializing constantly against human servitude, slavery became illegal in most Northern
states; in the South, however, with the advent of "King Cotton," it became more entrenched.

   Slavery festered at the center of a host of related problems—many of them reflected in
the prolonged debate over plans for colonizing black Americans outside the United States (see
January 5). Such plans resulted in the founding of Liberia and, later, in much less successful
settlements in Haiti. But to most black Americans, many of whom by then were descended from
several generations of blacks born in America, leaving their own country was not an agreeable
solution. Accepting emigration also meant conceding the battle for abolition—and the continuing battles that free African Americans were waging for equal rights. "This being our country,"
said black activist John Rock, "we have made up our minds to remain in it, and to try to make it
worth living in."

{ **JUNE 1** 1831: John Bell Hood (CSA) is born in Owingsville, Bath County, Kentucky.
1862: The Confederate army in northern Virginia has a new commander, Robert E. Lee. }

Heroes of the Colored Race.
Reconstruction-era depictions of
activists Blanche Kelso Bruce,
Frederick Douglass, and Hiram
Revels. Color lithograph, Joseph
Hoover, 1883

Throughout the Civil War, Northern black civilians and, from 1863, African American soldiers in the Union army fought for equality in the voting booth; in the schools; in recompense for doing the same jobs as whites; and in access to very simple things, such as a seat on a streetcar (see June 7 and 21). Through the persistent efforts of both blacks and whites, much progress was made. The major victory, of course, was the end of slavery. A giant step toward that end was taken when President Lincoln issued the Preliminary Emancipation Proclamation on September 22, 1862, and the Emancipation Proclamation itself on January 1, 1863. What the South termed the "peculiar institution" was finally and forever eradicated in the United States when the Thirteenth Amendment to the Constitution was ratified in December 1865. The Freedmen's Bureau, established in March of that year, instituted many programs for war refugees and former slaves in the South—including a pivotally important education program. Black men from Southern states were elected to state and national office. The future seemed filled with promise. But vast disappointment—and many more battles—lay ahead.

In 1902, Susie King Taylor, an escaped slave who was a teacher and laundress for an African American regiment during the Civil War, wondered, in a short book of wartime reminiscences, "if our white fellow men realize the true sense or meaning of brotherhood? . . . the war of 1861 came and was ended, and we thought our race was forever freed from bondage, and that the two races could live in unity with each other, but when we read almost every day of what is being done to my race by some whites in the South, I sometimes ask, 'Was the war in vain? Has it brought freedom, in the full sense of the word, or has it not made our condition more hopeless?'"

"The only place the American historian could find for the colored man was in the background of a cotton-field . . . ," the African American paper *Pacific Appeal* noted in September 1862. "But . . . old things are passing away, and eventually old prejudices must follow." That same month, Abraham Lincoln issued the Preliminary Emancipation Proclamation, following it on January 1, 1863, with the final Emancipation Proclamation—which President Jefferson Davis of the Confederacy immediately condemned as "the most execrable measure in the history of guilty man." As Northerners began (often grudgingly) to accept the abolition of slavery as an objective of the war, slavery continued to bolster the Southern war effort. "The institution of slavery in the South alone enables her to place in the field a force much larger in proportion to her white population than the North . . . ," the *Montgomery (Alabama) Advertiser* boasted on November 6, 1861. "The institution is a tower of strength to the South, particularly at the present crisis, and our enemies will be likely to find that the 'moral cancer' about which their orators are so fond of prating, is really one of the most effective weapons employed against the Union by the South."

A Cotton plantation on the Mississippi. Color lithograph, Currier & Ives, 1884

{ **JUNE 2** **1864:** As the battle of Cold Harbor, Virginia, continues, Union troops commanded by David Hunter fight at Covington, western Virginia, in what will become known as the Lynchburg campaign. }

Escaped slaves, and those freed by Union army action, were initially called "contrabands" (in 1861, Union general Benjamin F. Butler declared that they were "contraband of war"); after the Emancipation Proclamation was issued on January 1, 1863, they were called freedmen. By that time, tens of thousands of liberated African Americans were already within Union lines, and most Federal commanders had appointed general superintendents of contraband affairs to provide food, clothing, and shelter where necessary. In some places, schools were established for these former slaves, who, under Southern laws, had been forbidden any education. Approximately two hundred thousand free African Americans and freedmen from the North served in the Union army and navy; almost an equal number of contrabands supported the Northern war effort in other ways. Many were laborers, teamsters, cooks, carpenters, nurses, or laundresses. Others accepted more hazardous employment, as Vincent Colyer, superintendent of the poor for the Department of North Carolina, reported in 1864: "Upwards of fifty [African American] volunteers of the best and most courageous, were kept constantly employed on the perilous but important duty of spies, scouts, and guides. . . . They were pursued on several occasions by bloodhounds, two or three of them were taken prisoners; one of these was known to have been shot."

African American group. Salt print from the handmade album of engraver and sculptor Larkin Mead, Virginia, 1861–62

{ **JUNE 3** 1808: Jefferson Davis, president of the Confederate States of America, 1861–65, is born in Christian (Todd) County, Kentucky. }

For black men there are neither law, justice, humanity, nor religion. The Fugitive Slave Law makes mercy to them, a crime; and bribes the judge who tries them. An American judge gets ten dollars for every victim he consigns to slavery, and five, when he fails to do so. The oath of any two villains is sufficient, under this hell-black enactment, to send the most pious and exemplary black man into the remorseless jaws of slavery! His own testimony is nothing. He can bring no witnesses for himself. . . . Let this damning fact be perpetually told. Let it be thundered around the world, that, in tyrant-killing, king-hating, people-loving, democratic, Christian America, the seats of justice are filled with judges, who hold their offices under an open and palpable bribe, and are bound, in deciding in the case of a man's liberty, to hear only his accusers! In glaring violation of justice, in shameless disregard of the forms of administering law, in cunning arrangement to entrap the defenseless, and in diabolical intent, this Fugitive Slave Law stands alone in the annals of tyrannical legislation.

—Frederick Douglass, "What to the Slave is the Fourth of July?" speech, Rochester, New York, July 4, 1852

Effects of the Fugitive-Slave-Law. Lithograph on wove paper, Hoff & Bloede, 1850

On June 28, 1864, President Lincoln signed congressional legislation repealing the fugitive slave laws.

{ **JUNE 4** 1862: Along the Yazoo and the Mississippi rivers, frightened Southern planters burn huge stocks of cotton to prevent the material from falling into Union hands. }

From the onset of hostilities, slaves were impressed into service to support the Confederate war effort—often over the protests of their owners. Slave-labor brigades built fortifications and then, as shown in this William Waud drawing, installed the cannons that provided their firepower. Slaves hauled supplies, dug latrines, and, as the requirements of war expanded, were taken off the land to work in mines and factories, such as the Tredegar Iron Works in Richmond, Virginia, and munitions plants in Augusta, Georgia. Struggling to keep its vital rail lines in working order, the Confederacy also impressed slaves for railroad work. Early in the war, thousands of servants accompanied Southern officers to military camps, where they cooked, foraged, and did laundry for their masters. But this practice became less common as slave desertions increased.

Arms of ye Confederacie. A vitriolic indictment of the Confederacy and its dependence on slavery. Engraving on off-white card stock, 1862

Negroes mounting cannon . . . on Morris Island (South Carolina). Pencil, Chinese white, and black ink wash drawing on green paper by William Waud, 1861

{ **JUNE 5** **1864:** Brigadier General William E. "Grumble" Jones is killed in an engagement with General David Hunter's Union troops in the Shenandoah Valley. }

The attack on Ft Sumter 1861.

W. Wand

Scion of the Hamptons of South Carolina, among the largest slaveholding families in the Confederacy, Wade Hampton was a son and grandson of veterans of the American Revolution and the War of 1812. A lawyer and legislator with large holdings in land and slaves in Mississippi as well as his native state, Hampton was a political moderate who did not favor secession. But when his state left the Union, he immediately raised a mixed command of infantry, cavalry, and artillery known as Hampton's Legion. He remained a determined and resourceful army commander throughout the war. In the North, the equally determined and resourceful Frances Ellen Watkins Harper, born free but subject to the pervading racial discrimination of the time, continued her own lifelong battle for racial justice and sexual equality during the war. Giving speeches and reciting her pointed poetry, Harper sought ultimately to build up "true men and women" who would "make every gift, whether gold or talent, fortune or genius, subserve the cause of crushed humanity and carry out the greatest idea of the present age, the glorious idea of human brotherhood."

Wade Hampton (1818–1902). 1860–70

Frances Ellen Watkins Harper (1825–1911). Frontispiece in *Poems* (1898)

 JUNE 6 **1862:** Crowds along the Mississippi River at Memphis, Tennessee, witness the last "fleet action" of the war on the rivers: a smashing Union victory by Commodore Charles Davis's sixty-eight-gun fleet of five ironclads and four rams against eight weaker Confederate vessels. After the two-hour engagement, Federal troops take possession of Memphis.

The present position of the colored man is a trying one; trying because the whole nation seems to have entered into a conspiracy to crush him. But few seem to comprehend our position in the free States. The masses seem to think that we are oppressed only in the South. This is a mistake; we are oppressed everywhere in this slavery-cursed land. . . . We desire to take part in this contest, and when our Government shall see the necessity of using the loyal blacks of the free States, I hope it will have the courage to recognize their manhood. It certainly will not be mean enough to force us to fight for your liberty, . . . and then leave us when we go home to our respective States to be told that we cannot ride in the [street]cars, that our children cannot go to the public schools, that we cannot vote, and if we don't like that state of things, there is an appropriation to colonize us. We ask for our rights.

—John Rock, African American teacher, doctor, lawyer, and orator, excerpt from a speech, Boston, August 1, 1862

The American Declaration of Independence illustrated. Color lithograph designed by R. Thayer with an illustration by Dominique C. Fabronius, published by Louis Prang & Co., 1861

{ **JUNE 7** 1863: Union troops in Mississippi sack and burn the Brierfield Plantation of Jefferson Davis and his brother Joseph. }

On May 1, 1862, "political general" Benjamin F. Butler (the Union officer who had first defined escaped slaves as "contraband of war") assumed command of occupied New Orleans (see also May 11 and 12)—and immediately plunged into controversy. The worst furor was over his instantly infamous Order No. 28, issued on May 15, which declared that any woman whose attitude toward the city's occupiers was found wanting "shall be regarded and held liable to be treated as a woman of the town plying her avocation." Beginning in late September, Butler also oversaw the official mustering in of three regiments of Louisiana Native Guards, comprising men of Louisiana's free black population and former slaves. These black regiments included some seventy-five black captains and lieutenants and one major among their officers; however, this unprecedented step was reversed by Butler's successor, Major General Nathaniel P. Banks. Declaring that "the appointment of colored officers is detrimental to the service," Banks methodically drove the black officers out of the army with a campaign of slights, humiliations, and largely unfounded charges of incompetence. Only thirty-two other black officers were commissioned throughout the war—most of them chaplains and doctors.

Benjamin F. Butler (1818–1893). Photograph by the Brady National Photographic Art Gallery, 1860–65

"Camp Brightwood, DC—Contrabands in Second Rhode Island Camp: Capt. B. S. Brown (left), Lt. John P. Shaw, Co. F 2d Regt. Rhode Island Volunteer Infantry (center); and Lt. Fry (right) with African American men and boy." 1861–64

{ JUNE 8 **1862:** Stonewall Jackson's troops fight off a Federal attack in the battle of Cross Keys, Virginia. His thirty-eight-day Shenandoah Valley campaign ends the next day with a victory at Port Republic, Virginia. **}**

You have no idea of the state of things here. Go out in any direction and you meet negroes on horses, negroes on mules, negroes with oxen, negroes by the wagon, cart and buggy load, negroes on foot, men, women and children; negroes in uniform, negroes in rags, negroes in frame houses, negroes living in tents, negroes living in rail pens covered with brush, and negroes living under brush piles without any rails, negroes living on the bare ground with the sky for their covering; all hopeful, almost all cheerful, every one pleading to be taught, willing to do anything for learning. They are never out of our rooms, and their cry is for "Books! Books!" and "When will school begin?" Negro women come and offer to cook and wash for us, if we will only teach them to read the Bible. . . . Every night hymns of praise to God and prayers for the Government that oppressed them so long, rise around on every side—prayers for the white teachers that have already come—prayers that God would send them more. These are our circumstances.

—Thomas Calahan, United Presbyterian Church missionary in Louisiana, report in the *Liberator*, January 8, 1864

Fugitive African Americans fording the Rappahannock River in Virginia. Photograph by Timothy H. O'Sullivan, August 1862

{ **JUNE 9** 1863: For ten hours or more, Confederate troopers under Jeb Stuart clash with Brigadier General Alfred Pleasonton's Union horsemen at Brandy Station, Virginia, in the greatest cavalry battle on American soil. }

An often-abrasive career army officer, Brigadier General Thomas W. Sherman led the army units in the combined army-navy operation that established a Federal enclave around Port Royal, South Carolina, in November 1861 (see February 19). Ten thousand slaves, left behind by fleeing Confederates, became the responsibility of Union forces. Initially, the Port Royal contrabands who worked for the army did so as laborers, teamsters, or servants. But in spring 1862, a regiment of freed slaves was formed—without official sanction. It was quickly disbanded (see June 11). Later in 1862, however, an officially organized First South Carolina Volunteer Infantry was mustered in. Authority for its creation rested, in part, on the Second Confiscation Act, which the U.S. Congress passed on July 11. In Section 11, the act stipulated: "That the President of the United States is authorized to employ as many persons of African descent as he may deem necessary and proper for the suppression of this rebellion, and for this purpose he may organize and use them in such manner as he may judge best for the public welfare."

"Our Mess," Beaufort, South Carolina. Photograph by Timothy H. O'Sullivan, April 1862

Thomas W. Sherman (1813–1879). Photograph by the Brady National Photographic Art Gallery, 1860–65

{ **JUNE 10** **1863:** The steamer *Maple Leaf*, en route from Fort Monroe to Fort Delaware, is run ashore off Cape Henry, Virginia, by the Confederate prisoners it carries, and they escape. }

In May 1862, Major General David Hunter, commander of the Union's Department of the South, authorized raising a regiment of African American troops from the "contrabands" who had been abandoned by their fleeing Confederate masters after the Union's successful expedition to Port Royal, South Carolina. This initial attempt to form the First South Carolina Volunteer Infantry (Colored) was not successful: it had not been sanctioned by the Federal high command, and the former slaves were inducted involuntarily. A few months after the initial group was disbanded, the First South Carolina was formed again, this time under the authorization of the Second Confiscation Act (see June 10) and with actual volunteers. After a portion of the new regiment fought its first engagements, on November 2–18, 1862—raiding Confederate installations along the Georgia-Florida coast—the expedition's commanding officer, Colonel Oliver T. Beard, reported: "The colored men fought with astonishing coolness and bravery. . . . They behaved . . . gloriously, and deserve all praise."

Unidentified black soldier. Sixth-plate ambrotype, c. 1863–65

David Hunter (1802–1886). Photograph by the Brady National Photographic Art Gallery, 1860–65

 JUNE 11 **1861:** Unionist Virginia delegates meet at Wheeling to organize a pro-Union government, eventually leading to the creation of the state of West Virginia.

The fact that black soldiers faced special dangers from Confederate forces was reflected in the *Instructions for the Government of Armies of the United States in the Field*, issued in April 1863: "The law of nations shows no distinction of color, and if an enemy of the United States should enslave and sell any captured persons of their Army, it would be a case for the severest retaliation, if not redress." Enslavement was not the only danger; Southern soldiers often specifically targeted black troops. The most infamous case occurred on April 12, 1864, when Confederate soldiers led by Nathan Bedford Forrest—an exceptional cavalry commander and a former slave trader—attacked and captured Fort Pillow, Tennessee, on the Mississippi River. Many of the more than 250 U.S. Colored Troops defending the fort were reportedly murdered after they surrendered, along with some white defenders. Quickly termed a "massacre" by Northerners, Fort Pillow engendered a U.S. congressional investigation. Many Union soldiers, particularly blacks, adopted "Remember Fort Pillow!" as a battle cry.

"Rather die freemen, than live to be slaves—3rd United States Colored Troops." Photographic print of a painting by David B. Bowser, on carte de visite mount. c. 1864

Nathan Bedford Forrest (1821–1877). 1860–65

JUNE 12 **1862:** During the Union's Peninsula campaign in Virginia, Jeb Stuart's Confederate cavalry begins a four-day reconnaissance that develops into an extraordinary ride completely around General George B. McClellan's Army of the Potomac.

Even as they faced the probability of especially harsh treatment if captured by Confederate armies, African American soldiers were waging a sustained battle against discrimination in their own ranks. On August 25, 1862, the War Department order authorizing the first black regiments stated that black soldiers were to receive "the same pay and rations as are allowed by law to volunteers in the service." On June 4, 1863, however, the department reversed its decision, announcing that, thenceforth, black soldiers were to be paid the same as black *laborers*—$3 less than the $10 per month paid to white soldiers—and money for clothing was to be extracted from their pay, whereas white soldiers received an additional clothing allowance. Black soldiers could not leave the service if they objected to this abrupt change in policy. On the Northern home front, meanwhile, black civilians also battled discrimination: only five Northern states allowed blacks to vote on an equal basis with whites; five Northern states banned blacks from testifying in court against whites; at least one Northern state—Illinois—had passed a law banning black immigration into the state; school segregation was widespread. The struggle for equal civil rights would last long past the Civil War.

Quartermaster's Wharf, Alexandria, Virginia. c. 1863

{ **JUNE 13** 1861: The Confederate states observe a fast day, by proclamation of President Davis, to dramatize the necessary war effort. }

In January 1831, William Lloyd Garrison began publishing the nation's most important antislavery newspaper, *The Liberator*. "I will be as harsh as truth, and as uncompromising as justice," Garrison wrote—and he kept to his word, waging a war on slavery that continued until the Thirteenth Amendment to the U.S. Constitution was ratified in 1865. "My fanaticism," he declared in an 1854 speech, "is that I insist on the American people abolishing slavery or ceasing to prate the rights of man." Garrison's paper joined other white abolitionist publications, as well as black newspapers. America's black press had a history of advocacy for emancipation and civil rights dating back to the publication of *Freedom's Journal*, the first black newspaper, in 1827. During the Civil War, the most important black newspaper was the *Anglo-African* of New York, which forcefully called for equality beyond emancipation. *Douglass' Monthly*, published by Frederick Douglass in magazine format until 1863, was read by more whites than any other African American newspaper.

Masthead of *The Liberator*.
July 18, 1862

William Lloyd Garrison
(1805–1879). 1855–65

Unidentified African American woman and child. Photograph on carte de visite mount, 1860–70

{ **JUNE 14** 1811: Harriet Beecher Stowe, author of the influential antislavery novel *Uncle Tom's Cabin* (1852), is born in Litchfield, Connecticut. }

THE LIBERATOR.

Our Country is the World, our Countrymen are all Mankind.

WM. LLOYD GARRISON, Editor.

J. B. YERRINTON & SON, Printers.

VOL. XXXII. NO. 29.   BOSTON, FRIDAY, JULY 18, 1862.   WHOLE NO. 1641.

I am told that whenever the rebels take any black prisoners, free or slave, they immediately auction them off. . . . For instance, when, after the late battles at and near Bull Run, an expedition went out from Washington under a flag of truce to bury the dead and bring in the wounded, and the rebels seized the blacks who went along to help, and sent them into slavery, Horace Greeley said in his paper that the government would probably do nothing about it. What could I do?

Now, then, tell me, if you please, what possible result or good would follow the issuing of such a proclamation as you desire? Understand, I raise no objections against it on legal or constitutional grounds; . . . nor do I urge objections of a moral nature, in view of possible consequences of insurrection and massacre at the South. I view this matter as a practical war measure, to be decided on according to the advantages or disadvantages it may offer to the suppression of the rebellion.

—President Abraham Lincoln, reply to a committee of religious denominations
asking the president to issue a proclamation of emancipation,
September 13, 1862—nine days before he issued
the Preliminary Emancipation Proclamation

The only known copy of the first edition of Abraham Lincoln's preliminary Emancipation Proclamation, issued September 22, 1862

{ **JUNE 15** 1862: Jeb Stuart arrives triumphant in Richmond to report to General Robert E. Lee about his cavalry's ride around General George B. McClellan's Union forces on the Virginia Peninsula. }

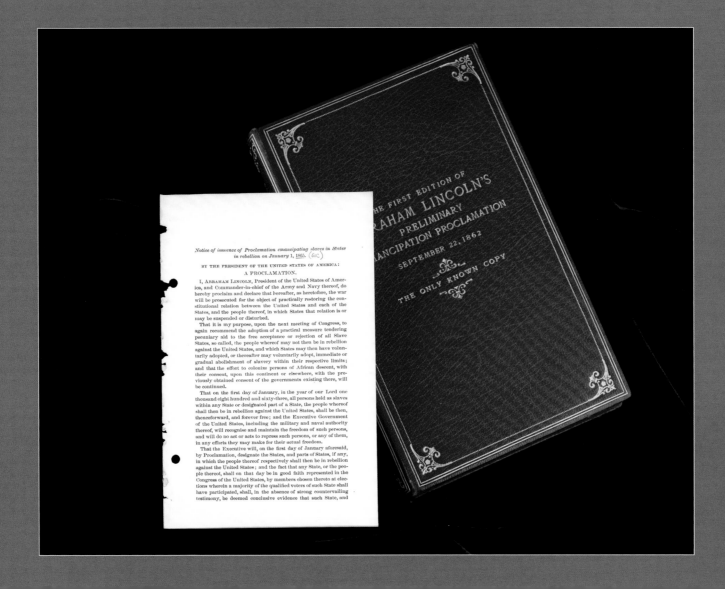

By virtue of the power and for the purpose aforesaid, I do order and declare that all persons held as slaves within said designated States and parts of States are, and henceforward shall be, free; and that the Executive Government of the United States, including the military and naval authorities thereof, will recognize and maintain the freedom of said persons.

And I hereby enjoin upon the people so declared to be free to abstain from all violence, unless in necessary self defense; . . .

And I further declare and make known that such persons of suitable condition will be received into the armed service of the United States to garrison forts, positions, stations and other places, and to man vessels of all sorts in said service.

And upon this act, sincerely believed to be an act of justice, warranted by the Constitution upon military necessity, I invoke the considerate judgment of mankind and the gracious favor of Almighty God.

—President Abraham Lincoln, Final Emancipation Proclamation,
January 1, 1863

President Lincoln writing the Proclamation of Freedom, January 1, 1863. Color lithograph on wove paper of a painting by David Gilmour Blythe, published by Ehrgott, Forbriger, & Co., 1863

{ **JUNE 16** 1862: Union troops under Brigadier General Henry W. Benham fail in a costly attack on Confederate works at Secessionville, South Carolina, a hamlet on an island near Charleston. }

"Our hearts were filled with an exceeding great gladness," wrote
a white teacher of freed slaves in the Union-occupied South Carolina Sea Islands of the joy
inspired by the issuance of the Emancipation Proclamation on January 1, 1863, "for . . . we
knew that Freedom was surely born in our land that day." African Americans and sympathetic
whites celebrated, formally and informally, throughout the North and the Union-occupied areas
of the South—although everyone knew this was just the crucially important first step. "It will
be seen that the President only makes provision for the emancipation of a *part* of an injured
race, and that the Border States and certain parts of the rebel States are excepted from the relief
offered to others by this most important document," the *Christian Recorder,* an African Methodist
Episcopal church newspaper in Philadelphia, editorialized. Nevertheless, the paper continued,
"We believe those who are not immediately liberated will be ultimately benefitted by this act,
and . . . we thank God and President Lincoln for what has been done, and 'take courage.'"

African American man reading
a newspaper report about the
Emancipation Proclamation.
Watercolor drawing by Henry
Louis Stephens, c. 1863

{ **JUNE 17** 1862: Braxton Bragg succeeds General P. G. T. Beauregard as commander of the Confederacy's Western Department. }

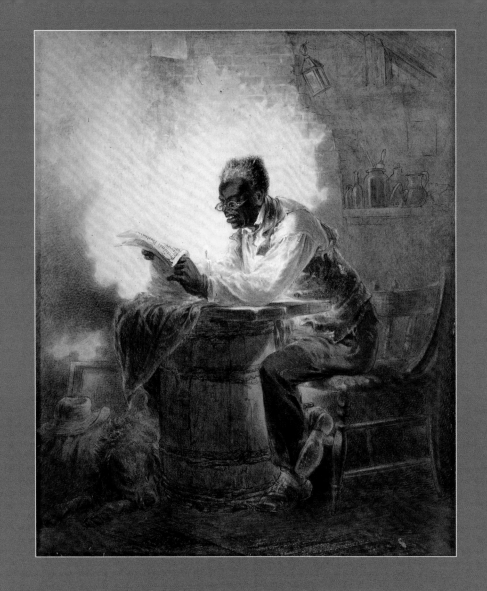

My company was examined and almost every one proved to be sound enough for soldiers. A dozen at a time were taken into a tent, where they stripped and were put through the usual gymnastic performance, after which they were measured for shoes and a suit, and then another dozen called in. Some of them were scarred from head to foot where they had been whipped. One man's back was nearly all one scar, as if the skin had been chopped up and left to heal in ridges. Another had scars on the back of his neck, and from that all the way to his heels every little ways; but that was not such a sight as the one with the great solid mass of ridges, from his shoulders to his hips. That beat all the anti-slavery sermons ever yet preached.

—Lieutenant Lawrence Van Alstyne, recruiting officer,
Ninetieth U.S. Colored Infantry (USA),
diary entry, November 6, 1863

Gordon as he entered our lines; Gordon under medical inspection; Gordon in his uniform as a U.S. soldier. Wood engravings of photographs by McPherson & Oliver of a runaway slave from Mississippi, in *Harper's Weekly,* July 4, 1863

{ **JUNE 18** **1862:** Northern troops commanded by Brigadier General George W. Morgan occupy the strategically valuable Cumberland Gap, where Virginia, Kentucky, and Tennessee meet. }

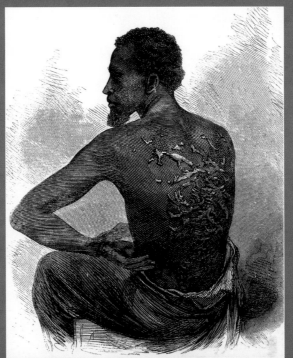

Fort Wagner on Morris Island was one of the main defenses of Charleston Harbor, South Carolina—and the scene of repeated Federal assaults in the summer of 1863. On July 18, six thousand Union troops commanded by Brigadier General Truman Seymour made a frontal assault on the fort. The Fifty-fourth Massachusetts Volunteer Infantry, the first African American regiment recruited in the North, headed the attack, seizing one small angle of the fort momentarily before the assault was repulsed. The regiment suffered terrible losses, including its commander, Colonel Robert Gould Shaw. Two days after the battle, Frederick Douglass's son Lewis, a sergeant in the Fifty-fourth, described it in a letter to his future wife: "Men fell all around me. A shell would explode and clear a space of twenty feet, our men would close up again, but it was no use we had to retreat, which was a very hazardous undertaking. How I got out of that fight alive I cannot tell. . . . I wish we had a hundred thousand colored troops we would put an end to this war." Federal forces finally occupied Fort Wagner on September 7.

The Beacon House (used as a Union headquarters and a signal station), Morris Island, South Carolina, after the struggle for Fort Wagner. Photograph by Haas & Peale, July–August 1863

Storming Fort Wagner, July 18, 1863. Color lithograph, Kurz & Allison, 1890

{ **JUNE 19** 1862: President Lincoln signs into law a congressional prohibition on slavery in the U.S. territories. }

Sergeant William H. Carney performed with such bravery under fire while a member of the Union's Company C, Fifty-fourth Massachusetts Volunteer Infantry, that he became the first African American soldier awarded the Medal of Honor (presented to him in May 1900). During the regiment's famous, ultimately unsuccessful assault on Fort Wagner on July 18, 1863 (see June 19), Carney rescued the Union colors in the midst of a hail of bullets. Despite suffering multiple wounds during the Federal retreat, Carney kept the banner aloft, insisting on holding on to it until he could turn it over to men of his own regiment—telling them, "Boys, the old flag never touched the ground." As the Fifty-fourth fought at Fort Wagner, Brigadier General Edward Augustus Wild, a medical doctor and Civil War combat officer who was a veteran of the Peninsula and Antietam campaigns, was avidly recruiting black soldiers and the white officers to lead them. (Among the recruited officers was James C. Beecher, half brother of Harriet Beecher Stowe.) Wild's African Brigade served in the hotly contested area around Charleston, South Carolina, participated in the campaign for Petersburg, Virginia, and ended the war as part of the force occupying the former Confederate capital of Richmond.

William H. Carney (1840–1908). c. 1900

Edward Augustus Wild (1825–1891). Steel engraving by A. H. Ritchie, date unknown

{ **JUNE 20** 1863: By presidential proclamation, West Virginia is admitted to the Union as the thirty-fifth state. }

Born Isabella Bomefree in New York, Sojourner Truth was emancipated under the laws of that state in 1827. When her son was sold into slavery in Alabama—which was illegal under New York law—Truth sued her former owner and won his return. In 1843, she adopted the name by which she is known and became an itinerant preacher and eloquent antislavery lecturer—and, during the Civil War, an active recruiter of African American soldiers after the North began allowing them to serve in the Union army. In 1863, she moved to Washington, D.C., where she aided black refugees. In 1865, she tested the enforcement of a new local statute prohibiting discrimination on streetcars: shoved and slammed against the door by a white conductor who did not want her on board, she took the man to court—and he lost his job. By that time, Fannie Virginia Casseopia Lawrence had become a minor celebrity in the North; her photograph, mounted on popular cartes de visite, was widely circulated. Born of a white father and a slave mother, the attractive child had been "redeemed" out of slavery by Catherine S. Lawrence in 1863, after the girl's father died. She was baptized by Harriet Beecher Stowe's brother.

Sojourner Truth (c. 1797–1883). c. 1864

Fannie Virginia Casseopia Lawrence, a "redeemed" slave child five years of age. Photographic print on carte de visite mount, c. 1863

{ **JUNE 21** **1863:** Heavy skirmishing marks the Confederate Army of Northern Virginia's advance northward toward Pennsylvania, with engagements at several locations in Virginia and at Frederick, Maryland. }

The United States knows our value as soldiers too well to suppose that we will sacrifice the position that we have gained by most arduous labor, and we, thoroughly comprehending our relation to the past glorious history of our race, and the verdict that must fall upon us in the future if we falter, will stand up for our rights, come what may. . . . Our debasement is most complete. No chances for promotion, no money for our families, and we little better than an armed band of laborers with rusty muskets and bright spades, what is our incentive to duty? Yet God has put it into our hearts to believe that we will survive or perish with the liberty of our country. If she lives, we live; if she dies we will sleep with her, even as our brave comrades now sleep with Col. Shaw within the walls of [Fort] Wagner.

—Excerpt from a letter by an African American soldier,
New York Weekly Anglo-African, April 30, 1864

Young African American orderly with a horse belonging to General John A. Rawlins, General Ulysses S. Grant's chief of staff. June 14, 1864

{ **JUNE 22** 1862: Thirty members of the Sisters of Charity order arrive at Fort Monroe, Virginia, to minister to the Army of the Potomac's sick and wounded. }

In 1863, Christian Abraham Fleetwood of Baltimore, a free African American who had joined the Union army, wrote in his diary: "This year has brought about many changes that at the beginning were or would have been thought impossible. The close of the year finds me a soldier for the cause of my race. May God bless the cause, and enable me in the coming year to forward it on." As a sergeant major in the Fourth U.S. Colored Infantry, Fleetwood was in charge of the left of the regiment's line at Chaffin's Farm, Virginia, on September 29, 1864, when an advance was ordered. Leading his portion of the line into withering fire that quickly decimated the Federal ranks, Fleetwood swept up the national colors after two color-bearers had fallen, persevered in the advance as long as possible, then rallied his remaining men around the colors when they returned to their own lines. "It was sheer madness," Fleetwood recalled later. "I have never been able to understand how [Corporal Charles] Veal [who had rescued the regimental colors] and I lived under such a hail of bullets." Fleetwood and Veal were awarded the Medal of Honor.

Make Way for Liberty! Color lithograph card by H. L. Stephens, in William A. Stephens, *Stephens' Album Varieties no. 3: The Slave in 1863* (1863)

Christian Abraham Fleetwood (1840–1914). 1865–1900

{ **JUNE 23** 1865: In Indian Territory, Cherokee leader Stand Watie becomes the last Confederate general to surrender his command. }

"MAKE WAY FOR LIBERTY.!"

Perhaps the most famous and well-organized settlement established for freed slaves, Freedman's Village, located on the grounds of Robert E. Lee's former estate in Arlington, Virginia, opened on December 4, 1863. The original tent city was supplanted by one hundred frame houses built by the Union army. Each one-and-a-half-story structure was split down the middle to form a duplex. Rent for each unit was $3 per month. The village itself became a "model" freedmen encampment, with parks, a home for the elderly, a hospital, and a school (with nine hundred students). Workshops were offered to provide the former slaves with new trades, such as blacksmithing and carpentry. The "temporary" village lasted nearly twenty years; in 1882, the U.S. Supreme Court ruled that it should be closed and the land used to expand Arlington National Cemetery.

Freedman's Village—Greene Heights, Arlington, Virginia. Pencil and Chinese white drawing on light olive paper by Alfred R. Waud, April 1864

 JUNE 24 1861: Two Union gunboats on the Potomac River shell Confederate positions at Mathias Point, Virginia.

Freedmans Village - Greene Heights Arlington. Va.

A R Waud

Born in Virginia, William Lewis Cabell resigned from the U.S. Army in spring 1861 to become a Confederate officer. After serving as chief quartermaster under P. G. T. Beauregard in the eastern theater, he was promoted to brigadier general and reassigned to the Trans-Mississippi Department. On April 18, 1864, Cabell and his Arkansas Brigade were part of a force of thirty-four hundred Confederates that encountered twelve hundred Union troops who were on a foraging expedition at Poison Springs, Arkansas. The Southerners defeated the Northern soldiers, but their victory was tainted by charges of murder: more than half the Union casualties were members of the First Kansas Colored Volunteers, and witnesses reported that some of these men were killed after they had surrendered or as they lay helplessly wounded. Although Confederates denied the charge, evidence supported it. Two weeks later, during another engagement in Arkansas, members of the Second Kansas Colored Volunteers shouted, "Remember Poison Springs!" as they overwhelmed a Confederate battery.

William Lewis Cabell (1827–1911). 1860–75

Unidentified African American soldier, holding a pistol. Ambrotype, 1860–70

{ **JUNE 25** 1864: During the long siege of Petersburg, Virginia, Federal engineers start digging a tunnel toward the Confederate lines—a massive project that will take five weeks—with the hope of placing explosives in it to blow apart the Southern earthworks. }

In June 1864, Lieutenant Colonel Henry Pleasants, commander of the Forty-eighth Pennsylvania Regiment—which included many coal miners—suggested tunneling under the entrenched Confederate lines at Petersburg, Virginia, and setting off a huge powder charge that would blow a gap in the defenses. In the face of much skepticism, the inventive plan was adopted. On July 23, the 511-foot tunnel was completed; four days later, eight thousand pounds of powder were in place. Preparations aboveground did not go so smoothly, however. When the explosion occurred—at 4:45 A.M. on July 30, killing some three hundred Confederates—Union troops charged directly into the huge crater it had created rather than advancing around it. Rallying quickly, Confederate forces fired down on the Federal soldiers—particularly targeting African Americans. Some wounded blacks were reportedly bayoneted. The valor of the U.S. Colored Troops on this and other occasions moved one of their white officers, Lewis Weld, to write to his mother two weeks later: "The colored troops are very highly valued here & there is no apparent difference in the way they are treated [by the Union]. . . . The truth is they have fought their way into the respect of all the army."

Scene of the explosion Saturday July 30th. Pencil and Chinese white drawing on light green paper by Alfred R. Waud, July 30, 1864

Within the mine. Col Pleasants superintending the arrival of powder. Pencil and Chinese white drawing on olive paper by Alfred R. Waud, c. July 29–30, 1864

{ **JUNE 26** 1863: General Jubal Early and some of his Confederate command enter Gettysburg, Pennsylvania. }

On December 15 and 16, 1864, U.S. Colored Troops were in the vanguard as the Union's Army of the Cumberland, under Major General George H. Thomas, charged out of Nashville, Tennessee, and dealt General John Bell Hood's Army of Tennessee a smashing blow from which it never recovered. The plaudits that the North's black soldiers won at Nashville added to the store of respect they were steadily accumulating among many of their white comrades-in-arms and civilians in the North. One soldier, a freedman from Tennessee, was also able to explain his purpose to a former owner, as he reported after the war: "I was in the battle of Nashville, when we whipped old Hood. I went to see my mistress on my furlough, and she was glad to see me. She said, 'You remember when you were sick and I had to bring you to the house and nurse you?' and I told her, 'Yes,'m, I remember.' And she said, 'And now you are fighting me!' I said, 'No'm, I ain't fighting you, I'm fighting to get free.'"

Unidentified African American soldier, in frock coat and kepi, posing before a painted background. Tintype, 1860–70

Battle of Nashville, Dec. 15–16, 1864. Color lithograph, Kurz & Allison, date unknown

{ **JUNE 27** 1864: The battle of Kennesaw Mountain, Georgia, a Confederate victory, temporarily checks General William T. Sherman's march to Atlanta. }

On February 18, 1865, the Twenty-first U.S. Colored Troops and two companies of the Fifty-fourth Massachusetts Volunteer Infantry were among the first Union troops to enter Charleston, South Carolina, where the war had begun nearly four years earlier. On April 3, the Fifth Massachusetts Colored Cavalry was in the vanguard of the Federal troops occupying the former Confederate capital of Richmond, Virginia. Fighting on two fronts, the Union's black soldiers had helped win signal victories on both: Southern armies were defeated and, with ratification of the Thirteenth Amendment in December 1865, slavery in the United States was at an end. Yet when the Army of the Potomac and General William T. Sherman's western armies marched in a spectacular Grand Review in Washington on May 23–24, 1865 (see December 15), the only African Americans among the marchers were freedmen walking with Sherman's troops. Not one of the 166 regiments of U.S. Colored Troops was included in this celebration. Existing prejudice and a volatile Reconstruction era would prolong the nation's racial discord—and America's black soldiers would be required to fight against prejudice at home as well as enemies abroad in future wars, well into the twentieth century.

Band of the 107th U.S. Colored Infantry, Arlington, Virginia. Photograph by William M. Smith, November 1865

{ **JUNE 28** 1863: General Robert E. Lee diverts Confederate forces from an intended drive on Harrisburg, Pennsylvania, to march them toward Gettysburg. }

A devout churchgoer and a teetotaler, Major General Oliver O. Howard—who was awarded the Medal of Honor for heroism at the 1862 battle of Seven Pines—once moved the much-less-straitlaced William T. Sherman to growl that Howard "ought to have been born in petticoats." A longtime opponent of slavery, Howard helped to found Howard University in Washington, D.C., in the late 1860s, and he was selected to oversee the Freedmen's Bureau at the end of the Civil War. Officially designated the Bureau of Refugees, Freedmen, and Abandoned Lands, the organization was established in March 1865 to help those displaced and impoverished by the war—both African Americans and Southern whites. Its many programs included distribution of food, clothing, and fuel; the establishment of Freedmen's United States Courts; and provision of medical care. It was also responsible for overseeing the creation of a school system for former slaves. Boasting some 250,000 students in forty-three hundred schools by 1870, the bureau's education program, which provided a foundation for black education in the South, was considered by many to be its greatest success.

Oliver O. Howard (1830–1909). 1860–65

The Freedmen's Union Industrial School, Richmond, Va. Wood engraving of a sketch by James E. Taylor, in *Frank Leslie's Illustrated Newspaper,* September 22, 1866

{ **JUNE 29** 1862: Union troops, driven from Savage's Station, east of Richmond, are forced to leave behind twenty-five hundred sick and wounded soldiers. }

By the end of the Civil War, Thomas Nast had emerged as America's most influential political cartoonist (see April 20). As he cast his eye on the postwar Reconstruction of the Union, he did not much like what he saw. As early as 1866, Nast vilified President Andrew Johnson's policies for allowing the South's prewar ruling class to regain its influence and for betraying the nation's African Americans in their fight for civil rights. Inspired by Shakespeare's tragedy, in this cartoon he casts the president as deceitful Iago betraying the dark-skinned American Othello. "You ask us to forgive the land owners of our island," a South Carolina freedman said to Freedmen's Bureau director Oliver O. Howard in 1865 (see also June 29). "*You* only lost your right arm in the war and might forgive them. The man who tied me to a tree and gave me 39 lashes and who stripped and flogged my mother and sister and who will not let me stay in his empty hut except I will do his planting and be satisfied with his price and who combines with others to keep away land from me well knowing I would have nothing to do with him if I had land of my own—that man, I cannot well forgive. Does it look as if he has forgiven me, seeing how he tries to keep me in a position of helplessness?"

Andrew Johnson's Reconstruction, and how it works. Wood engraving of a cartoon by Thomas Nast, 1866

{ **JUNE 30** **1865:** A military commission in Washington convicts all eight alleged Lincoln assassination conspirators. Four are sentenced to be hanged, three receive life sentences, and one is given six years in prison. }

ANDREW JOHNSON'S
RECONSTRUCTION,
AND HOW IT WORKS.

Th. Nast.

JULY: TURNING POINTS

The night of April 12–13, 1861, cannon fire in Charleston, South Carolina, turned the United States into a nation at war with itself. Friend turned against friend, sister against brother, father against son. On both sides, patriotic fervor turned into grim determination as the war lengthened. Month after harrowing month, skirmishes, guerrilla raids, and slogging marches culminated in battlefield clashes larger and bloodier than any seen before, or since, on the American continent. Foreign observers were horrified by the ever-increasing brutality: in January 1863, British correspondent Francis Charles Lawley, an eyewitness to several of the most ferocious Civil War battles, published in his newspaper, the *Times* of London, a heartfelt plea for European intervention:

> Will not England and France rush in to bring an end to this slaughter? . . . If [the civilized powers of Europe] could only witness the misery which is, from every acre of this once favoured continent, crying aloud to Heaven, it could scarcely be that they would risk some chance of failure rather than permit humanity to be outraged by a continuance of such excess of anguish as had visited no nation since the sword first leaped from its scabbard, and the human heart was first sown with the bitter seed of vindicativeness [*sic*] and hate.

{ **JULY 1** 1863: The battle of Gettysburg begins. }

Battle of Antietam, Army of the Potomac: Gen. Geo. B. McClellan, comm., Sept 17, 1862. Color lithograph, Kurz & Allison, 1888

Both North and South were concerned about European intervention: the South hoped for it; the North sought to prevent it. The North's victory at Antietam in September 1862, which allowed President Lincoln to issue the Preliminary Emancipation Proclamation from a position of strength (see April 15), made intervention by the antislavery European powers much less likely. This political and military turning point was followed by a nearly devastating Union defeat at Fredericksburg in December (see March 17) and another stunning loss at Chancellorsville in May 1863 (see March 22 and 23). At midyear, however, Union forces won two pivotal victories: at Gettysburg, Pennsylvania, and Vicksburg, Mississippi.

By the end of July 1863, Federal forces were in control of the entire Mississippi River—and Major General Ulysses S. Grant, whose skill and persistence had resulted in Vicksburg's surrender, had won the permanent favor of President Lincoln. After Grant was appointed general-in-chief of all Union armies (March 1864), the Union's military campaigns became the coordinated effort that the president had been advocating since 1862. Pressing Confederate forces simultaneously in all theaters (which made it impossible for the South to move reinforcements from one theater to another), the Union army and navy were strangling the Confederacy, as then General-in-Chief Winfield Scott had advocated in 1861 (see January 31). The Confederacy was being pierced, as well, by columns of Federal troops relentlessly destroying the South's war resources and pushing toward its remaining strategically important cities. "Where is this to end?" Confederate chief of ordnance Josiah Gorgas wrote in his diary on January 6, 1865. "No money in the Treasury, no food to feed Gen. Lee's Army, no troops to oppose Gen. Sherman, what does it all mean. . . . Is the cause really hopeless? Is it to be abandoned and lost in this way?"

The premier Civil War special artist-correspondent, Alfred R. Waud, had the unusual experience of being temporarily detained by Confederates near Centreville, Virginia, on September 27, 1862, ten days after the battle of Antietam. He took the opportunity to "make a sketch of one of the two crack regiments of the Confederate service." He later augmented his sketch with a written description of the First Virginia Cavalry:

First Virginia Cavalry halted during the invasion of Maryland. Pencil and Chinese white drawing on tan paper by Alfred R. Waud, September 1862

> They were not only as a body handsome, athletic men, but generally polite and agreeable in manner. With the exception of the officers, there was little else but homespun among them, light drab-gray or butternut color. . . . There were so many varieties of dress, half-citizen, half-military, that they could scarcely be said to have a uniform. . . . The horses were good; in many cases, they told me, they provided their own. Their arms were the United States cavalry sabre, Sharp's carbine, and pistols. Some few of them had old swords of the Revolution, curved, and in broad, heavy scabbards. . . . Their carbines, they said, were mostly captured from our own cavalry.

{ **JULY 2** 1863: The battle of Gettysburg continues as Confederates unsuccessfully attempt to overrun Little Round Top and Big Round Top. }

The Fourteenth Brooklyn Regiment, red-legged Zouaves, came into my line on a run, closing the awful gaps. Now is the pinch. Men and officers of New York and Wisconsin are fused into a common mass in the frantic struggle to shoot fast. Everybody tears cartridges, loads, passes guns or shoots. Men are falling in their places or running back into the corn. The soldier who is shooting is furious in his energy and eagerness to win victory. Many of the recruits who are killed or wounded only left home ten days ago.

—Major Rufus Dawes (USA), describing action at Antietam, as quoted in *History of the Fighting Fourteenth* [1911?]

Skirmish between the Brooklyn 14th and 300 Rebel Cavalry. Pencil and Chinese white drawing on green paper by Alfred R. Waud, September 17, 1862

 JULY 3 1863: The battle of Gettysburg ends in Confederate defeat.

Skirmish between the Brooklyn 14th and 300 Rebel Cavalry.

Recklessly brave in battle and much respected by his men, though sometimes abrasively critical of his fellow Confederate officers, Major General D. H. Hill was the intended recipient of what has become known as "Lee's Lost Order," prior to the battle of Antietam. Found—wrapped around some cigars—by Federal soldiers in a field that Hill's division had recently occupied, the Lost Order revealed Robert E. Lee's decision to split his forces as he moved into Maryland, information that should have enabled Major General George B. McClellan to deal Lee a decisive defeat by moving against each element of the divided Confederate forces in turn. But McClellan was characteristically overcautious in responding to this stroke of luck, and Lee was able to effectively counter the Union general's slow response. When blue and gray met at Antietam, Major General Edwin V. Sumner, a veteran of forty-two years of U.S. military service, personally led elements of his Second Corps as they assaulted Confederate lines, a piecemeal commitment of his troops that led to criticism following the battle. After the Union debacle three months later at Fredericksburg (see March 17), Sumner, ill and exhausted, asked to be reassigned. He died on March 21, 1863, reportedly toasting the Union on his deathbed.

Daniel Harvey Hill (1821–1889).
c. 1861–65

Edwin V. Sumner (1797–1863).
1855–65

{ JULY 4 } 1863: One day after the Confederate defeat at Gettysburg, Vicksburg surrenders to Federal forces. When Port Hudson, Louisiana, also surrenders, five days later, the Union controls the entire Mississippi River, and the Confederacy is cut in two.

We went into the fight with 301 men: of this number 136 were killed or wounded, leaving us, at the close of the day, but 165 men fit for duty. I fired between fifty and sixty rounds, and had a good mark to aim at every time. I did not waste any ammunition, I can assure you.

I suppose the battle of 'An-tee-tam' must be set down as the greatest ever fought on this continent. Each army numbered about 100,000 men, their lines extending between four and five miles. Our loss in killed and wounded will exceed 10,000 men. That of the rebels will never be known, but it exceeds ours by thousands. They spent the whole day after the battle in burying their dead and removing the wounded; and after their retreat the ground for miles was strewn with their dead, and houses and barns filled with their wounded.

We have been in the advance and on picket duty since the battle began till yesterday, and have been in active service since we left Falls Church, and the men are thoroughly worn out. . . . The rebels are in full view on the opposite bank of the Potomac.

—Sergeant Warren H. Freeman (USA), letter to his father, September 21, 1862

The Rebel dodge to cover the retreat into Virginia. Flag of truce to look after the wounded. Pencil and Chinese white drawing on tan paper by Alfred R. Waud, c. September 1862

{ **JULY 5** 1801: David Glasgow Farragut (USN), the first person in U.S. history to hold the rank of admiral, is born near Knoxville, Tennessee. }

The Rebel trying to cover the retreat ... Virginia ... he look into ... wounded A R Waud

In addition to its importance militarily and politically, the battle of Antietam was also a medical turning point: it was the first full-scale—and extremely successful—test of a new system to transport and care for the wounded, developed by Jonathan Letterman, medical director of the Union's Army of the Potomac. Working with the help of the civilian Sanitary Commission, Union doctors cared for Confederate wounded who fell into Northern hands, as well as for their own Federal soldiers, often initially treating their patients in makeshift facilities. One appreciative Union soldier who fought in the battle, John W. Jaques, noted in his diary after the battle: "The new organization—the Ambulance Corps, worked admirably, it was composed of men detailed from the regiments, some to drive the ambulances, conveying the wounded, a safe distance to the rear, or to the hospitals; and others as stretcher bearers to go on the battle field, and carry off the wounded to the ambulances; in the battle of Antietam, they could be seen with the green on their arm, faithfully tending to their duties."

"Confederate wounded at Smith's Barn, with Dr. Anson Hurd, 14th Indiana Volunteers, in attendance, Keedysville, MD—after Antietam." Photograph by Alexander Gardner, September 1862

{ **JULY 6** **1863:** Fighting occurs at Boonsboro, Hagerstown, and Williamsport, Maryland, as Lee withdraws from Gettysburg toward his army's home ground of Virginia. }

Former Illinois newspaper editor and congressman John A. McClernand, an often untactful general officer of less than stellar achievements, was photographed at Abraham Lincoln's side during the president's visit to General George B. McClellan's camp in early October 1862, soon after the battle of Antietam. Also in camp was the Chicago detective Allan Pinkerton, who had done some work for McClellan during the general's brief prewar civilian hiatus and was appointed intelligence chief for the Army of the Potomac when McClellan assumed command. Pinkerton and the agents of his Federal Secret Service (not to be confused with today's Secret Service) did provide useful information—but they undertook no long-term undercover assignments in the Confederacy and thus are sometimes blamed for McClellan's perpetual assumption that he was facing overwhelming Confederate strength. However, the general did have other intelligence sources.

Scottish immigrant Alexander Gardner, who took this picture, is credited with actually taking three-quarters of the photographs of the Army of the Potomac, even though he often has been overshadowed by Mathew Brady, his employer until 1863. One hundred of Gardner's photos were included in his *Photographic Sketch Book of the War* (1866), the first published collection of Civil War photographs.

Allan Pinkerton (1819–1884), at left, with President Abraham Lincoln and Major General John McClernand (1812–1890). Photograph by Alexander Gardner, October 3, 1862

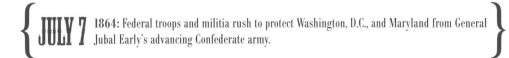

{ **JULY 7** 1864: Federal troops and militia rush to protect Washington, D.C., and Maryland from General Jubal Early's advancing Confederate army. }

Always slow to move aggressively, General George B. McClellan again frustrated the nation's commander in chief with his glacial pursuit of Robert E. Lee's Army of Northern Virginia after the battle of Antietam (see April 14). The president finally relieved McClellan of command in early November and named the reluctant Major General Ambrose Burnside to head the Army of the Potomac. Widely approved in Radical Republican circles, the removal of McClellan was widely unpopular with many of his troops. When the general took leave of them on November 10, reported Francis A. Donaldson, an officer with the 118th Pennsylvania, "whole regiments broke and flocked around him, and with tears and entreaties besought him not to leave them, but to say the word and they would soon settle matters in Washington. Indeed it was thought at one time that there would be a mutiny, but by a word he calmed the tumult and ordered the men back to their colors and their duty."

General McClellan accompanied by General Burnside taking leave of the Army of the Potomac. Pencil, Chinese white, and wash drawing on brown paper by Alfred R. Waud, November 10, 1862

{ **JULY 8** 1863: Confederates agree to surrender Port Hudson, Louisiana, the last Confederate garrison on the Mississippi, unconditionally. Formal ceremonies take place the next day. }

Allan Pinkerton's close association with General George B. McClellan caused the Pinkerton spy organization to lose favor when the general was removed from command. Lafayette Baker then assumed chief responsibility for counterespionage activities in Washington and its environs. After a period of uncertainty, Pinkerton's role as the Army of the Potomac's intelligence officer was taken over by Colonel (later, general) George H. Sharpe, who headed the newly designated Bureau of Military Information. The bureau's organization was based largely on a plan developed by former Pinkerton subordinate John C. Babcock, an architect who had joined Pinkerton's organization to sketch enemy fortifications as interrogated persons had described them. Conscientious and curious, Babcock may have been the only Pinkerton agent who ever did any scouting. As a result, the maps he drew won praise for their accuracy. The intelligence bureau he helped design between Pinkerton's departure and Sharpe's appointment became singularly effective at providing their commanding general with accurate information on Confederate railroads and supplies and on the activities of Robert E. Lee's army.

Secret Service officers at Army of the Potomac headquarters, Brandy Station, Virginia. Left to right: Colonel George H. Sharpe; John C. Babcock; unidentified; Lieutenant Colonel John McEntee. February 1864

{ **JULY 9** 1864: The battle of the Monocacy, Maryland: Lew Wallace's hastily assembled force of some six thousand Federals delays fifteen thousand Confederates under Jubal Early as they approach Washington, buying valuable time for the capital city to strengthen its defenses. }

Killed in May 1863 (see March 23), the victim of shots fired by his own men amid the confusion of combat in the uncertain light of dusk during the battle of Chancellorsville, Thomas Jonathan "Stonewall" Jackson was Robert E. Lee's reliable—and crushingly effective—right hand after Lee assumed command of the Army of Northern Virginia. A graduate of West Point and veteran of the Mexican War, Jackson was skillful, tenacious, and a beloved, if demanding, military commander. His stunningly successful 1862 Shenandoah Valley campaign (see March 6) provoked both fear and respect in the North—and added luster to his reputation in the South. "At dark a dispatch is received from Ginness Station, stating that Genl T J Jackson died at that place to day at a quarter past 3 o'clk," Confederate soldier W. W. Heartsill of Texas wrote in his journal on May 10, 1863. "'OUR STONEWALL JACKSON' none can feel the blow like the Virginians, they were completely wraped up in him and thought no man his equal. If I had not learned of the Nation's great loss, I should think that every person in The City of Richmond had to day burried their nearest and dearest friend. Lee's right hand is gone."

Last meeting of R. E. Lee and Stonewall Jackson. Color lithograph, Turnbull Bros., 1879

{ **JULY 10** 1863: Union forces land on Morris Island near Charleston, South Carolina, and begin a siege of Fort Wagner that will last until early September. }

The Union's Army of the Potomac had been placed in the hands of a new commander, Major General George Gordon Meade, only a few days before it faced Robert E. Lee's Army of Northern Virginia in the three-day battle at Gettysburg, Pennsylvania, one of the crucial turning points of the Civil War. Although Gettysburg had not been a deliberate choice as a battlefield, once the two forces engaged on the morning of July 1, 1863, Meade was able to bring the main body of his army into a strong, fishhook-shaped line in front of the town, as circumstances delayed the Confederates' two main attacks. When they occurred, late on July 2 (with an attempt by Lieutenant General James Longstreet's corps to turn the Federal left wing) and on July 3 (with a concerted assault on the Union center, subsequently known as "Pickett's charge"), Meade's shaken forces held fast. Lee began a withdrawal toward the Potomac River and was soon back in Virginia. "The results of this victory are priceless," exulted New York diarist George Templeton Strong. "The charm of Robert Lee's invincibility is broken. . . . Copperheads [Peace Democrats] are palsied and dumb for the moment at least. . . . Government is strengthened four-fold at home and abroad."

Field of Gettysburg, July 1st, 2nd & 3rd, 1863. Color lithograph by Theodore Ditterline, published by P. S. Duval & Son litho., 1863

 { JULY 11 1864: Confederates under Jubal Early invade the suburbs of Washington. **}**

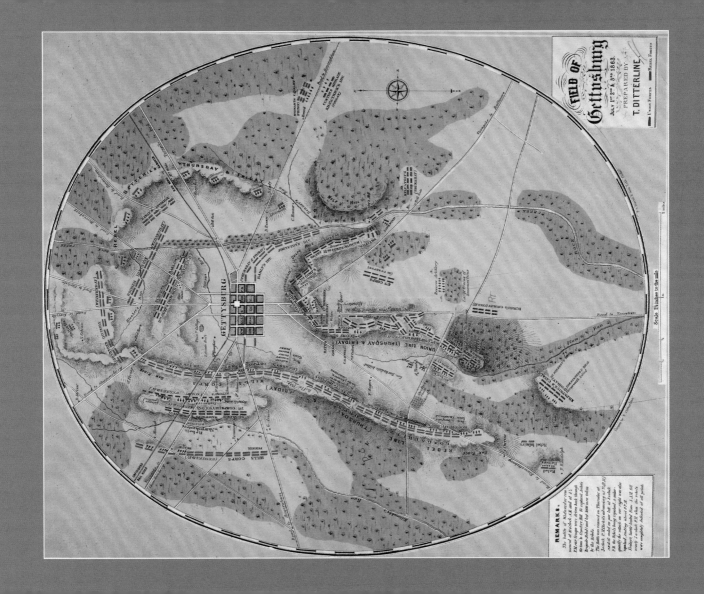

Sometimes called "a damned old goggle-eyed snapping turtle"

by his men, because of his spectacles and hair-trigger temper, career soldier George Gordon Meade (West Point, class of 1835) was also known as "Old Reliable," for his steadfastness in combat and competence in command. Assigned at the beginning of the war to the defenses of Washington, D.C., Meade served under Major General George B. McClellan during the Peninsula campaign and was severely wounded at Frayser's Farm (June 1862), one of the Seven Days battles. Only partially recovered, he fought at Second Bull Run (August 1862), was commended for his action at South Mountain (September 1862), and showed such initiative and insight during the battle of Chancellorsville (May 1863) that two of his fellow officers recommended him as the next commander of the Army of the Potomac. He was, in fact, ordered to replace General Joe Hooker—only three days before the battle of Gettysburg. Successful in this decisive encounter—though criticized for failing to press Robert E. Lee's army afterward— Meade remained in command of the Army of the Potomac for the rest of the war.

General George Gordon Meade (1815–1872), center, and staff on the steps of Wallack's house, Culpeper, Virginia. On Meade's right are General Andrew A. Humphreys, chief of staff, and Major J. C. Biddle, aide-de-camp. Photograph by Timothy H. O'Sullivan, September 1863

 { JULY 12 1864: As Federal reinforcements arrive at Washington, Jubal Early begins withdrawing his Confederate troops. **}**

It is my ninth battle, and the hardest I have been in yet. Our corps with the Eleventh fought the rebels at Gettysburg on the first day of the series of battles. After a stunning fight of about five hours our ammunition gave out, and being pressed by the enemy in overwhelming numbers, we fell back on the town. . . . While in full retreat I passed near a rebel officer lying on the ground; he was a very large man, badly wounded, and not able to move. He spoke to me and wished I would remove him to some place where he would be less exposed to the shot that was falling around. I declined for want of time and strength to lift him. Then he requested me to take his handkerchief and wipe the sweat from his face and around his eyes. This I did cheerfully, and it was all I could do for him. We were pursued by the rebels in large numbers, and there was considerable danger of his being hit by the balls intended for us. When exposed in this way to the hot sun and the perspiration starting out freely, it will soon form quite a thick crust, and unless wiped from the neighborhood of the eyes it soon becomes very painful.

—Sergeant Warren H. Freeman (USA), letter to his father, July 7, 1863

Edwin Forbes (1839–1895). Photograph on cabinet card, 1880–95

Gettysburg: Charge of Ewell's Corps on the Cemetery Gate, and Capture of Rickett's battery. Oil painting by Edwin Forbes, c. 1866

{ **JULY 13** 1821: Nathan Bedford Forrest (CSA) is born in Chapel Hill, Tennessee. }

Cavalry officer John Buford graduated from West Point in 1848 and embarked on years of frontier service as an officer of the Second Dragoons, during which he saw action against the Sioux and was commended for his efficiency as quartermaster during an eleven-hundred-mile forced march in the dead of winter. In 1861, another long march brought him back from the frontier to Civil War duty on the Union side, outside Washington. Promoted to brigadier general in 1862, he was soon in the thick of fighting in northern Virginia as Lee launched his Manassas campaign. In the retreat after Second Bull Run (August 1862), Buford was wounded so severely that he was reported killed. But by mid-September he was back on duty, named temporary chief of cavalry of the Army of the Potomac, then given command of a division. Buford's most notable service occurred in 1863 at Gettysburg, where, on July 1, his cavalry division delayed the advance of A. P. Hill's corps, buying precious time for Union forces to assemble. Buford was promoted to major general a few hours before his death, from typhoid, in Washington, D.C., on December 16, 1863.

Brigadier General John Buford (1826–1863), seated, with his staff. 1860–63

{ **JULY 14** 1861: The Federal blockade of Wilmington, North Carolina, begins. }

A terrific cannonade took place. . . . We had 120 pieces of artillery on one ridge; 400 pieces were firing at the same time. Skirmishing and occasional firing was kept up until 1 p.m., when the attack was furiously renewed and we drove the enemy from their works, but our supports were not near enough and the enemy rallied and regained them. Pickett's division took the hill on the right, but Pettigrew failed to sustain him. We were repulsed on all sides. . . . Our loss was very great, the men fighting with desperation and great valor. Many were killed and wounded. . . . The Generals had a council at General A. P. Hill's headquarters on the Cashtown Road, about sun-down, and decided to fall back. . . . I met Pickett's Division, returning after the battle, . . . no officers and all protesting that they had been completely cut up. A general movement of wagons, wounded, prisoners, etc., took place to the rear, and the unmistakable signs of a retreat were plentiful. There was a general feeling of despondency in the army at our great losses, though the battle is regarded as a drawn one.

—Major Jedediah Hotchkiss (CSA), diary entry, July 3, 1863

Pickett's Charge from a Position on the Enemy's Line, Looking toward the Union Lines. Oil painting by Edwin Forbes, c. 1866

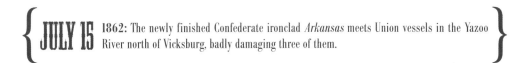

{ **JULY 15** 1862: The newly finished Confederate ironclad *Arkansas* meets Union vessels in the Yazoo River north of Vicksburg, badly damaging three of them. }

A West Point graduate (class of 1846) and a veteran soldier, Major General George Pickett will forever be chiefly associated with the massive frontal assault by some thirteen thousand Confederates against Union lines at Gettysburg on July 3, 1863, which his division spearheaded. The costly failure of "Pickett's charge" marked the end of that pivotal three-day battle and of Lee's second invasion of Northern territory. "It is all over now," Pickett wrote to his fiancée on July 4. "Many of us are prisoners, many are dead, many wounded, bleeding and dying. Your soldier lives and mourns and but for you, my darling, he would rather be back there with his dead, to sleep for all time in an unknown grave." Among the Union officers repelling Pickett's charge was fellow West Pointer (class of 1844) Major General Winfield Scott Hancock. On the first day of the battle, the unflappable and much-respected Union general maneuvered skillfully to delay Confederate action until more Federal troops could arrive. During Pickett's charge, Hancock was so badly wounded that he required six months to mend.

George Pickett (1825–1875). 1861–65

Winfield Scott Hancock (1824–1886). 1860–70

{ **JULY 16** 1863: Confederates under General Joseph E. Johnston abandon Jackson, Mississippi, to General William T. Sherman's superior Union forces. }

"Everywhere were evidences of mortal combat, everywhere wounded men were lying in the streets on heaps of blood-stained straw, everywhere there was hurry and confusion, while soldiers were groaning and suffering," wrote Union nurse Sophronia Bucklin about her arrival in Gettysburg, Pennsylvania, after the battle. There the seamstress from Auburn, New York, "washed agonized faces, combed out matted hair, [and] bandaged slight wounds." Among the Gettysburg wounded—and later awarded the Medal of Honor for his heroism in the battle—Joshua Lawrence Chamberlain had been a professor of "natural and revealed religion," rhetoric, and modern languages at Bowdoin College before the war. One of the Union's most remarkable and celebrated officers, Colonel Chamberlain led the Twentieth Maine in a stubborn defense of Little Round Top on the second day of the battle. At a crucial moment, with the regiment's ammunition gone, he led a furious bayonet charge that kept the critically important hill in Union hands.

Sophronia E. Bucklin (1810– after 1865). Engraving by J. C. Buttre in Sophronia E. Bucklin, *In Hospital and Camp . . .* (1869)

Joshua Lawrence Chamberlain (1828–1914). 1860–65

{ **JULY 17** 1864: Jefferson Davis relieves Joseph E. Johnston of command of the Confederate Army and Department of Tennessee and replaces him with John Bell Hood. }

You know all about the battle of Gettysburg. I need not repeat what I have written, nor what you have read in the papers. . . . Our march on Monday morning lay over a part of the battlefield on the left for the distance of a mile or more. The ground was still marked with newly made graves, with the bloated and disgusting bodies of horses with their mouths open and eye-balls protruding. Many human bodies were still unburied and the faces were black and the teeth grinning horribly. The trees were shattered by shot and shell. Wheat fields were trodden down. War had done its work; and the air was terribly offensive with the odor of thousands of rotting bodies. It was a relief to reach the outside of the terrible scene, to come again among beautiful farms, and through fields of ripe grain, and at last to reach Emmettsburg, where I enjoyed a good supper with a gentleman named McBride, a Catholic, who treated me with great kindness. I sat down with him and his family with feelings of no common pleasure.

—Lieutenant Colonel Alfred B. McCalmont
(USA), letter to his brother, July 9, 1863

Federal soldier disemboweled by a shell, on the battlefield at Gettysburg. 1863

Dead Confederate sharpshooter in the "Devil's Den," Gettysburg. Photograph by Alexander Gardner, July 1863

{ **JULY 18** 1863: Major General John G. Foster assumes command of the Union's Department of Virginia and North Carolina. }

... But in a larger sense, we cannot dedicate—we cannot consecrate—we cannot hallow—this ground. The brave men, living and dead, who struggled here, have consecrated it far above our poor power to add or detract. The world will little note nor long remember what we say here, but it can never forget what they did here. It is for us, the living, rather to be dedicated here to the unfinished work which they who fought here have thus far so nobly advanced. It is rather for us to be here dedicated to the great task remaining before us—that from these honored dead we take increased devotion to that cause for which they gave the last full measure of devotion; that we here highly resolve that these dead shall not have died in vain; that this nation, under God, shall have a new birth of freedom; and that government of the people, by the people, for the people, shall not perish from the earth.

—President Abraham Lincoln, Address at Gettysburg, Pennsylvania, at the dedication of the National Cemetery, November 19, 1863

Manuscript of the Gettysburg Address, 1863

{ **JULY 19** 1862: Confederates raid Brownsville, Tennessee. }

Four score and seven years ago our fathers brought
forth, upon this continent, a new nation, conceived
in liberty, and dedicated to the proposition that
"all men are created equal"

Now we are engaged in a great civil war, testing
whether that nation, or any nation so conceived,
and so dedicated, can long endure. We are met
on a great battle field of that war. We have
come to dedicate a portion of it, as a final rest=
ing place for those who died here, that the nation
might live. This we may, in all propriety do. But, in a
larger sense, we can not dedicate — we can not
consecrate — we can not hallow, this ground —
The brave men, living and dead, who struggled
here, have hallowed it, far above our poor power
to add or detract. The world will little note, nor long
remember what we say here; while it can never
forget what they did here.

It is rather for us, the living, to stand here, we here be dedica

ted to the great task remaining before us —
that, from these honored dead we take increased devotion to that cause for which
they here, gave the last full measure of devotion — that we here highly resolve these
dead shall not have died in vain; that
the nation, shall have a new birth of freedom, and that government of the people, by
the people, for the people, shall not perish from the earth.

In the western theater, General Ulysses S. Grant's second, ultimately successful campaign against the Confederate Mississippi River bastion of Vicksburg included two unsuccessful assaults on the city (May 19 and May 22, 1863) before the Federal troops began digging ever-more-elaborate trenches from which they held the city under siege. The city's inhabitants, soldiers and civilians alike, coped with dwindling food supplies, and besieged and besiegers both endured what came to be a near constant rain of gunfire; many civilians abandoned their homes for hillside caves. "The fighting is now carried on quite systematically," Confederate soldier Maurice Simons noted in his diary on June 13. "The work goes on just as regularly as . . . on a well regulated farm & the noise is not unlike the clearing up of new ground when much heavy timber is cut down! Add to that the nailing on of shingles by several men & one has a pretty good idea of the noise." As would occur at Petersburg, Virginia, a year later, Union soldiers set off a large explosion under Confederate lines in late June. As at Petersburg, many of the Federal troops became trapped, under fire, in the resulting crater; the survivors retreated. But by then the siege was almost over.

Siege of Vicksburg. Color lithograph, Louis Prang & Co., 1888

{ **JULY 20** 1864: General John Bell Hood fails his first big test of command as Southern forces attacking General George H. Thomas's Army of the Cumberland are defeated at the battle of Peachtree Creek, Georgia. }

Sunday, June 28th [Vicksburg, Mississippi]. Still in this dreary cave. Who would have believed that we could have borne such a life for five weeks? The siege has lasted 42 days and yet no relief—every day this week we have waited for the sound of Gen. [Joseph] Johnston's guns [indicating a Confederate relief column], but in vain.

      I don't believe I have ever given a description of our cave. Imagine to yourself in the first place a good sized parapet, about 6 feet high, a path cut through, and then the entrance to the cave—this is secured strongly with boards, it is dug the height of a man and about 40 feet under the hill. . . . In this cave we sleep and live literally under ground. I have a little closet dug for provisions, and niches for flowers, lights and books—inside . . . is our eating table with an arbor over it and back of that our fireplace and kitchen with table &c. In the valley beneath is our tent and back of it the tents of the generals. This is quite picturesque and attractive to look at but oh! How wearisome to live.

      —Mrs. W. W. Lord, resident of Vicksburg, diary entry, 1863

Cave life in Vicksburg. Etching by Adalbert John Volck, 1864

{ **JULY 21** **1861:** General Irvin McDowell's Union forces are defeated by Confederates under P. G. T. Beauregard and Joseph E. Johnston at the first battle of Bull Run (Manassas), Virginia. }

When, during the Mexican War of 1846–48, Lieutenant Ulysses S. Grant received official thanks for his role in the attack on Mexico City, the formal message was conveyed by Lieutenant John C. Pemberton. In 1863, Confederate general Pemberton faced Union general Grant across the defenses of Vicksburg. On July 3, Pemberton, his stocks of food nearly gone and with no hope of reinforcement, exchanged letters with Grant regarding terms for surrendering the city. After some negotiation, the two sides reached agreement, and at 10 A.M. on July 4, Pemberton surrendered the city and its garrison. (See also May 17.) "I rode into Vicksburg with the troops," Grant reported years later in his memoirs, "and went to the river to exchange congratulations with the navy upon our joint victory." Grant's dispatch to Washington reporting the surrender, coupled with the news of the victory at Gettysburg, "lifted a great load of anxiety, from the minds of the President, his Cabinet and the loyal people all over the North," Grant wrote. "The fate of the Confederacy was sealed when Vicksburg fell. Much hard fighting was to be done afterwards and many precious lives were to be sacrificed; but the *morale* was with the supporters of the Union ever after."

Ulysses S. Grant, on horse- back, Union army group in background. Color drawing by Charles Wellington Reed (Civil War Medal of Honor recipient), c. 1864

John C. Pemberton (1814– 1881). Photograph on carte de visite mount, 1861–90

{ JULY 22 1864: Union major general James B. McPherson is killed during the battle of Atlanta. **}**

In late September 1863, Federal troops were besieged in Chattanooga, Tennessee, by Confederates who had defeated them at the battle of Chickamauga (September 19–20), just across the state line in northwestern Georgia. To save the garrison and keep this crucial city in Union hands, Federal authorities rushed reinforcements and supplies across the country by train (see July 24). Ulysses S. Grant assumed command of the strengthened garrison, and he and his officers made plans to ease the flow of supplies into the city and break the Confederate hold on the surrounding heights. On November 14, William T. Sherman arrived with seventeen thousand more men; on November 23, Union forces knocked General Braxton Bragg's Confederate troops off Orchard Knob, a foothill of the Missionary Ridge range, and the next day other Federal troops advanced to seize Lookout Mountain; on November 25, General George H. Thomas's troops precipitated "the miracle of Missionary Ridge," when they exceeded their orders for a limited frontal assault and pushed the Confederates into full retreat. Now secured, Chattanooga would become the supply and logistics base for Sherman's 1864 Atlanta campaign.

Battle of Chattanooga—General Thomas' charge near Orchard Knob, Nov. 24 [sic], 1863. Color lithograph, Kurz & Allison, 1888

{ JULY 23 1862: Major General Henry W. Halleck assumes command of the armies of the United States. **}**

The Civil War was the first conflict in which railroads were used extensively to transport and support armies, and they made a tremendous impact on the conduct of the war. Both the Union and the Confederacy depended on rail transport of troops, supplies, and the sick and wounded; both made extensive efforts to disrupt the enemy's rail systems; and both experimented with new military uses for railroads—in particular, "rolling" artillery batteries. Perhaps the most stunning railroad operation of the war was the rush to relieve the Union troops under siege in Chattanooga, Tennessee (see July 23). Organized under the press of potential disaster, the reinforcements—twenty thousand troops and their equipment, horses, and artillery—were assembled, loaded, and safely transported twelve hundred miles from Virginia to Chattanooga within eleven days. The next year, railroads would be a vital supply line for General William T. Sherman's army during the Atlanta campaign.

Bridge on the Orange and Alexandria (Virginia) Railroad, as repaired by army engineers under Herman Haupt. Photograph by A. J. Russell, 1865

{ JULY 24 1864: Confederate forces under Jubal Early inflict heavy losses at the second battle of Kernstown, Virginia. }

Under orders from Ulysses S. Grant to "move against [Joseph E.] Johnston's army, to break it up, and to get into the interior of the enemy's country as far as you can, inflicting all the damage you can against their war resources," Major General William T. Sherman embarked on the most crucial series of operations in the western theater—the Atlanta campaign—in May 1864. Basically following the line of the Western and Atlantic Railroad from Chattanooga, Tennessee, to Atlanta, Georgia, Sherman dogged the Confederate Army of Tennessee through encounters at Snake Creek Gap (May 7–12); Resaca (May 14–15); and New Hope Church (May 25–27). At the battle of Kennesaw Mountain (June 27), Sherman, impatient with repeated unsuccessful attempts to turn his wily opponent's left flank, attacked the entrenched center of the Confederate army in a literally uphill fight in one-hundred-degree heat—which accomplished a surge in *Southern* morale when the attacks were repulsed at great cost to the Federal troops (see November 22). But as Grant was doing in his Overland campaign against Lee in the eastern theater, Sherman kept going, forcing Johnston ever closer to Atlanta.

Major General William T. Sherman (1820–1891), fourth from left, and staff. 1862–65

{ **JULY 25** 1864: Jubal Early's Confederates follow retreating Union forces to Bunker Hill, Virginia, where fighting erupts. }

Trying to preserve his Confederate troops, General Joseph E. Johnston moved so cautiously in blocking William T. Sherman's path to Atlanta that an impatient Jefferson Davis replaced him with John Bell Hood on July 17, 1864. Hood took command as Union troops closed in on the city, clashing with the Confederate general's troops at the battles of Peachtree Creek (July 20), Atlanta (July 22), and Ezra Church (July 28)—where the Confederates suffered an estimated 5,000 casualties to the Federals' 562. During the battle of Jonesboro (August 31–September 1), Sherman's troops cut the area's last Confederate rail link with the rest of the South, forcing Hood to retreat from Atlanta. Union troops entered Atlanta—the Confederacy's industrial, supply, and communications hub—on September 2, 1864. Sherman's telegram to President Lincoln that day—"Atlanta is ours, and fairly won"—sent Northern spirits soaring and gave a huge boost to Lincoln's campaign for reelection in November. Southern spirits plunged at this new loss. Diarist Mary Boykin Chesnut wrote, "Since Atlanta I have felt as if all were dead within me, forever. We are going to be wiped off the earth."

Siege of Atlanta. Officers observing action. Color lithograph, Louis Prang & Co., 1888

 JULY 26 1863: Confederate raider John Hunt Morgan surrenders his exhausted force of 364 men at Salineville, Ohio. Morgan and his officers are sent to the Ohio State Penitentiary, only to escape on November 27.

After engaging in a brief pursuit of John Bell Hood's Confederate army, now heading toward Tennessee, Major General William T. Sherman returned to the ravaged city of Atlanta to rest and strategize. Then, on November 15, Sherman embarked with his main force of sixty-two thousand men on a march from Atlanta toward Savannah and the Atlantic Ocean, to "demonstrate the vulnerability of the South." Planning to travel without a supply train, Sherman issued orders that his troops were to forage on the land. The orders also stated that they were to abide by certain rules even as they attempted to destroy the area's militarily useful resources: "In districts and neighborhoods where the army is unmolested, no destruction of such property [as houses, cotton gins, and grist mills] should be permitted; but should guerillas or bushwhackers molest our march, or should the inhabitants burn bridges, obstruct roads, or otherwise manifest local hostility, then army commanders should order and enforce a devastation more or less relentless, according to the measure of such hostility."

Federal army wagons at the Atlanta, Georgia, railroad depot. Photograph by George N. Barnard, 1864

Sherman's men tearing up railroad track, before leaving Atlanta, Georgia. Photograph by George N. Barnard, 1864

{ **JULY 27** 1861: Major General George B. McClellan assumes command of the Union's Division of the Potomac, after the Federal rout at the first battle of Bull Run. }

[Monday] we came through a mountainous region of country, beautiful in the distance, but dangerous traveling in the [railroad] cars. Some of our soldiers say they would rather fight their way back home than go back over that road. One box car ran off the track as we were coming through Bridgeport. Nobody killed but several wounded by jumping from the cars. . . . Sabbath morning came but the order for marching was countermanded (I know not why) and we had Brigade drill instead. I thought it wrong to drill on sabbath but I had no voice in the matter and said nothing.

—Private Douglas J. Cater (CSA), letter to his cousin Fanny, April 30, 1863

The vegetation had grown up tall and thick among the ruins so that sharp shooters could creep in and pick off the soldiers. . . . So Colonel Fiske asked me if I would take the job of collecting tools and cut the weeds down. . . . I took an army wagon and enough soldiers so that my words would mean something. . . . I breakfasted with a planter. . . . He was a violent Secesh as we called them. . . . We argued at the breakfast table on politics. He was sure we would never conquer the South. I was sure we should. I got half his hoes and all his scythes. I expect the bayonets were more eloquent than my words.

—Lieutenant George G. Smith (USA), diary entry, October 4, 1864

Private George Henry Graffam (age eighteen), Company B, Thirtieth Maine Infantry (USA). 1860–65 (rephotographed 1961)

Private Walter Miles Parker, First Florida Cavalry (CSA). 1860–65 (rephotographed 1961)

{ **JULY 28** 1861: Confederates occupy New Madrid, Missouri, an important defensive position across the Mississippi River from Tennessee and Kentucky. }

Grant is certainly a very extraordinary man. . . . He handles those around him so quietly and well, he so evidently has the faculty of disposing of work and managing men, he is cool and quiet, almost stolid as if stupid, in danger, and in a crisis he is one against whom all around, whether few in number or a great army as here, would instinctively lean. He is a man of the most exquisite judgment and tact. See how he has handled this Army. . . . He has humored us, he has given some promotions, he has made no parade of his authority, he has given no orders except through Meade, and Meade he treats with the utmost confidence and deference. The result is that even from the most jealously disposed and most indiscreet of Meade's staff, not a word is heard against Grant. The result is of inestimable importance. The army has a head and confidence in that head.

—Captain Charles Francis Adams (USA), letter to his father, May 29, 1864

"Council of War." General Grant, seated at the extreme left of the bench that is facing the camera, confers with his staff at Massaponax Church, Virginia. Photograph by Timothy O'Sullivan, May 21, 1864

{ **JULY 29** 1820: Clement Laird Vallandigham, a leader of the Peace Democrats ("Copperheads") during the Civil War, is born in New Lisbon, Ohio. }

Lieutenant General Ulysses S. Grant's relentless pursuit of Robert E. Lee's Confederate army during the spring 1864 Overland campaign pushed Lee's forces back on Petersburg and Richmond—but at such a terrible cost (sixty-five thousand Federal soldiers killed, wounded, or missing) that some Northerners, particularly Peace Democrats, began calling the Union general-in-chief a "butcher." Some of the worst fighting and heaviest casualties came at Cold Harbor, Virginia, where one assault alone, in the early morning of June 3, resulted in seven thousand Federal casualties. "I have always regretted that the last assault at Cold Harbor was ever made . . . ," Grant later wrote in his memoirs. "Indeed, the advantages, other than those of relative losses, were on the Confederate side. Before that, the Army of Northern Virginia seemed to have acquired a wholesome regard for the courage, endurance, and soldierly qualities generally of the Army of the Potomac. They no longer wanted to fight them 'one Confederate to five Yanks.' . . . This charge seemed to revive their hopes temporarily; but it was of short duration."

Battle of Cold Harbor. Color lithograph, Kurz & Allison, 1888

{ **JULY 30** 1864: Despite a huge mine explosion, Confederates fend off the second major frontal assault on Petersburg, Virginia, a clash that will become known as the battle of the Crater. }

Today we picked up, on the battle-field . . . the skull of a man who had been shot in the head. It was smooth, white, and glossy. A little over three months ago this skull was full of life, hope, and ambition. He who carried it into battle had, doubtless, mother, sisters, friends, whose happiness was, to some extent, dependent upon him. They mourn for him now, unless, possibly, they hope still to hear that he is safe and well. Vain hope. Sun, rain, and crows have united in the work of stripping the flesh from his bones, and while the greater part of these lay whitening where they fell, the skull has been rolling about the field the sport and plaything of the winds. This is war, and amid such scenes we are supposed to think of the amount of our salary, and of what the newspapers may say of us.

—Brigadier General John Beatty (USA), diary entry, December 27, 1863

Burial party on the battlefield of Cold Harbor. April 1865

 { **JULY 31** 1837: William Clarke Quantrill, Confederate guerrilla and outlaw, is born in Canal Dover, Ohio. }

AUGUST: ARMY LIFE

Approximately three million men (and, clandestinely, an estimated four hundred to six hundred women) served in the Union and Confederate armies during the Civil War. The overwhelming majority were volunteers who entered the service because of a sense of duty to their state or region or to the Union of American states—and, especially in the war's early days, in a quest for adventure or an eagerness to "see the elephant" (experience combat). These Union and Confederate "citizen soldiers" were drawn from an overall population of thirty-two million Americans whose shared "national profile" included an inherent distrust of large professional armies.

      The United States had come to depend on its part-time and imperfectly trained militias in times of emergency. And on both sides, the spirit of the militias prevailed early in the war. Men rallied to their respective colors, expecting to fulfill their obligations in a few months at most and return to their regular lives. As the war lengthened, however, many remained or reenlisted. Although both South and North instituted conscription, draftees amounted to only about 6 percent of Union soldiers, a somewhat higher percentage for Confederates. When conscripts or "bounty men" (men paid to enlist) did join the ranks, they often did not meet the standards of Union and Confederate volunteer-veterans: "I am sorry to say that we have got too many in the army that are not fighting for there [*sic*] country but for money," Corporal Matthew H.

{ **AUGUST 1** **1864:** Major General Philip H. Sheridan is named commander of the Army of the Shenandoah, charged with ridding the Shenandoah Valley of Confederates—especially Jubal Early. }

Going into bivouac at night.
Pencil and Chinese white drawing by Edwin Forbes, c. 1876

Perry from Massachusetts wrote to his mother in 1864, "and all they think of when they go into battle is how to . . . skulk behind the first stump . . . [and] keep out of danger."

Desertion waxed and waned in the armies of both sides throughout the war. Although statistics are incomplete, an estimated three hundred thousand soldiers, two-thirds of them Union men, are believed to have deserted during the course of the war. Many deserted temporarily; they took extra-long sick leaves or returned home to bring in harvests, to help their families fight off outlaws, or simply to visit during times when their units weren't campaigning. Particularly in the South, some men deserted infantry units and enlisted in cavalry regiments or in units assigned closer to their homes. Other deserters simply disappeared into the countryside. Some fled the country: in March 1864, the *Congressional Globe* reported one U.S. senator's statement that ten thousand to fifteen thousand Union deserters were living in Canada.

Yet most men stayed in the ranks, enduring the multiple terrors of full-scale battles, the dust and mud of marches, supply shortages, bad food, the insults of civilians, sneak attacks by guerrillas, injuries, the loss of comrades, and, particularly among Southern soldiers, uncertainties about what was happening at home. They also faced the invisible and little-understood enemies that caused disease. In this most costly American war—which was fought, according to Union surgeon general William A. Hammond, "at the end of the medical Middle Ages"—twice as many men died because of disease contracted while in the army as died in battle. "It would take volumes to write what we have to endure," Confederate lieutenant Richard Lewis wrote to his mother late in 1863, "and, after all, how cheerfully it is all borne up under—not near so much croaking and complaining as among the elegant men of leisure at home."

The mails here are like everything else, they go by military routine. We are only a mile and a half from the steamboat landing; but our letters go first to Brigade Head-quarters, then to Division Headquarters, one mile due west; then to Corps Headquarters, three miles further west; then to Grand Division Headquarters, a little further toward the Rappahan-nock, and finally to the Headquarters of the Army of the Potomac, stopping, I believe, at each Headquarters about twelve or twenty-four hours. After going through this interesting preliminary transition they are sent down to Falmouth and thence by rail over to the Potomac river from which they started. The system is admirable. One cannot help admiring its order, its regularity and precision; but like all other workings of the same system, it is impossible for a plain man to see how the great and desirable result of getting a letter to its destination is hastened by the process. There is a great deal more of method for the sake of method in the army, than of method for the sake of substance.

—Lieutenant Colonel Alfred B. McCalmont (USA), letter to his brother, February 4, 1863

(see also August 10, October 23)

Gen. Butlers Head Quarters—Army of the James. ("The Gen'ls Tent is the last one on the left, the House is used for the Adju-tant Gen's Telegraph & other officers.") Pencil, Chinese white, and black ink wash drawing by William Waud, October 1864

{ **AUGUST 2** 1861: The U.S. Congress passes legislation for the first national income tax: 3 percent on incomes exceeding $800. }

Gen Butlers Hewt-[?]

The most prominent city of the first state to secede, the site of a former U.S. arsenal that was producing ammunition for the Confederacy, and a prime port for blockade-runners, Charleston, South Carolina, was a particular target of Union military efforts throughout the war. Six thousand Federal troops landed east of the city in June 1862, but they were forced to retreat. In April 1863, Federal ironclads opened an unsuccessful six-month campaign against Charleston's defenses that included the legendary July 18 assault on Fort Wagner by the Fifty-fourth Massachusetts Regiment, composed of African American troops. Units of the Fifty-fourth and the Fifty-fifth Massachusetts were among the first Union troops to enter the city, on February 18, 1865. "The few white inhabitants left in the town were either alarmed or indignant, and generally remained in their houses," Colonel Charles B. Fox of the Fifty-fifth later wrote; "but the colored people turned out *en masse*. . . . On through the streets of the rebel city passed the column, on through the chief seat of that slave power, tottering to its fall. . . . The glory and the triumph of this hour may be imagined, but can never be described. It was one of those occasions which happen but once in a lifetime, to be lived over in memory for ever."

Fort Moultrie, Charleston Harbor. View from inside the fort. Black ink and watercolor drawing on tan paper by [Frank] Vizetelly. 1861

 AUGUST 3 1861: At Hampton Roads, Virginia, an observation balloon (used for reconnaissance) successfully ascends from the deck of a Federal vessel.

Halls Hill, Virginia: . . . I must tell you something about our new camp, for, though we are on the same ground, we have altered the looks of it materially. Each company's tents are in a line, and we have good wide streets between. These are all nicely graded and a trench dug round each tent and on each side of the street. Each side is set out with pine and cedar trees, and many of the tents have arches and bowers of evergreens before the doors. At the head of each street a grand arch is made with the letter of the company or some other device suspended, all made of the evergreen trees and branches. Company E, in the center, has the widest street and a little the nicest arch, as they have the colors.

    . . . I tell you these embellishments make our camp look very nice, and the streets are graded so nicely, and the ground in front of our camp is worn smooth and bare, so we have a splendid parade ground for company or battalion drills.

—Private Oliver Willcox Norton (USA), letter to his sister, December 19, 1861

Camp of the Forty-fourth New York Infantry, near Alexandria, Virginia. 1861–65

{ **AUGUST 4** 1861: A meeting is held in New York to combat intemperance in the Union army. }

Chaplains had served with American armies since the Revolution. But the prospect of incorporating large numbers of clergymen and other religious workers into the vastly expanded armed forces during the Civil War raised questions that many legislators found troubling. This was especially true in the South, where a number of state officials firmly believed that church and state should be strictly separated and that the churches themselves, rather than the government, should be responsible for supporting ministers in the army. Eventually, however, some twenty-three hundred chaplains served in the Union army and more than six hundred in the army of the Confederacy. In addition to their religious duties, chaplains on both sides comforted the wounded and dying, maintained camp libraries, counseled the troubled, cautioned soldiers against vice, and exhorted the faint of heart. In the Union army, chaplains also served as teachers, both to illiterate soldiers and to civilian contrabands (slaves found in, or who fled to, areas that the Union army had captured). Many chaplains, North and South, displayed remarkable courage in battle, often saving the lives of wounded men under fire. Three Union chaplains—Francis B. Hall, Milton L. Haney, and John M. Whitehead—were awarded the Medal of Honor.

Ninth Massachusetts Infantry camp, near Washington, D.C. Photograph by the Mathew Brady Studio, 1861

{ **AUGUST 5** 1864: Union forces under Admiral David G. Farragut defeat Confederates at the battle of Mobile Bay in Alabama. }

We ascertained, about noon, that a large body of the enemy's cavalry was drawn up in the plain and clouds of dust beyond showed that large bodies of troops were coming to the field. General [Stonewall] Jackson soon sent out flanking parties, . . . and we opened artillery on them from the centre. We drove off the cavalry and engaged the infantry and artillery and drove them from the field, although they came near flanking our left and driving it back, but Gen. A. P. Hill coming up routed them in turn. We took some 300 prisoners, one cannon, 12 wagon loads of ammunition and some 3,000 stand of small arms. The General and his whole staff were exposed to the hottest of the fire and all were busy trying to rally the left wing after it fell back, the General appealing to the men to follow him, and he led a body of them to the fight. . . . The cannonade continued until long after dark and was a splendid sight. The enemy left their dead and wounded on the field. The Yankee prisoners cheered Gen. Jackson as he rode past them coming back after the fight.

—Major Jedediah Hotchkiss (CSA), diary entry, August 9, 1862,
describing the battle of Cedar Mountain, Virginia

"August 9, 1862. Second Bull Run. A battery fords a tributary of the Rappahannock on its way to the fighting ground at Cedar Mountain." Photograph by Timothy H. O'Sullivan, August 1862

{ **AUGUST 6** 1811: Judah Philip Benjamin, a U.S. senator and then, successively, the attorney general, secretary of war, and secretary of state of the Confederacy, is born on St. Thomas in the West Indies. }

"A collection of untrained men," wrote Confederate general Richard Taylor, "is neither more nor less than a mob, in which individual courage goes for nothing. . . . Every obstacle creates confusion, speedily converted into panic by opposition." Hordes of untrained men poured into Confederate and Union camps early in the war, and many served under inexperienced or irresponsible officers who were incapable of training them. As the war lengthened, training vastly improved—helped along by a variety of manuals. *The Automaton Regiment* was created in 1863 by the artist, author, lawyer, and former army officer G. Douglas Brewerton to help new Union soldiers understand the basics of army life and battlefield maneuvers. That same year, black regiments were fast being formed, and on December 26, 1863, Federal authorities established the Free Military School for Applicants for the Command of Colored Troops in Philadelphia. The school's curriculum reflected the stringent requirements for officer candidates in the U.S. Colored Troops (all of them white at this time) that made most of these men—with the notable exception of some political appointees—among the best-prepared officers in the United States.

"Posts in line of Battle." Chart in *The Automaton Regiment: Infantry Soldiers' Practical Instructor* (1863)

Teaching the Negro recruits the use of the minie rifle. Wood engraving in *Harper's Weekly,* March 14, 1863

{ AUGUST 7 } **1861:** General John B. Magruder's Confederate troops burn the village of Hampton, Virginia, near Fort Monroe, while operating against General Benjamin F. Butler's Union forces.

KEY.

Posts in line of Battle.

Colonel

Colonel 35 paces in rear of file closers and opposite the centre of the Battalion.

Lt. Colonel

Lieut. Colonel 12 paces in rear of file closers and opposite the centre of the right wing.

Senior Major

Senior Major 12 paces in rear of file closers and opposite the centre of the left wing.

Junior Major

Junior Major 30 paces in rear of file closers and 5 paces to the right of the centre of the Battalion.

Surgeon

Surgeon On the left of the Colonel and 3 paces in his rear

Asst. Surgeon

Asst. Surgeon On the left of the Colonel and 3 paces in his rear.

Adjutant

Adjutant 8 paces in rear of file closers and opposite the right of the Battalion

Quarter Master

Quarter Master On the left of the Colonel and 3 paces in his rear.

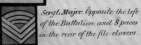

Sergt. Major Opposite the left of the Battalion, and 8 paces in the rear of the file closers.

	Right General Guide
	Left General Guide.
	Captain.
	First Lieutenant.
	Second Lieutenant.
	First Sergeant.
2	Second Sergeant.
3	Third Sergeant.
4	Fourth Sergeant.
	Color Sergeant.
	Color Corporals.
	All other Corporals.
	Groups of Four, or comrades in Battle.
	Drum Major.
	Field Music.
	Posted in rank of file closers. (rear rank.)
	Color and Guard (front rank) left of 5th Company.
	Lines indicating spaces. Centre file closers.

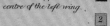
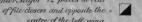

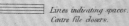
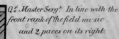

Qr. Master Sergt. In line with the front rank of the field music and 2 paces on its right.

HARPER'S WEEKLY.
A JOURNAL OF CIVILIZATION.

 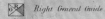

Vol. VII.—No. 324.]   NEW YORK, SATURDAY, MARCH 14, 1863.   [SINGLE COPIES SIX CENTS. $2.50 PER YEAR IN ADVANCE.

Entered according to Act of Congress, in the Year 1863, by Harper & Brothers, in the Clerk's Office of the District Court for the Southern District of New York.

TEACHING THE NEGRO RECRUITS THE USE OF THE MINIE RIFLE.—[See Page 174.]

"I don't believe we can have an army without music," said General Robert E. Lee—an indication of the important roles that music and musicians played in the armies of both sides during the Civil War. In battle, bugle signals were used to direct cavalry and artillery movements, and infantry drummers often risked their lives to "beat the rally," inspiring troops in the midst of combat. In camp, fifers and drummers memorized drum rolls and "calls" that got the men up, assembled them, announced work details, let the men know that the doctor was on duty, and generally regulated daily life. Men convicted of crimes or exhibiting cowardice in the face of the enemy were often drummed out of camp to the playing of the "Rogue's March." In both Union and Confederate forces, regulations decreed that musicians be trained as infantry. And in both, bandsmen served during combat as stretcher-bearers, couriers, and medical assistants—many performing those duties courageously. A number of buglers, drummers, and other musicians were cited for valor throughout the war; twenty-two Union musicians were awarded the Medal of Honor.

Band of the Eighth New York State Militia, Arlington, Virginia (detail). June 1861

An unidentified musician, Second Regulars, U.S. Cavalry. 1860–65 (rephotographed 1961)

{ **AUGUST 8** 1863: In the wake of defeat at Gettysburg, General Robert E. Lee offers to resign as commander of the Army of Northern Virginia, but President Davis rejects the offer three days later. }

Army camps attracted a wide range of visitors and hangers-on. "Camp followers" (civilians who followed armies for profit and employment) included laundresses, illegal whiskey dealers, bakers, barbers, private servants or slaves, and contract laborers. "Vivandières"—women, sometimes wearing their own stylized uniforms—performed various camp and nursing duties, and Union camps attracted thousands of "contrabands" and other refugees. Politicians, religious workers, newspaper reporters and artists, and photographers— either chronicling the war or seeking some profitable portrait-photo business—could often be found in camps. And soldiers were sometimes visited by friends or family members, who would stay for a few days or longer, depending on circumstances. "Are you making preparations to come out here this winter?" Dr. Spencer Glasgow Welch of the Confederate Thirteenth South Carolina Volunteers wrote to his wife on October 25, 1864. "Colonel Hunt will have his wife to come out again, and a great many other officers are arranging for their wives to come on soon. Some of them are here already, but I think it best for you to wait until winter puts a stop to military operations."

Camp of the Thirty-first Pennsylvania, near Washington, D.C. 1862

{ **AUGUST 9** 1862: The Union's Army of Virginia, under General John Pope, clashes with Stonewall Jackson's corps at the battle of Cedar Mountain, Virginia (see August 6). }

"Why don't some one from home write to me?" eighteen-year-old
Confederate lieutenant James B. Mitchell wrote to his Alabama family in 1863. "You must
not forget that I am always as anxious to hear from home as you are to hear from me." A vital
source of information and comfort for Civil War soldiers, the mail could be a source of material
sustenance as well—when it included "care packages" of food or clothing. Soldiers, in turn,
sometimes tucked portions of their pay into the eloquent, opinionated, and often artistically
embellished letters that they dispatched homeward, in what quickly became a veritable flood of
mail: on the Union side alone, some forty-five thousand letters *per day* were dispatched in the
East, and about twice that number in the western theater. At times, postal exchanges between
camp and home front were the means of long-distance debate. In October 1862, for example,
Union sergeant Josiah Chaney's wife urged him to come home rather than reenlist. The sergeant
was inclined to stay, and he explained his reasons: "It is not for you and I, or us & our dear
little ones, alone, that I was and am willing to risk the fortunes of the battle-field, but also for
the sake of the country's millions who are to come after us." (See also October 23.)

Illustrated letter from Union
soldier Charles Wellington Reed
(who received the Medal of
Honor for gallantry during the
battle of Gettysburg, less than
two weeks later). June 20, 1863

*Army Mail leaving Hd.Qts. Post
Office. Army Potomac.* Pencil
and Chinese white drawing on
tan paper by Alfred R. Waud,
c. March 1863

{ **AUGUST 10** 1861: Confederate troops are victorious at the battle of Wilson's Creek, the most significant battle of the Civil War in Missouri. }

Centreville June 20th 1863

Dear Mother

I received your nice[?] letter of the 16th last night having received it in the evening and your money...

Citizens of one of the most literate nations in the world, Civil War soldiers not only wrote letters, articles, and broadsides; they were also avid readers. Newspapers were particularly important. And illustrated periodicals, such as *Frank Leslie's Illustrated News* and *Harper's Weekly*, were so popular that newsboys arriving in camp with copies in their huge saddlebags were almost swept away by the chaos of soldiers attempting to buy one before they were gone. Soldiers were great admirers of good verbal and visual reporting, but they were quick to criticize when a paper was off the mark. Their responses ranged from sharp letters to the editor to grumbles and shakes of the head. "The march to-day . . . lay through a miserable looking country," Union lieutenant colonel Alfred B. McCalmont wrote to his brother in November 1862. "We could hear the drivers whipping and swearing, and sometimes see a wagon stuck fast in the mud. On the way a boy met us with the 'Philadelphia Inquirer,' and there was a great deal of laughing over one of the headings of army news which pithily stated . . . in large capitals, that the army's advance was not impeded by the rain."

Newspaperman. 1860–70

Reading the news—off duty. Rappahannock Station, March 12th 1864. Pencil drawing by Edwin Forbes, March 12, 1864

Newspaper vendor and cart in camp, somewhere in Virginia. Photograph by Alexander Gardner, November 1863

{ **AUGUST 11** 1862: In a bold raid, Confederate guerrillas capture Independence, Missouri. }

Line of Battle, Three miles southeast of Hagerstown, Md. . . . Since the great victory at Gettysburg we have been straining every nerve to overtake and strike the enemy before he leaves Maryland. Thousands of the men are barefoot, and officers, too, but they are bravely struggling on, footsore and hungry, enduring everything without a murmur, so we may finish the war now.

We had one of the greatest battles of the war, and a great victory, too. The old Third Brigade fought like demons, took four hundred prisoners, and laid the rebels in heaps before them. . . . Of thirteen hundred men . . . we lost 359 and no prisoners. . . .

Last night there was one of the grandest sights ever seen. The whole Army of the Potomac advanced two miles in line of battle, column by division, ten lines deep. As far as the eye could reach through fields of wheat, corn and clover that grand line was moving on.

—Private Oliver Willcox Norton (USA), letter to his sister, July 12, 1863

Pursuit of Lee's Army. Scene on the Road near Emmitsburg [in Maryland]. Marching through the Rain. July 7, 1863 (after the battle of Gettysburg). Oil painting by Edwin Forbes, c. 1866

{ **AUGUST 12** **1863:** President Lincoln refuses to give a new command to Major General John A. McClernand, a "political general" whom General Ulysses S. Grant had relieved of corps command at Vicksburg in June. }

"We are sitting by a fine rail fire," Captain William N. Berkeley from Virginia
wrote to his wife during General Robert E. Lee's 1863 invasion of Northern territory. "It seems
to do the men good to burn Yankee rails as they have not left a fence in our part of the country."
A wartime art form, foraging was a major aspect of army life for Confederate and Union soldiers
alike. Confederate foraging became a matter of increasing necessity as the Union adopted a
"hard war" policy that called for the destruction or confiscation of all materials that would be of
use to the Confederate armed forces. Southern soldiers often reacted creatively, as when troopers
under General Wade Hampton rustled twenty-five hundred cattle from under Union noses in
September 1864. But Southern civilians in Union-occupied territory often had little recourse.
"The Yankees commenced upon me after dinner by killing a calf or so, and I think another hog,
and toward night commenced tearing down my field fence all of which, I think, they tore down
to burn," Tennessee clergyman John Newton Waddel noted in his diary late in 1862. "They
will take my yard fence next. I try to put my trust in the Lord, but I do not feel as calm as I
did yesterday."

Stripping a rail fence for fires.
Pencil and Chinese white draw-
ing on brown paper by Alfred R.
Waud, 1862–65

Beef for the army—on the march.
Pencil drawing by Edwin Forbes,
February 4, 1864

{ AUGUST 13 1831: Nat Turner has the last in a series of visions; eight days later, he and other slaves start an insurrection in Southampton County,
Virginia; fifty-five whites and about one hundred blacks are killed before the rebellion is crushed. **}**

Stripping a rail fence for fires   A.R.W.

Rappahannock Station Va
Feb 14th 1864.

Julian Scott (1846–1901) lied about his age and enlisted in the
Third Vermont Infantry at fifteen years old. As a fifer/drummer, he should have been behind
the front lines during combat; however, at Lee's Mill, Virginia, in April 1862, while under fire,
he repeatedly rescued wounded men from a stream where, without his help, they would have
drowned. For that action, he was awarded the Medal of Honor. Scott's wartime sketches became
the bases of vivid postwar paintings, most of them depicting the life of the common soldier. The
Union men pictured in *Sold* have finally reached Confederate lines—only to discover that the
"Confederates" are clothes-draped dummies and the cannons are logs. Such "Quaker guns"
were often used to deceive enemy scouts—particularly by the Confederates, who suffered from
a comparative dearth of artillery. During the first two years of the war, Southern forces captured
more Union cannons than they received from Confederate armories or imports.

Sold. Color lithograph of a
painting by Julian Scott, published by Louis Prang & Co.,
1873

{ **AUGUST 14** **1861:** Union major general John Charles Frémont declares martial law in both the city and the county of St. Louis. }

We have been here so long that camp life seems a little stale to me; I want to be on the road; the excitement of marching, bivouacking, and battles I like, and would be perfectly contented to always live in this way, were it not for the anxiety I feel for Walter and Bob. The possession of Richmond, Vicksburg, and all their seaport towns would not atone for the death of one of them; my patriotism is not that great. I would willingly give my own life to save my country, but not the life of one of my brothers.

Camp of the Eighteenth Penn-
sylvania Cavalry. February 1864

—Lieutenant Eugene Carter (USA), letter to his parents, April 27, 1863

{ **AUGUST 15** 1864: Union forces capture the English-built Confederate cruiser *Georgia* off Lisbon, Portugal—after it was sold to an English shipowner and disarmed. }

Two months before the Union's bitter defeat—and Robert E. Lee's great Civil War triumph—at the battle of Chancellorsville, Virginia (May 1863), Edwin Forbes, "special artist" (see August 25) for *Frank Leslie's Illustrated News*, visited a Union officer's winter quarters in a forward position. Sketched off the line and in relatively cozy surroundings that included the comfort of a blazing fire, these officers and the men they commanded were on a type of duty that, while extremely boring at times, could also prove to be extremely dangerous. Constituting the advance guard for larger forces, pickets were often stationed closer to the enemy's guards than they were to their own units and were thus vulnerable in case of attack. Occasionally they also served as a "reception committee" for refugees and for deserters from the opposing army. Some pickets turned a blind eye to men deserting their own ranks—or became deserters themselves.

On picket—Officers' quarters in log house. Pencil drawing by Edwin Forbes, March 15, 1863

{ **AUGUST 16** 1862: Confederate raiders defeat Union troops in an action near Lone Jack, Missouri, but are then driven off by Northern reinforcements. }

Officially sanctioned civilian provisioners for the Northern and Southern armies, sutlers sold such valued "extras" as newspapers, tobacco, razors, tin utensils, food—and illegal alcohol. Many of these enterprising merchants were criticized for "skinning" the soldier clients who visited their tent- or cabin-housed stores, and the criticism was firmly rooted in fact. But most sutlers were businessmen rather than extortionists. And not a few of them (as well as unsanctioned, freelance peddlers) became victims of mischief themselves. "I have seen a crowd of soldiers gather around an unsuspecting victim," Union soldier David Lane noted in his diary in the summer of 1863, "a few shrewd, witty fellows attract his attention, while others pass out to their accomplices melons, peaches, tomatoes and vegetables, and when the poor fellow discovers the 'game' and gathers up his 'ropes' to drive away, the harness fall [*sic*] to the ground in a dozen pieces, the unguided mule walks off amazed, the cart performs a somersault and the poor peddler picks himself up and gazes on the wreck in silent grief."

A Sutler's Tent near H. Q. Pencil and Chinese white drawing on olive paper by Arthur Lumley, August 1862

{ **AUGUST 17** 1862: Facing starvation on their reservation in southwestern Minnesota, numerous Sioux begin a five-week uprising by killing settlers near Acton (see April 11). }

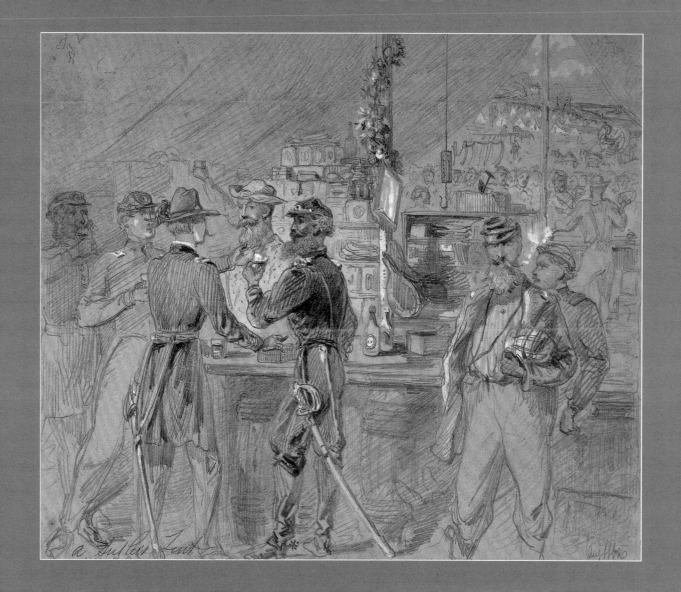

A Sutler's Tent

Thanksgiving day at home, all drills dispensed with, and the men permitted to leave the camp to spend the day, while those who could not afford it, had their Thanksgiving dinner in camp, of Government rations—Bean soup and hard bread.

—Private John W. Jaques (USA), diary entry, Thursday, November 28, 1861

I hope you all may have a happy Christmas, and I wish I had the means of sending some nuts and candy for Matthew and Galla. Many who spent last Christmas with wife and children at home will be missing this time—perhaps to join the happy group in merry Christmas never again. But let us be hopeful. . . . Now, dearest, good-bye till I see you again, or write. A kiss to the children as my Christmas gift.

—Major Elisha Franklin Paxton (CSA), letter to his wife, December 22, 1861

Thanksgiving in Camp. Pencil and Chinese white drawing on tan paper by Alfred R. Waud, November 28, 1861

Santa Claus in camp. Wood engraving signed by Thomas Nast, in *Harper's Weekly*, January 3, 1863

{ **AUGUST 18** 1864: The battle of the Weldon Railroad begins. (This important rail supply line runs south from the Federal siege lines around Petersburg, Virginia.) }

Camp near Fredericksburg. . . . We are now engaged in the laudable occupation of making ourselves comfortable; building log huts to protect ourselves from the cold storms of winter. . . . The eighteen thousand slaughtered husbands and sons who fell at Fredericksburg does not comprise our greatest loss. This whole army, for the time being, is thoroughly demoralized. It has lost all confidence in its leaders—a condition more fatal than defeat. . . . Have we made no advance? Surely we have made blunders, but will we not profit by them? We are learning the art of war—time is required to change a citizen into a soldier. Our officers are being weighed—the light weights cast aside or relegated to their class—and the good work will go on until one is found of size and weight to cope with Lee. 'Tis said, "Great generals are born, not made;" that true greatness is also modest, and does not vaunt itself; but our President is on the lookout for him and will find him—never fear—one who has the genius to plan, the will to do, the nerve to dare.

—Private David Lane (USA), diary entries, December 28–29, 1862

Returning from outpost duty.
Pencil drawing by Edwin Forbes,
c. 1876

{ **AUGUST 19** **1861:** The Confederate Congress agrees to an alliance with Missouri. The state now has two state governments, Federal and Confederate. }

In 1845, Alexander Cartwright published baseball rules for the Knickerbocker Club in New York that were widely adopted by teams around the country. By the time of the Civil War, baseball had replaced the British game of cricket as America's most popular sport. As it became one of the methods for relieving tension and the boredom of camp life during the war, the heretofore "gentleman's game" also became more egalitarian. In one early army versus civilian game, on July 2, 1861, members of the Seventy-first New York Regiment trounced the civilian Washington Nationals, 41–13, on the Ellipse behind the White House. Three weeks later, at First Bull Run, some of the regiment's team became casualties, while others became prisoners of war. This color lithograph indicates that some prisoners also played baseball, at least in one Confederate facility. Established in 1861, the camp at Salisbury, North Carolina, held relatively few prisoners at first; conditions were good, and mortality rates were low. But as the number of prisoners taken by both sides burgeoned, conditions in many camps, including Salisbury, deteriorated—sometimes precipitously.

Union prisoners at Salisbury, N. C. Color lithograph by Otto Boetticher, published by Sarony, Major & Knapp, 1863

{ **AUGUST 20** **1861:** Major General George B. McClellan, who replaced General Irvin McDowell right after the disaster at First Bull Run a month earlier, assumes command of the Union's newly organized Department and Army of the Potomac. }

"Tell cousin Lucy Dutton I would like very much to receive a letter from her and will take great pleasure in corresponding with her," Confederate soldier James W. Duke wrote to an unnamed cousin on August 31, 1864, adding, "if she has no aversion to corresponding with a prisoner of war." With the letter, Duke enclosed a color drawing of the Union's Rock Island, Illinois, prison camp, where he was being held. Located on an island in the Mississippi River, opposite Davenport, Iowa, the camp was widely known for hot, humid summers and bitterly cold winters. Between December 1863 and the summer of 1865, when it closed, 12,400 Confederates were imprisoned there. Some 2,000 died—most of them during an 1864 smallpox epidemic. To fight the tedium of confinement, Duke devoted at least some of his time to fashioning jewelry. "I received your kind letter acknowledging the receipt of the pin," he wrote to his cousin. "I am very glad to hear that you prize it so highly. . . . If you will send me some silver and buttons, I will have you some nice rings made."

Picture of our row of Barracks with a limited portion of the prison. Watercolor and ink drawing by "H. Junius," enclosed in a letter written by James W. Duke at Rock Island, Illinois, August 31, 1864

{ **AUGUST 21** 1863: Confederate guerrillas led by William Quantrill sack Lawrence, Kansas, killing about 150 men and boys and destroying more than $1.5 million in property. }

In January 1864, near Andersonville in south-central Georgia, slave laborers began to erect a stockade for Union prisoners. Officially designated Camp Sumter by the Confederates, Andersonville became the most infamous prison camp of the Civil War. Poor planning quickly resulted in an unhealthy morass: no provisions were made to manage waste disposal; the stream passing through the prison brought waste downstream from guards' camps and the cooking station; and there were no shelters for inmates. Designed to accommodate ten thousand prisoners, the camp held nearly thirty-three thousand by mid-August 1864. A multitude of diseases, exacerbated by malnutrition and exposure, claimed thirteen thousand lives—nearly 30 percent of all Northerners ever held prisoner at the camp. These conditions are now generally regarded as the results of an inept bureaucracy and limited resources. During the war, however, as the situation at the camp became known—and photographs of emaciated prisoners were reproduced and widely circulated—many Northerners believed that the Confederates were deliberately running Andersonville as a death camp. The camp's commander, Captain Henry Wirz, was later arrested, convicted of war crimes, and hanged on November 10, 1865.

Map of Andersonville, Georgia (depicting the prison camp). Print attributed to J. W. Cooper, date unknown

Union soldiers as they appeared on their release from the rebel prisons, from photographs made by order of Congress. Wood engraving in *Frank Leslie's Illustrated Newspaper,* June 18, 1864

{ **AUGUST 22** 1862: In a raid on Catlett's Station, Virginia, Jeb Stuart and his Confederates capture General John Pope's baggage train, including the Union general's papers. }

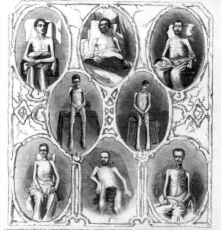

It is rather tough these cold and stormy nights, but a soldier is expected to stand it without flinching—that is duty. Visions of home, and the loved ones there reposing, during these solitary hours, of course spring up in the imagination, and if a tear comes unbidden to the eye, it only shows that in becoming soldiers we do not cease to be men.

—Sergeant Warren H. Freeman (USA), letter to his father, January 19, 1862

I never hear from home now. Home: Is there not magic in the word, poetry in the sound?

—Sergeant Rufus W. Cater (CSA), letter to his cousin, July 30, 1862

"The Soldier's Vision" (sheet-music cover). Color lithograph, Lee & Walker, 1862

Private Andrew F. Skidmore, Mount Vernon Guards, Company E, Seventeenth Virginia Infantry (CSA) (later killed at Yorktown, Virginia). 1861–62

{ **AUGUST 23** 1864: Fort Morgan, in Mobile Bay, Alabama, falls to Union forces after a nearly week-long siege. They now control the port, though not the city of Mobile. }

THE SOLDIER'S VISION.

MUSIC AND WORDS

BY

C. EVEREST.

Philadelphia LEE & WALKER 722 Chesnut St.

The most potent reason, or excuse, for playing cards, and one that seems to satisfy men who are strictly moral, is, "it serves to pass away the time." To most soldiers, when not on duty, time passes heavily. It is impossible to procure reading matter. Men do not always feel like talking. Most men cannot sit down by themselves and indulge in calm reflection—they must have some excitement—consequently, for want of something better, they gather in knots and shuffle cards.

—Private David Lane (USA), diary entry, February 11, 1864

If any member of the Regiment should so far lose sight of the interest and reputation of the service as to be caught horse racing or gaiming [*sic*] while on duty . . . the same shall be punished by court martial or otherwise.

—Colonel McCord [first name unknown] (CSA), excerpt from an order of June 17, 1863

General Patrick's punishment for gamblers. Pencil and Chinese white drawing on olive paper by Alfred R. Waud, October 1863

Officers of the 114th Pennsylvania Infantry playing cards, Petersburg, Virginia. August 1864

{ **AUGUST 24** **1862:** Near the Azores, about eight hundred miles west of Portugal, the Confederacy commissions the newly armed and supplied cruiser CSS *Alabama*, a few weeks after its departure from a shipyard in Liverpool, England, on a "test run"; under the command of Raphael Semmes, it will become the South's most effective commerce raider. }

The North's hardy band of "special artists" portrayed Civil War combat and army life with a verve and immediacy that the ponderous cameras of the day could not match. The artists' adventurous lives, according to one of them, Theodore Davis, involved "total disregard for personal safety and comfort; an owl-like propensity to sit up all night and a hawky style of vigilance during the day . . . [as well as] willingness to ride any number of miles [on] horseback for just one sketch." Davis was wounded twice as he sketched campaigns from Virginia through Vicksburg to Sherman's march through Georgia. The most prolific of the North's special artists, however, was Alfred R. Waud (whose brother, William, was also an artist-reporter). The only Northern special artist to carry a pistol along with his sketchbooks, pencils, and paints, Waud followed the Army of the Potomac in all its major campaigns—and toured the postwar South drawing vivid scenes of turbulent Reconstruction. James Walker, who was primarily an "easel artist" known for his carefully researched paintings, completed his celebrated panoramic oil, *Battle of Gettysburg: Repulse of Longstreet's Assault, July 3, 1863*, shortly after the war.

Theodore Davis (1840–1894) and James Walker (1818–1889), c. 1864

Alfred R. Waud (1828–1891). c. 1861–65

{ **AUGUST 25** 1863: Four days after Confederate guerrilla William Quantrill's bloody raid on Lawrence, Kansas, Federals force some twenty thousand people in four Missouri counties from their homes, which are then burned along with their crops. }

An immense amount of heroism among the wives of soldiers passed unnoticed, or was taken as a matter of course. For the soldier, he had his comrades about him, shoulder to shoulder. He had excitement. He had praise, if he did well. He had honorable mention, and pitying tears, if he fell nobly striving. But alas for his wife . . . who in giving her husband to her country gave everything; who had no friend to say "Well done!" as the lagging weeks of suspense crept on, and she stood bravely at her post keeping want and starvation at bay; . . . who shrouded her eyes from the possible future of her children should her strength give out under the pressure of want and anxiety. . . . This silent army of heroines was too often forgotten.

—Mary A. Livermore (1820–1905), U.S. Sanitary Commission worker, excerpt from her memoirs, *My Story of the War* (1887)

Marriage at the camp of the 7th New Jersey Volunteers, Army of the Potomac, Va. Pencil and Chinese white drawing on tan paper by Alfred R. Waud, March 18, 1863

{ **AUGUST 26** 1862: The Confederates in northern Virginia begin the Second Bull Run (Manassas) campaign. }

Well, [General Ambrose] Burnside has moved again, and got stuck in the mud. That is the short of it. The long of it was the five days it took us to get six miles and back to camp. It beat all the Peninsula mud I ever saw, and demonstrated the falsity of Burnside's theory that if twelve horses couldn't draw a cannon twenty-four could. The more horses the worse it was.

We got back to our old camps yesterday, and I apprehend we shall stay a while. The army cannot move in this climate in the winter, and perhaps the people will believe now that "Little Mac" [General George B. McClellan] was right in not moving last winter.

—Private Oliver Willcox Norton (USA), letter to his sister, January 25, 1863

Why the Army of the Potomac doesn't move, comprising four sketches: *The Relief, Going to Camp, Difficulties of Teaming, King Mud in Camp*. Pencil and Chinese white drawings on green paper by Alfred R. Waud, c. January 1863?

{ **AUGUST 27** 1809: Hannibal Hamlin, U.S. vice president under Abraham Lincoln, March 1861–March 1865, is born in Paris Hill, Maine. }

The Relief   Going to Camp

Difficulties of Moving

Kives Found in Convivial

Some mornings I would go along the picket line, and I could see the rebels on the opposite side of the river. . . . Sometimes one or two would desert to us, saying, they "had no negroes to fight for." Others would shoot across at our picket, but as the river was so wide there was never any damage done. . . .

I learned to handle a musket very well while in the regiment, and could shoot straight and often hit the target. I assisted in cleaning the guns and used to fire them off, to see if the cartridges were dry, before cleaning and reloading, each day. I though this great fun. I was also able to take a gun all apart, and put it together again.

—Susie King Taylor, a former slave who became a nurse, laundress, and teacher with the First South Carolina Volunteers (USA), an African American regiment, excerpt from her memoirs, 1902

Headquarters, U.S. Fifth Army Corps, Harrison's Landing, James River, Virginia. (The African American woman standing at right is identified on the photograph's border—not shown—as "Mrs. Fairfax.") 1862

{ **AUGUST 28** 1861: Union forces capture Fort Hatteras, North Carolina, on the second day of bombardment, thus sealing off a significant blockade-running route. }

Our company have been on picket duty for the last two days of the week, the lines being on the bank of the river. The enemy are disposed to be very friendly, and try frequently to exchange papers with us, but we are not allowed to hold any communications with them. The day that I was on picket, two men came down to the river, somewhat intoxicated, and invited some of the Yankees over. . . . I was a little afraid the General might find it out, as the orders were so strict in regard to their crossing, and I can tell you I made the Yankee boys get back to their own side in a hurry.

—Lieutenant Richard Lewis (CSA), letter to his mother, January 18, 1863

Pickets trading between the lines. Drawing by Edwin Forbes, c. 1876

The lines here are so close the men talk with each other, and have agreed to warn each other when the officers come around. At other times it is more like visiting than anything else. It is terribly hot in the rifle pits. I made the rounds to-day, and had a chat with a middle-aged Johnnie. He said we were not at all like they had been told, and there were some who believed we had horns on our heads, and had feet like cattle. Now that they know better they don't want to fight us, and will only do so when obliged to.

—Lieutenant Lawrence Van Alstyne (USA), diary entry, June 18, 1863

{ **AUGUST 29** **1863:** In Charleston Harbor, South Carolina, the Southern submersible *H. L. Hunley* sinks on a test run; five men are lost, while three others escape. Repeatedly raised and then sunk during tests (see October 15), it will go down for the last time, on February 17, 1864, after destroying a Union ship with a torpedo, or mine, protruding from its prow. }

Pickets trading.

Recently, while on picket guard, during the stillness of midnight, . . . I heard a slight rustle among the leaves, and on turning my head in the direction from whence the sound came, I perceived a slight movement . . . and felt quite sure that some object must be approaching; the first impulse was that it might be a cowardly rebel creeping up, rifle in hand, to pick off his man. And though usually insensible to fear, still I will admit that I felt the cold chills, and a slight perspiration coming on; but I did not leave my seat, only brought my rifle to the "make ready," and in a moment after a great black dog sprang over the fence quite near me, and went on his way regardless of my presence. I congratulated myself in that I did not blaze away at this imaginary danger and thereby alarm the whole camp, as is often done by the raw recruit when there is much less cause.

—Sergeant Warren H. Freeman (USA), letter to his father, July 5, 1862

The Chickahominy—Sumners Upper Bridge. Watercolor drawing by William McIlvaine, 1862

{ **AUGUST 30** 1862: The second battle of Bull Run (Manassas), like the first about a year earlier, ends in defeat for the Union. }

Who would have dreamed in '61 that those of us who started out to finish the war in the course of a three month' service, would still be in the field three years afterwards, with the task still unaccomplished? . . . Over one half of our original number has disappeared from the muster rolls; killed in action; died of wounds, of disease, of fatigue and exposure, or perhaps resigned, unable to stand in the constant shock of arms. This old state of Virginia has become a vast cemetery, in which thousands of once bright and ambitious men belonging to the army of the Potomac now lie scattered in its shady nooks or somber woods. . . . Amongst the survivors, the excitement and enthusiasm of early days has long since passed away, but the resolve still remains, and until the work is done this army will never lay down its arms.

—Major Josiah Marshall Favill (USA), diary entry, January 1, 1864

Federal encampment on the Pamunkey River, Cumberland Landing, Virginia. May 1862

{ AUGUST 31 1822: Fitz-John Porter (USA) is born in Portsmouth, New Hampshire. **}**

SEPTEMBER: WAR IN THE WEST

Action in the western theater, between the western slope of the Appalachian Mountains and the Mississippi River, as well as the trans-Mississippi theater, west of the river, brought Ulysses S. Grant and his most trusted and capable subordinate, William Tecumseh Sherman, to national attention. George H. Thomas, James B. McPherson, William Rosecrans, and Don Carlos Buell were other prominent Union generals in what was then called the West. Braxton Bragg, Albert Sidney Johnston, Joseph E. Johnston, Nathan Bedford Forrest, John Bell Hood, and Edmund Kirby Smith are leading Confederate generals who served there.

Wilson's Creek, Shiloh (Pittsburg Landing), Stones River (Murfreesboro), two Union campaigns against Vicksburg, Chickamauga, the Confederate siege of Union-occupied Chattanooga, and the battles that broke that siege are among the major clashes in the West. Once the Union secured Chattanooga, Tennessee, it became an important center of logistical support during Sherman's relentless campaign into the Southern heartland. This campaign forced the surrender of Atlanta and eventually led to the near destruction of the Confederate Army of Tennessee at Nashville by Union troops under George H. Thomas, while Sherman took Savannah, Georgia, and moved into South and North Carolina.

With the fall of Vicksburg, Mississippi, in July 1863, Southern armed forces west of the Mississippi were cut off from the rest of the Confederacy. The Confederate commander in the

{  **SEPTEMBER 1** 1864: Confederate troops rapidly evacuate Atlanta, destroying munitions, some railroad equipment, and other supplies that they had no time to take with them. }

The Battle of Pittsburg, Tenn. April 7th, 1862. Also called the battle of Shiloh, this two-day clash resulted in more casualties than all other previous U.S. wars combined. Hand-colored lithograph, Currier & Ives, 1862

theater, General Edmund Kirby Smith, used some creative methods, such as providing cotton to Mexico in exchange for supplies, to maintain his military department. Supply difficulties in what became known, among some, as "Kirby Smithdom" were exacerbated by the influx of a host of Southern refugees—who found comparatively little North-South conflict in the area but, instead, were confronted with raids by increasingly aggressive Comanche and Kiowa war parties.

Guerrilla warfare, which occurred in all theaters, was rampant in the West. In this irregular conflict, Confederate partisan rangers and guerrilla and "counter-guerrilla" bands on both sides raided, looted, and generally harassed each other, army supply and communications facilities, and civilian settlements. Formed spontaneously, or under the Confederate Partisan Ranger Act (April 21, 1862) or the general orders of various military department commanders, the bands ranged from military organizations with strict rules of conduct (such as John Singleton Mosby's Forty-third Virginia Battalion, better known as "Mosby's Rangers") to murderous outlaw gangs (such as the men who rode with Missouri's Bloody Bill Anderson).

In Alabama in 1862, Colonel John Beatty's Union troops were frequent targets of Confederate irregulars, apparently with the support of local citizens. "I said to them that bushwhacking must cease," he wrote in his diary in May. "Hereafter every time the telegraph wire was cut we would burn a house; every time a train was fired upon we should hang a man; and we would continue to do this until every house was burned and every man hanged between Decatur and Bridgeport. . . . We proposed to hold the citizens responsible for these cowardly assaults, and if they did not drive these bushwhackers from amongst them, we should make them more uncomfortable than they would be in hell."

The Confederates who clashed with Ulysses S. Grant's Union soldiers at the brutal battle of Shiloh, Tennessee, were initially led by Albert Sidney Johnston, commander of the South's huge Western Department and a veteran soldier noted for his integrity. Constantly facing forces superior to his own, Johnston had lost Forts Henry and Donelson and then was forced to withdraw from Nashville. When these reverses caused some in Richmond to demand that he be replaced, President Davis refused, saying, "If Sidney Johnston is not a general, I have none." "I had known Johnston slightly in the Mexican war and later as an officer in the regular army," Grant later wrote in his memoirs. "His contemporaries at West Point, and officers generally who came to know him personally later and who remained on our side, expected him to prove the most formidable man to meet that the Confederacy would produce." Grant's postwar reflections, however, led him to judge that Johnston had been "vacillating and undecided in his actions. . . . I do not question [his] personal courage . . . , or his ability. But he did not win the distinction predicted for him by many of his friends." Wounded in the leg at Shiloh, Johnston bled to death on the first day of the battle. P. G. T. Beauregard, whose bombardment of Fort Sumter had begun the Civil War a year earlier, then assumed command.

Albert Sidney Johnston (1803–1862). 1860–62

Gen. Ulysses S. Grant (1822–1885). Color lithograph by Dominique C. Fabronius, 1867

{ **SEPTEMBER 2** 1864: Union forces under Major General William T. Sherman occupy Atlanta. }

Union forces occupied the important railroad hub of Corinth, Mississippi, after Confederate forces evacuated the city in May 1862. On October 3–4, Corinth was attacked by twenty-two thousand Confederates under Major Generals Sterling Price and Earl Van Dorn, who hoped to retake the city as a base for operations into Tennessee. Heat and water shortages—along with three earthquake tremors—increased the challenge to the Confederate troops as they assaulted General William Rosecrans's twenty-three thousand Union troops, but the Southerners pushed the defenders back to their interior line. The Federal troops regrouped, however, and held firm against renewed assault. On the second day, fighting was particularly intense around Battery Robinett, which Confederate troops led by Colonel William P. Rogers briefly overwhelmed; then a counterattack, in which Rogers was killed, retook the Union battery. A brief, unsupported thrust into Corinth that same day resulted in more Southern casualties, as Confederates who had entered the city were caught in a cross fire. Those who could retreat did so, and the main Confederate force soon withdrew, leaving Corinth in Federal hands. Some five thousand Union and Confederate soldiers were killed or wounded in the battle.

Confederate dead in front of Battery Robinett, Corinth, Mississippi, the morning after the attack. Photograph by N. Brown (?), October 4, 1862

{ **SEPTEMBER 3** **1861:** A Confederate force commanded by Leonidas Polk moves from Tennessee into Kentucky, ending that state's proclaimed neutrality in the war (see November 29). }

When Admiral David G. Farragut's naval squadron fought its way past defending fortresses and captured New Orleans (see May 11 and 12), most citizens of the Confederacy's largest city were deeply distressed (as were people throughout the South). But other local residents were deeply relieved to have the Stars and Stripes flying again from the city's flagpoles. Prominent among them was Mrs. Nellie Maria Dewey Taylor, a native of New York State whose family had moved to New Orleans before the war. A teacher, she had been dismissed from her school for unequivocally expressing Unionist sympathies. ("I am, always have been, and ever shall be, for the Union," she reportedly said.) After facing down a mob that threatened to burn her house, she maintained her quiet devotion to the Union under pressures that led her son to return from safe haven at a school in the North and enlist in the Confederate army so the ill treatment would end. (He served with distinction and survived the war.) With the city back in Federal hands, Mrs. Taylor returned to teaching and also became a ministering angel, assisting the sick and wounded in Union hospitals.

The Battle of New Orleans.
Color lithograph, Lee & Walker, 1862–65

David G. Farragut (1801–1870). Photograph by the Brady National Photographic Art Gallery, 1860–65

Mrs. Nellie Maria Dewey Taylor. Illustration in *Woman's Work in the Civil War: A Record of Heroism, Patriotism and Patience* (1867)

{ **SEPTEMBER 4** **1864:** John Hunt Morgan, a Confederate cavalry commander and raider renowned in the South, is shot and killed in a Federal raid on Greeneville, Tennessee. }

On January 9, 1863, as the struggle for control of the Mississippi River continued, thirty-two thousand Federal troops commanded by Major General John McClernard and a supporting naval squadron under Commander David Dixon Porter reached the Confederate bastion of Fort Hindman on the Arkansas River, about fifty miles from its confluence with the Mississippi. Constructed in 1862 with the labor of some five hundred slaves, the fort, and the Confederate garrison's initial stout defense on January 10, proved a formidable obstacle for McClernand's soldiers. Fierce bombardment from the naval squadron was the decisive factor in the Confederates' surrender the next day, yielding five thousand prisoners, a number of guns, and large stores of supplies to the Union. "I was at first disposed to disapprove of this move as an unnecessary side movement having no especial bearing upon the work before us," Ulysses S. Grant wrote in his postwar memoirs. "But when the result was understood I regarded it as very important. Five thousand Confederate troops left in the rear might have caused us much trouble and loss of property while navigating the Mississippi." Coming only four weeks after the Union's terrible defeat at Fredericksburg, Virginia, the success at Fort Hindman also helped boost morale in the North.

Bombardment and capture of Fort Hindman, Arkansas Post, Ark. Jany. 11th 1863. Hand-colored lithograph, Currier & Ives, 1863–1907

{ **SEPTEMBER 5** 1863: Under pressure from the United States, the British government decides not to deliver two ironclads, called the "Laird Rams," that are under construction for the Confederates. }

The first prisoners taken in the Civil War were U.S. Army regulars assigned to the Texas frontier who were compelled to surrender after that state seceded in February 1861. In 1863, Confederates established Camp Ford at Tyler, Texas. The largest prisoner-of-war camp west of the Mississippi River, the unsheltered stockade housed some six thousand Federal soldiers during its two years of operation. A good supply of fresh water and steady rations of cornmeal and beef contributed to one of the lowest mortality rates of any camp. Very few prisoners escaped from Camp Ford, but, as in other theaters of operation, a number were exchanged for Confederate personnel. Regular man-for-man prisoner exchanges slowed to a trickle between fall 1863 and February 1865, however, chiefly because of the Confederacy's refusal to exchange black Union soldiers or their white officers. "Exchanging man for man and officer for officer, with the exception the rebels make," Secretary of War Edwin M. Stanton wrote in November 1863, "is a substantial abandonment of the colored troops and their officers . . . and would be a shameful dishonor to the Government bound to protect them."

Noncommissioned officers of the Nineteenth Iowa Infantry, exchanged prisoners from Camp Ford, Texas, photographed at New Orleans on their arrival. 1863–65

{ **SEPTEMBER 6** 1819: William Starke Rosecrans (USA) is born in Delaware County, Ohio. }

Louisiana quickly became a fertile ground for guerrilla warfare, as well as combat between Union and Confederate regulars, after Union forces occupied part of the Confederate state in May 1862. On September 27 in New Orleans, the First Regiment of the Louisiana Native Guards, U.S. Army, comprising free black Louisianians and former slaves, became the first black regiment to be officially mustered into U.S. military service; it was rapidly followed by the Second and Third Native Guards. These regiments initially included black officers (a policy that was quickly reversed; see June 8). Among them was Captain André Cailloux (1825–1863), a former slave who had become a prosperous free man. Literate, fluent in both English and French, Cailloux proved to be an exceptional—and exceptionally courageous—leader. During the determined but unsuccessful assault on the Confederate bastion of Port Hudson that occurred on May 27, 1863, he continued to fight after he was wounded, until he was killed in the battle. The valor of Cailloux and the other black soldiers who fought at Port Hudson—some 20 percent became casualties—was widely reported in the North and became a major factor in the growing acceptance of black troops (see also September 13).

"Wilson Chinn, a branded slave from Louisiana. . . ." Photograph by Kimball, 1863

Pickets of the First Louisiana "Native Guard," guarding the New Orleans, Opelousas and Great Western Railroad. Wood-cut illustration in *Frank Leslie's Illustrated Newspaper*, March 7, 1863

{ **SEPTEMBER 7** 1864: General William T. Sherman orders civilians in Atlanta to evacuate the city so that he might more easily feed and supply his Union army. }

Purchased in New Orleans Dec 1863
DeBendd Keim

FRANK LESLIE'S
ILLUSTRATED
NEWSPAPER

No. 388—Vol. XV.]   NEW YORK, MARCH 7, 1863.   [PRICE 5 CENTS.

SCENES IN LOUISIANA.

Our Artist has sent us some sketches which illustrate, in a striking degree, the novel phases of life, both military and civil, which the present struggle is evolving. The fact of black regiments being actively employed is not a novelty, since they have been for some time part of the British military system, which, with its usual com-

mon sense, avails itself of every aid in the pursuit of its objects. Our Artist says that among the cypress swamps of Louisiana negro soldiers are invaluable, and accompanies his sketch of the picket of the First Louisiana native troops, guarding the New Orleans, Opelousas and Great Western Railroad, with some remarks which we quote:

"In this swamp in the wilderness the 'nigger soldier' are eminently useful. The melancholy solitude, with the spectral cypress trees, which

seem to stand in silent despair, like nature's sentinels waiting in the air wreaths of gray funereal moss, to warn all human beings of the latent pestilence around, though unendurable to our soldiers of the North, seems no objection to these sable soldiers, for the swampy forest has no terrors to them, impervious to miasma, they are only the home of the coon, the possum and the sugarhouse, so that with 'de gun del Massa Sam gib um,' they have around them all the essential elements of colored happiness, 'except hollen' anxiety.'"

The Old Slave Laws.

In strange illegitimations of the use to which the colored race may be put, the new régime has empowered Provost Marshal Col. French to put in force the old Slave Laws of Louisiana. Our Artist says: "The first result of the Emancipation Proclamation has been attended with a paradoxical effect, namely, a revival of the old Slave Laws of Louisiana. On the evening in question, all the negroes found in the streets after nine o'clock with-

PICKET OF THE FIRST LOUISIANA "NATIVE GUARD" GUARDING THE NEW ORLEANS, OPELOUSAS AND GREAT WESTERN RAILROAD—FROM A SKETCH BY OUR SPECIAL ARTIST.

On July 17, 1862, Major General Thomas C. Hindman, commander of the Confederates' Trans-Mississippi Department, issued General Order No. 17, which included a call for citizens "to organize themselves into independent companies . . . to cut off federal pickets, scouts, foraging parties, and trains, and to kill pilots and others on gunboats and transports, attacking them day and night." "Persons acting as guerrillas . . . ," Union major general Ulysses S. Grant declared that same month, "are not entitled to the treatment of prisoners of war." Partisans and guerrillas had become such a problem that Union general-in-chief Henry W. Halleck called upon legal scholar Francis Lieber for an informed opinion regarding guerrilla warfare. The resulting essay, *Guerrilla Parties Considered with Reference to the Laws and Usages of War*, distinguished between partisans (authorized troops entitled to due process of law) and "self-constituted guerrillas" ("brigands" and "assassins" entitled to no more than summary execution). This essay was the genesis of General Order No. 100, issued on April 24, 1863. Also known as the Lieber Code, the order was the world's first formal guideline for the conduct of armies in the field.

A jerilla [guerrilla] / a deserter. Pencil drawing by Alfred R. Waud, c. 1863

Thomas C. Hindman (1828–1868). 1861–65

Henry W. Halleck (1815–1872). Photograph by John A. Scholten, 1860–65

{ **SEPTEMBER 8** **1863:** A small group of Confederates repulses an attack by four Union gunboats and transports at Sabine Pass, on the Texas-Louisiana border. }

The three-day battle of Stones River (Murfreesboro), Tennessee, on December 31, 1862, and January 2–3, 1863, pitted some forty-seven thousand men of the Union's Army of the Cumberland, under the command of Major General William S. Rosecrans, against General Braxton Bragg's thirty-eight-thousand-man Confederate Army of Tennessee. The bitter clash, resulting in about twenty-four thousand Union and Confederate casualties (more on the Northern side), was regarded as a Union "win"—badly needed after the North's rending defeat on December 13, 1862, at Fredericksburg, Virginia. On January 1, there was a lull in the fighting. "Both armies want rest," Union brigadier general John Beatty noted in his diary, "both have suffered terribly. Here and there little parties are engaged burying the dead, which lie thick around us. . . . A little before sundown all hell seems to break loose again, and for about an hour the thunder of the artillery and volleys of musketry are deafening; but it is simply the evening salutations of the combatants. The darkness deepens; the weather is raw and disagreeable. Fifty thousand hungry men are stretched beside their guns again on the field. Fortunately I have a piece of raw pork and a few crackers in my pocket. No food ever tasted sweeter."

Battle of Stone [sic] River, near Murfreesborough, Tenn, Dec. 31, 62. Jan 2–3, 1863. . . . Color lithograph, Kurz & Allison, 1891

{ SEPTEMBER 9 } **1863:** Threatened by Union general William S. Rosecrans's Army of the Cumberland, Confederate general Braxton Bragg withdraws his Army of Tennessee from Chattanooga, Tennessee, and the Federal army occupies part of the town while pressing ahead—spreading itself thin in the mountainous area to the south.

It seems strange how our aversion to seeing suffering is overcome in war,—how we are able to see the most sickening sights, such as men with their limbs blown off and mangled by the deadly shells, without a shudder; and instead of turning away, how we hurry to assist in alleviating their pain, bind up their wounds, and press the cool water to their parched lips, with feelings only of sympathy and pity.

—Susie King Taylor, laundress and nurse with the First South Carolina
Volunteers (USA), excerpt from her memoirs, 1902

The Night after the Battle.
Hand-colored lithograph,
Currier & Ives, 1862

The last day of '64, and much coveted peace seemingly as distant as ever. If it were not for the knowledge that there is an end to all things, and that some day there will be an end to this, it would be unbearable. The past year has equaled any of its predecessors for carnage and bloodshed. Our land is drenched with the blood of martyrs!

—Kate Cumming, nurse with the Army of Tennessee
(CSA), journal entry, December 31, 1864

{ **SEPTEMBER 10** 1836: Joseph (Fightin' Joe) Wheeler (CSA) is born in Augusta, Georgia.
1863: Confederates evacuate Little Rock, the capital of Arkansas. }

We were attacked here on June 7, . . . by a brigade of Texas troops about 2,500 in number. We had about 600 men to withstand them—500 of them negroes. . . . Our regiment had about 300 men in the fight. . . . I never felt more grieved and sick at heart than when I saw how my brave soldiers had been slaughtered. . . . I never more wish to hear the expression, "the niggers won't fight." Come with me 100 yards from where I sit, and I can show you the wounds that cover the bodies of 16 as brave, loyal and patriotic soldiers as ever drew bead on a Rebel. . . . The enemy charged us so close that we fought with our bayonets, hand to hand. . . . It was a horrible fight, the worst I was ever engaged in—not even excepting Shiloh. The enemy cried "No quarter!" but some of them were very glad to take it when made prisoners. . . . What few men I have left seem to think much of me because I stood up with them in the fight. I can say for them that I never saw a braver company of men in my life. . . . They fought and died defending the cause that we revere.

—Captain M. M. Miller (USA), letter to his aunt, published in the *New Orleans Union*, July 14, 1863, describing his experience with the Ninth Regiment of Louisiana Volunteers of African Descent at the battle of Milliken's Bend, Louisiana (June 7, 1863)

Freedom for all—6th United States Colored Troops. Photographic print on carte de visite mount, c. 1864

Connecticut's Twenty-ninth Volunteer Infantry Regiment (Colored), Beaufort, South Carolina. Photograph by Sam A. Cooley, 1864

{ **SEPTEMBER 11** **1861:** General Robert E. Lee begins the five-day Cheat Mountain campaign in western Virginia, which ends in a Confederate withdrawal that mars Lee's reputation for a few months. }

The need for intelligence regarding Confederate movements and intentions prompted Major General Ulysses S. Grant to appoint one of his division commanders, Major General Grenville Dodge, to head the intelligence-gathering activities in the western theater. Dodge had already proved himself a singularly adept "spymaster." In 1862, while serving in Missouri, he had formed a "Corps of Scouts" that gathered valuable information for the Union's Army of the Southwest. Carefully trained by Dodge, these scouts largely avoided the miscalculations and exaggeration of Confederate troop strength that characterized Allan Pinkerton's operations in the East. For Grant, Dodge established a highly effective and widespread network of more than one hundred spies whose identities were carefully concealed (though a number were discovered). Extreme caution was his hallmark: he sent information, in code, only by messenger—avoiding the telegraph, which he knew could be tapped (see March 24).

Secret Service by Wm. Gillette. Poster for a spy drama set in the Civil War. Color lithograph, Strobridge Lith. Co., 1896

Grenville M. Dodge (1831–1916). Photograph by the Brady National Photographic Art Gallery, 1860–65

{ **SEPTEMBER 12** 1818: Richard Jordan Gatling, inventor of the first machine gun (Gatling gun) for use in the Civil War, is born in Hertford County, North Carolina. }

SECRET SERVICE

BY Wm. Gillette

"It Looks Like A Plot On Our Telegraph Lines!"

The enemy opened a blistering fire of shell, canister, grape, and musketry. . . . At every pace, the column was thinned by the falling dead and wounded. . . . No matter how gallantly the men behaved, no matter how bravely they were led, it was not in the course of things that this gallant brigade should take these works by charge. Yet charge after charge was ordered. . . . The last charge was made about one o'clock. At this juncture, Capt. Callioux [*sic*] was seen with his left arm dangling by his side,—for a ball had broken it above the elbow,—while his right hand held his unsheathed sword gleaming in the rays of the sun; and his hoarse, faint voice was heard cheering on his men. A moment more, and the brave and generous Callioux was struck by a shell, and fell far in advance of his company. . . . Seeing it to be a hopeless effort, . . . the troops were called off. . . . The self-forgetfulness, the undaunted heroism, and the great endurance of the negro, as exhibited that day, created a new chapter in American history for the colored man.

—William Wells Brown, excerpt from *The Negro in the American Rebellion* (1867), describing the Union assault on Port Hudson, Louisiana (May 27, 1863), six weeks before the Confederate bastion finally surrendered (see also May 23, September 7)

Port Hudson from the opposite bank of the river and *The Union forces entering the breast-works to take possession of Port Hudson, July 9, 1863.* Wood engravings in *Harper's Weekly,* August 8, 1863

{ **SEPTEMBER 13** 1863: Southern cavalry seize twenty crewmen of USS *Rattler* who are attending church at Rodney, Mississippi. }

"General Grant is still knocking for admittance at the 'Gates of Jericho,'" Union private David Lane wrote in his diary in the summer of 1863, referring to the siege of Vicksburg, Mississippi. "Were I to credit what I hear, . . . I would believe he has already made the seventh circuit of that doomed city with his terrible ram's horn in full blast, and now . . . has paused on a 'commanding eminence' to witness the final consummation of his plans. But the continuous thundering of his artillery and the occasional rattle of musketry convince me that, in these latter days, the tumbling down of formidable walls is not so easily accomplished as in the olden times. . . . The whole country for fifteen miles around Vicksburg is little less than a fortification." After Vicksburg surrendered at last, on July 4, and Port Hudson fell five days later, the North controlled the entire Mississippi River. The Confederacy's leading generals did not view this as a tremendous logistical setback, as few supplies or Confederate troops crossed the river and controlling it did not provide the North with important new lines of operation. But, as President Davis understood, it was a tremendous blow to Southern morale and cast a heavy shadow on the South's hope that the Confederacy would achieve victory soon. (See also May 17, July 20–22.)

Quarters of General John A. Logan's Union division in the trenches in front of Vicksburg, Mississippi. 1861–65

{ **SEPTEMBER 14** 1862: Union forces push Confederates back at the battles of South Mountain and Crampton's Gap, Maryland. }

The Metropolitan came along on its way from Vicksburg and took us off. It is said General Grant and staff are on board. I am looking out for General Grant, for I have a great curiosity to see him. . . . I have enquired out all those [officers] that make the biggest show and none of them were him. . . . I finally gave it up and went up on the hurricane deck. . . . A solitary soldier, with nothing on him to tell of rank, had his feet cocked up on the rail and I joined him. He asked if I knew whose fine place it was we were passing, and just then an officer came after him. . . .

[Upon reaching New Orleans,] after supper we went up to the St. Charles and found it crammed with army officers and city officials, and that General Grant was among them. . . . I worked my way in, determined not to miss this chance, and imagine my astonishment when I saw it was the fellow I had sat beside on the upper deck of the Metropolitan. A couple of small stars on his shoulder was his only mark of rank. Of all the men I saw on the Metropolitan he was the last one I should have called General Grant.

—Lieutenant Lawrence Van Alstyne (USA), diary entries, September 2 and 3, 1863

Levee and steamboats, Vicksburg, Mississippi. Photograph by William Redish Pywell, February 1864

{ **SEPTEMBER 15** 1862: Stonewall Jackson's Confederates capture Harpers Ferry, Virginia, taking about twelve thousand prisoners. }

Placed in command of the Confederate Department of East Tennessee in early 1862, West Point graduate Edmund Kirby Smith was victorious at the battle of Richmond, Kentucky, on August 30–September 1, during the Confederate invasion of that state. In 1863, he was named commander of the Trans-Mississippi Department—which was cut off from the rest of the Confederacy less than six months later, when the Union gained complete control of the Mississippi River. Smith oversaw the successful defense against the Union's 1864 Red River campaign, led by former Speaker of the U.S. House of Representatives Nathaniel P. Banks, in cooperation with Rear Admiral David Dixon Porter, who commanded the naval contingent. From March through May, this joint expedition sought to block the flow of supplies from Shreveport, Louisiana, the site of Smith's headquarters, into Texas. After some initial successes, Banks's progress slowed. On April 8, his troops were defeated by eight thousand Confederates under Major General Richard Taylor at the battle of Mansfield (Sabine Crossroads), south of Shreveport, and Banks began to pull back—continuing despite his defeat of Taylor's Confederates at nearby Pleasant Hill the next day. The Red River expedition ended in failure.

Edmund Kirby Smith (1824–1893). 1860–65

Nathaniel Prentiss Banks (1816–1894). 1861

{ **SEPTEMBER 16** 1862: Preparing for an imminent Union attack, General Robert E. Lee gathers his Confederate forces and forms lines along Antietam Creek, near Sharpsburg, Maryland. }

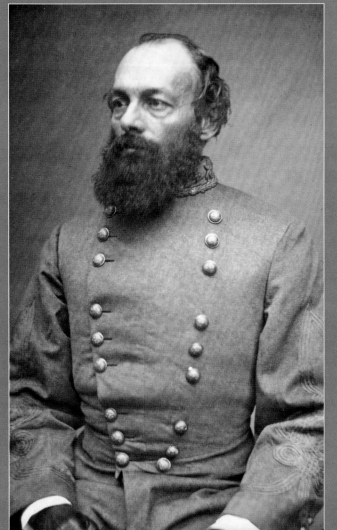

"The cavalry constitute the eyes and ears of the army." Lieutenant General Daniel H. Hill told his Confederate troops in 1863. "The safety of the entire command depends upon their vigilance and the faithfulness of their reports." Because of the range and accuracy of Civil War weapons, cavalry engaged in few sweeping frontal assaults. Intelligence gathering, protecting their army's flanks from enemy approach, and presenting a screen against the reconnaissance of the other side's cavalry were among the major functions of mounted forces. The information that cavalry gathered could be quickly transmitted by telegraph, which both sides used extensively (see also March 24). The Union employed the larger telegraph net, comprising commercial telegraph companies, the Military Telegraph Service, and, for the first two years of the war, the Signal Corps Field Telegraph. Signal Corps telegraphers used the Beardslee telegraphic device, pictured here, which transmitted messages by way of a dial. Less reliable than the more common key device, the Beardslee was discarded when the Signal Corps telegraph unit came under the supervision of the Military Telegraph Service in late 1863.

Cavalry Orderly, Rappahannock Station. Painting on canvas by Edwin Forbes, January 28, 1864

Signal telegraph machine and operator. Pencil and Chinese white drawing on tan paper by Alfred R. Waud, c. December 1862

{ **SEPTEMBER 17** 1862: The battle of Antietam (Sharpsburg)—the costliest one-day battle of the war, with a total of more than twenty-two thousand killed, wounded, or missing—halts the Confederate advance into the North. }

Signal Telegraph Machine and operation - Fredericksburg

Cavalry raids were a prominent feature of warfare in the western theater. On April 17, 1863, Colonel Benjamin H. Grierson set out from La Grange, Tennessee, at the head of seventeen hundred Federal cavalry troops. Moving through Mississippi, Grierson reported that by May 2, when they reached Union-occupied Baton Rouge, Louisiana, his men had "destroyed between 50 and 60 miles of railroad and telegraph, captured and destroyed over 3,000 stand of arms, and other army stores and Government property to an immense amount." They had also diverted the attention of Confederate forces from General Ulysses S. Grant's main movement toward Vicksburg. In July 1863, Brigadier General John Hunt Morgan, the widely known Confederate raider, diverted fourteen thousand Federal troops when he staged an incursion into Ohio—the longest cavalry raid of the war, covering more than seven hundred miles in twenty-five days. Convinced that bringing the war into the Northern homeland was the only way to relieve pressure on the Confederacy, Morgan and his "Terrible Men" cut a wide and destructive swath. Defeated at Buffington Island on July 19, Morgan was subsequently caught and imprisoned as a common criminal—but he escaped in late November.

Benjamin H. Grierson (1826–1911). 1861–65

The late Rebel General John Morgan (1825–1864). Reproduction of a drawing. 1900–1950

{ **SEPTEMBER 18** 1862: After his defeat at Antietam, General Robert E. Lee pulls his Confederate army out of Maryland under cover of night. }

Born John Joseph Klem in Newark, Ohio, nine-year-old Johnny Clem was allowed to tag along with the Twenty-second Michigan Regiment in 1861, and he first entered Civil War records as a footnote to news reports on the April 1862 battle of Shiloh. The next year, "Johnny Shiloh" became better known as "the drummer boy of Chickamauga" when, during this Union defeat, he exhibited the same stubborn courage as his commanding general, George H. Thomas ("the Rock of Chickamauga"). Another Federal officer present at the battle, Richard W. Johnson, described Clem's action in a letter to his own young son: "Johnny would not run . . . and presently a rebel Colonel with several orderlies came up to him. The Col. said 'you little Yankee, throw down your gun and surrender.' He replied, 'Johnny Clem never surrenders,' and at the same time fired and killed the Colonel and then escaped. . . . As soon as his Colo. heard of the gallant conduct of Johnny he made him a sergeant and I saw him yesterday stepping around giving orders as big as if he were grown." Eventually a career army man, Clem retired as a general in 1915.

Chickamauga (Union line advancing through forest toward Confederates). Having pursued Braxton Bragg's Confederates from Chattanooga, Union troops retreated to that city after their defeat in this battle. Chinese white and black ink wash drawing on tan paper by Alfred R. Waud, 1863

Johnny Clem (1851–1937). c. 1865

{ **SEPTEMBER 19** 1864: Union troops under Phil Sheridan defeat Jubal Early's Confederates in the third battle of Winchester, Virginia. }

CHICKAMAUGA.

Besieged in Chattanooga by General Braxton Bragg's Confederate army after the Union defeat at the battle of Chickamauga (see September 19), the men of the North's Army of the Cumberland, with their backs to the Tennessee River, fortified their front with trenches and rifle pits. The Confederates were determined to starve the Federal troops out of this important city, which could be used as a Union gateway for movement into Georgia; the Federals were just as determined to stay in possession and break the siege (see October 20). Major General Ulysses S. Grant, recently named commander of the Union's newly created Military Division of the Mississippi, arrived in Chattanooga on October 22, 1863. By November 1, the supply situation had been alleviated by the Cracker Line Operation (October 24–November 1, 1863), during which a new supply line was established, via the Tennessee River, from Bridgeport, Alabama. Secretary of War Edwin M. Stanton's quick dispatch of reinforcements from Virginia (see July 24), and the mid-November arrival of Major General William T. Sherman with seventeen thousand men gleaned from the Vicksburg and Memphis garrisons, gave the Federals sufficient strength to strike, in late November, in a series of battles that broke the siege (see July 23, September 22). Chattanooga remained in Union hands for the rest of the war.

Chattanooga, Tennessee. Colored manuscript map by G. H. Blakeslee, c. 1862–64

{ **SEPTEMBER 20** 1863: On the second day of the battle of Chickamauga, Confederates exploit a gap in Union lines and cause a confused Northern retreat. }

By 1864, Federal authorities had established several facilities for housing Confederate prisoners in Tennessee. Most of them were held at the Tennessee State Penitentiary and Maxwell House, a converted hotel, in Nashville. As many as seventy-five hundred men were imprisoned in these two facilities. Neither the Union nor the Confederacy subscribed to a uniform code of treatment for prisoners such as the twentieth century's Geneva Conventions. Bound only by ill-defined and flexible concepts such as "civilized warfare," the captors on both sides routinely neglected their captives. Cut off from their comrades, chronically underfed and ill, and lacking basic provisions for physical and mental health, prisoners of war fought a daily battle to stay alive. At times they received help from civilians, as noted by Confederate W. W. Heartsill, who was confined in a Union prison in Illinois: "Mrs Nutt arrived here to day from Louisville Ky; where she has succeeded in procuring a good supply of clothing for all the prisoners confined here. . . . Her kind actions are indelibly engraven upon the heart of every prisoner."

Confederate prisoners at railroad depot, Chattanooga, Tennessee. 1864

{ **SEPTEMBER 21** 1863: Retreating after defeat at Chickamauga, Union troops occupy a strong defensive position in and around Chattanooga, Tennessee. }

Encouraged by Union commander Ulysses S. Grant to show initiative as Federal forces waged their successful campaign to break the Confederate siege of Chattanooga, General Joseph Hooker led three divisions on November 24, 1863, against Confederates holding Lookout Mountain, southwest of the city. One small Confederate division under General Carter Stevenson held the summit, supported by troops under Generals Edward C. Walthall and John C. Moore protecting the slopes. Fog moved in as the Federals began their assault at about 8 A.M. It continued to inhibit both forces during the day, so that much of this "battle above the clouds" was heard but not seen by observers at Grant's headquarters. Southerners put up stiff resistance around Cravens' farm, below the summit, but in the afternoon, Stevenson was ordered to withdraw from the mountain to reinforce Confederates then battling General William T. Sherman's Union forces to the northeast. All Confederate troops were successfully withdrawn by 8 P.M. By the end of the next day, after heavy fighting on Missionary Ridge, the siege of Chattanooga had been broken.

Battle of Lookout Mountain.
Color lithograph, Kurz & Allison, 1889

{ **SEPTEMBER 22** 1862: Issuing his Preliminary Emancipation Proclamation, President Lincoln declares that all slaves in rebellious states shall be free as of January 1, 1863. }

The complete organization of the regiment occupied about two months, being finished by Jan. 1ˢᵗ, 1864. The field, staff and company officers were all white men. All the non-commissioned officers,—Hospital Steward, Quartermaster, Sergeant, Sergeant-Major, Orderlies, Sergeants and Corporals were colored. They proved very efficient, and had the war continued two years longer, many of them would have been competent as commissioned officers. . . .

General George H. Thomas, though a Southerner, and a West Point graduate, was a singularly fair-minded, candid man. He asked me one day soon after my regiment was organized, if I thought my men would fight. I replied that they would. He said he thought "they might behind breastworks." I said they would fight in the open field. He thought not. "Give me a chance General," I replied, "and I will prove it."

—Colonel Thomas J. Morgan, Fourteenth U.S. Colored Infantry (USA),
excerpt from a reminiscence published in 1885 (see also September 28)

Camp of Tennessee Colored Battery, Johnsonville, Tennessee. 1864

{ **SEPTEMBER 23** 1829: George Crook (USA) is born near Dayton, Ohio. }

"If we must be enemies, let us be men, and fight it out as we propose to do, and not deal in hypocritical appeals to God and humanity," Union general William T. Sherman wrote to Confederate general John Bell Hood on September 10, 1864. Fighting it out was what Sherman proceeded to do. While some of his forces, under Major General George H. Thomas, prepared for battles at Franklin and Nashville, Tennessee, that would smash Hood's army, Sherman himself made ready to lead other forces out of Atlanta (see July 25–27) on what would become known as his March to the Sea. A friend of the South, but not of the Confederacy's attempt to dismember the Union, Sherman described his attitude toward the citizens of the land he would be moving through in a letter to Union major general Henry W. Halleck, also written that September: "If the people raise a howl against my barbarity and cruelty, I will answer that war is war, and not popularity-seeking. If they want peace, they and their relatives must stop the war."

William Tecumseh Sherman (1820–1891). 1860–70

One of fifty-one manuscript maps drawn by Major R. M. McDowell, chief topographical engineer, left wing, U.S. Army of Georgia, illustrating Sherman's March to the Sea and then through the Carolinas and Virginia, 1865

{ **SEPTEMBER 24** 1862: Fourteen Northern governors meet at Altoona, Pennsylvania, and support emancipation. }

One of General William T. Sherman's foremost concerns during his Atlanta campaign was the security of his rail supply line from Chattanooga and Nashville, Tennessee. A chief reason for his worry was Major General Nathan Bedford Forrest, the Confederacy's most feared cavalry commander. The first force that Sherman dispatched to deal with Forrest suffered a humiliating defeat at Brice's Cross Roads, Mississippi, on June 10, 1864—a defeat mitigated by the actions of three African American regiments that held back the Confederates and allowed the balance of the Union force to escape. A furious Sherman ordered a second try the following month, telling Major General Andrew J. Smith, then in La Grange, Tennessee, to "follow Forrest to the death, if it cost 10,000 lives and breaks the Treasury." Smith's attempt yielded better results. Engaging a force comprising Forrest's corps and two thousand reinforcements at the battle of Tupelo (Harrisburg), Mississippi, on July 14, Smith's troops dealt with a series of uncoordinated Confederate charges and inflicted many casualties. Short on rations, Smith did not pursue and destroy the Confederates. But Forrest had been wounded in the battle, and Sherman's anxiety about his supply line was at least temporarily relieved.

Andrew Jackson Smith
(1815–1897). 1861–65

Two brothers-in-arms (identities unknown). Tintype, 1860–70

{ **SEPTEMBER 25** 1864: Phil Sheridan's Union troops advance toward Staunton and Waynesborough, Virginia, and force Jubal Early's Confederates to retreat before them. }

On November 21, 1864, General John Bell Hood led thirty-nine thousand Confederates, including Nathan Bedford Forrest's cavalry, into Tennessee, intending to defeat Major General George H. Thomas's Federal forces, crush General William T. Sherman's base of logistical support, and, perhaps, move through Kentucky and toward the rear of the Union force that was besieging Petersburg, Virginia. Instead, while Sherman marched toward the Atlantic coast at Savannah, Georgia, Federal forces under Major General John M. Schofield soon met Hood's army head-on at Franklin, Tennessee. Hood insisted on a disastrous frontal assault against entrenched positions, which resulted in sixty-two hundred Confederate casualties (to about twenty-three hundred on the Union side). Among the dead were six Confederate generals (Patrick R. Cleburne, States Rights Gist, H. B. Granbury, John Adams, O. F. Strahl, and John C. Carter). With five other generals wounded and one captured, the command structure of Hood's army was severely damaged. Yet when Federal forces withdrew to Thomas's lines at Nashville, Hood immediately followed, and the Confederates formed lines around the city.

John M. Schofield (1831–1906). 1860–65

Battle of Franklin [Tennessee,] November 30, 1864. Color lithograph, Kurz & Allison, 1891

{ **SEPTEMBER 26** 1863: President Lincoln and others are distressed when the *New York Post* reveals the movement of reinforcements to Chattanooga. }

Deemed "a bold fighter" by General Robert E. Lee, General John Bell
Hood suffered the amputation of his right leg after the battle of Chickamauga but soon returned
to service, commanding a corps under General Joseph E. Johnston. He assumed command of
the Confederate western army after Johnston was relieved on July 17, 1864. Pressed by General
William T. Sherman's advancing forces, Hood was unable to save Atlanta, then led his Army
of Tennessee to rending defeats at the battles of Franklin (November 30, 1864) and Nashville
(December 15–16, 1864). He resigned a month later. "I like him for his bravery and untiring
energy," one of his soldiers, Douglas J. Cater, wrote to a cousin, "but he lacked caution and
seemed to care nothing for the lives of his men." Hood's opponent at Nashville did not lack
caution. George H. Thomas, a native of Virginia who remained loyal to the Union, was so
deliberate in his preparations before the battle of Nashville that an impatient General Ulysses
S. Grant considered replacing him. But Thomas emerged to win a smashing victory—providing
another reminder to Northerners who persisted in questioning his loyalty that Thomas, "the
Rock of Chickamauga," was one of the Union's most effective and reliable generals.

John Bell Hood (1831–1879).
1860–65

George H. Thomas (1816–1870).
1860–65

{ SEPTEMBER 27 **1809:** Raphael Semmes, Confederate naval commander responsible for the destruction or capture of sixty-five Union ships,
is born in Charles County, Maryland. **}**

As soon as the fog lifted, the battle began in good earnest. Hood mistook my assault for an attack in force upon his right flank, and weakening his left in order to meet it, gave the coveted opportunity to Thomas, who improved it by assailing Hood's left flank, doubling it up, and capturing a large number of prisoners. Thus the first day's fight wore away. . . . When the second and final assault was made, . . . I watched that noble army climb the hill with a steady resolve which nothing but death itself could check . . . and the enemy seeing that further resistance was madness, gave way and began a precipitous retreat. . . . When General Thomas rode over the battle-field and saw the bodies of colored men side by side with the foremost, on the very works of the enemy, he turned to his staff, saying: "Gentlemen, the question is settled; negroes will fight."

> —Colonel Thomas J. Morgan, Fourteenth U.S. Colored Infantry (USA), excerpt from a reminiscence published in 1885 (see also September 23)

The Federal outer line, Nash-ville, Tennessee. Photograph by George N. Barnard, December 1864

{ **SEPTEMBER 28** **1863:** Union generals Alexander McDowell McCook and T. L. Crittenden are relieved of their corps commands in the Army of the Cumberland after the defeat at Chickamauga. Both are exonerated of any wrongdoing by courts of inquiry—but the shadow of Chickamauga will dim their command prospects through the rest of the war. }

After the battle of Nashville (December 15–16, 1864), where his Union cavalry helped rout General John Bell Hood's army, Brevet Major General James H. Wilson began assembling the largest Union mounted force of the war—13,480 men—for a strike at the important munitions and manufacturing center of Selma, Alabama. In March and April 1865—as Major General William T. Sherman's army was completing its march into North Carolina and the Army of the Potomac was preparing for its final moves against Petersburg and Richmond, Virginia—Wilson led the successful raid, opposed by 8,000 to 9,000 Confederates under Nathan Bedford Forrest. After a three-pronged assault, the well-fortified Selma fell on April 2. As Wilson's men extended their raid into other areas of the Deep South, Major General Joseph "Fightin' Joe" Wheeler was leading his Confederate cavalry troops in hit-and-run opposition to Sherman's relentless progress into North Carolina. A West Point graduate, Wheeler had commanded the Nineteenth Alabama Infantry at the battle of Shiloh in 1862, then transferred to the cavalry, where his effective leadership earned him the official thanks of the Confederate Congress in 1863. Daring and resourceful, Wheeler was the ranking Confederate cavalry commander in the western theater by May 1864.

James H. Wilson (1837–1925). 1860–65

Joseph Wheeler (1836–1906). 1860–65

{ **SEPTEMBER 29** 1862: A Federal brigadier general named Jefferson C. Davis fatally shoots a fellow Union officer, Brigadier General William "Bull" Nelson, during a quarrel in a hotel in Louisville, Kentucky. }

On May 10, 1865, the Fourth Michigan Volunteer Cavalry, one element of
the force that General James H. Wilson had led into Alabama (see September 29), received
intelligence that the fleeing Confederate president, Jefferson Davis, was in their vicinity,
near Irwinville, Georgia. Moving in on his camp, the Union soldiers surrounded Davis as he
attempted to escape. He surrendered, saying simply, "God's will be done." A rumor quickly
spread that Davis was disguised as a woman at the time, and Northern cartoonists gleefully
portrayed the scene. "Much was said at the time about the garb Mr. Davis was wearing when he
was captured," Ulysses S. Grant later wrote in his memoirs. "I cannot settle this question from
personal knowledge of the facts; but I have been under the belief, from information given to me
by General Wilson shortly after the event, that when Mr. Davis learned that he was surrounded
by our cavalry he was in his tent dressed in a gentleman's dressing gown."

"Jeff's Race for the Last Ditch"
(illustration on a sheet-music
cover). Lithograph on wove
paper, 1865

{ **SEPTEMBER 30** 1864: General Robert E. Lee's troops unsuccessfully counterattack Fort Harrison, Virginia, from which Confederates had been ousted by Union troops the day before. }

OCTOBER: BEHIND THE LINES

"I regret to learn that mother feels so badly on account of my joining the army," new Massachusetts recruit Warren H. Freeman wrote to his father on January 9, 1862. "The news came suddenly and unexpectedly upon her, I know. . . ." The war assaulted the lives of most Americans, North and South, with much that was sudden, unexpected, and wrenching. Millions of households were bereft of husbands and sons as the huge armies were assembled, and more deeply bereft as their men were wounded or died in service. Industries were restructured; agriculture became an arm of support and a target for enemy armies. The South suffered increasing shortages of everything from paper to medicine, cotton to railroad ties. In both South and North, women assumed unfamiliar roles, becoming farmers, nurses, teachers, leaders of relief organizations, public speakers, commercial clerks, or government workers— often supporting their own families as well as their armies in the field. Civilians of both sides presented new regiments with homemade flags, collected food and clothing for the men in uniform, and raised money that bought everything from gunboats to artificial limbs.

  In the North, particular effort was extended to help former slaves who entered Union lines by the thousands. African American churches established special relief associations; educational and work programs also were developed. In the South, hundreds of thousands of white refugees moved across the land, trying to evade battles or Union occupation. On both sides,

{ OCTOBER 1 **1864:** Weighed down by the $2,000 in gold she is carrying (along with dispatches), the famed Confederate spy Mrs. Rose O'Neal Greenhow drowns when the blockade-runner she is traveling in goes aground near Fort Fisher, North Carolina, and her small boat overturns as she tries to evade capture. **}**

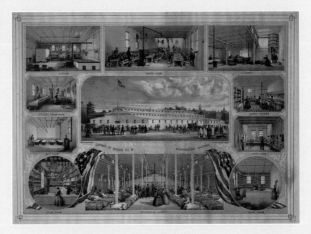

Citizens Volunteer Hospital, Philadelphia. Color lithograph by James Queen, published by P. S. Duval & Son, 1860s

civilian distress sometimes erupted into violent demonstrations, none worse than the draft riot that made New York City a battleground in 1863 (see October 22). In the midst of all the disruptions, poets and novelists wrote of the war, musicians composed patriotic songs, painters and lithographers created commemorative art. Thousands of people on both sides wrote letters and filled diaries, in which their war experiences, their angers, joys, and sorrows, were preserved for future generations.

Working in and visiting army camps, operating special hostels for traveling soldiers, bringing relief to the more fortunate among the hundreds of thousands of prisoners of war—and, in the South, enduring the encroachments of Union troops—many civilians gained a firm understanding of the boredom, chaos, multiple corruptions, and terrifying uncertainties of war. Those who helped collect the wounded after battles, who worked in hospitals or on medical transport trains and ships, gained devastating knowledge of its terrible cost and brutality. These medical workers confronted "every form of wound (the mere sight of some of them having been known to make a tolerably hardy visitor faint away)," civilian volunteer Walt Whitman wrote in the midst of the war. "One has much to learn to do good in these places."

Washington, D.C., became a watchful and spy-conscious capital city after war broke out. Guards checking credentials sometimes arrested travelers who simply *seemed* suspicious; Allan Pinkerton and his detectives spied on suspected spies; and congressional committees were soon established to oversee the conduct of the war—and to root out traitors. The House Committee on the Judiciary investigated loyalty problems, while the House Select Committee on the Loyalty of Clerks and Other Persons Employed by the Government created bureaucratic tempests by inviting Federal employees to testify against suspected colleagues, then seeking the dismissal of those accused of disloyalty—without allowing them to confront their accusers. In fact, the city *was* filled with spies and gossips who provided information to the South. Thomas Nelson Conrad, for example, the headmaster of a Georgetown boys' school, passed information for months to Confederate soldiers across the river in his native Virginia, using a signal system of his own devising that involved raising and lowering the window shades at his school.

Guards examining passes near Georgetown, Washington, D.C. 1865

{ **OCTOBER 2** 1800: Nat Turner, a slave and leader of an insurrection at Southampton, Virginia, is born in Southampton County. }

Civilian support groups on both sides were an important factor throughout the war. In the North, the relief efforts of thousands of local groups were coordinated by the U.S. Sanitary Commission, a nationwide organization established in June 1861 in conjunction with the Federal government. The commission was charged with inspecting and improving sanitary conditions in the camps and hospitals, as well as providing supplies, nursing care, and other services for the sick and wounded. Headquartered in Washington, the commission ultimately established regional headquarters in ten Northern cities, which in turn facilitated the creation of thousands of local aid societies, or auxiliaries. Although the national organization was headed by such men as the Reverend Henry W. Bellows and the renowned landscape architect Frederick Law Olmsted, the commission's work was carried out primarily by women. As president of the Brooklyn Relief Association, Marianne F. Stranahan directed a program that provided valuable supplies and assistance to the Woman's Central Association of Relief—a precursor of the Sanitary Commission. Margaret E. Breckinridge volunteered as a nurse in 1862 and spent much of her service on Mississippi River hospital boats before succumbing to illness in 1864.

Nurses and officers of the U.S. Sanitary Commission, Fredericksburg, Virginia. May 1864

Miss Margaret Elizabeth Breckinridge (1832–1864), above right, and Mrs. Marianne F. Stranahan (dates unknown). Illustrations in *Woman's Work in the Civil War: A Record of Heroism, Patriotism and Patience* (1867)

{ **OCTOBER 3** 1863: The U.S. War Department orders the enlistment of Negro troops in the slave states of Maryland, Missouri, and Tennessee. }

Camp at Avery House, Va. . . . The evening has resumed the general semblance of all other evenings in this region. Some men are singing Methodist hymns, members of the band in their quarters are practicing on snatches of music with various kinds of horns. Trains of cars occasionally hurry past a short distance in the rear of our camp, and the pickets keep up their steady monotonous firing. . . .

   . . . A salute of one hundred guns was fired this morning by a battery in the rear of our camp in honor of the victory of [General George H.] Thomas at Nashville. I am in hopes that another will soon announce the taking of Savannah. The late successes in different quarters give us much reason to hope that the war will be ended. The Confederacy is evidently getting weaker. During the year just closing the Rebels have had only one or two victories of a small kind to set off against almost a dozen very decided Federal triumphs, and although there has been no great result achieved in this quarter it is plain that Grant's army has been steadily gaining ground all the time.

   —Colonel Alfred B. McCalmont (USA), letters to his brother, December 16 and 18, 1864

Headquarters of Genl. Warren at Col. Avery's house—near Petersburg. Pencil and Chinese white drawing on tan paper by Alfred R. Waud, 1864

{ **OCTOBER 4** 1862: The two-day battle of Corinth, Mississippi, ends with a Confederate withdrawal from this important railroad center. }

Head quarters of Genl Warren at Cold Harbor — on route to home — army...

During the months-long Union siege of Petersburg, Virginia, General-in-Chief Ulysses S. Grant established his headquarters at City Point, Virginia, a well-positioned town along the James River. There, his military "family" included Brigadier General John A. Rawlins, who had become Grant's aide-de-camp in 1861 and remained his right-hand man throughout the war. Like Grant, Rawlins was a devoted family man, and, following a general custom during the war, family members visited them whenever practicable. These photographs, taken in late 1864 or early 1865, record two such visits to City Point. Grant poses with his wife, Julia, and one of their four children, Rawlins with his second wife, Mary (his first wife had died in 1861), and one of his three children. Grant's eldest son, Frederick, had also visited his father during the 1863 siege that led to the fall of Vicksburg. "He looked out for himself and was in every battle of the campaign," Grant wrote in his memoirs. "His age, then not quite thirteen, enabled him to take in all he saw, and to retain a recollection of it that would not be possible in more mature years."

General Ulysses S. Grant with his wife and child. 1864–65

General John A. Rawlins (1831–1869) with his wife and child. 1864–65

{ **OCTOBER 5** **1863:** The Confederate torpedo boat *David*, with a four-man crew, attacks and damages the Federal ironclad *New Ironsides* outside Charleston Harbor, South Carolina. }

During the Civil War, many soldiers captured on the battlefield were accorded "parole," a status based on the French *parole d'honneur*. A man who pledged to his captors that he would not fight against them until he had officially been exchanged for one of their soldiers would report to a camp run by his own army, where such a camp was available (or, where one was not, to other quarters away from the front), until the exchange was complete. Union sergeant Warren H. Freeman, who had been captured during the battle of Gettysburg, described this unique type of military limbo in a letter to his father on July 26, 1863, after he reported to a Union parole camp in West Chester, Pennsylvania: "The guard that do duty over us are raw Pennsylvania militia, and seem disposed to grant us, not only a full run of the camp, but the largest degree of liberty. Consequently some of the men have gone home, others work for the farmers in the neighborhood at haying, etc." Paroles and exchanges were affected by administrative difficulties, battlefront conditions, and political considerations. Irreconcilable differences between North and South about the status of black soldiers all but halted exchanges by the fall of 1863. They did not resume with any regularity until February 1865.

Parole Camp, Annapolis Md. Color lithograph, E. Sachse & Co., 1864

{ **OCTOBER 6** 1861: The Union navy captures the Confederate blockade-runner *Alert* off Charleston, South Carolina. }

One of many Southern women who assisted the Confederate war effort, Mrs. Felicia Grundy Porter began her war work by establishing hospitals in Nashville, Tennessee. As president of the Benevolent Society of Tennessee, she arranged concerts and tableaux for the people of cities and towns throughout the state and used the proceeds from ticket sales to buy artificial limbs for amputee soldiers. She later expanded her activities, becoming president of the Women's Relief Society of the Confederate States.

Though known as the "Angel of the Battlefield," Northerner Clara Barton generally acted as a nurse only when she could wrest time away from procuring desperately needed provisions and distributing them to the front lines. She contributed her own money, as well as securing donations of money and goods from others, and established a parcel-post service for soldiers that was maintained throughout the war. In 1864, she became superintendent of nurses in the army of General Benjamin F. Butler, and the following year she headed a search for missing soldiers that succeeded in identifying the bodies buried in more than 90 percent of the graves at the cemetery in Andersonville, Georgia.

Mrs. Felicia Grundy Porter (b. 1820). Date unknown, published in 1911

Clara Barton (1821–1912). Date unknown

{ OCTOBER 7 **1864:** Violating Brazilian neutrality and international law, USS *Wachusett* rams and then captures the Confederate commerce raider CSS *Florida* within the port of Bahia, Brazil. The incident sparks a diplomatic protest and a subsequent condemnation by U.S. Secretary of State William H. Seward of the unauthorized action. **}**

The anxiety of all classes for the safety of Richmond is now intense, though a strong faith in the goodness of God and the valour of our troops keeps us calm and hopeful. A gentleman, high in position, panic-struck, was heard to exclaim, yesterday: "Norfolk has fallen, Richmond will fall, Virginia is to be given up, and to-morrow I shall leave this city, an exile and a beggar." Others are equally despondent, and, as is too frequently the case in times of trouble, attribute all our disasters to the incompetency and faithlessness of those entrusted with the administration of public affairs. Even General Lee does not escape animadversion, and the President is the subject of the most bitter maledictions. I have been shocked to hear that a counter-revolution, if not openly advocated, has been distinctly foreshadowed, as the only remedy for our ills.

—Mrs. Judith W. McGuire, diary entry, May 14, 1862

The ruins of Hampton, Virginia. Watercolor drawing by William McIlvaine, 1862

 **{ OCTOBER 8** **1861:** Brigadier General William T. Sherman is named to command the Union's Department of the Cumberland, headquartered at Louisville, Kentucky; he replaces Brigadier General Robert Anderson, who had been the commander at Fort Sumter, South Carolina, when the Civil War began there. **}**

As Northern troops moved through the South, they caused tens of thousands of white Southern civilians to flee their homes out of fear of invasion, lack of food, the spread of disease, and forced military evacuation, or in the wake of the destruction of their homes, towns, and cities. An estimated two hundred thousand people within the Confederacy became refugees, often facing insecurity, poverty, and hunger. Many of the refugees were women and children, who often tried to stay with their property until they had no choice but to move. "It is remarked that there never were so many women and children traveling as there are now," Southern nurse Kate Cumming wrote in her diary on February 10, 1863. "Numbers of ladies, whose husbands are in the army, have been compelled to give up their homes for economy and protection, and seek others among their relatives. . . . We have a large floating population—the people who have been driven from their homes by the invader."

Their belongings piled atop a wagon, a group of Southern refugees prepares to get out of the path of advancing Northern armies. 1860–65

{ **OCTOBER 9** 1864: Union cavalry under George Custer and Wesley Merritt engage and rout Confederates at Tom's Brook (Round Top Mountain), Virginia. }

Appointed "superintendent of women nurses" in June 1861, the humanitarian Dorothea Dix was charged with the responsibility "to select and assign women nurses to general or permanent military hospitals, they not to be employed in such hospitals without her sanction and approval, except in cases of urgent need." Dix's single-mindedness in establishing the army's first professional nursing corps—and, perhaps, her insistence that her nurses be at least thirty years old and "plain-looking"—led some of her recruits to dub her "Dragon Dix."

After the fall of Port Hudson, Louisiana, in the summer of 1863, Confederate brigadier general William N. R. Beall was imprisoned at Johnson's Island, Ohio, a camp plagued by such deficiencies in food that prisoners formed a "rat club," which snared rodents to supplement their rations. Released in 1864, he embarked on an unusual project: with the permission of Union authorities, he set up a cotton brokerage in New York. Ships affiliated with Beall's endeavor were permitted to leave Southern ports loaded with cotton, which Beall then sold. The proceeds went for food, clothing, and blankets for Confederates in Union prison camps.

Dorothea Lynde Dix (1802–1887). Date unknown

William N. R. Beall (1825–1883). 1860–65

{ **OCTOBER 10** 1862: President Jefferson Davis asks Virginia for a draft of forty-five hundred black workers to complete the fortifications around the Confederate capital of Richmond. }

Appointed U.S. surgeon general in April 1862, Dr. William Alexander Hammond immediately set about reforming U.S. Army medical services, implementing a medical inspection system, greatly expanding hospital facilities, building government pharmaceutical laboratories to ensure adequate supplies, and supporting the development of an ambulance corps to offer emergency treatment and remove wounded soldiers from the field. With fewer resources, Confederate authorities were also trying to improve medical services. Civilian assistance remained crucial for both sides. In a letter to her mother, Katharine Wormeley, a nurse with the U.S. Sanitary Commission, described bringing Union wounded off the Virginia Peninsula in 1862:

> Imagine a great river or Sound steamer fitted on every deck, every berth and every square inch of room covered with wounded men, even the stairs and gangways and guards filled with those who are less badly wounded; and then imagine fifty well men, on every kind of errand, rushing to and fro over them, every touch bringing agony to the poor fellows, while stretcher after stretcher came along, hoping to find an empty place, and then imagine what it was to keep calm ourselves.

Hospital attendants collecting the wounded after the engagement; within our lines near Hatchers Run. Pencil, Chinese white, and black ink wash drawing by William Waud, September–October 1864

William A. Hammond (1828–1900). Photograph by the Brady National Photographic Art Gallery, 1860–65

{ OCTOBER 11 1861: Brigadier General William S. Rosecrans assumes command of the Union's Department of Western Virginia. **}**

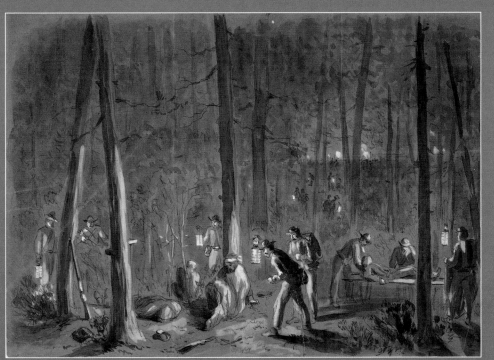

I joined an ambulance train that was just starting to go to the relief of our starving and wounded men, near Centreville. . . . I soon perceived that the drivers were men of the lowest character, evidently taken from the vilest purlieus of Washington, merely as common drivers. . . . About mid-day we arrived, and found our men in a most piteous condition, lying everywhere. . . . I found the drivers did not feel it to be their duty to help the sufferers, but sulked, or swore, or laughed, as it pleased each. . . . Of course, I repeated all these facts in a letter to the Surgeon-General. He assured me that I could not tell him anything new—that he had, months since, foretold to the Secretary of War the horrors that would occur with such a set of wretches as usually were found in a body of ambulance drivers—that he had vainly endeavored to obtain *some system*, but there was none now. . . . I want now . . . to create a public sentiment that will compel the Government to attend to this matter, and to have a real ambulance corps.

—Dr. Henry I. Bowditch, address to the Boston Society
for Medical Improvement, September 22, 1862

Bringing wounded soldiers to the cars after the battle of Seven Pines. Pencil and Chinese white drawing on tan paper by Arthur Lumley, June 3, 1862

Shortly after his speech, Dr. Bowditch wrote that his eldest son, "having been mortally wounded . . . lay helpless on the ground, for some time. . . . Two surgeons saw him, but they evidently had no means for carrying off the wounded officer, and it is believed *no one connected with an Ambulance Corps ever approached him there*." Lieutenant Bowditch died.

{ **OCTOBER 12** **1861:** The Union navy's first ironclad, the gunboat *St. Louis*, is launched at Carondelet, Missouri. (On February 16, 1862, it will destroy Tennessee ironworks along the Cumberland River.) }

As armies campaigned on the battlefield, Dr. Jonathan Letterman, medical director of the Army of the Potomac, and U.S. Surgeon General William Hammond campaigned to create an effective, army-wide Ambulance Corps. As late as August 1862, the lack of well-drilled and organized ambulance teams meant that many wounded lay unattended on the field for days after a battle. By the battle of Antietam on September 17, however, this had begun to change. The much-improved Ambulance Corps developed by Letterman employed specially trained military drivers and litter-bearers who were part of the Medical Department (previously, drivers had been part of the Quartermaster Corps), and ambulance units had a more centralized organization. Bureaucratic resistance yielded to public pressure (see October 12), and the Ambulance Corps Act of March 11, 1864, applied the improved system to all U.S. armies. The absence of a comparable Confederate ambulance corps (Stonewall Jackson's medical director, Hunter H. McGuire, did develop a successful "infirmary corps")—as well as a shortage of ambulances in the resource-strapped South—resulted in greater confusion and suffering for Confederate wounded.

Workmen in front of the Ambulance Shop, Washington, D.C. April 1865

{ **OCTOBER 13** 1864: By a margin of only 375 votes out of nearly 60,000 cast, Maryland voters adopt a new state constitution abolishing slavery. }

In 1862, Union forces began converting railroad cars into hospital trains. Twenty-four stretchers per rail car were suspended by sturdy bands of rubber that attached to interior posts. There were also cook and dispensary cars and a car to transport surgeons. Although the Confederates also used rail transport, their system was less developed, and as the war progressed, their rail lines were increasingly disrupted. Trains transported more than 250,000 wounded soldiers throughout the war.

Mary J. Safford was described by U.S. Sanitary Commission official Mary A. Livermore as perhaps "the *very first woman* who went into the camps and hospitals, in the country; I know she was in the West. She systematized everything in Cairo [Illinois]. . . . At Pittsburg Landing [Shiloh], where she was found in advance of other women, she was hailed by dying soldiers, who did not know her name, but had seen her at Cairo, as the 'Cairo Angel.'" After the war, Safford studied medicine in New York and Europe and became the first female practicing physician in Florida.

The Interior of a hospital [rail-road] car. Wood engraving of a sketch by Theodore R. Davis, 1864

Miss Mary J. Safford (1834–1891). Illustration in *Woman's Work in the Civil War: A Record of Heroism, Patriotism and Patience* (1867)

{ **OCTOBER 14** **1863:** Confederates under General A. P. Hill strike retreating elements of the Army of the Potomac at Bristoe Station, Virginia, in an inconclusive engagement. }

USS *Columbia* was a former Confederate blockade-runner

before its capture in 1862; thereafter, until it ran aground and was wrecked, it was part of the U.S. Navy's North Atlantic Blockading Squadron—and thus part of the largest blockade ever undertaken by any nation to that time. Proclaimed by President Lincoln on April 19, 1861, the blockade of 3,549 miles of Southern coastline and 180 inlets at first required resources that the Union navy did not possess. (Its chief early consequence was to discourage foreign nations from trading with the Confederacy, under threat of provoking war with the United States.) Its effects soon increased dramatically, however—engendering the new maritime industry of blockade-running. Although many blockade-runners were successful, they could not bring in enough medicine, munitions, and other essential supplies to the Confederacy. In fact, many carried much more profitable consumer items; coffee, for example, which cost $249 a ton in Nassau in the Bahamas, was sold in the South for $5,500. Although it never succeeded in shutting down all of the South's foreign trade, the Union blockade did exacerbate shortages and thus contributed to the runaway inflation that eventually crippled the Confederacy's war effort.

Columbia ashore Sullivans Island. Pencil and watercolor drawing on olive paper by Alfred R. or William Waud, January 13, 1863

{ **OCTOBER 15** 1863: In Charleston Harbor, South Carolina, the Confederate submersible *H. L. Hunley* sinks for a second time during a practice dive; eight men die, including Hunley, the inventor, but once again the vessel is raised and repaired. }

In January 1864, President Lincoln received, from Frank P. Bailey of Zanesville, Ohio, a type of request that had become familiar to him: "The ladies are going to have a Soldiers Fare & they want me to make a Bust of you I cannot find any true picture of you & I want to know if you will for the sake of the soldiers send me a picture I am a poor Boy & cannot go to war so I wanto [*sic*] do all I can for them." That same year, the president agreed to pose in person for a portrait bust to be created by a diminutive, curly-haired, seventeen-year-old Post Office clerk, Vinnie Ream—who would also sculpt such Civil War figures as General George Armstrong Custer (see March 4), the Radical Republican congressman Thaddeus Stevens (see December 22), and New York editor Horace Greeley (see April 5) before she was twenty-one. After Lincoln was assassinated, Congress awarded Ream a $10,000 contract for a full-length, standing statue of the president to be placed in the Capitol Rotunda; she thus became the first woman commissioned to execute a sculpture for the U.S. government. Her statue of Lincoln still stands in the Capitol's Statuary Hall, and her statue of Civil War naval hero Admiral David G. Farragut is a central feature in Washington's Farragut Square.

President Abraham Lincoln. Photograph by Anthony Berger, Brady National Photographic Art Gallery, February 9, 1864

Vinnie Ream [Hoxie] (1847–1914) with Lincoln portrait bust. c. 1865

{ **OCTOBER 16** 1859: Fervent abolitionist John Brown leads an unsuccessful raid on the government arsenal at Harpers Ferry, Virginia. }

"I will introduce myself to your notice as one of the Prisoners in the late Indian War in Minnesota," Sarah F. Wakefield wrote to Abraham Lincoln on March 23, 1863. She went on to inform the president that a Sioux man, Chaskadan, who had been her friend and had saved her family during the August–September 1862 Sioux uprising (see April 11), "was executed in place of the guilty man this man is now at Mankato living, while a good honest man lies sleeping in death. . . . My Husband . . . thinks the mistake was intentional on the part of a certain 'Officer' at Mankato. . . . God and you Sir, protect and save them [the Sioux] as a people." Four days later, a delegation of Southern Plains Indians visited the White House. This time of war between North and South was also a period of high tensions between Indian nations and the white Americans who were slowly absorbing their territories. Within two years of this visit, all the Indians in the front row of this photograph were dead; only one died of natural causes, while the other three were killed by U.S. troops—two of them in the massacre at Sand Creek, Colorado, on November 29, 1864.

Southern Plains delegation, White House Conservatory. Interpreter William Simpson Smith and agent Samuel G. Colley are standing at left, the white woman standing at far right is often identified as Mary Todd Lincoln, and the Indians in the front row are (left to right) War Bonnet, Standing in the Water, and Lean Bear of the Cheyenne, and Yellow Wolf of the Kiowa; the Indians in the second row are unidentified. March 27, 1863

{ **OCTOBER 17** 1863: President Lincoln issues a proclamation calling for three hundred thousand more volunteers for the Union armies. }

As the war lengthened and Southern sacrifices increased,
criticism of President Jefferson Davis grew from muted to intense—at least in some quarters.
The *Richmond Examiner,* for example, accused the president of everything from laziness to
incompetence. But it was in Charleston, South Carolina, where the war had begun, that editorial commentary reached a fever pitch. Ardent states' rights advocate Robert Barnwell Rhett
Jr., editor of the *Charleston Mercury,* was vicious in his relentless attacks on Davis and the
government, charging the president with inefficiency, ineptitude, poor prosecution of the war,
and even worse military and political appointments. This last charge was not surprising, given
that the editor's father, fire-eater Robert Barnwell Rhett Sr.—the "Father of Secession" and a
frequent contributor to the *Mercury*—had been passed over when Davis chose his cabinet
(see also January 2). The Rhetts' *Mercury* diatribes undermined Confederate morale and
provoked the Confederate first lady, Varina Davis, to declare that she hated the *Mercury*'s editor
more than she did any Republican.

Jefferson Davis (1808–1889).
c. 1861–65

Robert Barnwell Rhett Jr.
(1828–1905). Photographic
print on carte de visite mount,
1860–70

{ OCTOBER 18 1862: John Hunt Morgan and his Confederate raiders defeat Union cavalry near
Lexington, Kentucky, and capture the city's garrison before moving on. **}**

Frances Ann Kemble, a celebrated English-born actress,

championed abolition during the war with the publication of her *Journal of a Residence on a Georgian Plantation* (1863), an account of the cruelty of slavery as she perceived it as the former wife of slave owner Pierce Butler. In 1838 and 1839, Kemble and Butler lived in a plantation house that closely resembled that of Confederate general Thomas Drayton (pictured here). Kemble wrote her impressions in a diary—which Butler prevented her from publishing at the time. She finally did so five months after the Emancipation Proclamation, her purpose being primarily to persuade Great Britain not to support the Confederacy. "Scorn, derision, insult, menace—the handcuff, the lash—the tearing away of children from parents, of husbands from wives . . . the labor of body, the despair of mind, the sickness of heart—these are the realities which belong to the system, and form the rule, rather than the exception, in the slave's experience," she wrote. Her words were read aloud in the British House of Commons. The reception given to the American edition was equally enthusiastic—in the North.

Frances Anne (Fanny) Kemble (1809–1893). Steel engraving, c. 1873

"Mansion of the rebel Genl. Thomas F. Drayton, Hilton Head, S.C." Photograph by Henry P. Moore, May 1862

{ OCTOBER 19 **1864:** A small Confederate raiding party, operating from Canada and led by Lieutenant Bennett H. Young, robs three banks in nearby St. Albans, Vermont, of more than $200,000; after local citizens fight and then pursue the group, Young and about half of his men are arrested in Canada and some of the money is recovered. **}**

Throughout the war, particularly in the North (where materials for printing were much more plentiful), publishers did a brisk business in war mementos and patriotic souvenirs. Honored in this 1864 lithograph, the Union's Army of the Cumberland was responsible for all of Tennessee east of the Tennessee River, as well as northern Alabama and northern Georgia. Victorious in its first major battle (Stones River or Murfreesboro, December 31, 1862–January 3, 1863), the army retreated into siege conditions at Chattanooga, Tennessee, after a defeat at the battle of Chickamauga, nearby in Georgia, in September 1863. "[The] long lines of [Confederate] camp fires almost encompass us," Brigadier General John Beatty wrote in his diary on October 3. "But the camp fires of the Army of the Cumberland are burning also. Bruised and torn by a two days' unequal contest, its flags are still up, and its men still unwhipped. It has taken its position here, and here, by God's help, it will remain." Under a new commander, Major General George H. Thomas, the Army of the Cumberland was instrumental in breaking the siege in November. Published before that event, this *Roll of Honor* features the commander whom General Thomas replaced, Major General William S. Rosecrans (see also September 26–28).

Roll of Honor, Army of the Cumberland. Color lithograph, Middleton, Strobridge & Co., 1863

{ OCTOBER 20 } 1864: For the second straight year (after sporadic observances on various dates and in various parts of the nation), President Lincoln specifically proclaims the last Thursday in November "a day of Thanksgiving and Praise to Almighty God." In 1941, Congress will change this to the fourth Thursday in November.

In 1863, as Russia faced the prospect of war with Great Britain and France over events in Russian Poland, officials under Czar Alexander II dispatched their fleet to ports in the United States, with which Russia had enjoyed cordial diplomatic relations for more than a decade (see April 8). Some Russian vessels arrived in New York in September 1863; others docked in San Francisco in October. Although the ships had been sent to be well placed for action should the tense situation in Europe erupt into war, the effect on morale throughout the American North was electric: the fleet's arrival was viewed as a gesture of support for the Union. Naval facilities were placed at the Russians' disposal; deputations from Northern states arrived to honor the visitors; balls and receptions were held, with ladies dressed elegantly in fashions like those pictured here. The Russians, in turn, helped extinguish a large fire that broke out in San Francisco—where they also offered to deploy to prevent a (falsely) rumored attack by Confederate commerce raiders. The Russian fleet remained in U.S. ports through April 1864, when the threat of a European war had passed. "Russia . . . has our friendship," Secretary of State William H. Seward wrote on December 23, 1863, "because she always wishes us well, and leaves us to conduct our affairs as we think best."

Czar Alexander II (1818–1881), a friend of the United States— and an inspiration: in 1861, he emancipated the Russian serfs. Photograph by Levitskii, St. Petersburg, Russia, 1870–80

The great Russian ball at the Academy of Music, New York City, November 5, 1863. Wood engraving signed by (Winslow) Homer, in *Harper's Weekly,* November 21, 1863

Godey's Fashions for February 1865. Hand-colored engraving, Kimmel, 1865

{ **OCTOBER 21** 1861: Union forces suffer a dramatic, costly defeat at the battle of Ball's Bluff (Leesburg), Virginia; among the more than nine hundred Federal casualties is Colonel Edward D. Baker, a senator from Oregon and a friend of President Lincoln's (see February 17). }

Riots were an occasional feature of Civil War civilian life. In the South, they were primarily the result of food shortages or tensions between Unionists and staunch Confederates. In the North, they were prompted by resistance to the draft, racial tensions, and the opposition by Peace Democrats, or "Copperheads," to the conduct of the war. The North's worst draft riot occurred in New York City on July 13–16, 1863—as the casualty lists from the battle of Gettysburg were being published. When names of those chosen in the draft lottery were announced, tensions burst into violence. The draft office was burned by a mob primarily consisting of Irish laborers who could not afford to buy their way out of the draft and who feared that when they entered the army, their jobs would be permanently expropriated by black men. Over four ugly days, they rampaged through the streets of the city, attacking the property of Republicans and abolitionists, burning police stations and the Colored Orphan Asylum, and murdering black people. They also fought against Union troops sent to suppress them—some of whom had come directly from the Gettysburg battlefield. More than one hundred people were killed before order was restored.

Rioters sacking the brownstone houses in New York. Reproduction of an illustration in the *New York Illustrated News,* July 25, 1863

Mob lynching a black man during the 1863 New York draft riot. Reproduction of a newspaper illustration, 1860s

{ **OCTOBER 22** 1862: Confederate cavalry take London, Kentucky. }

Both North and South viewed an uninterrupted postal service as a great morale booster for soldiers and civilians alike. In the Confederate states, Postmaster General John H. Reagan used the routes and offices established by the U.S. Post Office Department, raised basic postage to more than three times that of the North, cut jobs, and enticed several U.S. postal employees to join the Confederate cause to keep Southern mail moving. He also extended a privilege to Southern troops that their Northern counterparts did not have: sending mail free of charge (the recipient paid the postage). But Reagan was not able to maintain the system's efficiency as rail lines were cut, shipments of mail and stamps were destroyed, and paper supplies dwindled to nothing. The Northern postal system, on the other hand, was able to handle an ever-increasing volume of mail with growing efficiency. Postmaster General Montgomery Blair devised an effective mail service to and from military posts and instituted compulsory payment of postage by the sender. He also created the postal draft system for sending money orders, which allowed soldiers to receive money or to send some of their pay home. (See also August 2 and 10.)

Group in front of post office tent at Army of the Potomac headquarters, Falmouth, Virginia. Photograph by Timothy H. O'Sullivan, April 1863

{ **OCTOBER 23** **1864:** The last real Confederate effort in Missouri ends in defeat at the hard-fought battle of Westport. }

Civil War photographers took an estimated one million photographs between 1860 and 1865. The vast majority of these images were taken by Northern cameramen. A lack of supplies and operating capital made Southern photographers—who were much less numerous than those based in the North in the prewar years—all but nonexistent after the early years of the war. Of the North's photographers, Mathew Brady is perhaps the best known. Well established as a portrait photographer by 1861, he organized a corps of photographers when war broke out, assigned them to cover different armies and areas of operation, and secured permits from the Union authorities to make this possible. All expenses incurred in the enterprise were to be paid by Brady, not the government; however, his photographers did enjoy some marked cooperation, including use of army transports and railroads. To broaden the scope of his photographic record as much as possible, Brady also purchased the work of other cameramen in the field. These itinerant photographers generally traveled in odd covered wagons stuffed with their cumbersome gear—distinctive conveyances that the soldiers quickly dubbed "whatisit wagons."

One of Mathew Brady's photographer's wagons, in front of Petersburg, Virginia. c. 1864

{ **OCTOBER 24** **1861:** Western Union completes the first transcontinental telegraph. The telegraph will become an essential tool for Civil War commanders—and will provide newspapers with nearly instantaneous (though not always accurate) accounts of battlefield events. }

In December 1861, the poet Julia Ward Howe was visiting Washington, D.C., with her husband, the educator and reformer Samuel Gridley Howe. Morale in the city had been considerably dampened over the previous six months by the Union defeats at Wilson's Creek in Missouri and First Bull Run and Ball's Bluff in Virginia. One evening, after the group she was with sang "John Brown's Body," someone suggested that she should write new words for the air—"good words for a stirring tune." "Battle Hymn of the Republic" was published in the February 1862 issue of *Atlantic Monthly*. When set to the music of "John Brown's Body," Howe's poem became the single most memorable song to emerge from the Civil War. At about the same time this new Union song was circulating, "Our National Confederate Anthem: God Save the South" was being printed in Richmond—with one of the rare illustrated sheet-music covers issued under the Confederacy. At least two different tunes—by C. T. De Coeniel (pictured here) and Charles W. A. Ellerbrock—were composed for the words by Marylander George H. Miles, writing under the name Earnest Halpin: "God save the South! / . . . Her altars and firesides! / God save the South! / Now that the war is nigh / Now that we're arm'd to die / Chanting our battle cry / Freedom or Death!"

Julia Ward Howe (1819–1910). c. 1900

"Our National Confederate Anthem: God Save the South" (sheet-music cover). Lithograph by Ernest Crehen, c. 1862

{ **OCTOBER 25** **1861:** The keel of the revolutionary Union ironclad USS *Monitor* is laid at Greenpoint, in Brooklyn. }

Best known today for the landscapes and marine subjects that were his primary interests, the volatile artist Winslow Homer (1836–1910) was among the artist-reporters who followed the Union armies. Homer's presence in army camps was intermittent (he was an employee of *Harper's Weekly* but refused to work full time). When he was with the army—notably during General George B. McClellan's 1862 Peninsula campaign and the beginning of General Ulysses S. Grant's 1864 Overland campaign, both in Virginia—he preferred to sketch soldiers' everyday lives rather than the battle scenes he supplied to *Harper's* for publication. One depiction, *The surgeon at work at the rear during an engagement,* was one of the first pictures to give attention to army doctors. *Life in Camp,* a series of twenty-four of Homer's more humorous depictions of army life, was published in 1864 by Louis Prang & Company of New York and sold to civilians and soldiers as war souvenirs. A pioneer in color reproduction, Prang published his first Civil War image (an engineer's plan of Charleston Harbor) as soon as the war began. Throughout the conflict, his company published maps, battle plans, war-related portraits, and Civil War sheet music with illustrated covers.

Images from *Life in Camp.* Color lithograph souvenir cards reproducing illustrations by Winslow Homer, published by Louis Prang & Co., 1864

{ OCTOBER 26 1864: Confederate guerrilla Bloody Bill Anderson (whose small band includes future outlaws Jesse and Frank James) is killed in an ambush near Richmond, Missouri. **}**

SURGEONS CALL.

UPSET HIS COFFEE.

RIDING ON A RAIL.

AN UNWELCOME VISIT.

OUR SPECIAL.

GOOD BYE.

DRUMMER.

THE RIFLE PIT.

WATER CALL.

BUILDING CASTLES.

STUCK IN THE MUD.

TOSSING IN A BLANKET.

THE FIELD BARBER.

THE GIRL HE LEFT BEHIND HIM.

TEAMSTER.

EXTRA RATION.

HARD TACK.

LATE FOR ROLL CALL.

A SHELL IS COMING.

THE GUARD HOUSE

FORDING.

HOME ON A FURLOUGH.

A DESERTER.

IN THE TRENCHES.

Dearest Mother— . . . I believe I mentioned a young man in Ward F, Armory-square, with a bad wound in the leg, very agonizing—had to have it propt up, and an attendant all the while dripping water on night and day. . . . He was of good family—handsome, intelligent man, about 26, married; his name was John Elliot, of Cumberland Valley, Bedford co., Penn.—belonged to 2nd Pennsylvania Cavalry. . . . The surgeons put off amputating the leg, he was so exhausted, but at last it was imperatively necessary to amputate. Mother, I am shocked to tell you that he never came alive off the amputating table. . . . Poor young man, he suffered much, very, *very* much, for many days, and bore it so patiently—so that it was a release to him. Mother, such things are awful—not a soul here he knew or cared about, except me—yet the surgeons and nurses were good to him. . . . Mother, how contemptible all the usual little worldly prides and vanities, and striving after appearances, seems in the midst of such scenes as these— such tragedies of soul and body. To see such things and not be able to help them is awful—I feel almost ashamed of being so well and whole.

—Poet and Union nurse Walt Whitman, letter, May 13, 1863

Walt Whitman (1819–1892). Frontispiece in *The Wound Dresser* (1898), a collection of his Civil War letters

A ward in Armory Square Hospital, Washington, D.C. 1861–65

{ OCTOBER 27 1864: In a daring adventure, Lieutenant William B. Cushing and his fifteen-man Union crew, in a steam launch with a torpedo (mine) protruding from it at the end of a pole, sink the Confederate ironclad *Albemarle* at Plymouth, North Carolina. **}**

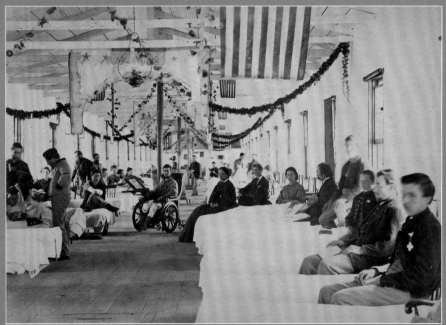

Among the first female physicians in the United States, Mary Edwards Walker applied for a commission as an army surgeon at the beginning of the Civil War. Despite her medical degree (1855), she was permitted at first to serve only as a volunteer nurse, but in 1862 she was allowed to become a volunteer field surgeon. Dressed in uniform, with a surgeon's sash, she tended Union wounded at Fredericksburg, Chickamauga, and Chattanooga; however, she remained unsuccessful in her quest to secure an official commission as an army doctor (an army medical board pronounced her "utterly unqualified for the position of medical officer"). Nevertheless, in 1864, Major General George H. Thomas appointed her assistant surgeon of the Fifty-second Ohio Infantry Regiment, the first such position awarded to a woman—over the outraged objections of male doctors, one of whom called the appointment a "medical monstrosity." She tended both soldiers and civilians (and may have operated as a spy) until her capture by Confederates. She was released in a prisoner exchange after four months. Dr. Walker remains the only woman who has received the Medal of Honor. It was originally conferred in 1866, rescinded in 1916, and restored in 1977.

Wounded soldiers from the battle of the Wilderness, at Fredericksburg, Virginia. May 1864

Dr. Mary Edwards Walker (1832–1919), wearing her Medal of Honor. Date unknown

{ **OCTOBER 28** 1862: Major General John C. Breckinridge (President James Buchanan's vice president and the 1860 presidential nominee of the Southern faction of the Democratic Party) assumes command of the Confederate Army of Middle Tennessee. }

"All the newspaper intelligence to-day is cheering. I am delighted by the nomination of McClellan," Lieutenant Colonel Alfred B. McCalmont wrote to his brother on August 31, 1864. "If some great and decisive result is not attained by our armies in a month he will be elected, which will be a glorious event." The election for U.S. president had loomed large in both the North and the South throughout the year. Many Southerners and Northern Peace Democrats had high hopes that former Union general-in-chief George B. McClellan would defeat Abraham Lincoln and immediately negotiate to end the war. However, more than one "great and decisive result" attained by the Union armies in September and October, coupled with other events, defeated these hopes. "The smoke has cleared away and we are beaten!" McClellan wrote to his mother on November 11. "Personally I am glad that the dreadful responsibility of the government of the nation is not to devolve upon my shoulders." The following January, he and his much-beloved wife, generally called Ellen, embarked on an extended tour of Europe. "The feeling for the General in England is enthusiastic," she reported to her father. "They look upon him as *the* American general." (See also February 16, April 24 and 25.)

The true issue or "That's what's the matter." A rare pro-Democratic political cartoon, depicting presidential aspirant George B. McClellan as the intermediary between Presidents Abraham Lincoln and Jefferson Davis. Lithograph on wove paper, Currier & Ives, 1864

George B. McClellan (1826–1885) with his wife, Mary Ellen Marcy McClellan. Date unknown

{ **OCTOBER 29** 1861: The largest combined land-sea expedition mounted by the United States to date—about twelve thousand troops and seventy-seven vessels—leaves Hampton Roads, Virginia, for the Carolina coast and Port Royal, South Carolina. }

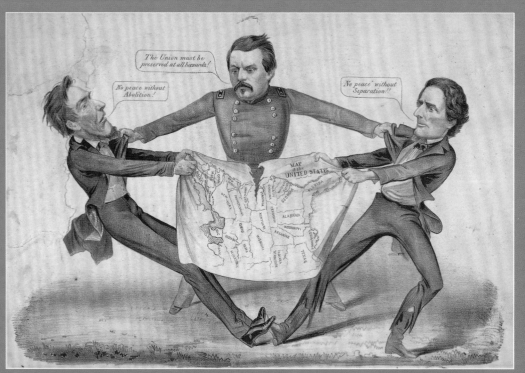

"The foolish, yet absolute, devotion of the women to the Southern cause does much to keep it alive," Union colonel John Beatty wrote in his journal in May 1862. "It encourages, nay forces, the young to enter the army, and compels them to continue what the more sensible Southerners know to be a hopeless struggle." Throughout the war, women in the South generally faced much greater difficulties than their Northern counterparts: most of the war was fought on Southern ground, the economy was devastated by the demands of war, and disruption and shortages plagued even the formerly wealthy. Despite hardships, however, most white Southern women remained devoted to the Confederate cause; as Union victory loomed, their trepidation was laced with stubborn defiance. "To go back into the Union!!!" Emma Holmes of South Carolina exclaimed to her diary in April 1865. "No words can describe all the horrors contained in those few words. . . . We could not, we would not believe it. Our Southern blood rose in stronger rebellion than ever and we all determined that, if obliged to submit, never could they *subdue* us."

Richmond ladies going to receive [U.S.] government rations. Wood engraving of a sketch by Alfred R. Waud, in *Harper's Weekly,* June 3, 1865

{ **OCTOBER 30** 1863: Unconditional Unionists in Arkansas—a Confederate state that is now largely under Federal control—meet at Fort Smith and name a representative to the U.S. Congress. }

I saw battle-corpses, myriads of them,

And the white skeletons of young men, I saw them,
I saw the debris and debris of all the slain soldiers of the war,
But I saw they were not as was thought,
They themselves were fully at rest, they suffer'd not,
The living remain'd and suffer'd, the mother suffer'd
And the wife and the child and the musing comrade suffer'd,
And the armies that remain'd suffer'd.

—Walt Whitman, excerpt from
"When Lilacs Last in the Dooryard Bloom'd," 1866

The Soldier's Memorial. Hand-colored lithograph, Currier & Ives, 1863

Officers and soldiers on the battlefield of Second Bull Run, attempting to recognize the remains of their comrades. Pencil drawing by Edwin Forbes, 1863

{ **OCTOBER 31** 1864: By presidential proclamation about a week before Election Day, Nevada becomes the thirty-sixth state in the Union. }

NOVEMBER: VALOR AND SACRIFICE

From the quiet courage of civilians and soldiers who did their duty faithfully through years of routine and hardship to the stunning bravery demonstrated time and again by combatants on both sides in the heat of battle, the Civil War was a testament to the capacity of "common" people to exhibit uncommon valor. Confronted with multiple dangers and the swirling chaos of war, angered by reports of war profiteering (and, in the South, by impressment of food and livestock), beset by arguments that constantly erupted over political and military matters—millions of Americans, North and South, persevered in their quest for victory until the outcome was incontestable. Pursuing similar ideals—interpreted very differently—the two sides in the divided and intensely religious American community fervently prayed for support to the same sustaining God.

"It is fitting that religion herself should with gentle voice whisper her benediction upon your flag and your cause," the Reverend Benjamin Palmer, of New Orleans First Presbyterian Church, said to departing Confederate soldiers. "It is a war of defense against wicked and cruel barbarism . . . a war of religion against a blind and bloody fanaticism. . . . May the Lord of Hosts be with you as a wall of fire, and shield your head in the day of battle."

"This is not a war waged in the interest of any base passion," the Reverend Henry Ward Beecher preached to a Brooklyn congregation in November 1861, "but truly and religiously in

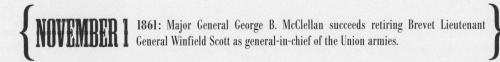

{ **NOVEMBER 1** 1861: Major General George B. McClellan succeeds retiring Brevet Lieutenant General Winfield Scott as general-in-chief of the Union armies. }

*Battle of Williamsburg—Gen.
Hancock's charge, May 5, 1862.*
Color lithograph, Kurz & Allison,
1893

the defence of the highest interests ever committed to a nation's keeping. . . . God
is loading up magazines for us. God has poured money into our coffers. . . . Let all
nations stand off! Sweep around the ring and stand off spectators, and now let these
gigantic forms stand, Liberty and God—Slavery and the Devil, and no more put hand
or foot into that ring until they have done battle unto the death!"

In four years of increasingly brutal conflict, more than 620,000 soldiers
sacrificed their lives on the battlefield, in disease-riven camps, or on the march.
Thousands more who were wounded returned, sometimes again and again, to the field.
This war saw the birth of the highest decoration awarded to U.S. military personnel,
the Medal of Honor, established as a permanent medal in 1863. Bestowed, at first,
without adequate or uniform criteria (some medals were rescinded by a military
board in 1916), the Medal of Honor was awarded to 1,519 men—and one woman—
who acted with exceptional courage during the war. Confederates did not have an equivalent
decoration during the war—in part, because of discomfort over singling some men out over
others. ("We have an army of brave men," said General Robert E. Lee.) On October 3, 1863,
however, General Order No. 131 did establish a Confederate Roll of Honor. Comprising more
than 2,000 names when fighting stopped in 1865, the roll contains no descriptions of specific
acts of heroism. But Civil War history is rich with accounts of the valor of individual Confederate
soldiers, who, like their Union counterparts, faced the horrors of war and the possibility of
violent death with courage and resolution.

Leading a charge in the Mexican War (1846–48), Phil Kearny sustained a wound that led to the amputation of his left arm. Serving with the French cavalry in 1859, he displayed courage that won him the Cross of the Legion of Honor. Appointed a Union brigadier general of volunteers in 1861, Kearny added to the esprit de corps of his men by having them wear a distinctive red "Kearny patch." "You are marked men," he said; "you must be ever in the front." During the 1862 Peninsula campaign, Kearny was cited for bravery at the battle of Williamsburg, and his leadership at a later battle inspired Edmund Stedman to write the poem "Kearny at Seven Pines." On September 1, 1862, as Union troops clashed with Confederates during a violent rainstorm at the battle of Chantilly (Ox Hill), Virginia, elements of Kearny's division charged up to bolster General Isaac I. Stevens's men after Stevens was killed (see March 12). Shortly thereafter, riding up to investigate a rumored gap in Federal lines, General Kearny himself was killed—depriving the army of a leader whom former Union general-in-chief Winfield Scott had described as "the bravest man I ever knew."

Philip Kearny (1814–1862). 1855–62

General Kearney's gallant charge, at the Battle of Chantilly, Va 1ˢᵗ of September 1862. Color lithograph by Augustus Tholey, 1862–67

NOVEMBER 2 **1861:** In the volatile border state of Missouri, Major General John C. Frémont is relieved of command of the Union's Western Department by order of President Lincoln. The president is particularly disturbed by Frémont's unauthorized August 30 proclamation freeing the slaves of any Missourian who took up arms against the Union.

One of the few "fleet actions" of the war, the battle of Plum Run Bend (Tennessee), as it is sometimes called, pitted seven Union ironclad mortar boats commanded by Captain Charles H. Davis against eight unarmored boats of the makeshift Confederate River Defense Fleet on May 10, 1862. Despite the odds against them, the Confederates, under the bold command of Captain James E. Montgomery, rammed and sank the ironclads *Cincinnati* and *Mound City* (which were later raised). Not in ramming range of other Union boats, the Confederates kept up fire with their guns and sharpshooters for half an hour and then withdrew toward Fort Pillow, the only other river defense for Memphis, Tennessee, besides the Confederate fleet. On June 3–5, the Confederates withdrew from the fort, and in the battle on June 6 that preceded the surrender of Memphis that morning, three of the Confederate boats were destroyed and four were captured; only one escaped.

African American sailor (identity unknown) holding a double-case image of Confederate soldiers. Ambrotype, 1860–70

Brilliant naval victory on the Mississippi River, near Fort Wright, May 10th 1862. Hand-colored lithograph, Currier & Ives, 1862

{ **NOVEMBER 3** 1816: Jubal Anderson Early (CSA) is born in Franklin County, Virginia. }

Suddenly we found out that the enemy was firing on us from the rear. . . . Our men faced about, formed, and advanced on them. . . . Our colonel fell dead at the first fire and the major immediately after. Our senior captain was shot and we were almost without officers. My two tent mates were wounded, and after that, they tell me, I acted like a madman. God only knows why or how I came out alive. I had three guns shot to pieces in my hands, a rammer shot in two, and I was struck in three places by [musket] balls. . . . Through Monday and Tuesday we were constantly exposed to the shells and grape of the enemy. About sundown Tuesday night the remnant of our brigade went out again to the front. Here the rebels swarmed out of the woods, seemingly without end, and though again and again repulsed, and the field piled with the dead . . . they still came on, determined to drive us from our position, but they could not do it. . . . Our last corporal, Walter Ames, who brought the colors safely off the bloody field of Gaines' Mill, was shot through the heart while waving them in front of our lines in this last fight.

—Private Oliver Willcox Norton (USA), letter, July 5, 1862, describing the fighting on the Virginia Peninsula, from June 26 through the July 1 battle of Malvern Hill

Private Edwin Francis Jemison, Second Louisiana Regiment (CSA) (later killed at the battle of Malvern Hill, Virginia Peninsula, July 1, 1862). 1861–62 (rephotographed 1961)

Federal wounded at a field hospital at Savage's Station, Virginia Peninsula. Photograph by James F. Gibson, June 30, 1862

{ **NOVEMBER 4** 1862: With the conquest of Vicksburg in mind, General Ulysses S. Grant's forces occupy the important transportation links of La Grange and Grand Junction, Tennessee. }

During the battle, the Surgeons of the different divisions established their field hospitals in the farm houses with their barns and out-buildings scattered over the field of battle, which extends some six miles irregularly along Antietam Creek. . . . As soon after the fighting as was possible, the wounded who were scattered over the vast area embraced by the battle-field and the space between it and the Potomac River, over which the Confederates retreated, were taken charge of. . . . The scene was a busy one. Men were actively engaged in collecting the wounded, ambulances were hurrying to the rear, many of the slightly wounded were staggering to hospital-wards, and burial parties were busy digging long burial trenches. The evidences of the battle were everywhere, bullet marks on corn, twigs, and fences, trees shattered in their trunks, and the dead scattered far and wide. In a day or so, visitors and the friends of the injured thronged to the field.

—Major John H. Brinton, surgeon (USA), excerpt from his memoirs (1914),
describing the battle of Antietam, September 17, 1862

Citizen volunteers assisting the wounded in the field of battle. Pencil and Chinese white drawing on olive paper by Alfred R. Waud, September 17, 1862

{ **NOVEMBER 5** 1818: "Political general" Benjamin Franklin Butler (USA) is born in Deerfield, New Hampshire. }

As the fog rolled away and the sun came out, the enemy were seen advancing from the town in great force. . . . [They] made a desperate attempt to gain these heights. Assault after assault was made, each time with fresh columns and increased numbers. They never succeeded, however, in getting nearer than seventy or eighty yards to the stone wall, from which the brave Georgians and Carolinians saluted them with a fire that no mere human force could face and live. We repulsed the foe with a slaughter that is without parallel in this war. I went over the ground this morning, and the remaining dead, after two-thirds of them had been removed, lay twice as thick as upon any other battlefield I have ever seen.

—Peter Alexander, correspondent for the *Charleston (South Carolina) Courier*, describing the battle of Fredericksburg, 1862 (see also March 17 and 18)

Rebel pickets dead, in Fredericksburg. Pencil drawing on cream paper by Alfred R. Waud, December 1862

"Inscription for the dead at Fredericksburgh [*sic*]," by Herman Melville, New York. 1863

{ NOVEMBER 6 1860: After a particularly complex and heated campaign (see January 15 and 16), Abraham Lincoln is elected president of the United States, with more than 1.8 million votes and 180 electoral votes (28 more than he needed to win). **}**

Rebel Pickets dead in Fredericksburg.
Ponton Bridge, Union Batteries firing on the rebel works
back of the City—down the hill in the background of picture

Inscription
For the Dead
At Fredericksburgh.

A dreadful glory lights an earnest end;
In jubilee the patriot ghosts ascend;
Transfigured at the rapturous height
    Of their passionate feat of arms,
Death to the brave's a starry night,—
    Strewn their vale of death with palms.

Herman Melville

After seeing husbands, sons, brothers, and friends off to the army, many women, South and North alike, found myriad ways to help the war effort themselves. Mary Morris Husband, for example, volunteered at a Philadelphia hospital before traveling to Virginia to nurse a son who had become ill during the Union's 1862 Peninsula campaign. She proceeded to treat wounded soldiers from Antietam through Chancellorsville, Gettysburg, and the 1864 Overland campaign; she also helped soldiers falsely accused of desertion and other infractions appeal their sentences. When Union troops entering Richmond in April 1865 saw that she was there, they gave out with a lusty cheer: "Hurrah for Mother Husband!"

In 1863, Confederate nurse Kate Cumming worried over the wounded in her care, who "were put on the train about three or four days ago, . . . and many of them have not had their wounds dressed during that time." In 1864, her worries expanded to include the approaching enemy: "Not a day passes but we hear of some brutal outrage committed by these vandals. . . . I have been told that . . . Cassville [Georgia] . . . has been laid in ruins, and other outrages committed, all because some of the ladies thoughtlessly insulted the prisoners who passed through there about two years ago."

The Brave Wife. Hand-colored lithograph, Currier & Ives, date unknown

Mrs. Mary Morris Husband (1820?–1894). Illustration in *Woman's Work in the Civil War: A Record of Heroism, Patriotism and Patience* (1867)

{ **NOVEMBER 7** **1837:** Elijah Parish Lovejoy (b. 1802), abolitionist and editor of the *Alton (Illinois) Observer*, is killed by a proslavery mob while trying to protect his presses from being destroyed for the fourth time. He will become known as the "martyr abolitionist." }

A Maryland resident whose drawings expressed his fervent support of the South, Adalbert John Volck created this sentimental depiction of Southern sacrifice in 1863. Although recasting bells into ordnance was probably a rare occurrence, many Southern civilians did regularly reach into their ever-shrinking stores to support their troops, often raising money via raffles or bazaars. In Columbia, South Carolina, just weeks before it was occupied during General William T. Sherman's advance, a fund-raising bazaar featured booths named for each Confederate state. "To go there one would scarce believe it was war time," one observer wrote; "the tables were loaded with fancy articles—brought through the blockade, or manufactured by the ladies." Many Southern women manufactured wares for more personally pressing reasons: "Our ladies, who have been brought up in the greatest luxury, are working with the hands to assist their families," Virginia native Judith McGuire wrote in her diary in 1863. "Some young ladies plait straw hats for sale; I saw one sold this morning for twenty dollars—and . . . so far from being ashamed of it, they take pride in their own handiwork."

Offering of Bells to be Cast into Cannon. Etching by Adalbert John Volck, 1863, published 1864

{ **NOVEMBER 8** 1864: Abraham Lincoln is reelected president of the United States, with Andrew Johnson of Tennessee as vice president. Lincoln wins 212 electoral votes; his opponent, Democrat George B. McClellan, receives 21. }

After earning the admiration of his commander, Stonewall Jackson, during Jackson's hallmark 1862 Shenandoah Valley campaign, veteran soldier Richard S. Ewell was so badly wounded during the Second Bull Run campaign (August 1862) that his leg required amputation. Undaunted, he returned to duty—though he had to be strapped to his horse when he rode. One of Lee's three corps commanders, Lieutenant General Ewell held the Confederate left at Gettysburg. But he was injured again in 1864, this time so severely that he could no longer command in the field. Yet he continued to serve, directing Richmond's defenses until the city fell.

Young volunteer Warren H. Freeman of the Thirteenth Massachusetts Volunteers (whose brother Eugene was an engineer in the Union's transport service) wrote often to his parents as he moved through the thick of warfare in the eastern theater, from Second Bull Run to the siege of Petersburg. His letters reflect the determination that characterized many of the volunteers of both sides—as well as their growing war weariness: "I think mother must be about sick of these tales of blood," he wrote in August 1864, "certainly I am; but what can I do? I say as little, and endeavor to describe in the least revolting manner the horrible scenes around me. I trust I may be spared the task of speaking of or participating in any more such conflicts."

Richard S. Ewell (1817–1872). 1860–65

Warren Hapgood Freeman (b. c. 1844). Frontispiece in *Letters from Two Brothers Serving in the War for the Union to Their Family at Home in West Cambridge, Mass.* (1871)

{ **NOVEMBER 9** 1825: A. P. (Ambrose Powell) Hill (CSA) is born in Culpeper, Virginia. }

Truly brothers-in-arms, George A. Custer and Thomas W. Custer served in different theaters until 1864, when Tom joined his brother's command as a second lieutenant. In 1865, during the final pursuit of General Robert E. Lee's army, Tom Custer was awarded two Medals of Honor for capturing Confederate flags during the battles at Namozine Church (April 3) and Sayler's Creek (April 6). His elder brother, meanwhile, had become one of the Union army's youngest and most celebrated generals, noted for the aggressive leadership he first displayed during the 1862 Peninsula campaign (see March 4). General Custer also served with distinction at the May 11, 1864, battle at Yellow Tavern, Virginia, where the dashing and much-beloved Confederate cavalry general Jeb Stuart (see also March 8 and 21), having pressed his men hard to place them between Federal troops and Richmond, received a mortal wound. "For seven days Lee declined to give any official announcement of this tragedy," Bennett H. Young wrote in *Confederate Wizards of the Saddle* (1914). "General Lee was unwilling to let his fighters know that death had called the illustrious cavalry chieftain at the moment when they most needed the inspiration of every Confederate leader."

George Armstrong Custer (1839–1876), seated, with his wife, Elizabeth Bacon Custer, and his brother, Thomas W. Custer. 1861–76

James Ewell Brown (Jeb) Stuart (1833–1864). 1860–64

{ **NOVEMBER 10** **1862:** Relieved of command on November 5, Major General George B. McClellan bids an emotional farewell to the Union's Army of the Potomac (see July 8). }

Before we were aware of it, almost, we were engaged in our first cavalry charge. . . . At our left, as far as eye could reach, were seen bodies of our cavalry advancing with quick movements toward the enemy's cavalry. . . . In our front and moving rapidly toward us were the enemy's troops that had just driven the other regiments of our brigade from the field. . . . A little to the right of our front was a rebel battery, which turned its attention to us as we emerged from the woods. . . . A shell from the battery on our right comes screaming with harsh voice along our line . . . and seeming so near as to make it impossible, almost, for the left of the company to escape its effects—and bursts quarter of a mile away. . . . On we went; my battalion, in response to an order, wheeling half-right, going for and driving the enemy away from the battery, and passing by the lonely and now quiet guns that a moment before were so loudly talking, while the remainder of the regiment keeps its original direction. And see! the rebel force in our front is in full retreat, and the charge has turned to a chase.

—Lieutenant Edward P. Tobie (USA), excerpt from his reminiscence (1882)

Cavalry charge near Culpeper Court House, Va. Pencil drawing by Edwin Forbes, September 14, 1864

{ **NOVEMBER 11** 1864: Union troops at Rome, Georgia, destroy bridges, foundries, warehouses, and other property useful to the Confederates and then proceed toward Atlanta. }

With profound gratitude toward the God of battles, by whose blessings our enemies have been humbled and our arms rendered triumphant, your commanding general avails himself of this his first opportunity to express to you his admiration of the heroic manner in which you have passed through the series of battles which to-day resulted in the surrender of the enemy's entire army. The record established by your indomitable courage is unparalleled in the annals of war. Your prowess has won for you even the respect and admiration of your enemies. . . . Should the assistance of keen blades, wielded by your sturdy arms, be required to hasten the coming of the glorious peace for which we have been so long contending, the general commanding is proudly confident that in the future, as in the past, every demand will meet with a hearty and willing response. Let us hope that our work is done, and that, blessed with the comforts of peace, we may soon be permitted to enjoy the pleasure of home and friends.

For our comrades who have fallen, let us ever cherish a grateful remembrance.

—Major General George Armstrong Custer (USA), statement to
"Soldiers of the Third Cavalry Division," April 9, 1865

Officers of the Fifth U.S. Cavalry, in the vicinity of Washington, D.C. Photograph by William Morris Smith, June 1865

{ NOVEMBER 12 **1861:** Bought in England, the Confederate blockade-runner *Fingal* arrives in Savannah, Georgia, with military supplies. Subsequently converted to an ironclad and renamed CSS *Atlanta*, the ship will surrender after sixteen crew members are wounded during a fierce engagement with two Union vessels on June 17, 1863. **}**

"There is a woman in the town [Fairfax Court House, Virginia] by the name of Ford, not married, who has been of great service to Gen. [Jeb] Stuart in giving information &c—so much that Stuart has conferred on her the rank of major in the rebel army," averred a letter printed in the *New York Times* on March 14, 1863. The vivacious Antonia Ford had indeed been given an *honorary* commission by General Robert E. Lee's flamboyant cavalry commander, and she treasured the document. She also undoubtedly provided information to Confederate officers—among them, partisan raider John Singleton Mosby (see March 20)—that she had overheard from Union men occupying her town. The Federal officer who escorted her to Washington's Old Capitol Prison the day before the letter appeared in the *Times*, Major Joseph C. Willard, was part owner of Willard's Hotel (see January 29). He was also deeply smitten with Miss Ford—who, gradually, returned his affections. But she would not marry him while he was in uniform: "[My] parents and relatives would be mortified to death; acquaintances would disown me." In March 1864, after Willard resigned his commission, they were married at Washington's Metropolitan Hotel.

Lace cap and collar made by Antonia Ford Willard while in prison on charges of spying for the Confederate army. c. 1863

Antonia Ford Willard (1838–1871). Date unknown

General Stuart's new aid [*sic*]. Depiction of Antonia Ford (Willard). Wood engraving in *Harper's Weekly*, April 4, 1863

{ **NOVEMBER 13** 1814: Joseph "Fighting Joe" Hooker (USA) is born in Hadley, Massachusetts. }

"Sylvia's Lovers" is the new novel by Mrs. Gaskell—a story of English life, told with the eloquent fervor and dramatic power for which the authoress of "Mary Barton" has long since established her fame. It has been greeted with great

DO YOU GIVE IT UP?

What Christian name reads both ways the same? *Hannah.*

Why is Ireland likely to become very rich? *Because its capital is always doubling (Dublin).*

GENERAL STUART'S NEW AID.

"The rebel cavalry leader, STUART, has appointed to a position on his staff, with the rank of Major, a young lady residing at Fairfax Court House, who has been of great service to him in giving information," etc.—*Daily Paper.*

At TWO o'clk am; we are aroused by the "Long Roll" and to make matters worse the rain is falling in torrents, tents are soon struck and long before light we are slipping and splashing through the rain and mud, no one can understand why the "long roll" was beat; some say that Colonel Mills is mad because the men straggled so yesterday. The men are all worn out by yesterdays march and this addition of rain and mud completely uses us up. Let a soldiers clothing and blankets get thoroughly saturated with water and it will add thirty pounds to his burden; then take a step of twentyeight inches and slip back twenty of them, try it all day long and see how pleasant it is. (not to a soldier.)

—W. W. Heartsill, Lane Rangers (CSA), journal entry, June 3, 1863

A stormy march (artillery)—
Spotsylvania Court House.
Pencil drawing by Edwin Forbes,
May 12, 1864

{ **NOVEMBER 14** **1862:** In New Orleans, a proclamation calls for the election of members of the U.S. Congress from the portions of Louisiana that are under Union control. }

May 12th 64

This is a fast day, proclaimed by the President of the Confederate States, and has been observed as a Sabbath in the Camp. Mr. Lacy preached at our headquarters. . . . His allusions to General [Stonewall] Jackson in his prayers were very fine. . . . After sermon Dr. Coleman of Johnson's Division . . . said the finest tribute [to Jackson] he had ever heard was from a Mrs. Neal, at Yerby's near Hamilton's Crossing. . . . She said her opinion of him had entirely changed after his family came there and she saw the stern warrior unbend himself and fondle his child and talk artlessly to it, and how deeply and fondly he loved his wife, coming there, often . . . and that she got to thinking of the efforts the Yankees would make to capture him. . . . She rushed up to his room and said: "General; why don't you bring a guard with you. . . . It is not right for you to expose yourself thus. Your life does not belong to you, you belong to the country." He smiled and she proceeded. "After this war is over and we have achieved our independence, I don't care how soon you die" (and here she covered up her face and wept bitterly . . .). "For *this* world has no honor commensurate with your merits."

—Major Jedediah Hotchkiss (CSA), diary entry, August 21, 1863

(see also March 23, July 10)

Stonewall Jackson and His Boyhood Home, situated on the West Fork River, Lewis Co., WVA. Color lithograph, Henderson-Achert Litho. Co., 1889

Thomas Jonathan "Stonewall" Jackson (1824–1863) at Hamilton's Crossing, near Fredericksburg, Virginia. Photograph by Minnes of Richmond, April 1863

{ **NOVEMBER 15** **1861:** The Young Men's Christian Association (YMCA) organizes the U.S. Christian Commission for service to Federal soldiers. }

I went on hunting for the field infirmary, and when I found it . . . I at once went to work assisting in amputations, and continued at it all day and until late at night. . . . We knew nothing of Stonewall Jackson's being shot the night before. . . . After all the wounded were attended to I was very tired and went to sleep late that night in a tent. I would wake up cold during the night and reach out for a jug of whiskey and take a swallow and go back to sleep again. . . . The next morning (Monday the 4th) . . . several handsome young Yankee surgeons in fine uniforms came over with a white flag, and I went to where they were attending to their wounded. While there I talked with a wounded man from Ohio, and saw one of our soldiers cut a forked limb from a tree and make a crutch for a Yankee who was wounded in the foot.

—Dr. Spencer Glasgow Welch (CSA), letter, May 9, 1863,
describing his experiences during the battle of Chancellorsville

*Steam mill on the battlefield,
used as a medical depot* (battle
of Chancellorsville, Virginia).
Pencil and Chinese white drawing on brown paper by Alfred R.
Waud, May 1–4, 1863

{ **NOVEMBER 16** **1864:** General William T. Sherman and sixty thousand Union troops leave a burned-out Atlanta, beginning what will become known as Sherman's March to the Sea. }

the battlefield used as a medical depot. H. R. Wa...

Louisiana's Francis Tillou Nicholls left the U.S. Army in 1856, one year after his graduation from West Point, to pursue a career in law. He abandoned his burgeoning law practice for the duration of the Civil War to serve in the Confederate army. After fighting at First Bull Run, Nicholls served under Stonewall Jackson in the 1862 Shenandoah campaign—during which he was wounded so severely that his left arm had to be amputated. After convalescence, he returned to field duty in command of the Second Louisiana Brigade. At the battle of Chancellorsville in May 1863, an exploding artillery shell tore off his left foot. Nicholls continued to serve behind the front lines. In July 1864, he was appointed superintendent of the conscript bureau of the Trans-Mississippi Department. As he was traveling west, Admiral David G. Farragut's naval squadron waged its fierce battle at Mobile Bay on August 5, 1864. On board Farragut's flagship, USS *Hartford*, Landsman John H. Lawson was badly wounded in the leg as a Confederate shell exploded on the deck. Refusing treatment, he remained at his post throughout the battle—a Union victory that closed the important Confederate port at Mobile (see May 28). Lawson was subsequently awarded the Medal of Honor.

Francis Redding Tillou Nicholls
(1834–1912). 1861–65

John H. Lawson (1837–1919).
c. 1900

{ **NOVEMBER 17** 1863: Confederates in Tennessee besiege Knoxville while continuing their siege of Chattanooga to the southwest. }

The Union troops advanced some distance into the woods, when a hot, and sharp, contest with musketry ensued, laying many a poor fellow low; we could not use our artillery, as there would be danger of injuring our own men, who were hotly engaged in the woods. . . . We advanced in *line of batle* [*sic*], over an open field, across a deep ditch, whose banks were very steep, and entered the *Wilderness*, where the battle was raging; . . . we advanced through thick underbrush, for some distance, when we halted; soon, the rebels, who could not be seen any distance through the thick woods, simultaneously poured a volley in to our first line, which caused it to break, and they fell back on the second, but soon rallying, they again formed in line, and drove the rebels some distance, and long after dark, the firing having ceased, we laid down on our *arms*, to rest from a fatiguing day's work. We lost heavily in killed and wounded.

—Private John W. Jaques (USA), diary entry, May 5, 1864 (see also March 25 and 26)

Battle of the Wilderness—Desperate fight on the Orange C. H. Plank Road, near Todd's Tavern, May 6th, 1864. Color lithograph, Kurz & Allison, 1887

William W. Heath, Company H, Fourth Vermont Infantry (USA) (later killed at the battle of the Wilderness, May 5, 1864). 1860–64 (rephotographed 1961)

{ **NOVEMBER 18** 1864: President Davis tells General Howell Cobb, who is at Macon, Georgia, to "get out every man who can render any service even for a short period" to oppose General William T. Sherman's March to the Sea. }

Field Hospital near Spottsylvania Court House, Va. . . . I thought our

fighting was over, for we had driven the Yankees off the field at the Wilderness . . . but we had another big fight with them the next day (8th instant) near this place. Then on the 10th another big fight here, and then one again yesterday that was the most terrific battle I have ever witnessed. . . . We were behind breastworks, but the Yankees charged into them in many places, fighting with the greatest determination, and it strained us to the utmost to hold our own. Such musketry I never heard before, and it continued all night, engaged with our brigade. It was perfectly fearful. I never experienced such anxiety in my life. It was an awful day, and it seemed to me as if all the "Furies of Darkness" had come together in combat. Everybody who was not firing was pale with anxiety, but our noble soldiers stood their ground, fighting with the utmost desperation. The Yanks certainly tried their best . . . and they made us try our best too. . . . I hope the Yankees are gone and that I shall never again witness such a terrible day as yesterday was.

—Dr. Spencer Glasgow Welch (CSA), letter, May 13, 1864 (see also March 27)

The toughest fight yet. The fight for the salient (at Spotsylvania, Virginia). Pencil, Chinese white, and black ink drawing on green paper by Alfred R. Waud, May 12, 1864

{ NOVEMBER 19 1863: At the dedication ceremony for a new national cemetery, following a two-hour oration by the statesman and clergyman Edward Everett, President Lincoln delivers a short, surpassingly eloquent speech that will become known as the Gettysburg Address. **}**

The toughest fight yet — the fight for the Dallas

A.R. Waud

After the fierce fighting at Spotsylvania Court House, Virginia (see November 19), General Ulysses S. Grant's Army of the Potomac and General Robert E. Lee's Army of Northern Virginia had little respite before clashing again with similar ferocity in a series of engagements farther south at Cold Harbor—culminating in the costly and unavailing Union assault on June 3 that Grant viewed ever after with regret (see July 30). Lengthening casualty lists provoked new levels of criticism over the slow and brutal push toward Richmond. In Washington on June 7, a troubled and weary Walt Whitman wrote to his mother of the new masses of wounded coming in from the terrible battles of the Overland campaign: "They are crowded here in Washington in immense numbers, and all those that come up from the Wilderness and that region, arrived here so neglected, and in such plight, it was awful. . . . One new feature is that many of the poor afflicted young men are crazy. Every ward has some in it that are wandering. They have suffered too much, and it is perhaps a privilege that they are out of their senses." Stubbornly, however, Grant and his soldiers pressed on toward the James River and Richmond—contested, with equal stubbornness, by Lee and his men.

Ulysses S. Grant and his war horse Cincinnati, Cold Harbor, Virginia. June 4, 1864

{ **NOVEMBER 20** 1862: General Robert E. Lee arrives at Fredericksburg, Virginia, as the buildup of Union and Confederate troops along the Rappahannock River continues. }

Dear Father and Mother, . . .

It is very strange, as well as painful, to see how little is thought of death in the army; it is rarely alluded to. I remember one of our boys—he was in the same mess with me; he used to speak about some statistics of other wars, how many pounds of lead and iron it took to kill a man, and how few were killed in proportion to the number engaged, and what a good chance there was to get off whole—his name was Henry Holden, and he was the first man killed in my company at Bull Run.

—Sergeant Warren H. Freeman (USA), letter, March 11, 1864

Dead Confederate soldiers at the scene of Richard S. Ewell's attack near Spotsylvania Court House. May 19, 1864

{ **NOVEMBER 21** 1861: President Davis appoints Judah P. Benjamin Confederate secretary of war. Exactly one year later, Davis appoints James A. Seddon to the same post. }

Pushing toward Atlanta in 1864, Major General William T. Sherman, repeatedly frustrated in his attempts to turn the left flank of General Joseph E. Johnston's Confederate army, hurled his men at the entrenched center of the Southern force at the battle of Kennesaw Mountain in Georgia. Trying to advance uphill in one-hundred-degree heat, the Union forces were repulsed at great cost. Among those paying the heavy price of this encounter was Colonel Daniel McCook Jr. of the Fifty-second Ohio. A former law partner of Sherman's, the colonel was also one of the "Fighting McCooks"—seventeen siblings and cousins who served in the war, seven of them as generals. Shot in the chest at point-blank range as he moved up the mountain, McCook was removed from the field and transported back to Ohio. He died at a brother's home four days before his thirtieth birthday. His promotion to brigadier general was confirmed the day before he died.

Battle of Kenesaw [sic] Mountain, June 27, 1864. Color lithograph, Kurz & Allison, 1891

Daniel McCook Jr. (1834–1864). 1861–64

{ **NOVEMBER 22** 1864: General Henry W. Slocum's wing of General William T. Sherman's army occupies Milledgeville, the Georgia state capital. }

In July 1864, General Jubal Early led fifteen thousand Confederates down the Shenandoah Valley toward Washington, D.C. As General Ulysses S. Grant dispatched reinforcements from Virginia, General Lew Wallace scraped together a force of some six thousand Union soldiers by the Monocacy River near Frederick, Maryland. Most of these troops were new and no match for the Confederate veterans. But Wallace and his emergency force managed to buy some valuable time for Washington to prepare for its unwanted visitors. "The enemy resisted our passage most of the day," Confederate major Jedediah Hotchkiss wrote in his diary on July 9. The next day, he made "a sketch of the Monocacy Battle Field, then followed the army . . . toward Washington." Early's men created a sensation when they arrived at the outskirts of the capital city on July 11. Visiting Fort Stevens, part of Washington's defensive lines, the following day, President Lincoln became so interested in seeing the invaders that a young captain, sometimes identified as Oliver Wendell Holmes Jr. (the future associate justice of the U.S. Supreme Court), yelled, "Get down, you damn fool, before you get shot!" The president obeyed. This was the only occasion when he came under direct fire from Confederate forces.

Sketch of the Battle of Monocacy. Color manuscript map by Jedediah Hotchkiss (CSA), July 10, 1864

{ **NOVEMBER 23** 1803: Theodore Dwight Weld (1803–1895), "The Great Abolitionist," is born in Hampton, Connecticut. }

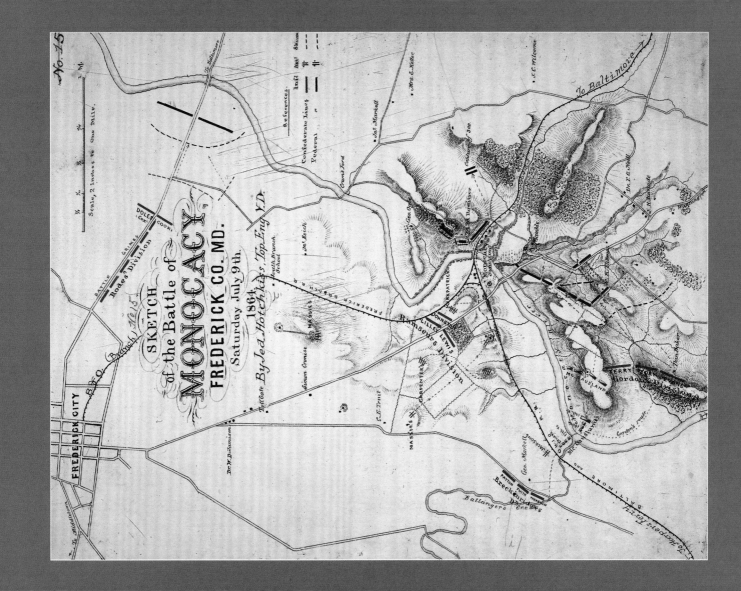

About the 20ᵗʰ of September, 1864, I was sent to the Valley of Virginia. This was then the condition of affairs: In the latter days of July and early August, a cavalry raid had been made by the enemy across the Potomac and Maryland into Pennsylvania. The town of Chambersburg was burned, and the enemy withdrew into Virginia. At this time, General Sheridan, by Grant's order, was placed in command of a considerable force on the upper Potomac, from Harper's Ferry westward and southward. He was opposed by the southern general Early, and a good deal of maneuvering took place. . . . The enemy's wounded fell into Sheridan's hands, and were scattered over a large area of country. He also captured a large number of prisoners. . . . The devastation of the Shenandoah Valley and the Valley of Virginia then followed, the country being rendered useless to the enemy as a base of military operations or for material supplies. In fact it was left in such a state, that to use the words of Sheridan, "A carrion crow in his flight across must either carry his rations or starve." War's stern necessity!

—Major John H. Brinton, surgeon (USA), excerpt from his memoirs (1914)

(see also March 28)

Sheridan's army following [Jubal] Early up the Valley of the Shenandoah. Pencil drawing on light green paper by Alfred R. Waud, August 1864–March 1865

{ **NOVEMBER 24**   1862: General Joseph E. Johnston is assigned to the major Confederate command in the western theater, comprising all or part of six states. }

Sheridan's army following Early up the Valley of the Shenandoah.

A. R. Waud

The first major encounter between Major General Phil Sheridan's new Army of the Shenandoah and General Jubal Early's Confederates after the latter's incursion into Northern territory was the third battle of Winchester (Opequon Creek), Virginia, on September 19, 1864. Outnumbered by nearly three to one, Early's men resisted stubbornly during this encounter, until a Union division got beyond their left flank and charged—beginning an assault that fragmented the Confederate ranks and led to their retreat. Although Sheridan had made some potentially disastrous tactical errors during the battle, he was able to report to General Ulysses S. Grant that he had sent Early's forces "Whirling through Winchester."

Sheridan's Final Charge at Winchester. Color lithograph, Louis Prang & Co., 1886

{ NOVEMBER 25 1864: Confederate agents set fires in at least ten New York hotels and in Barnum's Museum; none does serious damage. **}**

By the time he graduated from West Point at the head of his class in 1863, John Rodgers Meigs had already distinguished himself in combat, while on leave from the academy, as a volunteer at the first battle of Bull Run. Son of the U.S. Army quartermaster general, Montgomery C. Meigs, and Louisa Rodgers Meigs—herself a member of a leading American military family—the young lieutenant of engineers was attached, after graduation, to Major General Philip Sheridan's command. Cited several times for gallantry in action during the Shenandoah Valley campaign in 1864, he quickly won promotion to brevet major. On October 3, 1864, while traveling with two enlisted men, he was accosted within Union lines by three Confederates, reportedly guerrillas, and killed—one of the enlisted men later stated that Meigs had been murdered. The presumed assassination of such a well-regarded and prominent young officer incited retaliation from Sheridan—some homes near the site of Meigs's death were burned—and a grief-stricken General Meigs offered a reward for his son's killer. The small statue that he commissioned of his son, depicted exactly as he fell, is now a poignant Civil War memorial in Arlington National Cemetery.

John Rodgers Meigs (1842–1864). Watercolor, c. 1862

Mrs. Louisa Rodgers Meigs and Montgomery Meigs (1816–1892). 1860–70

{ **NOVEMBER 26** 1861: A convention at Wheeling, in Unionist western Virginia, adopts a constitution for a new state to be created by secession from Virginia and called West Virginia. }

Having been instrumental in the Union conquest of the Mississippi River (see May 5, 12, and 17), Admiral David Dixon Porter was summoned to the East Coast to command the naval arm of the combined force that was to attack the formidable Fort Fisher, protecting the Confederate port city of Wilmington, North Carolina—an essential avenue for conveying supplies to General Robert E. Lee's besieged army at Petersburg, Virginia. A first attempt by this largest army-navy force of the war, in late December 1864, was unsuccessful: when Confederate reinforcements began to arrive, land force commander Major General Benjamin F. Butler withdrew units that had established a beachhead. In this, Butler defied General-in-Chief Ulysses S. Grant's explicit orders to maintain any foothold achieved and institute a siege of the fort, if it could not be taken immediately. Porter, whose ships had provided continual artillery support, "complained bitterly of having been abandoned by the army just when the fort was nearly in our possession," Grant wrote in his postwar memoirs, "and begged that our troops might be sent back again to co-operate, but with a different commander. . . . I selected A. H. Terry to command." (See also May 31.)

Rear Admiral David Dixon Porter, center, and staff aboard the Union admiral's flagship, USS *Malvern*, at Hampton Roads, Virginia. December 1864

{ **NOVEMBER 27** 1863: General John Hunt Morgan and several of his officers manage to escape from the Ohio State Penitentiary and reach Confederate territory. }

Jan 15.... The bombardment of Fort Fisher began again on Friday....

Jan. 18. . . . The prospect is growing darker & darker about us. On Sunday night Fort Fisher fell by assault. After having repulsed the enemy until half past six, it fell at 10 o'clock by a night attack most of the garrison being captured. A distinguished Virginian, Mr. [J. P.] Holcombe [of Bedford County], tells me there is a strong disposition among members of congress to make terms with the enemy, on the basis of the old Union, feeling that we cannot carry on the war any longer with hope of success. Wife & I sit talking of going to Mexico to live out there the remnant of our days.

Jan. 25, I have outlived my momentary depression, & feel my courage revive when I think of the brave army in front of us, sixty thousand strong. As long as Lee's army remains intact there is no cause for despondence. As long as it holds true we need not fear.

—Brigadier General Josiah Gorgas, chief of ordnance (CSA), diary entries, 1865 (see also May 31)

Capture of Fort Fisher. Color lithograph, Louis Prang & Co., 1887

{ **NOVEMBER 28** 1861: The Confederate Congress officially admits heavily divided Missouri to the Confederate States of America. }

A West Point graduate who left the army after only six months to study for the clergy, Leonidas Polk was a bishop of the Protestant Episcopal Church in 1861. Yet his conviction that the South was fighting in a sacred cause led him to abandon his clerical duties and accept a commission as major general in the Confederate army. His first major action—the politically disastrous incursion into the neutral state of Kentucky in September 1861—reflected some of the inexperienced, and sometimes contentious, general's military weaknesses; dedication and courage were among his strengths. Engaged in resisting General William T. Sherman's march toward Atlanta, he was killed by artillery fire at Pine Mountain, Georgia, on June 14, 1864.

One of Sherman's most reliable generals, Major General James B. McPherson was riding up to check on his lines during the battle of Atlanta on July 22, 1864, when he was shot and killed by Confederate riflemen. A talented soldier respected by his fellow officers and beloved by his men, McPherson had been a mainstay in western campaigns since serving as a field engineer during General Ulysses S. Grant's conquests of Forts Henry and Donelson in Tennessee. "Poor Macpherson's loss grieved me very much," former general-in-chief George B. McClellan wrote to Sherman. "It must have been a serious personal as well as official one to you."

Leonidas Polk (1806–1864). 1860–64

James B. McPherson (1828–1864). Photograph by the Brady National Photographic Art Gallery, 1860–64

{ **NOVEMBER 29** 1864: At Spring Hill, Tennessee, a Union army under the command of General John Schofield somehow manages to withdraw along a turnpike past Confederate general John Bell Hood's army without suffering an attack—a confusing incident that has become known as the "Spring Hill Affair." }

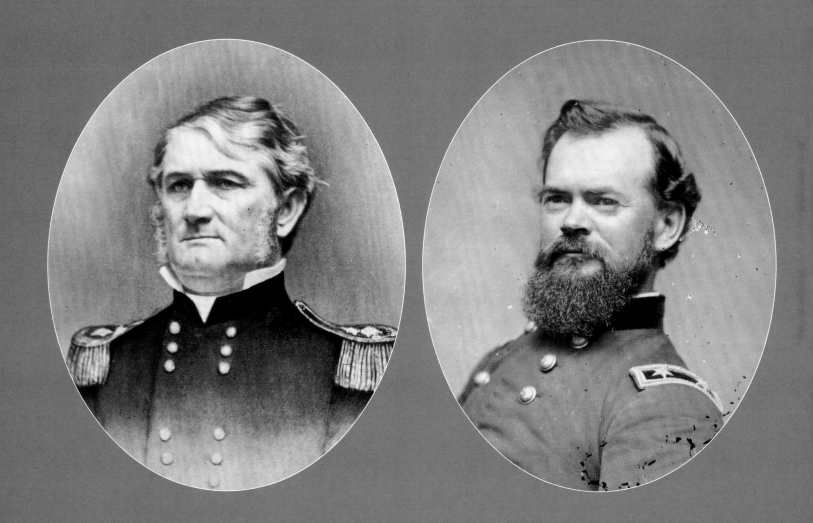

Washington was a little delirious. Everybody was celebrating. . . . Every day there was a stream of callers who came to congratulate the President, to tell how loyal they had been. . . . Because of the general joyousness, I was surprised when, late on the afternoon of the 14th, I accompanied Mr. Lincoln on a hurried visit to the War Department, I found that the President was more depressed than I had ever seen him. . . . Afterward Mrs. Lincoln told me that when he drove with her to the Soldiers' Home earlier in the afternoon he had been extremely cheerful, even buoyant. She said that he had talked of the calm future that was in store for them . . . when, his term over, they would go back to their home in Illinois. . . . Mr. Lincoln said to me: "Crook, do you know, I believe there are men who want to take my life?" . . . He came out of the Secretary's office in a short time. Then I saw that every trace of the depression . . . had vanished. He talked to me as usual. He said that Mrs. Lincoln and he, with a party, were going to the theatre to see *Our American Cousin.*

—William H. Crook, Lincoln's bodyguard, excerpt from "Lincoln's Last Day," as "written down by" Margarita Spalding Gerry, *Harper's Magazine,* September 1907

Abraham Lincoln at His Desk. Reproduction of a painting by Howard Pyle, illustration in "Lincoln's Last Day." *Harper's Magazine,* September 1907

Ford's Theatre program for Friday evening, April 14, 1865

{ **NOVEMBER 30** 1863: Gathering his defeated Confederate army in northwestern Georgia, General Braxton Bragg learns that President Davis has accepted his resignation. }

DECEMBER: AN UNEASY PEACE

The year 1865 opened with expectations in the North for victory at last, and with despair in the South—accompanied by continuation of a fighting spirit. But that spirit received a shattering blow when General Robert E. Lee was forced to surrender his Army of Northern Virginia during the second week of April, only a few days after the fall of Petersburg and the Confederate capital, Richmond. Although other Confederate forces remained in the field, Lee's surrender marked the virtual end of the war.

Less than a week after Lee met with General-in-Chief Ulysses S. Grant at Appomattox Court House, Virginia, to settle the terms of surrender, Northerners were devastated by the assassination of President Abraham Lincoln. His successor, Andrew Johnson, seemed at first to hold views that might be compatible with the plans of congressional Radicals who favored more punitive measures toward the South than President Lincoln had wished to impose. Johnson quickly grew more conciliatory toward former Confederate leaders, however—even as he proved implacably resistant to confirming and protecting the rights of African Americans. In 1868, Johnson's increasingly stormy relations with Congress culminated in his impeachment and trial (see December 22). The next president, Ulysses S. Grant, contended with storms of anti-black

The fall of Petersburg, Va. After withstanding a ten-month siege, Petersburg fell on April 2, 1865–but Robert E. Lee was able to withdraw the remnants of his army. The Confederates were quickly pursued by Union troops. Color lithograph, Kurz & Allison, c. 1890

{ **DECEMBER 1** 1861: The Union gunboat *Penguin* captures the blockade-runner *Albion* off Charleston, South Carolina, and confiscates her valuable cargo of arms, food, and military equipment. }

A. P. (Ambrose Powell) Hill (1825–1865). Riding outside Petersburg to rally his men on April 2, 1865, he was shot and killed by two Union soldiers. Engraving, date unknown

and anti-Republican violence in the South during his two terms of office, as former Confederate leaders waged a persistent, and ultimately successful, battle to reacquire political influence in the Southern states.

As political battles continued, surviving soldiers of the North and the South returned to their civilian pursuits—with Southerners also confronting the huge task of rebuilding their ravaged region. Black veterans and other African Americans in both the South and the North—although bolstered by the Thirteenth, Fourteenth, and Fifteenth Amendments to the Constitution and the knowledge that slavery had been eradicated in the United States—still faced many more decades of fighting for equality.

In the postwar years, many soldiers, sailors, former army nurses, and others wrote their memoirs or published their wartime letters and diaries—providing future generations with an especially rich historical record. Poets and lyricists sang of the war, playwrights and novelists wrote of it, artists depicted it on canvas, lithographers sold prints of heroic and nostalgic wartime scenes. As scars slowly healed and bitterness dissipated, veterans of both North and South came together at reunions, sharing memories they had gathered on opposite sides of Civil War battlefields. In 1913, surviving veterans of the battle of Gettysburg returned to Pennsylvania for the fiftieth anniversary of that pivotal North-South encounter and were honored by a number of prominent Americans, including President Woodrow Wilson. In one of the many speeches given, Dr. Nathaniel Cox of Indiana's Reunion Committee harkened back to another gathering at Gettysburg, on November 19, 1863: "That great patriot who loved his country and his fellowman, who stood on these hills a half century ago, and dedicated this hallowed ground in simple language that will live forever, had a vision of this scene, when he uttered these prophetic words, 'This nation, under God, shall have a new birth of freedom, and that government of the people, by the people, and for the people, shall not perish from the earth.'"

To increase the pressure on Petersburg, General-in-Chief Ulysses S. Grant determined to cut the railroad lines that brought supplies into the city, as soon as possible. The Weldon Railroad, closest to the Union lines in the summer of 1864, connected Petersburg to Weldon, North Carolina. "This road was very important to the enemy," Grant later wrote in his memoirs. "The limits from which his supplies had been drawn were already very much contracted, and I knew that he must fight desperately to protect it." The first Union attempt to cut it, in late June, failed. The second attempt, in mid-August, also met fierce resistance, with the major fighting in the battle of the Weldon Railroad (Globe Tavern) taking place on August 18–19—but the Confederates were unable to shake General Gouverneur K. Warren's Union forces loose from the position they had assumed astride the railroad line. "Warren . . . fortified his new position, and our trenches were then extended from the left of our main line to connect with his new one," Grant reported. "Lee made repeated attempts to dislodge Warren's corps, but without success, and with heavy loss."

General Warren fortifying his lines on the Weldon road. Pencil and Chinese white drawing on olive paper by Alfred R. Waud, September 1864

{ **DECEMBER 2** **1863:** After the Confederate defeats at and around Chattanooga, Tennessee, General Braxton Bragg turns over command of the Army of Tennessee temporarily to Lieutenant General William Hardee at Dalton, Georgia. General Joseph E. Johnston will succeed Hardee two weeks later. }

General Warren fortifying his lines on the Weldon R.R.

A R Waud

Since being declared the capital of the Confederate States of America in May 1861, Richmond, Virginia, had been a prime target of the Union. By April 1, 1865, with Federal forces advancing on all fronts, Richmond was doomed to fall. "I think it is absolutely necessary that we should abandon our position tonight," General Robert E. Lee, in nearby Petersburg, telegraphed President Davis in Richmond before dawn on April 2. During the day, a messenger fetched Davis from Sunday church services to receive the news that Lee had begun retreating from Petersburg. By 11 P.M., Davis and most of his cabinet had left Richmond and the capital was in chaos. Streets and rail stations were packed. Fires that were started to destroy important papers and supplies or were set by looters soon burned out of control. The center of the city became an inferno rocked by the explosions of shells in the arsenal and of gunboats being scuttled on the river. Richmond's proud role as the seat of government of a hopeful Confederacy was at an end.

The fall of Richmond, VA on the night of April 2, 1865. Hand-colored lithograph, Currier & Ives, 1865

{ **DECEMBER 3** 1826: George Brinton McClellan (USA) is born in Philadelphia. }

I had about one thousand mounted men and a battery. I got out to the Darbytown road, and by this time heavy explosions were heard towards Richmond, like the sound of heavy, distant fighting. Finding the enemy's lines deserted and no orders coming I concluded something was up and it was best to push ahead; so we went through the lines and took the Richmond road. . . . To have led my regiment [the Fifth Massachusetts Cavalry (Colored)] into Richmond at the moment of its capture is the one event which I should most have desired as the culmination of my life in the Army. That honor has been mine. . . . I also had to ride round a portion of the line of defences, crossing the celebrated Chickahominy swamp and visiting the scene of McClellan's old operations. The rebel earthworks are the strongest I ever saw and the city is wonderfully defensible. There, at last, however were those works, the guns still mounted and unspiked, with the ammunition beside them, taken at last without the loss of a man.

—Brigadier General Charles Francis Adams Jr. (USA),
letter to his father, April 10, 1865

A collection of captured Confederate artillery on the wharves of Richmond, awaiting shipment north. Spring 1865

{ **DECEMBER 4** 1862: General Joseph E. Johnston assumes overall command of Confederate forces in the western theater. }

After General Robert E. Lee's Confederate army broke out of Petersburg, Virginia, hotly pursued by the Army of the Potomac, an exchange of messages between General-in-Chief Ulysses S. Grant and Lee led to a historic meeting between them at the home of Wilmer McLean in the village of Appomattox Court House on April 9. (A last weak attempt by Lee's greatly reduced Army of Northern Virginia to break out of the Union army's pincers had been stopped dead that morning.) At the McLean house, the terms of surrender were agreed to—among them, that Confederate officers could keep their sidearms, their private horses, and their baggage. Later, aware that many of the surrendering soldiers were farmers and would not be able to put in crops without horses, Grant instructed his officers to "let any Confederate, officer or not, who claimed to own a horse or mule take the animal to his home." Grant also agreed to provide food for Lee's hungry troops. After the formal surrender ceremony took place on April 12 (four years to the day from the Confederate bombardment of Fort Sumter), the Civil War in Virginia was over; however, other Confederate troops remained in the field. President Andrew Johnson would not proclaim hostilities to be "virtually at an end" until May 10.

Surrender at Appomattox. The room in the McLean House, . . . in which Gen Lee surrendered to Gen. Grant. Tinted lithograph, Major & Knapp Lith. Co., 1867

{ DECEMBER 5 1839: George Armstrong Custer (USA) is born in New Rumley, Ohio. **}**

Officially appointed general-in-chief of all Confederate armies on January 31, 1865, the Army of Northern Virginia's revered commander, Robert E. Lee, followed his graceful surrender to Union general-in-chief Ulysses S. Grant with an equally graceful farewell to his Confederate troops. "The war being at an end, the Southern States having laid down their arms, and the questions at issue between them and the Northern States having been decided," he wrote to Captain Josiah Tatnall some five months later, "I believe it to be the duty of every one to unite in the restoration of the country, and the reestablishment of peace and harmony." Maintaining this resolve, Lee became president of Washington College (later renamed Washington and Lee University, in his honor) in Lexington, Virginia, as he and fellow Southerners grappled with the huge task of postwar rebuilding and reconciliation. "The truth is this," Lee wrote shortly before his death in 1870. "The march of Providence is so slow and our desires so impatient; the work of progress so immense and our means of aiding it so feeble; the life of humanity is so long, that of the individual so brief, that we often see only the ebb of the advancing wave and are thus discouraged. It is history that teaches us to hope."

General R. E. Lee's Farewell Address. Tinted lithograph, Charles H. Walker, 1893

{ **DECEMBER 6** 1833: John Singleton Mosby (CSA) is born in Edgemont, Virginia. }

The calamity which has fallen upon us in the total destruction of our government is of a character so overwhelming that I am as yet unable to comprehend it. I am as one walking in a dream, & expecting to awake. I cannot see its consequences, nor shape my own course, but am just moving along until I can see my way at some future day. It is marvelous that a people that a month ago had money, armies, and the attributes of a nation should to-day be no more, & that we live, breathe, move, talk as before.

—Josiah Gorgas, former chief of ordnance (CSA), diary entry, May 4, 1865

Children amid the ruins of Charleston, South Carolina, one of many Southern cities ravaged by the war. April 1865

{ **DECEMBER 7** **1862:** Confederate raider John Hunt Morgan, with fourteen hundred men, surprises a Federal garrison at Hartsville, Tennessee, taking eighteen hundred prisoners. }

On February 28 [18?], 1865, the remainder of the regiment were ordered
to Charleston, as there were signs of the rebels evacuating that city. Leaving Cole Island, we
arrived in Charleston between nine and ten o'clock in the morning, and found the "rebs" had set
fire to the city and fled, leaving women and children behind to suffer and perish in the flames.
The fire had been burning fiercely for a day and night. When we landed, under a flag of truce,
our regiment went to work assisting the citizens in subduing the flames. It was a terrible scene.
For three or four days the men fought the fire, saving the property and effects of the people,
yet these white men and women could not tolerate our black Union soldiers, for many of them
had formerly been their slaves; and although these brave men risked life and limb to assist them
in their distress, men and even women would sneer and molest them whenever they met them.

—Susie King Taylor, nurse and laundress, Thirty-third U.S. Colored Infantry
(USA), excerpt from her memoirs, 1902

*Marching on!—The Fifty-fifth
Massachusetts Colored Regiment
singing John Brown's March in
the Streets of Charleston, February 21, 1865.* Wood engraving
in *Harper's Weekly,* March 18,
1865

{ **DECEMBER 8** 1863: President Lincoln issues a Proclamation of Amnesty and Reconstruction, pardoning participants "in the existing rebellion" if they take an oath of loyalty to the Union. }

Fort Sumter, in Charleston Harbor, South Carolina—the site of the beginning of the Civil War, when Confederate forces besieged and finally fired upon Major Robert Anderson's small U.S. garrison in April 1861—became a focal point for Union action in 1863 and remained a prime target of Federal bombardments until the Confederates evacuated the city and its fortifications on February 17, 1865. On April 14, 1865, four years to the day after he had surrendered the fort, Anderson, now a general, participated in a happier Fort Sumter ceremony, hoisting over the reclaimed bastion the same flag he had been forced to lower in 1861. The Reverend Henry Ward Beecher, brother of *Uncle Tom's Cabin* author Harriet Beecher Stowe, delivered a speech before the gathering of Northern officers and dignitaries, and the solemn yet joyful ceremonies continued into the evening. As they were concluding with fireworks, President Lincoln, in Washington, D.C., was preparing to go to Ford's Theatre to see a performance of the comedy *Our American Cousin.*

Crowd inside Fort Sumter, Charleston, South Carolina. April 14, 1865

Abraham Lincoln (one of his last sittings for a photo). Photograph by Alexander Gardner, April 10, 1865

{ **DECEMBER 9** 1863: Black Union troops at Fort Jackson, Louisiana, mutiny briefly over one white officer's alleged mistreatment of his soldiers. }

In 1858, the celebrated actress and theater manager Laura Keene produced a comedy by Tom Taylor called *Our American Cousin*. The first play in modern history to enjoy a long run, it became a Keene staple. On April 14, 1865, she was on stage performing the play at Ford's Theatre in Washington, D.C.—a performance that President Lincoln was heartily enjoying with his wife—when the Confederate fanatic John Wilkes Booth, a well-known actor, entered the presidential box and shot Lincoln in the head, fatally wounding him. Lincoln's personal bodyguard, William H. Crook, was absent that night—as were General and Mrs. Ulysses S. Grant, who had been in Washington that day and had been invited to join the Lincolns. "I replied to the President's verbal invitation to the effect, that if we were in the city we would take great pleasure in accompanying them," Grant later wrote in his memoirs, "but that I was very anxious to get away and visit my children, and if I could get through my work during the day I should do so. I did get through and started by the evening train on the 14th, sending Mr. Lincoln word, of course, that I would not be at the theatre. . . . When I reached . . . Philadelphia, I found people awaiting my arrival there; and also dispatches informing me of the assassination." (See also April 29–30, November 30.)

Ford's Theatre, with guards posted at the entrance and crepe draped from windows. April 1865

Laura Keene (1820?–1873). 1855–65

(See also April 29–30, November 30.)

{ **DECEMBER 10** 1861: In Richmond, the Confederate Congress admits Kentucky to the Confederacy, the last of the thirteen states that the South considers part of the Confederate States of America (represented by thirteen stars on the Confederate flag). Like Missouri, however, the border state of Kentucky officially remains in the Union. }

A member of America's leading theatrical family (which included his father, Junius Brutus Booth, and his brother Edwin), the actor John Wilkes Booth developed a markedly different political viewpoint from that of his celebrated relatives. After Abraham Lincoln's reelection, Booth's devotion to the Southern cause and his hatred of the president became fanatic. "For four years have I waited, hoped and prayed, for the dark clouds to break," he wrote to his brother-in-law John S. Clarke in November 1864; "to wait longer would be a crime. . . . God's will be done. I go to see, and share the bitter end." By April 1865, Booth's beliefs had blossomed into a deadly plot in which he was the major player—mortally wounding President Lincoln at Ford's Theatre in Washington. Shouting, "Sic semper tyrannis" ("Thus always to tyrants"), as he leaped to the stage (breaking his leg in the process), Booth managed to escape from the theater and, on horseback, cross a bridge over the Potomac River into Virginia. The U.S. government worked swiftly to capture him and his fellow conspirators—one of whom, David Herold, was trapped with Booth on April 26 when Federal troops surrounded the barn near Port Royal, Virginia, in which they were hiding. Herold surrendered but Booth refused, even as the barn was set on fire. By most reputable accounts, the first presidential assassin in American history was killed by a single shot, fired into the barn—against orders—by Sergeant Boston Corbett. (See also December 14 and 16.)

Cover of *Booth, the Assassin*, a nineteenth-century "dime novel." Date unknown

Satan tempting Booth to the murder of the President. Lithograph on wove paper, J. L. Magee, 1865

{ **DECEMBER 11** **1861:** Charleston, South Carolina, already suffering under the Federal blockade and facing a threat from the Union occupation of nearby Hilton Head, is struck by a disastrous fire that sweeps through its business district. }

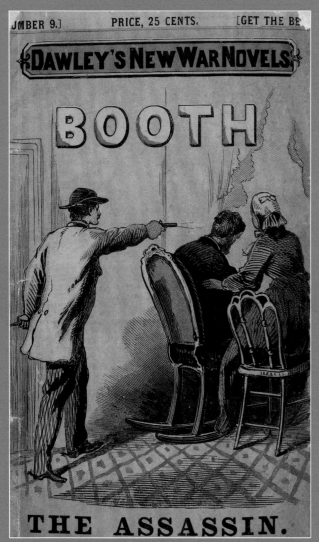

DAWLEY'S NEW WAR NOVELS

BOOTH

THE ASSASSIN.

Plunged into mourning by Abraham Lincoln's death—with many
people calling for retribution against the South—grieving Northerners waited in long lines to
view the body in the eleven cities (in Maryland, Pennsylvania, New York, Ohio, Indiana, and
Illinois) where it stopped along the way from Washington to Springfield, Illinois. "The hearse . . .
was almost entirely of plate-glass, which enabled the vast crowd on the line of the procession
to have a full view of the coffin," reported the 1865 publication *The Lincoln Memorial*. "The
supports of the top were draped with black cloth and white silk, and the top of the car itself was
handsomely decorated with black plumes." In addition to the throngs that poured into the cities
at which the train stopped, thousands more people lined the train tracks. "In out-of-the-way
places, little villages, or single farm-houses," *The Lincoln Memorial* noted, "people came out
to the side of the track and watched. . . . Every five rods along the whole line were seen these
mourning groups, some on foot and some in carriages, wearing badges of sorrow, and many
evidently having come a long distance to pay this little tribute of respect, the only one in their
power, to the memory of the murdered president."

*Funeral Car of President Lincoln,
New York April 26, 1865.* Watercolor drawing, © P. Relyea, 1879

{ **DECEMBER 12** 1862: On the Yazoo River, north of Vicksburg, Mississippi, the Union ironclad
Cairo strikes a mine (then called a torpedo) and sinks—but the crew escapes. }

On the morning of April 15, 1865, shortly after Abraham Lincoln died, Attorney General James Speed called on Vice President Andrew Johnson (see also April 26) at his rooms in the Kirkwood House hotel and delivered a letter signed by members of the cabinet that outlined the events of the previous night and declared: "By the death of President Lincoln, the office of President has devolved, under the Constitution, upon you." Johnson chose to have Chief Justice Salmon P. Chase administer the oath of office in his rooms, with a few cabinet officers and congressmen present. He addressed them briefly after officially becoming the seventeenth president: "Gentleman . . . I feel incompetent to perform duties so important and responsible as those which have been so unexpectedly thrown upon me. . . . The only assurance that I can now give of the future, is by reference to the past. . . . The best energies of my life have been spent in endeavoring to establish and perpetuate the principles of free government, and I believe that the government, in passing through its present trials, will settle down upon principles consonant with popular rights more permanent and enduring than heretofore."

Andrew Johnson (1808–1875). Photograph attributed to Jessie Whitehurst, c. 1860

Andrew Johnson taking the oath of office in the small parlor of the Kirkwood House, Washington. Wood engraving in *Frank Leslie's Illustrated Newspaper,* January 6, 1866

{ **DECEMBER 13** 1818: Mary Ann Todd (Lincoln), the wife of Abraham Lincoln, is born in Lexington, Kentucky.
1862: General Ambrose Burnside's Army of the Potomac suffers a bloody defeat at the battle of Fredericksburg, Virginia. }

I met an officer ... who has been ... in charge of nine or ten persons who are implicated in the assassination plot. His account of his duties, of the treatment of the prisoners and of their behavior made me shudder. The prisoners were confined in separate cells, and each had a hood or mask fastened over his or her head and face. They saw no one. No one could see their features. . . . This morning the whole party were taken to court-martial, and were still hooded. They were there placed near and facing each other. The masks were all suddenly removed. . . . There is something in the idea of such a meeting calculated to curdle a man's blood.

The trial of these persons before a court-martial is a very bold stretch of power. I cannot see that it is either necessary or wise. I should have given trial by jury its true position. As long as we have a Constitution it is worth sticking to. As for the criminals I should care very little whether they were hanged, strangled or drowned.

—Brevet Brigadier General Alfred B. McCalmont (USA), letter to his brother, May 9, 1865

The Military Commission that tried the accused conspirators in the assassination of Abraham Lincoln. Standing, left to right: Brigadier General Thomas M. Harris, Major General Lew Wallace, Major General August V. Kautz, and Colonel Henry L. Burnett (assistant judge advocate). Seated, left to right: Lieutenant Colonel David R. Clendenin, Colonel C. H. Tompkins, Brigadier General Albion P. Howe, Brigadier General James Ekin, Major General David Hunter (presiding officer), Brigadier General Robert S. Foster, John A. Bingham (assistant judge advocate), and Judge Joseph Holt (judge advocate). Photograph by Alexander Gardner, 1865

{ **DECEMBER 14** 1861: Brigadier General H. H. Sibley assumes command of the Confederate forces along the upper Rio Grande and in the New Mexico and Arizona territories. }

As the military tribunal that was trying those accused of conspiring in the assassination of the president conducted its solemn business, people flooded into the nation's capital for a happier occasion: the Grand Review, on May 23 and 24, 1865. During this huge celebration of the Union's preservation, regiment after regiment of the Grand Armies of the Republic paraded along Pennsylvania Avenue and read the banner attached to the Capitol: "The only national debt we never can pay is the debt we owe to the victorious soldiers." The eastern theater's Army of the Potomac marched on the first day, General William T. Sherman's troops of the western theater on the second. Although more than 160 African American regiments had been formed during the war, and the courage and accomplishments of black soldiers had been widely celebrated by the Northern press, no black regiments were included in this massive celebration. Within a year, the U.S. Army would be reduced from one million men to about eighty thousand, on its way to a regular peacetime strength of about twenty-seven thousand. Most of those initially mustered out were white; a disproportionate number of black units remained in service as part of an army of occupation in the South.

Thomas Hawkins, sergeant major, Sixth U.S. Colored Troops. He received the Medal of Honor for action at Chaffin's Farm, Virginia, September 29, 1864, but was among nearly two hundred thousand African Americans excluded from the Grand Review. Date unknown

The Grand Review at Washington, May 23d 1865. The glorious Army of the Potomac passing the head stand. Color lithograph by E. Sachse & Co., published by C. Bohn, 1865

{ **DECEMBER 15** 1863: Confederate major general Jubal A. Early is assigned to the Shenandoah Valley District. }

The military tribunal that convened in early May 1865 tried David Herold, Lewis Paine (sometimes spelled Payne; he had attacked and severely wounded Secretary of State William H. Seward), Samuel Arnold, George Atzerodt (assigned by Booth to kill Vice President Johnson, he could not bring himself to make the attempt), Michael O'Laughlin, Dr. Samuel Mudd (who had set Booth's broken leg the day after the assassination and did not inform authorities that he had treated the assassin), Edmund Spangler, and Mary Surratt (the owner of the boardinghouse where Booth's cohorts, including her son, John, had plotted the assassination). Each was convicted. Atzerodt, Herold, Paine, and Mary Surratt were hanged on July 7 at the Washington Arsenal prison (now Fort McNair); Arnold, O'Laughlin, Mudd, and Spangler received prison sentences. O'Laughlin died of yellow fever in 1867, but President Johnson pardoned the others in 1869. John Surratt, who had fled the country after the assassination, was captured in Egypt in 1866 and returned to the United States for trial. He was freed a year after the jury deadlocked eight to four in favor of acquittal.

A crowd witnesses the hanging of the Lincoln assassination conspirators, Washington, D.C. Photograph by Alexander Gardner, July 7, 1865

{ **DECEMBER 16** 1864: The battle of Nashville ends with General George H. Thomas's Union troops smashing General John Bell Hood's Confederate Army of Tennessee, which manages to retreat but is no longer an effective fighting force. }

The Confederacy is conquered; its days are numbered; Virginia is lost to us, and North Carolina must soon follow; and state after state under the hostile tread of the enemy, must re-enter the old union. The occasion, the emergency, the dire necessities and misfortunes of the country, the vast interests at stake, were never contemplated by those who framed the Constitution. They are all outside of it; and in the dissolution of the confederacy and the wreck of all their hopes, the States and the people will turn to you whose antecedents and whose present position and powers constitute you, more than any other living man the guardian of their honor and their interests, and will expect you not to stand upon constitutional limitations but to assume and exercise all powers which to you may seem necessary and proper to shield them from useless war, and to save from the wreck of the country all that may [be] practicable of honor, life & property.

—Secretary of the Navy Stephen R. Mallory (CSA), letter to President Jefferson Davis, April 24, 1865

Fate of the rebel flag. Color lithograph of a painting by William Bauly, published by Sarony, Major & Knapp, 1861

The casemate, Fortress Monroe. Jeff Davis in prison (two guards attending). Pencil and Chinese white drawing on tan paper by Alfred R. Waud, 1865

 **DECEMBER 17** 1863: President Lincoln sends the U.S. Congress a plan by the Freedmen's Aid Society to set up a Federal Bureau of Emancipation in order to assist free blacks; no action is taken until the Freedmen's Bureau is established in March 1865.

Our republican institutions were regarded as experiments up to the breaking out of the rebellion, and monarchical Europe generally believed that our republic was a rope of sand that would part the moment the slightest strain was brought upon it. Now it has shown itself capable of dealing with one of the greatest wars that was ever made, and our people have proven themselves to be the most formidable in war of any nationality. . . .

      The war has made us a nation of great power and intelligence. We have but little to do to preserve peace, happiness and prosperity at home, and the respect of other nations. Our experience ought to teach us the necessity of the first; our power secures the latter.

      I feel that we are on the eve of a new era, when there is to be great harmony between the Federal and Confederate. I cannot stay to be a living witness to the correctness of this prophecy; but I feel it within me that it is to be so.

    —Ulysses S. Grant, excerpt from his memoirs (1885–86), written as he was dying of cancer

Our heaven born banner. Color lithograph of a painting by William Bauly, published by Sarony, Major & Knapp, 1861

{ **DECEMBER 18** 1865: Secretary of State William H. Seward declares that the Thirteenth Amendment to the U.S. Constitution, which abolishes slavery and has been ratified by twenty-seven states, is now in effect. }

"What a beautiful world it is, this bright June morning," recently mustered-out Union veteran David Lane wrote in his journal on June 8, 1865, "and how familiar the sights and sounds that greet my senses. . . . I am almost home; just around the corner." For Union veterans, delight at resuming their civilian lives was augmented by receipt of an average of $250 in final and undrawn pay and bounties, as well as a generous pension from the U.S. government for those who qualified. The Federal government also established fifteen National Homes for Disabled Volunteer Soldiers between 1867 and 1933, and the various states also established homes for the orphaned children of Union casualties.

Returning to their homes in the midst of a devastated land, Confederate soldiers had no government to pay them or any pension to look forward to. Southern state governments and volunteer groups did make an effort to provide artificial limbs, but not until Reconstruction ended in 1877 could these governments offer pensions to Confederate veterans and provide soldiers' homes to house those in need.

Home again. Tinted lithograph by Dominique C. Fabronius of a painting by Trevor McClurg, 1866

{ **DECEMBER 19** 1814: Edwin McMasters Stanton, U.S. secretary of war in 1862–68, is born in Steubenville, Ohio. }

"I want to go home so bad," **black soldier Tilman Hardy** wrote in a letter in 1866. "It seems to me that I have been gone from home 70 years & longer." After months of postwar duty in the ravaged and resentful South, most African Americans still in uniform felt the same way. Gradually, most returned to civilian life—after following army regulations and traveling the sometimes long distance to the place they had mustered in so that they could be properly mustered out. Some Northern U.S. Colored Troops were given parades and celebrations before disbanding; most that had formed in the South were not. The much-respected white commander of one such regiment, Lieutenant Colonel C. T. Trowbridge of the First South Carolina Volunteers (Thirty-third U.S. Colored Infantry), issued lengthy general orders as his men prepared for release from the service, celebrating their proud record and including a caution: "I adjure you, by the associations and history of the past, and the love you bear for your liberties, to harbor no feelings of hatred toward your former masters. . . . The church, the school-house, and the right forever to be free are now secured to you, and every prospect before you is full of hope and encouragement."

Negro soldiers mustered out at Little Rock, Arkansas. Pencil and Chinese white drawing on green paper by Alfred R. Waud, c. 1866

{ **DECEMBER 20** 1860: In Charleston, the South Carolina Convention unanimously passes a formal declaration of secession, making that state the first to declare that it is no longer part of the United States of America. }

Off with your gray suits, boys—

Off with your rebel gear—
They smack too much of the cannons' peal,
The lightning flash of your deadly steel,
The terror of your spear. . . .

Down with the cross of stars—
Too long hath it waved on high;
'Tis covered all over with battle scars,
But its gleam the Northern banner mars—
'Tis time to lay it by.

—Lieutenant Falligant (no first name given),
excerpts from "Doffing the Gray" (quoted in an 1867 collection)

The Confederate Note Memorial.
Color lithograph, Gray Ellis,
c. 1902

{ **DECEMBER 21** 1864: General William T. Sherman and his Union army enter Savannah, Georgia, with no opposition, completing their March to the Sea. }

By 1867, President Andrew Johnson was increasingly at odds with members of Congress who favored radical Reconstruction measures in the South—particularly the powerful chairman of the House Ways and Means Committee, the fiery Radical Republican Thaddeus Stevens of Pennsylvania. Stevens's early hope that Johnson would adopt the Radical program changed to open hostility as the president proposed generous terms for Reconstruction and aired openly racist views in regard to civil rights (decrying, for example, the dangers "which must result from the success of the effort now making to Africanize the half of our country"). Seizing upon Johnson's abrupt February 1868 dismissal of Secretary of War Edwin M. Stanton (which violated procedures laid out under the 1867 Tenure of Office Act), Stevens led a successful movement to impeach Johnson—though ill health prevented the congressman from participating fully in the president's trial. Stevens's health deteriorated further after Johnson's acquittal in the Senate (by one vote). When Stevens died in August, he was buried in a Negro cemetery in Pennsylvania, his epitaph reading, in part, "I have chosen this, that I might illustrate in my death the principles which I advocated through a long life—Equality of Man before his Creator."

Thaddeus Stevens (1792–1868). 1850–68

The last speech on impeach-ment—Thaddeus Stevens closing the debate in the House, March 2. Wood engraving of a drawing by Theodore R. Davis, in *Harper's Weekly*, March 21, 1868

{ **DECEMBER 22** **1864:** General William T. Sherman sends President Lincoln a message: "I beg to present you, as a Christmas gift, the city of Savannah." }

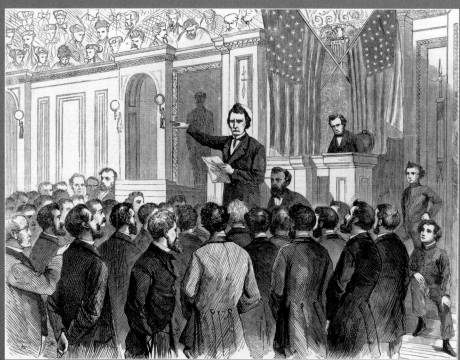

We believe that the highest welfare of this great country will be found in erasing from its statute-books all enactments discriminating in favor of or against any class of people, and by establishing one law for the white and colored people alike. . . . In the matter of government, the object of which is the protection and security of human rights, prejudice should be allowed no voice whatsoever.

—Proclamation of the National Convention of Colored Citizens of the United States, 1864

Distinguished Colored Men.
Color lithograph, A. Muller & Co., 1883

The African American leaders portrayed in the lithograph on the facing page are, at center: Frederick Douglass (1817?–1895), author, editor, orator, reformer, and diplomat; top row: Robert Brown Elliott (1842–1884), an architect of South Carolina's Reconstruction government, and Blanche K. Bruce (1841–1898), U.S. senator from Mississippi, 1875–81; and clockwise from above center: William Wells Brown (1814–1884), author and activist; R. T. (Richard Theodore) Greener (1844–1922), educator, lawyer, consular officer, and reformer; Rt. Rev. Richard Allen (1760–1831), founder of the Free African Society and the African Methodist Episcopal Church; J. H. (Joseph Hayne) Rainey (1832–1887), the first African American seated in the U.S. House of Representatives; E. D. (Ebenezer Don Carlos) Bassett (1833–1908), educator and diplomat; John Mercer Langston (1829–1897), educator, diplomat, and politician; P. B. S. (Pinckney Benton Stewart) Pinchback (1837–1921), activist, state legislator, and a founder of the Louisiana Republican Party; and Henry Highland Garnet (1815–1882), clergyman, editor, temperance leader, and diplomat.

{ **DECEMBER 23** 1864: A Union fleet from Fort Monroe, Virginia, scattered by storms and heavy seas, reunites at a rendezvous near Wilmington, North Carolina, for an attack on Fort Fisher. }

The Thirteenth Amendment to the U.S. Constitution, banning slavery in the United States, was ratified on December 18, 1865. The Fourteenth Amendment, framed in part to protect the rights of black Americans, was ratified on July 28, 1868. And March 30, 1870, saw ratification of the Fifteenth Amendment, which guaranteed black men the right to vote. Encouraged by the valor of the Union's African American soldiers and the eloquence of orators such as Frederick Douglass, Sojourner Truth, and John Rock during the war, the movement toward equal rights in the Reconstruction era was furthered in the postwar years by activists such as Mississippi's U.S. senators Blanche K. Bruce and Hiram Revels (who assumed the Senate seat once held by Jefferson Davis). By the time Reconstruction ended in 1877, however, progress had slowed and in some cases been reversed, especially in areas where the Ku Klux Klan and similar groups intimidated blacks and whites who favored equal rights for all Americans. The long and often bitter struggle toward a truly egalitarian society was to continue.

The Fifteenth Amendment, celebrated May 19th 1870. Lithograph with watercolor on wove paper, Thomas Kelly, 1870

{ **DECEMBER 24** 1864: The Union fleet bombards Fort Fisher, North Carolina, which guards Wilmington, the last major Confederate port still operating. }

Even before the Civil War ended, violence erupted in the South against the freedmen and those who tried to help them. Educational facilities, white and black teachers, black Union soldiers, and white Unionists were among the frequent targets. The violence continued as the troubled Reconstruction era began. In Memphis, Tennessee, riots against blacks raged from April 30 to May 2, 1866; forty-six African Americans were killed and more than eighty were wounded. "Soon we shall have no more black troops among us," predicted a local newspaper. "Thank heaven the white race are once more rulers of Memphis." Three months later, on July 30, when New Orleans Radicals tried to reconvene the convention that had passed the Union-occupied state's constitution in 1864, in order to disenfranchise some Confederates and enfranchise some blacks, riots resulted in the deaths of thirty-four blacks and three whites, with more than one hundred others injured. Agents of the Freedmen's Bureau (who had varying diplomatic skills and degrees of integrity) were sometimes able to defuse volatile situations. But many agents were themselves the targets of violence.

The Freedmen's Bureau. Wood engraving of a drawing by Alfred R. Waud, in *Harper's Weekly*, July 25, 1868

{ **DECEMBER 25** 1864: Union troops from the Federal fleet are landed to take Fort Fisher, North Carolina, but the assault fails and they are withdrawn. }

In 1867, Radical Republicans in Congress enacted their vision of
Reconstruction with a series of Federal laws, which inspired a new wave of violent resistance
in the South. Secret terrorist societies were determined to overturn these reforms by creating a
climate of fear. Most prominent among these groups was the Ku Klux Klan. Rooted in a social
club started in late 1865 or 1866 by young whites in Pulaski, Tennessee, the Klan had spread to
most Southern states by 1867, and former Confederate cavalry general Nathan Bedford Forrest
was named as its Grand Wizard. Employing everything from psychological intimidation to
arson, whippings, and murder, the Klan's masked cadres sought to destroy the Republican-
instituted Reconstruction infrastructure and reestablish unquestioned white supremacy in the
South. Klansmen murdered Republican congressman James M. Hinds of Arkansas, three South
Carolina state legislators, and some two hundred African Americans in one Louisiana parish
alone. Louisiana and Georgia went to the Democrats in the 1868 presidential election (won by
Republican Ulysses S. Grant), because Republican voters had been so intimidated that they
stayed away from the polls.

Visit of the Ku-Klux. Wood
engraving of a drawing by Frank
Bellew, in *Harper's Weekly*,
February 24, 1872

*Two members of the Ku-Klux
Klan in their disguises.* Wood
engraving in *Harper's Weekly*,
December 19, 1868

{ **DECEMBER 26** 1862: Union troops attack a guerrilla camp in Powell County, Kentucky. }

In 1871, after previous legislation to protect the rights of black
Americans in the South had proved ineffective, Congress passed the so-called Ku Klux Klan
Act (third Enforcement Act), with President Ulysses S. Grant's full support. Using powers given
to him under this act, the president suspended habeas corpus in nine South Carolina counties
and used other enforcement measures that made the 1872 election, which returned him to the
White House, a remarkably fair political contest in the South. Yet powerful white Southerners
continued their march toward "redeeming" all Southern states—returning them, as close as
possible, to the prewar status quo. In the 1876 presidential election, former Union brigadier
general Rutherford B. Hayes finally prevailed in his extended, and much-disputed, presidential
contest with Samuel J. Tilden, in part as a result of background negotiations between Southern
Democrats and Northern Republicans. Hayes's election, and his willingness to recognize
the political claims of former Confederate leaders (that of former Confederate general Wade
Hampton to the governorship of South Carolina, for example), marked the end of the already
waning Reconstruction era. "Every state in the South," observed African American Henry
Adams, "had got into the hands of the very men that held us as slaves."

*The "Strong" Government
1869–1877—The "weak" gov-
ernment 1877–1881.* Illustration
by J. A. (James Albert) Wales in
Puck, May 12, 1880

{ **DECEMBER 27** 1860: One day after Major Robert Anderson finishes transferring his garrison from the less defendable Fort Moultrie,
outraging secessionists, the U.S. flag is raised over Fort Sumter in Charleston Harbor while South Carolina troops occupy all
other Charleston forts. }

In 1867, Edward A. Pollard of Virginia published *The Lost Cause: A New Southern History of the War of the Confederates: A Full and Authentic Account of the Rise and Progress of the Late Southern Confederacy—the Campaigns, Battles, Incidents, and Adventures of the Most Gigantic Struggle of the World's History*. "Lost Cause" quickly became a popular catchphrase among the white population of the South. Nostalgia for the Lost Cause inspired the creation of popular art that ranged from stirring lithographs on Confederate themes to portraits of Confederate heroes on advertising labels. (Northern heroes were also used to sell products; in 1874, for example, Ulysses S. Grant, then president of the United States, was depicted in his Civil War uniform in a full-color ad for "Grant's Tobacco.") In the midst of these waves of nostalgia and commerce, the South's greatest hero, Robert E. Lee, continued to urge Southerners to "unite in honest efforts to obliterate the effects of the war, and to restore the blessing of peace . . . promote harmony and good feeling; qualify themselves to vote; and elect to the state and general Legislatures wise and patriotic men, who will devote their abilities to the interests of the country, and the healing of all dissensions."

Robert E. Lee (1807–1870). Photograph by Levin C. Handy, May 1869

Six advertising labels for "Lost-Cause" Perline, manufactured by Barnum & Starbird, Louisville, Kentucky, bearing the images of, from top, left to right: P. G. T. Beauregard and Robert E. Lee; Jefferson Davis and John Hunt Morgan; Joseph E. Johnston and Thomas J. Jackson. Photographic prints on engraved labels, 1860–80

{ **DECEMBER 28** **1862:** The Union's Army of the Frontier pushes back Confederates at Dripping Springs, Arkansas, and captures the town of Van Buren. }

Well before the Charleston batteries fired on Fort Sumter, plays that centered on the growing divisions between North and South were being produced—including, in the North, several productions based on Harriet Beecher Stowe's *Uncle Tom's Cabin* (see January 10 and 11). During the Civil War, patriotic tableaux and war-related plays were written and staged for home-front audiences, sometimes with a speed that absolutely ensured poor quality. Less than a month after the first battle of Bull Run, for example, the play *Bull Run* by Charles Gayler was on the boards at New York's Bowery Theater. After the actual conflict ended, it continued on theater stages, with such productions as *The Fall of Vicksburg: A Drama of the Great Rebellion* (1866) by John A. Parra, *The Color Guard* (1870, "a military drama in five acts with accompanying tableaux") by Colonel A. R. Calhoun, and *The Volunteer* (1871, "respectfully dedicated to the Grand Army of the Republic") by "comrades of Sedgwick Post No. 1, Department of Connecticut." This poster for *Her Atonement* dates from the 1880s, during a marked resurgence of interest in the Civil War. Other war-related plays of the era included *The Great Rebellion* (1881), an ambitious five-act work by Cyrenus Osborne Ward, and *Loyal Mountaineers: or The Guerrilla's Doom* (1889) by J. Culver.

Her Atonement by Anson P. Pond. Color lithograph of a theatrical poster, Strobridge & Co., 1883

{ **DECEMBER 29** **1808:** Andrew Johnson, seventeenth president of the United States (1865–69), succeeding Abraham Lincoln, is born in Raleigh, North Carolina. }

HER ATONEMENT BY ANSON P. POND

OFF TO THE WAR '62

"MY SON! MY SON!" HOME AGAIN '65 "THAT MAN'S THE MURDERER"

In 1867, as people decorated the graves of the Confederate dead at Magnolia Cemetery in Charleston, South Carolina, they heard a recitation of the Southern poet Henry Timrod's "Ode": "Stoop, angels, hither from the skies! / There is no holier spot of ground / Than where defeated valor lies. . . ." An essayist and correspondent for Southern newspapers during the Civil War, Timrod was one of many poets and novelists, North and South, whose postwar work reflected the nation's war experience. In the North, the poet and lecturer Edwin Markham recited a work of his at the May 30, 1922, dedication ceremonies for the Lincoln Memorial—the culmination of a long and stormy process that began in 1867. Every aspect of the memorial's development had been subject to intense debate. "Lincoln, the Man of the People," among Markham's most popular and best-known poems, spoke of "the Captain with the mighty heart" who "Held on through blame and faltered not at praise. / And when he fell in whirlwind, he went down / As when a lordly cedar, green with boughs, / Goes down with a great shout upon the hills, / And leaves a lonesome place against the sky."

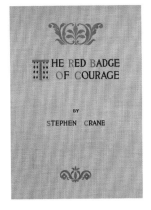

Cover of *The Red Badge of Courage: An Episode of the American Civil War* (1895). Written by Stephen Crane (1871–1900), this is one of the best-known and most enduring novels set in the Civil War.

Henry Timrod (1828–1867). Date unknown

Edwin Markham (1852–1940). May 30, 1922

{ **DECEMBER 30** 1862: USS *Monitor*, the Northern hero of the battle with CSS *Virginia* (formerly the *Merrimack*), founders off Cape Hatteras, North Carolina, in heavy seas; sixteen officers and men are lost. }

My Comrades of the Confederate Army, my friends and veterans of the Federal Army, . . . I am filled with emotion as I look upon survivors of the armies of the Civil War and remember that here, at Gettysburg, was fought one of the greatest and most decisive battles of the Civil War. We are not here with battle flags, charging brigades, roaring cannon, rattling musketry, and dead and dying soldiers, but we are here with friendship and fraternity, good will and glorious peace. A half century has made those who wore the Blue and those who wore the Gray stand together as friends, and behold the Bow of Peace and promise in the sky, and look with pleasure upon the flag of our country, as it presents the stars of Re-United States and represents reunited people. . . . While those of us who were soldiers when the battle of Gettysburg was fought will always remember the glory and the gloom of that period, we may well thank God, today, that the benediction of peace and reconciliation spreads over our great Republic, and we realize that the immortal words now most conspicuous are, "One country, one constitution, one flag, and one destiny."

—James B. McCreary, governor of Kentucky, remarks at the Gettysburg Reunion, 1913

"The Blue and the Gray at Gettysburg, Assembly Tent" (fiftieth-anniversary reunion, Gettysburg, Pennsylvania). 1913

Cover of *Blue and Gray* magazine, March 1893

{ **DECEMBER 31** 1815: George Gordon Meade (USA) is born in Cádiz, Spain. }

ACKNOWLEDGMENTS

The American Civil War: 365 Days is a product of years of "rummaging" through the astounding and diverse Civil War collections of the Library of Congress, in which joyful endeavor I am always guided by Library staff whose knowledge and love of the materials in their various domains are inspiring. I am particularly grateful to Harry Katz, former head curator in the Prints and Photographs Division, and Mary Ison, head of the Prints and Photographs Reference Section; to the encyclopedically knowledgeable Civil War specialist John Sellers and the late Mary Wolfskill, head of the Reference and Reader Section, in the Manuscript Division; to Clark Evans, in the Rare Book and Special Collections Division; and to the staff of the Geography and Map Division, guardians of a trove of Civil War cartographic treasures.

The Library is indebted to Gary W. Gallagher for his illuminating introduction to the book, and I am most grateful for his comments on the manuscript. Picture editor Vincent Virga provided invaluable guidance regarding the selection and arrangement of images. Editor Richard Slovak brought knowledge and love of the Civil War era to the project; his thought-provoking questions and excellent suggestions did much to improve the text. Many thanks are also due to Harry N. Abrams, Inc., project manager Deborah Aaronson, whose vision helped inspire and shape the development of the book, and to designer Eric J. Diloné, who has created a vivid and artistic setting for this complex of text and disparate images. Any errors in *The American Civil War: 365 Days* are the author's responsibility alone.

Finally, I salute my colleagues in the Library of Congress Publishing Office, with special gratitude to Director of Publishing Ralph Eubanks and to Linda Osborne and Susan Reyburn, whose epic work on the *Library of Congress Civil War Desk Reference* and thoughtful comments on the draft text of *The American Civil War: 365 Days* are reflected in this book.

—M. E. W.

BIBLIOGRAPHY

DAILY EVENT NOTATIONS

The Library of Congress general and specialized collections include thousands of studies of the Civil War and remembrances of it. One of these resource volumes, *The Civil War Day by Day: An Almanac, 1861–1865*, compiled by E. B. Long with Barbara Long (Garden City, N.Y.: Doubleday & Company, 1971), was the primary and most valuable resource in assembling the notations on daily events included in this book.

TEXT: PRINCIPAL SOURCES AND FURTHER READING

HISTORIES

Brockett, L. P., and Mary C. Vaughan. *Woman's Work in the Civil War: A Record of Heroism, Patriotism and Patience*. Boston: R. H. Curran, 1867.

Browning, Robert M., Jr. *From Cape Charles to Cape Fear: The North Atlantic Blockading Squadron during the Civil War*. Tuscaloosa, Ala., and London: University of Alabama Press, 1993.

Current, Richard N., Paul D. Escott, Lawrence N. Powell, James I. Robertson Jr., and Emory M. Thomas, eds. *Encyclopedia of the Confederacy*. New York: Simon & Schuster, 1993.

Faust, Patricia L., ed. *The Historical Times Illustrated Encyclopedia of the Civil War*. New York: Harper & Row, 1986.

Furgurson, Ernest B. *Freedom Rising: Washington in the Civil War*. New York: Alfred A. Knopf, 2004.

Gallagher, Gary W. *The Confederate War*. Cambridge, Mass.: Harvard University Press, 1997.

Glatthaar, Joseph T. *Forged in Battle: The Civil War Alliance of Black Soldiers and White Officers*. New York: The Free Press, 1990.

Golder, F. A. "The Russian Fleet and the Civil War." *American Historical Review* 20, no. 4 (July 1915): 801–12.

Grimsley, Mark. *The Hard Hand of War: Union Military Policy toward Southern Civilians, 1861–1865*. Cambridge and New York: Cambridge University Press, 1995.

Heidler, David S., and Jeanne T. Heidler, eds. *Encyclopedia of the American Civil War: A Political, Social, and Military History*. Santa Barbara, Calif.: ABC-CLIO, 2000.

Klein, Maury. *Days of Defiance: Sumter, Secession, and the Coming of the Civil War*. New York: Alfred A. Knopf, 1997.

McPherson, James M. *Battle Cry of Freedom*. New York: Oxford University Press, 1988.

———. *For Cause and Comrades: Why Men Fought in the Civil War*. New York: Oxford University Press, 1997.

———. *The Negro's Civil War: How American Blacks Felt and Acted during the War for the Union*. New York: Ballantine Books, 1991. First published 1965.

Pennsylvania Commission. *Fiftieth Anniversary of the Battle of Gettysburg, Report of the Pennsylvania Commission*. Harrisburg: Commonwealth of Pennsylvania, December 1913.

Perry, James M. *A Bohemian Brigade: The Civil War Correspondents—Mostly Rough, Sometimes Ready*. New York: John Wiley & Sons, 2000.

Tevis, C. W. *History of the Fighting Fourteenth*. Brooklyn: Brooklyn Eagle Press, [1911?].

Tsouras, Peter G.. *Military Quotations from the Civil War in the Words of the Commanders*. New York: Sterling Publishing Co., 1998.

Wagner, Margaret E., Gary W. Gallagher, and Paul Finkelman, eds. *The Library of Congress Civil War Desk Reference*. New York: Simon & Schuster, 2002.

PUBLISHED DIARIES, LETTERS, SPEECHES, AND MEMOIRS OF CIVIL WAR FIGURES

Beatty, John. *The Citizen Soldier, or Memoirs of a Volunteer*. Cincinnati: Wilstach, Baldwin & Co., 1879 (most recent edition, 1998).

Bowditch, Henry I. *A Brief Plea for an Ambulance System for the Army of the United States, as drawn from the extra sufferings of the late Lieut. Bowditch and a wounded comrade*. Boston: Ticknor & Fields, 1863.

Brinton, John H. *Personal Memoirs of John H. Brinton, Major and Surgeon U. S. V., 1861–1865*. New York: Neale Publishing Co., 1914 (most recent edition, 1996).

Carter, Robert Goldthwaite. *Four Brothers in Blue, or Sunshine and Shadows of the War of the Rebellion*. Washington, D.C.: Press of Gibson Bros., 1913 (most recent edition, 1999).

Chesnut, Mary Boykin. *Mary Chesnut's Civil War.* Edited by C. Vann Woodward. New Haven, Conn.: Yale University Press, 1981.

Cumming, Kate. *A Journal of Hospital Life in the Confederate Army of Tennessee, from the Battle of Shiloh to the End of the War.* Louisville, Ky.: J. P. Morton, & Co.; New Orleans: W. Evelyn, 1866 (most recent edition, retitled *Kate: The Journal of a Confederate Nurse*, 1998).

Dawson, Sarah Morgan. *A Confederate Girl's Diary.* Boston and New York: Houghton Mifflin Co., 1913 (most recent edition, retitled *Civil War Diary of Sarah Morgan*, 1991).

Favill, Josiah Marshall. *The Diary of a Young Officer Serving with the Armies of the United States during the War of the Rebellion.* Chicago: R. R. Donnelley & Sons, 1909.

Ford, Worthington Chauncey, ed. *A Cycle of Adams Letters, 1861–1865.* Boston and New York: Houghton Mifflin Co., 1920.

Freeman, Warren Hapgood, and Eugene Freeman. *Letters from Two Brothers Serving in the War for the Union to Their Family at Home.* Cambridge, Mass.: printed for private circulation, 1871.

Hotchkiss, Jedediah. *Make Me a Map of the Valley: The Civil War Journal of Stonewall Jackson's Topographer.* Edited by Archie P. McDonald. Dallas: Southern Methodist University Press, 1973.

[Johnson, Andrew]. *Life, Speeches and Services of Andrew Johnson, Seventeenth President of the United States.* Philadelphia: T. B. Peterson & Brothers, 1865.

Lane, David. *A Soldier's Diary: The Story of a Volunteer, 1862–1865.* Printed privately by David Lane, 1905.

Lewis, Richard. *Camp Life of a Confederate Boy of Bratton's Brigade, Longstreet's Corps, C. S. A.* Charleston, S.C.: News and Courier Presses, 1883.

McCalmont, Alfred B. *Extracts from Letters written by Alfred B. McCalmont . . . from the Front during the War of the Rebellion.* Printed for private circulation by his son, Robert McCalmont, [1908?].

Norton, Oliver Willcox. *Army Letters, 1861–1865.* Printed for private circulation, 1903.

Simms, William Gilmore, ed. *War Poetry of the South.* New York: Richardson & Co., 1867.

Taylor, Susie King. *Reminiscences of My Life in Camp with the 33d United States Colored Troops, Late 1ˢᵗ S. C. Volunteers.* Boston: published by the author, 1902 (most recent edition, 2004).

Tobie, Edward P. *Service of the Cavalry in the Army of the Potomac.* ["Personal Narratives of Events in the War of the Rebellion No. 14—Second Series."] Providence, R.I.: N. B. Williams & Co. / Soldiers and Sailors Historical Society of Rhode Island, 1882 (later edition, 1988).

Van Alstyne, Lawrence. *Diary of an Enlisted Man.* New Haven, Conn.: Tuttle, Morehouse & Taylor Co., 1910.

Welch, Spencer Glasgow. *A Confederate Surgeon's Letters to His Wife.* New York and Washington, D.C.: Neale Publishing Co., 1911 (later edition, 1954).

Whitman, Walt. *The Wound Dresser: A Series of Letters Written from the Hospitals in Washington during the War of the Rebellion.* Edited by Richard Maurice Bucke. Boston: Small, Maynard & Co., 1898 (later edition, 1978).

Wormeley, Katharine Prescott. *The Cruel Side of War.* Boston: Roberts Bros., 1898.

LIBRARY OF CONGRESS MANUSCRIPT DIVISION

Cater, Rufus, and Douglas Cater, Confederate soldiers (letters).

Hotchkiss, Jedediah, Confederate cartographer (papers, including diary; see also published wartime diary, above).

Johnson, Richard W., Union officer (letter regarding Johnny Clem).

Lincoln, Abraham (presidential papers).

Lord, Mrs. W. W. (typescript of diary regarding the siege of Vicksburg).

Mitchell, James Billingslea, Confederate officer (letters).

Porter, David Dixon, Union naval officer (papers).

Reed, Charles Wellington (papers).

Waddel, John Newton, Confederate civilian (diary).

Whitman, Walt (papers; see also published letters, above).

Willard Family (papers, including those of Joseph C. and Antonia Ford Willard).

For a much more complete list of the Library's Civil War manuscript collections (numbering more than a thousand), see Sellers, John R., comp. *Civil War Manuscripts: A Guide to Collections in the Manuscript Division of the Library of Congress.* Washington, D.C.: Library of Congress, 1986.

PICTURE CREDITS

To order reproductions of images in this book: Note the Library of Congress negative number provided with the image (LC-USZ6-, USZ62-, or LC-B indicates a black-and-white negative; LC-USZC2-, USZC4-, or LC-USZC6- indicates a color transparency, and LC-DIG- indicates a digital file). Where no negative number is given, note the Library division and the title of the item. Duplicates may be ordered from the Library of Congress, Photoduplication Service, Washington, DC, 20540-4570, 202/707-5640; fax: 202/707-1771. Visit the Photoduplication Web Site at http://www.loc.gov/preserv/pds/ for further information. An **asterisk** follows the LC number or division reference of every image restored for this book.

KEY: Prints and Photographs Division, P&P; Rare Book and Special Collections Division, RBD; Geography and Map Division, G&M; General Collections, GC; Manuscript Division, MSS; Music Division, MUS

JANUARY 1: LC-USZC4-1724. 2: (Webster) LC-USZ62-110139*; (Rhett) LC-USZ62-129740. 3: LC-USZ62-92043. 4: (Brown) LC-USZC4-11786; (Walker) LC-USZC4-10802. 5: (Coker) LC-USZC4-6768; (Fish Town) LC-USZC4-8195. 6: LC-USZC4-2851. 7: (Lash) LC-USZC4-2524; (Parting) LC-USZC4-2525. 8: (Platform) LC-USZC4-12569; (Brooks) LC-USZ62-9010; (Sumner) LC-USZ62-128709. 9: (Burns) LC-USZ62-90720; (Williamson) LC-USZC4-12565. 10: LC-BH82-5279*. 11: LC-USZC4-1298. 12: (Scott) LC-USZ62-5092; (Taney) LC-BH82-402; (Buchanan)

LC-BH82101-6628. 13: (Lincoln) LC-USZ62-16377; (Douglas) LC-USZ62-110141*. 14: (photo) LC-USZ62-7816; (drawing by Bernarda Bryson) P&P—Art © Estate of Bernarda Bryson Shahn / Licensed by VAGA, New York, N.Y. Reproduced with permission. 15: LC-USZC4-7997. 16: LC-USZC4-4616*. 17: LC-USZC4-2621. 18: LC-USZ62-48564. 19: LC-USZ62-92048. 20: (portrait) LC-USZC4-11370; (speech) LC-USZ62-109704. 21: RBD. 22: LC-USZC4-1557. 23: (broadside) LC-USZ62-11191; (Seward) LC-USZ62-106731. 24: LC-USZC4-7942. 25: (Ruffin) LC-USZ62-123816; (Crittenden) LC-USZ62-110095. 26: LC-USZC4-528. 27: (Anderson) LC-USZ62-129737; (Beauregard) P&P. 28: (March) LC-USZC2-3767; (All Hail) LC-USZC2-3773. 29: LC-USZC2-1289. 30: LC-B813-2094. 31: G&M*.

FEBRUARY 1: LC-USZC4-1446. 2: (photo) LC-B812-3175; (litho) LC-USZC2-2231. 3: LC-USZC4-1736. 4: (USA) LC-USZ62-6225; (CSA) RBD. 5: (Lincoln and son) LC-USZC4-2777; (Mrs. Lincoln) LC-BH824-4575. 6: LC-USZ62-86311. 7: LC-USZC4-12566. 8: LC-B8184-10358. 9: LC-USZC4-7985. 10: LC-B817-7339*. 11: G&M. 12: LC-USZC4-691. 13: G&M. 14: (McDowell) LC-B8172-1630; (Johnston) LC-USZ62-9247. 15: LC-USZC4-1767. 16: LC-B8184-10111. 17: (Baker) LC-USZ62-90165; (Ball's Bluff) LC-USZC2-2229. 18: G&M. 19: LC-USZC2-3134. 20: (P. Drayton) LC-BH82-5399; (T. Drayton) LC-B8184-10642; (slaves) LC-DIG-ppmsca-04324. 21: LC-USZC4-1764. 22: LC-USZ62-90934. 23: GC*. 24: LC-USZC4-6316. 25: LC-USZC4-1910. 26:

(CSA) GC; (USA) GC. 27: LC-USZC4-1729. 28: LC-USZC4-996.

MARCH 1: (McClellan) LC-USZC2-3791; (Lincoln) LC-USZ62-5803. 2: LC-USZC4-6698. 3: (Davis) LC-USZ62-11618; (Lee) LC-B8172-0001. 4: LC-B8171-0389. 5: LC-USZC4-8105. 6: LC-USZ62-14015. 7: G&M. 8: LC-USZC4-6699. 9: LC-B8171-0377. 10: LC-USZC4-1033. 11: LC-USZC4-3257*. 12: (Stevens) LC-B8171-0164; (Starke) LC-USZ62-84333. 13: LC-USZC4-1738. 14: (Greenhow) LC-USZ62-3131; (Cushman) LC-USZ62-7989. 15: LC-USZC4-6675. 16: LC-USZC4-5629. 17: LC-USZC4-1757. 18: LC-USZC4-1820. 19: LC-USZC4-2392. 20: (Mosby) LC-BH83-2410; (Sheridan) LC-B812-2881. 21: (Heroes) LC-USZC4-7943*; (Cadets) LC-USZ62-129739. 22: (Hooker) LC-B8172-6385*; (Cavalry) LC-USZC4-4776. 23: LC-USZC4-1760. 24: LC-B8171-2351. 25: LC-USZC4-1308. 26: LC-B811-4037. 27: GC. 28: (Early) LC-BH821-1022; (Cedar Creek) LC-USZC4-1468. 29: LC-B8171-3302*. 30: LC-USZC4-1759. 31: (Rebs) LC-USZC4-8106; (Point Lookout) G&M.

APRIL 1: LC-USZC4-1734. 2: LC-USZ62-3559. 3: (Hamlin) LC-USZ62-109919*; (Stephens) LC-BH832-582. 4: LC-USZ62-5263. 5: LC-USZ62-110182. 6: G&M*. 7: LC-USZC4-4671. 8: (de Stoeckl) LC-BH82-5273; (Clay) LC-USZ62-109862*. 9: LC-USZC4-1330. 10: (Boudinot) LC-BH83-968*; (Parker) LC-USZ62-14456. 11: LC-USZC4-2995. 12: (Anthony) LC-USZ61-84; (Dickinson) LC-BH82-5035. 13: (Aunt Phillis) LC-USZ62-107753; (spelling book) RBD. 14: LC-B8171-7951*. 15: MSS. 16: (Harris) LC-USZ62-118561; (Beaty) LC-USZ62-118556. 17: (Russell) LC-BH82-5087; (d'Orléans) LC-B8172-3818. 18: LC-USZC4-6732. 19: (Vallandigham) LC-BH82-4408; (Burnside) LC-B8172-1625*. 20: (Nast) LC-BH83-2571; (broadside) RBD. 21: (Brownlow) LC-BH83-232*; (Unionists) LC-USZ62-95984. 22: (Stanton) LC-B8172-2208; (Benjamin) LC-USZC4-12291. 23: (J. Sherman) LC-USZ6-2001; (cartoon) LC-USZ62-31164. 24: (Dem.) LC-USZC2-2485; (Rep.) LC-USZC2-2492. 25: LC-USZC4-7807. 26: LC-USZ62-1983. 27: (Cleburne) LC-USZ62-12995; (Cobb) LC-USZ62-110081*. 28: LC-USZC4-2438. 29: RBD. 30: LC-USZC4-5341.

MAY 1: LC-USZC2-1984. 2: (Welles) LC-USZ62-72777; (Mallory) LC-B8172-1743. 3: (Semmes) LC-USZC4-2385; (*Sumter*) LC-USZC4-4177. 4: (*Hunchback*) LC-USZ62-94045; (powder monkey) LC-B8171-4016*. 5: David Dixon Porter Papers, MSS. 6: (Foote) LC-USZ62-67469; (Waddell) LC-B8184-10672. 7: (Wilkes) LC-USZ61-1986; (Slidell) LC-USZC4-11108; (Mason) LC-USZ62-109846. 8: LC-USZC4-708. 9: LC-USZC4-7979. 10: (Worden) LC-USZ62-17153; (Buchanan) LC-B8172-1428. 11: LC-USZC4-2286. 12: David Dixon Porter Papers, MSS. 13: LC-B8184-10488. 14: LC-USZC4-5820. 15: LC-USZC2-2253. 16: LC-USZ62-97261. 17: LC-USZC4-1754. 18: LC-B8171-2321. 19: (*Merrimac*) LC-USZC2-2252; (*Monitor*) GC. 20: LC-B8184-10098. 21: LC-USZ62-117998. 22: (Maffitt) LC-USZ62-72757; (Porter) LC-B8184-7945. 23: LC-USZC4-4420. 24: LC-B8171-7697. 25: LC-B8171-3413. 26: LC-USZC4-11456. 27: LC-USZC4-3418. 28: LC-USZC4-781. 29: (Infernal machines) LC-USZC4-12570; (Lashed) LC-USZC4-1887. 30: LC-USZ62-77201. 31: LC-USZC2-1986.

JUNE 1: LC-USZC2-1720. 2: LC-USZC4-1065. 3: LC-USZC4-4575*. 4: LC-USZC4-4550. 5: (Arms) LC-USZC4-12568; (mounting cannon) LC-USZC4-690. 6: (Hampton) LC-B813-6770; (Harper) LC-USZ62-118946. 7: LC-USZC4-10347. 8: (Butler) LC-B8172-1406; (Camp Brightwood) LC-USZC4-6158. 9: LC-B8171-0518*. 10: (Our Mess) LC-B811-208; (T. W. Sherman) LC-B8172-1626. 11: (soldier) LC-USZC4-4608; (Hunter) LC-B8172-1820. 12: ("Rather die") LC-USZ62-23098; (Forrest) LC-B8171-2908. 13: LC-B8184-440. 14: (masthead) LC-USZ62-33470; (Garrison) LC-BH82-5004; (woman and child) LC-USZ62-132210. 15: RBD. 16: LC-USZC4-1425. 17: LC-USZC4-2442. 18: LC-USZ62-98515. 19: (Beacon House) LC-B8156-19; (Fort Wagner) LC-USZC4-507. 20: (Carney) LC-USZ62-118558; (Wild) LC-USZ62-84332. 21: (Truth) LC-USZ62-119343 (different pose); (Lawrence) LC-USZ62-110710. 22: LC-USZ62-131082. 23: (Liberty!) LC-USZC4-2519; (Fleetwood) LC-USZ62-44731. 24: LC-USZC4-8109. 25: (Cabell) LC-BH83-637; (soldier) LC-USZ62-132209. 26: (scene of explosion) LC-USZC4-10794; (in the mine) LC-USZC4-12564. 27: (soldier) LC-USZ62-132204; (battle of Nashville) LC-USZC4-506. 28: LC-B8171-7861. 29: (Howard) LC-B8172-3719; (school) LC-USZ62-33264. 30: LC-USZC4-4591.

JULY 1: LC-USZC4-1768. 2: LC-USZC4-2394. 3: LC-USZC4-3130. 4: (Hill) LC-B8184-10569; (Sumner) LC-BH82-46. 5: LC-USZC4-4398. 6: LC-B8171-0588. 7: LC-B8171-7929. 8: LC-USZC2-3810. 9: LC-B8171-7202. 10: LC-USZC4-995. 11: G&M. 12: LC-B8171-7330. 13: (Forbes) LC-USZ62-120894; (Gettysburg) LC-USZC4-1005. 14: LC-BH831-1329. 15: LC-USZC4-977. 16: (Pickett) LC-USZ6-284; (Hancock) LC-USZ62-13703. 17: (Bucklin) GC; (Chamberlain) LC-BH831-934. 18: (Union) LC-

USZC4-1830; (Confederacy) LC-B817-7096. 19: MSS. 20: LC-USZC2-499. 21: LC-USZ62-100070. 22: (Grant) MSS; (Pemberton) LC-USZ62-130838. 23: LC-USZC4-1763. 24: LC-USZC4-4589. 25: LC-B813-1999. 26: LC-USZC4-3194. 27: (wagons) LC-B811-2718; (tearing up track) LC-B811-3611. 28: (Graffam) LC-B8184-10339; (Parker) LC-B8184-10374. 29: LC-B8171-0731. 30: LC-USZC4-1519. 31: LC-USZC4-4595.

AUGUST 1: LC-USZC4-2058. 2: LC-USZC4-12567. 3: LC-USZC4-7941. 4: LC-B8184-B172. 5: LC-USZC4-4605. 6: LC-B8171-0520. 7: (Posts) RBD; (*Harper's*) LC-USZ62-118150. 8: (band) LC-B8184-4545 (full picture, cropped for publication); (musician) LC-B8184-10685 (Photograph reproduced with the permission of Marius Pelladeau). 9: LC-B8171-2405. 10: (Reed letter) MSS; (army mail) LC-USZC4-12571. 11: (newspaperman) LC-B814-1378; (reading) LC-USZC4-4217; (vendor) LC-B8171-0617. 12: LC-USZC4-1003. 13: (stripping fence) LC-USZC4-4275; (beef) LC-USZC4-4200. 14: LC-USZC4-4968. 15: LC-USZ62-92389. 16: LC-USZC4-4224. 17: LC-USZC4-5246. 18: (Thanksgiving) LC-USZ62-6929; (Santa) LC-USZ62-122770. 19: LC-USZC4-7515. 20: LC-USZC4-3036. 21: MSS. 22: (map) LC-USZC4-1332; (soldiers) LC-USZ62-130792. 23: (cover) MUS; (Skidmore) LC-B8184-10045, reproduced courtesy of the United Daughters of the Confederacy. 24: (punishment) LC-USZC4-4185; (officers) LC-B8171-7145. 25: (two artists) LC-USZ62-65086; (Waud) LC-USZ62-533. 26: LC-USZC4-4089. 27: LC-USZC4-4276. 28: LC-USZ62-122103. 29: LC-USZC4-12600. 30: LC-USZC4-6676. 31: LC-B8171-1214.

SEPTEMBER 1: LC-USZC2-1964. 2: (Johnston) LC-B813-6595; (Grant) LC-USZC4-678. 3: LC-B811-

1292. 4: (battle) LC-USZC2-3770; (Farragut) LC-B813-1561; (Taylor) GC. 5: LC-USZC2-1987. 6: LC-B811-1288. 7: (Chinn) LC-USZ62-90345; (pickets) LC-USZ62-105562. 8: (jerilla) LC-USZC4-10792; (Hindman) LC-USZ62-99327; (Halleck) LC-B8172-6377. 9: LC-USZC4-1756. 10: LC-USZC2-2886. 11: (Freedom) LC-USZC4-6156; (troops) LC-BH822-341. 12: (poster) P&P; (Dodge) LC-B8172-1672. 13: LC-USZ62-132450. 14: LC-USZC4-7948. 15: LC-B8171-0391*. 16: (Smith) LC-B8172-2013; (Banks) LC-USZ62-122438. 17: (orderly) LC-USZC4-993; (telegraph) LC-USZC4-2277. 18: (Grierson) LC-USZC4-7991; (Morgan) LC-USZ62-94183. 19: (Chickamauga) LC-USZC4-2540; (Clem) LC-USZ62-11596. 20: G&M. 21: LC-B811-2653. 22: LC-USZC4-1755. 23: LC-B8171-2646*. 24: (Sherman) LC-B813-6534; (map) G&M. 25: (Smith) LC-USZ62-90950; (soldiers) LC-USZ62-132208*. 26: (Schofield) LC-B8172-1944; (Franklin) LC-USZC4-1732. 27: (Hood) LC-B813-6594; (Thomas) LC-B8172-6480. 28: LC-B8171-2639. 29: (Wilson) LC-B8172-2074; (Wheeler) LC-B8172-1974. 30: LC-USZ62-91845 (cropped for publication).

OCTOBER 1: LC-USZC4-3193. 2: LC-B8171-0290. 3: (group) LC-B8171-0741; (portraits) GC. 4: LC-USZC4-4272. 5: (Grant) LC-B8184-10267; (Rawlins) LC-B8171-3400. 6: G&M. 7: (Porter) LC-USZ6-1335; (Barton) LC-USZ62-19319. 8: LC-USZC4-6705. 9: LC-B811-306*. 10: (Dix) LC-USZ62-9797; (Beall) LC-B8172-1973. 11: (attendants) LC-USZC4-3609; (Hammond) LC-B8172-1558. 12: LC-USZC4-5243. 13: LC-B8171-7834. 14: (hospital car) LC-USZ62-708; (Safford) GC. 15: LC-USZC4-7944. 16: (Lincoln) LC-USZ62-15651; (Hoxie) LC-USZ62-10284. 17: LC-USZ62-11880. 18: (Davis) LC-B8184-4146;

(Rhett) LC-USZ62-4890. 19: (Kemble) LC-USZ62-69903; (mansion) LC-DIG-ppmsca-04325. 20: LC-USZC4-5152. 21: (czar) LC-USZ62-128131; (ball) LC-USZ62-77757; (Godey's) LC-USZC4-5145. 22: (rioters) LC-USZ62-127304; (lynching) LC-USZ62-125930. 23: LC-B8171-7396. 24: LC-B8184-B-5077. 25: (Howe) LC-USZ62-46364; (anthem) LC-USZ62-33407. 26: LC-USZC4-11459, LC-USZC4-11460. 27: (Whitman) LC-USZ62-85567; (hospital) LC-USZC4-7976. 28: (soldiers) LC-B8184-740; (Walker) LC-B5-950306. 29: (cartoon) LC-USZC4-12609; (McClellans) LC-B8172-1765. 30: LC-USZ62-116427. 31: (memorial) LC-USZC4-1841; (officers) LC-USZC4-3261.

NOVEMBER 1: LC-USZC4-1758. 2: (Kearny) LC-BH82-4011*; (Chantilly) LC-USZC4-12604. 3: (sailor) LC-USZ62-132206; (victory) LC-USZC4-4250. 4: (Jemison) LC-B8184-10037; (wounded) LC-B8171-0491. 5: LC-USZC2-3821. 6: (pickets) LC-USZC4-5529; (inscription) MSS. 7: (wife) LC-USZC2-792; (Husband) GC. 8: LC-USZC4-5340. 9: (Ewell) LC-B813-6583-C; (Freeman) GC. 10: (Custers) LC-USZ62-114798; (Stuart) LC-B813-6772-B. 11: LC-USZC4-12601. 12: LC-B817-7661. 13: (Willard and cap) MSS; (Harper's) LC-USZ62-100253. 14: LC-USZC4-5989. 15: (home) LC-USZC4-1523; (Jackson) LC-B8184-10612. 16: LC-USZC4-8277. 17: (Nicholls) LC-USZ62-90482; (Lawson) LC-USZ62-118553. 18: (battle) LC-USZC4-1748; (Heath) LC-B8184-10537 (Photograph reproduced with the permission of Marius Pelladeau). 19: LC-USZC4-5969. 20: LC-USZC4-4579*. 21: LC-USZ62-104043. 22: (battle) LC-USZC4-1766; (McCook) LC-USZ62-104988. 23: G&M. 24: LC-USZC4-5797. 25: LC-USZC4-1965. 26: (son) LC-USZC4-6071; (mother, detail) LC-USZ62-

120544; (father) LC-B813-6417 B. 27: LC-B8171-7227. 28: LC-USZC4-2384. 29: (Polk) LC-B813-1320; (McPherson) LC-B813-6415*. 30: (Lincoln) GC; (program) LC-USZ62-32073.

DECEMBER 1: (Petersburg) LC-USZC4-1520; (Hill) LC-USZ62-13697. 2: LC-USZC4-12599. 3: LC-USZC4-602. 4: LC-B8184-10272. 5: LC-USZC4-1321. 6: LC-USZC4-1524. 7: LC-B8171-3448. 8: LC-USZ62-105560. 9: (Sumter) LC-B8171-3140; (Lincoln) LC-USZ61-1938. 10: (theater) LC-B8171-7765; (Keene) LC-BH82-4848 B. 11: (novel) RBD; (Booth tempted) LC-USZ62-8933. 12: LC-USZC4-2337. 13: (Johnson) LC-DIG-ppmsca-05704; (oath) LC-USZ62-10122. 14: LC-USZ62-14086. 15: (Hawkins) LC-USZ62-118559; (review) LC-USZC4-2459. 16: LC-B8171-7798. 17: (Flag) LC-USZC4-12419; (imprisoned) LC-USZC4-1157. 18: LC-USZC4-12417. 19: LC-USZC4-1987. 20: LC-USZC4-2042. 21: LC-USZC4-1522. 22: (Stevens) LC-USZC4-7987; (speech) LC-USZ62-106848. 23: LC-USZC4-1561. 24: LC-USZC4-973. 25: LC-USZ62-105555. 26: (visit) LC-USZ62-127756; (Klansmen) LC-USZ62-119565. 27: LC-USZC4-2623. 28: (Lee) LC-USZC4-7982; (labels) LC-USZC4-6501. 29: P&P. 30: (Badge) RBD; (Timrod) LC-USZ61-813; (Markham) LC-USZ62-64974. 31: (reunion) LC-USZ62-88416; (cover) GC.

INDEX

Only prominently mentioned (or quoted) individuals, as well as places, ships, and the like, are listed. Southern names of some battles are noted parenthetically.

To the intrepid Civil War–era artist-correspondents, the roving practitioners of what was then the new art of photography, and the soldier-artists of both North and South, whose work sheds eloquent light on a pivotal era in American history.

Project Manager: Deborah Aaronson
Editor: Richard Slovak
Designer: Eric J. Diloné
Production Manager: Jane Searle

Library of Congress Cataloging-in-Publication Data

Wagner, Margaret E.
  The American Civil War : 365 days / Margaret E. Wagner.
    p. cm.
  Includes bibliographical references and index.
  ISBN 10: 0–8109–5847–3 (hardcover : alk. paper)
  ISBN 13: 978–0–8109–5847–0
1. United States—History—Civil War, 1861–1865—Pictorial works. 2. United States—History—Civil War, 1861–1865. 3. United States—History—Civil War, 1861–1865—Sources. I. Title.

E468.7.W23 2006
973.7022'2—dc22
                    2005025645

Introduction © Gary W. Gallagher
All other text and images © 2006 Library of Congress

Printed and bound in China
10 9 8 7 6 5 4 3 2

HNA
harry n. abrams, inc.
a subsidiary of La Martinière Groupe

115 West 18th Street
New York, NY 10011
www.hnabooks.com